Captain Rod and Susan is

COASTAL LORAN COORDINATES

Volume 3: Pacific Coast, Alaska to Mexico

International Marine Publishing Company
Camden, Maine

Published by International Marine Publishing Company

10 9 8 7 6 5 4 3 2 1

Copyright © 1990 Rodney J. and Kyong S. Stebbins

Reproduction or publication of the content in any manner, without express permission of the publisher, is prohibited. No liability is assumed with respect to the use of the information herein. International Marine books are published by International Marine Publishing Company, a division of TAB BOOKS Inc. The name "International Marine" and the International Marine logo are trademarks of TAB BOOKS Inc. Printed in the United States of America.

Publications produced by WEAK INDUSTRIES, Inc. and TAB BOOKS, Inc. are not able to, nor intended to, supplant individual training, responsibility, any other navigational aids, charts, or judgment of the user, nor will the publisher, copyright owners, retailers, dealers, or distributors assume any responsibility whatsoever for damages arising from the use of this publication by anyone. The purchaser and users of this publication agree that, with the implementation of this publication, they will hold harmless WEAK INDUSTRIES, Inc., and TAB BOOKS, Inc., their owners, agents, publishers, distributors/dealers, retailers, and subsidiary corporations from damages arising from the use of information contained herein.

International Marine Publishing Company offers software for sale. For information and a catalog, please contact TAB Software Department, Blue Ridge Summit, PA 17294-0850.

Printed by Arcata Graphics, Kingsport, TN
Contributing authors: Will Cerney and Pierce Hoover

To add loran coordinates for reefs, wrecks, havens, ports, and passes to this book, write:

Rod and Susie Stebbins
WEAK INDUSTRIES, Inc.
9132 Blairmoor Road
Tampa, FL 33635-1322

Additional copies and information about this publication can be obtained from:

INTERNATIONAL MARINE PUBLISHING COMPANY
Division of TAB BOOKS, Inc.
Blue Ridge Summit, PA 17294-0850
(800)822-8158

WEAK INDUSTRIES, Inc.
9132 Blairmoor Road
Tampa, FL 33635-1322

Library of Congress Cataloging-in-Publication Data

Stebbins, Rodney J.
   [Coastal loran coordinates]
   Captain Rod and Susie Stebbins' coastal loran coordinates.
     p.   cm.
   Contents: v. 3. Pacific Coast.
   ISBN 0-87742-277-X (v. 3)
    1. Loran — United States — Tables. 2. Boats and boating — United States.
I. Stebbins, Susie S. II. Title. III. Title: Coastal loran coordinates.
VK561.U5S74 1990   90-4031
623.89'32'0973 -- dc20   CIP

ABOUT THE AUTHORS

The Captain of the intrepid vessel Sancho and the husband of wonderful First Mate Susie is a retired civil engineer who specialized in concrete construction and consulting for fun and profit.

During his professional career as a consulting engineer, he traveled the wide world, working for many agencies whose concrete structures were in need of repair. He sat on five American Concrete Institute Committees and two Transportation Research Board Committees (researching epoxies, fibers, testing methods, polymers, and shotcrete) for a bit more than 12 years.

In the winter of 1981, the Stebbinses left Chicago, Illinois, with all of their belongings trailing behind them in trucks.

When they arrived in Tampa, Rod and Susie asked for directions to the salty Gulf of Mexico. Without hesitation, they drove to the beach, changed into their swimsuits, and, as one might predict of any tourist who arrives in the winter, they soaked themselves and got salty.

The next day, Rod and Susie went out looking not for a house, but for a boat. Their furniture and boat, dubbed Sancho, arrived almost simultaneously a few days later. While Susie put the house together, Rod got Sancho ready. In the process, Rod was transformed from a mild-mannered engineer into the man Susie lovingly calls her "Captain Bligh." In an unceremonious manner, Sancho was launched and christened with diet Coke and a trip to the Florida Keys.

The loran coordinates that were collected on their very first trip, right on through those recorded during their voyages in the year 1989, are contained in this book. In addition, many were donated by friends who believe that a loran without a destination is just about as sorry as "a Sancho without his Don Quixote."

The First Mate in this operation is the talented and pretty wife of Captain Rod. Only five feet tall, Susie is a giant on the boat. She stands her watch (day or night), navigates, drives, washes and polishes the boat, is usually the first in the water, outfishes most everyone else, and prepares the finest meals anywhere from almost anything she gathers from the sea. What's more, she takes time out for romance, sunrises, and sunsets.

When the Stebbinses first moved to Florida, Susie couldn't swim at all and believed that water deeper than two or three feet was strictly for the fish. By 1982, Susie was taking lessons in scuba diving, and in the spring of 1983, Susie, armed with her wetsuit and scuba equipment, joined her husband in exploring the deep. Together they form a highly complementary diving team.

During the next several years, they logged over 800 dives while identifying reefs and wrecks. As one might guess, Susie is the delight of this team.

Now in his fourth incarnation, the first Sancho was a 22-foot Glastron. The next four were Sea Rays that grew gradually from 24 to 27 to 30 feet in length, finally becoming the present-day Sancho, a 36-foot flybridge model.

Throughout his various reincarnations, Sancho has carried his charges all along the eastern seaboard. He has spent a four-month vacation in the Bahamas, a three-and-a-half-month vacation in the Florida Keys, and two weeks in the Dry Tortugas. Each year Sancho makes several trips from Tampa, Florida, to various points on the Florida coast.

An integral part of the team, Sancho has his vices too. He has a serious drinking problem that seems to be without end. In eight years, Sancho has consumed over 120,000 gallons of gasoline, and has logged an average of between 950 to 1,125 engine hours each year for seven years.

Sancho is Rod and Susie's "incomparable friend," perpetual in purpose and gracefully classic in line. He is a willing participant in the quest for the "impossible dream." With Sancho at the ready, Rod and Susie know their voyage will never end.

Also known as the Damned Cat, Garfeldasteinski is the only unwilling participant in the quest for coordinates, sunsets, sunrises, sunnin', funnin', divin', fishin', campin', and boatin'.

Captain Rod says, "The only reason the Damned Cat goes with us is because the First Mate loves to have her pet with her. If you were to ask the Damned Cat what she thinks about the whole idea, she would quickly hiss, spit twice, turn tail, and get seasick."

Looking at the Stebbins family, an outsider might think the crew just about the most unlikely combination of humanity imaginable.

Susie is a pretty Oriental lady, petite in stature, nicely groomed, conservative in dress, and swift to smile. Rod, on the other hand, is a born captain type: tall and portly, he is most often attired in boating shoes, shorts, and sport shirts, wears a short silver beard, and plays his "Captain Bligh" character with gusto. In the quiet of the evening, Susie reminds Captain Rod that he can continue to play captain just as long as he has her permission.

Captain Hal Carter of the Grouper Trouper of Seffner, Florida, has this to say about traveling with the Stebbinses: "It's similar to traveling with a Captain Bligh who has a purpose and a mission. Captain Rod was destined to be a captain; he barks orders with great conviction at the First Mate, yells at the Damned Cat, and demands that everything be in its place.

"Susie is the finest boat cook and First Mate any Captain Bligh could ever hope for. What the captain lacks, she more than makes up for in charm, willingness, and ability.

"While both insist on careful attention to details, each has a certain faraway manner that calms seas and assures those who meet them that there are good and colorful things left to dream about. Their dream is to traverse the plentiful waters of the eastern seaboard and to view the gorgeous colors of the crystal-clear waters of Florida.

"The Florida waters are better for the likes of the Stebbinses voyaging upon them. The world still has room for dreamers."

CONTENTS

CHAPTER 1:	Introduction	1
CHAPTER 2:	Finding A Waypoint	3
CHAPTER 3:	Loran Navigation	7
CHAPTER 4:	Boating Buddies	31
CHAPTER 5:	The Lowdown On Diving	38
CHAPTER 6:	Making Passes	40
CHAPTER 7:	Heavenly Havens	117
CHAPTER 8:	Plentiful Ports	121
CHAPTER 9:	Reaching Rocks	130
CHAPTER 10:	Lovely Ledges	136
CHAPTER 11:	Reefs	139
CHAPTER 12:	Wrecks	144
CHAPTER 13:	Fine Fish'n	146
CHAPTER 14:	Sea Bounty	160
CHAPTER 15:	Daffynitions	165
CHAPTER 16:	Waypoint Log	168

CHAPTER 1

INTRODUCTION

This very handy publication was intended, from its inception, to be not much more than a book of destinations. This simply means that there are no predetermined routes given and the book won't tell you how to get to a rock, ledge, wreck, reef, or sea buoy. Instead, it lets you know that these things exist and provides the coordinates for them in the simplest method that exists today.

Each state, province, or island group is listed within each chapter alphabetically. Each county is listed within each state alphabetically, and coordinates are arranged by decreasing latitude. This feature should make it a lot easier for trailer-boaters to use this book.

Water depths are listed for reference only and should not be considered absolutely accurate, as we have not yet been able to authenticate many water-depth listings.

The contents of the book are broken down into subject categories, as found in the table of contents. All the coordinates were accumulated with the ASF (Automatic Secondary Factor) in the off position. To ensure maximum loran accuracy, turn the ASF off when searching for the waypoints listed herein. Chapter 6 is the possible exception, depending on your loran unit; read Chapter 3 and the Chapter 6 introduction before using the coordinates in Chapter 6.

The chapter on passes lists all the sea buoys that can be found from San Diego County up the Pacific Coast to the Aleutian Islands. Also included are latitude and longitude coordinates for Hawaii, the Caroline Islands, the Marianas, the Marshall Islands, Samoa, and the Philippines. Loran coverage is not available in the islands, but the latitude-longitude coordinates will prove useful with any navigation system, including Satnav and GPS. In addition to the sea buoys, most of the first few markers that lead into each of the principal passes themselves are listed.

All the other chapters, including those on havens, ports, rocks, ledges, reefs, wrecks, and fishin' are self-explanatory with regard to what is contained in each. Each chapter is a beginning, and as with the other regional volumes of *Coastal Loran Coordinates*, we anticipate that all the chapters will grow in future editions.

CREWS WHO CRUISE

To assist us in our search for coordinates, we have chartered boats manned with retired husband-and-wife teams much like us. Each boat has the ability to take its passengers to dive spots to verify findings, and each of the members of these teams — known as our "WEAK" crews — love to fish, cruise, and camp along the way. All of them work very hard and have made significant contributions to the sport of recreational boating — to say nothing of their invaluable ability to search out and verify coordinates for this publication. Without our WEAK crews, the three regional volumes of *Coastal Loran Coordinates* could not exist.

First, we thank the several commercial fishermen who tested coordinates for us along the Pacific Coast. A very special thanks must go out to Captain Joe Potts, his lovely wife Sandy, and their 34-foot Sea Ray Brandy for their presence and encouragement; to Captain Hal Carter and his Grouper Trouper for his editing and constant scouring; to Captain Eddy Garcia, his wife Joanie, and their 43-foot Morgan Lady Joan for their great efforts and the one year they spent at sea assisting us on the coasts of Louisiana, Mississippi, and Texas.

We'd also like to thank the Fisherman Doctor David Deam for his contributions and encouragement, and Captain Terry Farner, his fishing family, and their vessel Special K for their fishing coordinates and constant vigilance. Last, but far from least, our thanks go to Captain Jim "London" Zonlick, his team, and their 36-foot Sea Ray Hunky Dory, for their diving and photographic expeditions during the 1988 season, and to Captain Ed Suarez, Jr. of Columbia, Maryland, for his help and expertise in locating and documenting wrecks. Their help is invaluable to us.

The combined efforts of our WEAK crews have helped us produce the finest loran coordinate reference books available. The growth of the Texas to Maine volume over the past couple of years is readily apparent. Our first edition was printed in April of 1986 and included 650 coordinates. Within 60 days we released an additional 200 coordinates, adding those we'd collected for the Florida Keys and the Bahamas. Our May 1987 edition contained more than 1,600 coordinates, and our May 1988 edition contained nearly 4,000 neat places to go. In 1989 our publication grew to more than 8,000 destination coordinates, and the 1990 edition contains more than 14,000, making it the largest publication of its kind available on the market at this time. We hope for similar growth in the future for *Volume 3: Pacific Coast, Alaska to Mexico.*

ONWARD AND UPWARD

All in all, everyone is looking forward to 1990, when we can get underway again. We are still at the helm seeking sunsets and romantic havens to hole up in. So if you see our 36-foot Sea Ray Sancho, please rap on the door and join us for a cool one. If you see any of our hard-working WEAK crews plying about, please treat them to a cool one, as they provided many of the coordinates for our most enjoyable spots.

Good luck to you in your search, and may all you discover bring you great happiness.

CHAPTER 2

FINDING A WAYPOINT

When we think of finding a location on a map or chart, we usually think of the intersection of two visible bearings, like the meeting of two highways. Finding our way with a loran isn't too different, except that the destination is out in the middle of the puddle and there probably isn't anything to see except water, waves, and more water. That tends to make most of us wonder if we really have arrived!

Large objects such as wrecks, ledges, holes, domes, spikes, and mounds can readily be seen on a chart paper recorder or a video depth monitor, and your depth finder will tell you when you have arrived. But sometimes small items such as subtle bottom structure changes and gradual depth changes can't be seen on a sounder, and, as a result, it's easy to overlook a good fishing location.

With practice, you can learn to identify the type of bottom that is below the boat. Steel hulls may look like a malfunction, sandy bottoms will look different than rocky bottoms, and so on. Learn to operate your machinery, because this publication is not designed to teach you all about individual types of equipment; instead, it simply provides the destination coordinates.

COMMON MISTAKES
Before we discuss the techniques for arriving at a location, it is important that we help you understand that movement, however small, can make finding things quite frustrating. When it appears that you are dead in the water and that you are going nowhere fast, you are actually moving away from the very target you just came to find!

It is important to learn the limitations and functions of your chosen loran, to learn a reasonable method of determining when you're about to arrive at your chosen destination, and when, in fact, you're at ground zero.

Probably the most common mistake made in using the loran is failing to understand what the mission is. Ground zero is *not* the exact spot where you must drop anchor all of the time. If you're looking to fish or dive near a ledge, for example, it's only important that the divers be able to get to the ledge easily from the boat.

We like to place a marker on the ledge and then anchor the boat "downstream" from it. When the divers go down the anchor line, they can check their compasses and swim in the same direction to the ledge, which is upstream, while they are at their strongest.

When we are going to fish a ledge, we most always troll a zigzag course along the ledge, hoping to tease a fish into striking one of the $4.75 phony foods laced with sharpened barbed hooks. (It often seems to us that these hooks are placed strategically to warn the fish to stay away!)

Probably the next biggest mistake you can make with your loran is to operate the unit with the Automatic Secondary Factor (ASF) enabled (on) instead of disabled (off). Hard on the heels of this mistake is entering the coordinates incorrectly, like putting time delays (TDs) into the latitude/longitude (LAT/LON) mode and vice versa, making errors in interpolation, making errors in reading coordinates taken from the charts, forgetting to "seed" the loran, selecting the improper transmitting stations, and assuming that the loran is always right.

We have accepted invitations to assist our readers in understanding their lorans and the system. Without exception, within two hours they have all been able to take up "loraning" by themselves.

It seems that most people are intimidated by the way their loran's instructions are presented. It also seems that the people who write the instructions either know nothing about boating and what the loran is to be used for, or wrote the manual in a foreign language and then gave it to a fourth grader to translate.

OUR METHOD

Now that we have bitten the hand that feeds us, let's discuss finding our spots. The need for accuracy varies from chapter to chapter. If you are looking for a sea buoy in the fog, as might be described in the chapter on passes, or if you are looking for wrecks or reefs, it goes without saying that the "targets" (destinations) are smaller by comparison to the areas found in the chapters on rocks and fishing, which may include rocky or fishing areas that are acres across.

Once you've learned the basics of the loran, it is possible for you to find the large fields of rocky and fishing areas listed in this book, and, with a little practice, small objects are a piece of cake, too.

We do a lot of evening and night boating, now that we have made friends with our electronics. We are not as intimidated about finding our way home at night now that we have come to understand a few simple facts and techniques.

Our first night trip was a voyage for the books. Wow, were we concerned! To say that we were uptight would be a gross understatement. We had visions of falling into trenches, of night serpents snapping at our wake, of running out of gas, of having mechanical failures, and of just about everything else we could dream up — all of this after we had made exactly the same trip during daylight hours several times to make certain we would not fall off the edge of the world.

Now that we have made many such trips, we have made up "trip cards" that list each coordinate necessary to make a safe voyage. These trip cards remain on the boat, ready to be used should the visibility deteriorate due to haze, smog, fog, or rain. The confidence we have gained by using these cards, coupled with the use of our loran, has allowed us to use the boat much as we might use the car.

One of the first lessons we learned about traveling by loran with limited visibility is that it is best to slow to a speed that allows us to avoid hitting something or someone should we come upon them suddenly. We cruise at a speed of about six knots, which allows us to hear horns and whistles over the noise of our engines.

One evening, as we plowed through the fog, we almost rammed into a small boat that had set anchor due to the limited visibility. The fact that he had a small flashlight (which was getting weaker by the moment) was the only thing that prevented us from causing great damage. As it turned out, we were able to assist the boaters by towing them to a safe anchorage well out of harm's way, where we both stayed until the next morning.

GROUND ZERO

Hitting ground zero means to reach zero-zero on the nautical miles to the destination displayed on the screen of the loran. Probably the only time it is necessary to be that accurate is when finding a marker, a sea buoy in very limited visibility, or when it is necessary to find an unmarked reef or wreck. Suffice it to say that markers and sea buoys are already marked, so we will discuss finding the reefs, wrecks, and other small objects where accuracy is required.

The first step is to slow down. When we are within 0.20 nautical miles of our destination, we slow Sancho to idle speed while holding the compass heading to the destination. We change the screen of the loran so that we can see the notation "Distance to Destination," and watch it count down to 0.00, being very careful to hold the heading.

There we deploy a marker, which is nothing more than an empty plastic milk bottle tied to a stout cord with a five-pound chunk of lead tied to the other end.

Once it is anchored, we make a wide swing to the right so that we can approach the marker with the bow into the wind. Once again, we're looking for 0.00 while monitoring the white line recorder for indications of the wreck or reef. When we have made a positive identification with the white line, disregarding 0.00, Susie sets the second marker in place after the Captain yells, "Now, honey!" Sancho then continues into the wind far enough to set the bow anchor, yet close enough to allow his stern to lie close the second marker.

If we are going to fish, we set markers to tell us if we are drifting right or left of the spot. If we are going to dive the site, we are positioned in a way that's best to protect the divers during their descent and ascent.

Incidentally, don't forget to have the dive flags up when the divers are in the water and to take them down again when the divers are out of the water, just in case someone else wants to approach the site.

Share the site by communicating about your activities with other boats in the area. Most important, leave the site clean, undisturbed, and unmarked. It takes the sea a long time to heal from an indiscretion.

When we leave, we lift our markers, secure the lines, and stow them for the next time. On the way home, we usually take a moment or

---

WIT & WISDOM

Hull speed for a displacement hull can be calculated by multiplying the square root of the length of the water line (feet) by approximately 1.4, with the average range for the multiplier actually being 1.3 to 1.5.

two to have a cold drink and to apologize to each other for all of the screaming and hollering we did during the anchoring exercises. I don't think we have ever made a good anchorage without one of us yelling out an unnecessary command or the other replying with an equally unnecessary something-or-other. Must be a part of boating, because it seems everyone does it.

When searching for good fishing or diving sites, look for the things that don't seem to fit the scenery, like a pile of rocks in the middle of a sand bar. That pile of rocks might be the first clue to a find of wealth; then again, it might just be a pile of rocks. This is the excitement that comes with exploring and researching destinations.

We will stay at the helm for a few more years and we will keep updating this guide. We trust all of our efforts will bring lots of exciting adventures for both the novice boater and the seasoned salt.

It's all done by researching and digging; then slow down and try to piece together the clues that are everywhere.

CHAPTER 3

LORAN NAVIGATION

By Will Cerney and Pierce Hoover

A special thanks to Sport Fishing Magazine for permission to reprint this text, which was compiled from articles in the magazine.

In the old days, sea captains subdued sextants, calibrated chronometers, and labored over log tables just to get an estimation of where in the world they were. Many an old salt would have been grateful for a machine that could simply tell him what part of the ocean he was in with any degree of accuracy.

With the advent of Satnav, loran, and, soon, GPS, oceangoing skippers now take it for granted that they can punch a few buttons and get their vessel's position almost anywhere in the world, all without doing any complicated mathematics or perching on the deck to take a sun sight.

In US coastal waters, it is the loran system that provides the quickest, least expensive, and most reliable electronic means of positioning a vessel. In the days of loran A and the early days of loran C, the machines could do nothing more that get a fix — it was up to the skipper to mark his charts, make his calculations, and navigate his vessel accordingly.

But with the miniaturization of computer technology has come a new breed of machines. The modern loran can do a lot more than just give loran numbers to be plotted on a grid. Skippers now rely on their lorans to steer them to and from their fishing grounds and harbors, to keep track of distances and speeds, and to store information on favorite fishing locations.

Such electronic assistance is a great boon to sailors, cruising skippers, and fishermen, who can now spend more time searching for secluded anchorages or fishing, and less time fiddling with charts.

The only problem is, some folks think a loran can take over and do all the navigating for them. True, you can punch a few numbers into a loran and it will take you there and back without any understanding on your part.

But at the very least, skippers who run offshore should have some idea of how their machines figure distances and headings, and they should be familiar with basic navigational techniques such as plotting and dead reckoning. A captain shouldn't rely on any one device, even a loran, to guide his boat, and he should be able to make his way home safely if the loran fails.

To operate safely offshore using a loran system as a primary tool of piloting, a skipper needs to have a clear understanding of what those numbers he punches into his machine mean, and of how the loran processes those numbers to help him steer to and from his destination.

THE LORAN SYSTEM

The word loran is an acronym for LOng RAnge Navigation. It is an electronic radio navigation system first developed during World War II as loran A. The system we now use is loran C, which was developed in the 1960s and put into service in the 1970s.

While the name says long range, loran C is really considered a medium-range system. For very precise, close-in navigational fixes, the offshore oil industry often uses such costly systems as portable microwave positioning, while ships at sea rely on the somewhat less precise fixes given by Omega and satellite navigation receivers. Loran C falls between the extreme accuracy of short-range microwave and the lesser accuracy of present-day worldwide systems.

With loran C, you can get a position up to 1,200 miles from the transmitting facility. When things are working right, loran can establish your position to within 100 to 1,000 yards of your actual location (this is known as accuracy), but if you know where you are, it can bring you back to within 50 to 75 feet of the same spot the next time (this is known as repeatability). Loran's excellent repeatability is ideally suited to fishermen searching for that choice piece of bottom they ran across last trip, and its accuracy is good enough to plot a course to distant harbors with confidence.

Loran coverage is not worldwide, but it is in operation along both coasts of the United States and Canada as well as the Great Lakes, in Hawaii, Europe, the Far East, and various other areas of the northern hemisphere. This coverage comes from several groups of loran transmitters known as chains. Each chain is made up of a master transmitter and several slaves that work together to provide position information. While all loran transmitter chains broadcast at the same frequency (100 KHz), they each have a unique signal pulse rate (known as a Group Repetition Interval, or GRI) that tells your machine which transmitter group it is listening to. But before we get into TDs, GRIs, and all the other terms, let's find out how a loran knows where you are.

LORAN THEORY

Loran is a time delay location system. In other words, it works on the assumption that radio signals travel at constant speeds and the longer it takes a signal to reach you, the farther you are from the source. By using three separate signal sources in a given loran chain, your unit can determine your position with a good deal of accuracy.

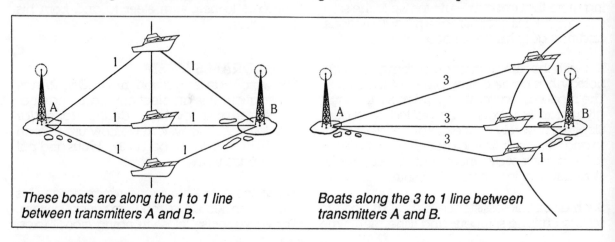

These boats are along the 1 to 1 line between transmitters A and B.

Boats along the 3 to 1 line between transmitters A and B.

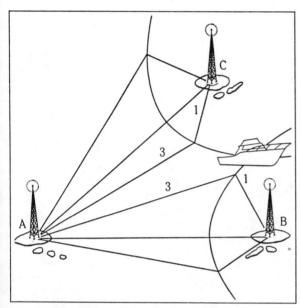

This boat is at the intersection of the AB 3 to 1 line and the AC 3 to 1 line.

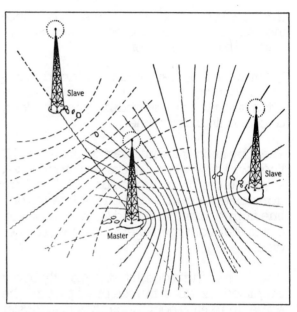

A simple loran chain, with a master and two slave transmitters.

To understand the process, let's imagine two loran transmitters are set on islands several hundred miles apart. A direct line between these transmitters is known as the base line. Now, let's imagine that we are on a boat at the mid-point of that base line, halfway between the two islands. If both loran transmitters fired simultaneous signals (which they really don't), we would receive the signals at the same time.

The same would hold true if we moved at an angle 90 degrees to the base line, since the two stations would still be the same distance from our boat, no matter where we were along that line. We can call that line of all points equidistant from the two transmitters the one-to-one line, since it is established by measuring the time delay from transmission to reception. Technicians would call our one-to-one line a time delay line, or TD.

It makes sense that if we move our imaginary boat along the base line until we are closer to one transmitter than the other, we will get that signal sooner. If we are three times as far from one transmitter as from the other, the signal from the closer transmitter will get there three times as quickly. Plotting a line of all points that are three times as far from one transmitter as the other produces a curve, which we'll call the three-to-one time delay (TD) line, since it measures the amount of time it takes the signal to get from the transmitter to our position.

But even though the receiver knows we are somewhere along that three-to-one TD curve, it can't tell what part of the curve it is on. Finding the exact location along that curve requires a third transmitter.

What we need, then, is a third island transmitter that can work with one of our two existing transmitters to establish a position along a second time delay line.

Then, by finding the intersection of the two TD lines, we know where we are. So if the receiver says you are on a three-to-one TD line from transmitters A and B, and on the three-to-one line from transmitter A and C, you know you are at the exact spot where those two TD lines cross.

A real loran chain doesn't work exactly as our simplified one does, but the principles are the same. In reality, each chain has one master transmitter and several slave transmitters. TD lines are always based on readings between the master and one of the slaves, and the transmitters don't fire at the same time. Instead, the master fires and each slave follows at a predetermined interval. Each slave has a distinct delay interval and every loran chain in the world has a different group repetition interval (GRI); in other words, the interval at which the master and each of the slaves transmit their signals.

The northeastern United States, for example, works on a GRI of 9960, while the southeastern US uses a GRI of 7980 and the California coast operates on 9940. What these numbers represent is the time interval in which the master fires, is answered by each of the slaves, and fires again. These numbers are expressed in microseconds; a microsecond is one-millionth of a second!

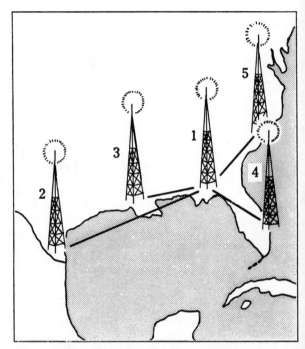

The southern loran chain. The master station (1) is in Malone, FL, with slave stations in (2) Raymondville, TX, (3) Grangeville, LA, (4) Jupiter, FL, and (5) Carolina Beach, NC.

To delve a bit farther into GRI, let's look at the southeastern US chain. The master, which is in Malone, Florida, fires once every 79,800 microseconds, and each of the four slaves — known as W, X, Y, and Z — follows after a predetermined delay. The W slave in Grangeville, Louisiana, fires 11,000 microseconds after the master; the X in Raymondville, Texas, follows after 23,000 microseconds; the Y in Jupiter, Florida, at 43,000 microseconds; and the Z in Carolina Beach comes last, at 59,000 microseconds.

So when a fisherman comes over the radio

and tells you he is in the 13,500 line at the 46,600, he is using the W and Y slaves in conjunction with the master to establish his position along the TD lines formed by W and the master and by Y and the master.

We should point out that there is no direct relationship between TD numbers and distance, because the lines curve and cross at different angles throughout the coverage area.

A modern loran can interpret signals down to hundredths of a microsecond, which can represent a distance as small as two or three boat lengths. For greatest accuracy, the TD lines used should intersect at as near a 90-degree angle as possible. Some modern lorans have a feature known as ATS (Automatic Transmitter Selection) or ASS (Automatic Slave Selection), which automatically selects the best TD line crossover angle for the particular location.

OPERATING SEQUENCE

The loran should be turned on and should be working before you start your day on the water. Unless your boat has a separate battery system for electronics, you should start your engines before turning on the loran. Otherwise, the sudden voltage drop created by the starter motor can blank out the loran and you will have to run through the cycling process again.

After you turn the loran on, it may take several minutes to lock onto the transmitters, depending on signal strength and local noise. If your machine has automatic transmitter selection, it will automatically select the two slave transmitters in the chain it considers to have the best crossing angle for your particular location. If you want to use a different slave, you will need to put the machine on manual select to make the change.

If you have a couple of minutes, you might run the loran through a signal-to-noise ratio (SNR) check. The SNR button checks each transmitter and tells you how strong the signal is in relation to interference and electrical noise. A low SNR reading means the transmitter signal is weak or you have a lot of interference. In either case, you might be in for trouble. Different manufactures have different values for SNR, and you should know the optimum and minimum values for your loran.

Once the loran is cycled out or locked on, you should make sure it is giving you a good reading by checking its output against a couple of known positions. A logical first checkpoint would be the dock, and you should know your dockside position and check it against what the machine says to make sure it knows you are in the same place as usual.

A good second checkpoint would be a marker or buoy outside the harbor or at the mouth of the channel. Before you get underway, enter that second checkpoint as waypoint one and you can run a check on your navigational functions, such as range and bearing. You might also want to leave that position in the memory to use as a destination on the trip home.

NAVIGATION FEATURES

Early lorans did nothing more than establish a position and display it in TD coordinates, which then had to be plotted on a loran C overprinted chart. Since then, a number of memory and navigation features have been built into loran units. Navigational units now convert TD coordinates to latitude and longitude and display the position as "lat" and "lon" readings.

It is possible to operate a loran in the latitude/longitude mode exclusively, and some users successfully plot courses and find fishing holes without ever knowing what a TD is. But it is important to remember that lat and lon are calculated from the loran's TDs, and are only as accurate as the TD coordinates themselves. We'll talk more about that later; for now, just remember that all loran machines measure position in TDs, even if they display it as latitude and longitude.

Most modern lorans have a built-in memory that stores TD or lat/lon information. This is quite useful for fishermen, who want to record their exact position when they find a fishing spot they like. If the fisherman saves that location in the loran's memory, it can consistently bring him back to within 50 or 75 feet of the same location in most coastal areas.

TD or lat/lon coordinates for a known location, such as an island, can also be entered into the loran and used to steer a course. But as with any method of navigation, a loran should never be relied on as an absolute or solitary source of piloting information. The two most common problems arising from using loran memory in navigation are wrong numbers and lack of navigational understanding.

If a wrong number is accidentally keyed into

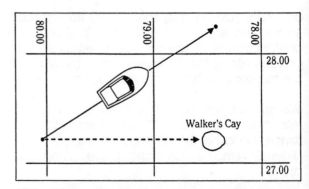

This skipper punched a wrong number into his loran without checking it and is not going to Walker's Cay.

the memory, the loran will take you to a place you don't want to visit. This problem becomes especially severe if the operator doesn't understand charts and lacks basic navigational skills.

Let's suppose, for example, that a boat owner without any navigational know-how plans a trip from Florida over to Walker's Cay in the Bahamas. A buddy gives him the numbers for Walker's Cay — latitude 27-14.38, longitude 78-24.08 — and tells our friend that there's nothing more to it than entering the numbers and going where the loran tells him to go.

But if our boat owner hits an eight instead of a seven when he is punching his latitude coordinates without double-checking (thus getting 28-14.38), the machine will tell him to go to a point 60 nautical miles north of the island (each degree of latitude equals 60 nautical miles). Add to that the possibility of a loran failure halfway through the trip and you can see that our friend has some problems.

A basic understanding of charts and dead reckoning is essential to piloting with a loran, and every skipper should make the effort to understand the relationship of the coordinates he feeds into his loran and the actual locations these numbers represent.

RANGE AND BEARING
When driving a boat, the direction from one spot to another is always expressed in terms of a compass heading between zero and 360 degrees, known as the bearing, while the actual distance between the two points is expressed in nautical miles, known as the range. For example, a boat at the mouth of Miami's Government Cut has range and bearing to the island of Bimini of 40 miles at 80 degrees.

Simple enough. Just steer a compass course of 80 degrees and 40 miles later you're in Bimini, right? Well, sort of. As you would expect, nothing is as simple as it seems. For starters, the bearing isn't necessarily the course you will need to steer by your compass to reach your destination.

Cross currents, polar magnetic variation, and compass irregularities work together to create differences between the numerical heading expressed on a chart and the compass heading you will actually need to steer to reach your destination. Before we get on with loran use, we'll have to take a short side trip to see how these various factors come into play.

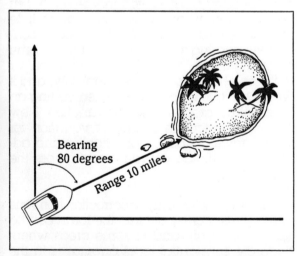

Range and Bearing: The island lies 10 miles from the boat; this distance is known as the range. The direction is 80 degrees from true north, which is known as the bearing.

TRUE AND MAGNETIC NORTH
Navigators speak of "magnetic north" and "true north," and it should be realized that the two aren't always the same thing. When you look at a chart plotted with latitude/longitude lines, north is always "up," in a direction parallel to the lines of longitude.

If you look at a globe, you will see that longitude lines aren't actually parallel; instead, they converge at the north pole. For the sake of mapmaking, we think of longitude lines as running parallel, a process known as a Mercator projection. This type of projection creates some irregularities when using navigation charts over long distances, but it has to do with other things besides true and magnetic north (to explain that, we'd have to get into spherical trigonometry).

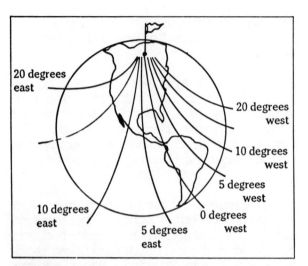

Magnetic variation occurs because the magnetic and true north poles are not identically located, and variation increases from 0 degrees along the west coast of Florida to as much as 20 degrees on other coastlines.

Whether you are using a globe or a Mercator projection chart, true north always refers to the direction to the top of the earth — the north pole. Readings taken from a chart are therefore automatically expressed in true north bearings.

It just so happens that one of the earth's centers of magnetic attraction lies near the north pole. Magnetic pieces of metal (like compasses) point to this magnetic north pole, which actually lies several hundred miles to the south of the real north pole. In some areas of the world, true and magnetic north are almost the same, while they differ by as much as 20 degrees in other locales.

In any one area, the angle of difference between true and magnetic north can be calculated, and it is known as the local magnetic variation. Navigators have long been aware of this fact, and add or subtract the magnetic variation difference when calculating what compass course to steer.

To make things even more complicated, scientists have discovered that this magnetic north pole moves a little bit every year. This means the magnetic variation in any particular area is increasing or decreasing by slight amounts each year.

To get range and bearing information from your loran, you must enter a destination (waypoint). The machine, which already knows where you are, calculates the distance and direction to your destination. The direction (bearing) is calculated in true north, but because lorans are now such smart little machines, many of them automatically convert the bearing to magnetic north. On some older machines, the magnetic variation for your area had to be entered annually, and it would have to be changed when visiting an area with a greater or lesser variation. New machines calculate magnetic variation for your particular spot automatically, and adjust that variation as you move across the earth's surface.

By the way, the automatic correction from true to magnetic north built into the loran can be turned on or off, and in some areas where there are substantial local anomalies in the magnetic field, it might be a good idea to turn the correction off and do the calculations for yourself.

COURSE ADJUSTMENTS

And now we come to the important point of all this explanation, the point that gets a lot of beginning navigators in trouble. Skippers, take heed: your loran is a smart little machine, but it can't tell you what number on your particular compass you should steer by to reach your destination. Sure, it can give you the bearing, either in true or magnetic north, but that bearing may be substantially different from the actual course you need to steer by the compass.

Cross currents, wind, and tides all need to be taken into consideration when figuring what course to run, but in addition to these variables, these is often an error in the compass itself, caused by objects on the boat.

Compasses are affected by objects in the local environment. Place a large metal object right next to the compass and you can see this for yourself. Radios with external speakers, video screens, metal equipment housings, tools, steel (but not aluminum) drink cans left on the console, and a host of other objects can affect a magnetic compass. (Wires forming a circuit that surrounds the compass create a magnetic field. To solve the problem, wires are run together in "twisted pairs." This way, the fields from the two wires will cancel each other out.)

The fluctuations of a magnetic compass are known as deviation, and wise old salts and sailors sometimes take the time to calculate precise compass deviations for their boats. Since deviation often will change with the boat's heading, the only way to figure deviation is to run between several points where you know the actual heading (say, from buoy one to buoy two, which you know is 170 degrees), then note the difference between what you know and what your compass reads for each heading. (Also, bear in mind that compass deviation will change when you reposition any of the objects that are affecting it.)

Thus, in the old days navigators calculated the course to steer by figuring the true north bearing and then by adding or subtracting both magnetic variation and compass deviation for the desired course heading. Next, they took into account tides, current, and the ship's leeway, finally arriving at a heading that was essentially an educated and precisely calculated guess. Sounds like a lot of work, doesn't it?

Trying to figure compass deviation and drift for all headings quickly takes all the fun out of boating. But since we're now using a loran to help with our navigation, we can do something that would make traditionalists who rely entirely on their magnetic compass and their esoteric navigational skills throw up their hands in horror.

As far as we're concerned, the compass is mostly an aid to steering. Sure, we should try to keep deviation to a minimum by mounting the compass away from interfering magnetic objects, and we should note any large deviations the compass may show, but with the loran on board, we don't have to rely on painfully exact course calculations and precise compass courses to get us to our destination.

Instead, we will give the loran the coordinates of our desired destination, let it do the figur-

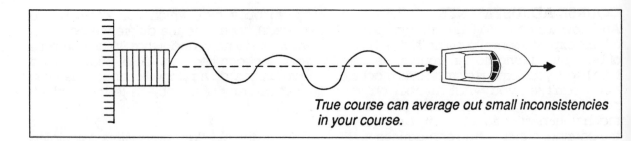

True course can average out small inconsistencies in your course.

ing, and then take off on an approximate compass heading. Once underway, we will use the compass mostly as a guide to steer by, keeping the bow in line with a number on the compass card. (If you are on a steady course, heading in the right direction, it really doesn't matter what that number is.) To keep on track, we will use the navigation software built into the loran — features like true course, ground speed, estimated time of arrival, and cross track error. Most loran users already know something about these functions, but we'll go over them just to make sure.

TRUE COURSE

You're heading out to the ledge, running at 24 knots. A buddy calls up on the VHF and asks what course you're running. You glance at the compass and tell him you're heading due east.

Well, maybe you are and maybe you aren't. The only thing you know for sure is that the needle on your compass lines up with the big E when you look at it. What about magnetic variation, and what about that windshield wiper motor that sits right next to the compass? Isn't the tide turning north at four knots, and didn't you make a few swings in the last few minutes to dodge floating junk?

The only way to know the real direction you have been traveling in is to use your loran. The setting known as true course (TC) can tell you what track you have been making across the ocean bottom.

To do this, the loran records your present position (waypoint zero), waits a little while, takes another position (waypoint one), then calculates the actual bearing between the two points. The machine keeps doing this at predetermined intervals, and when it has enough samples, it averages these waypoints to calculate your true bearing over the past few minutes, taking into account all the little jogs you took to avoid floating logs and any other helm changes you might have made. If you hold a steady course on the compass, the loran will give you an exact heading. If your course wavers slightly, the machine will give you an average course for the predetermined time interval it samples.

One very important, and often overlooked, element of this process is the length of the sampling interval the loran uses to calculate true course. On slow vessels, such as sailboats, the sampling interval must be fairly long to get a good average heading. But if the same long sampling period is used on a sportfisherman running at 30 knots, the TC function will

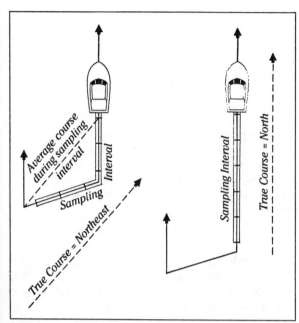

The true course setting has a built-in lag factor, which may cause the machine to appear inaccurate at times. In figure one, the skipper has turned the boat and is heading due north, but his loran still shows his true course as northeast. This is because of the lag of sampling intervals, which follows the boat's course like a string of railroad cars. In figure two, the sampling interval has "turned the corner." In other words, the lag of the true course samples has now adjusted to the new course.

lag far behind any helm changes and will not accurately represent your present course.

As a rule of thumb, the faster the boat is traveling, the shorter the sampling interval (known as the time filter) should be. If you consistently overrun your fishing hole (we'll explain why you do that in a minute), it might be an indication that your time filter is set for too long an interval, and you should make necessary adjustments, or discuss it with a knowledgeable electronics dealer.

GROUND SPEED

When your loran takes sample readings, it not only calculates bearing, it also keeps track of the distance you have traveled. When you set the loran in ground speed (GS) mode, it divides distance by time to figure boat speed. Once again, it is using a predetermined sampling interval, and displays average speed during that interval.

The loran's ground speed calculations are based on a straightline course, and, like the true course calculation, it is most accurate when you are maintaining a constant course. Zigzags and course changes will affect the average speed, just as they affect TC readings. In addition, the sampling interval your loran is set for will create a lag between present speed and average speed for the duration of the sampling period.

That may sound complicated, but it's easy to see it for yourself. Next time you are out on your boat, put your loran in GS mode, get up to speed for awhile, and then chop the throttle. You will notice that the loran takes a while to slow down, because it is averaging your present slow speed and your former fast speed. The longer it takes the loran's GS indicator to drop down to your present speed, the longer your sampling period (time filter). If you think that your loran's sampling period is too long, you might want to shorten it.

Now that you know how a loran figures course

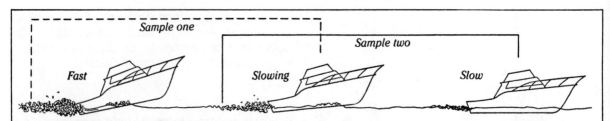

Ground speed is measured by tracking the boat's speed for a certain interval of time and averaging it. In sample one, the ground speed reading will be high, even though the skipper has come off a plane just as he got his ground speed reading. This is because he has been running fast through most of the sampling period. In sample two, the boat has been moving slowly through most of the sampling period, so the ground speed reading will be very close to the boat's actual speed.

and speed, you will see why so many fishermen overrun their waypoints. When you punch a destination in and tell the machine to give you direction to get there, it stays busy throughout the trip figuring true course, average speed across the bottom, and a whole lot of other things. As we've seen, all these calculations take time, and that lag time can cause you to overshoot your mark.

Let's say, for example, that your machine is set up to sample waypoints for 30 seconds to figure out headings and speed and cross track error and all those other things. That means that in range and bearing mode, it won't recognize you are at your destination until 30 seconds after you get there. If you are blasting along at 30 knots, that 30-second delay means you have overshot your point by a quarter of a mile. That's why smart skippers slow down a half mile or so before they get to their destination — this gives the loran time to catch up.

Of course, if you switch the machine back to latitude/longitude or TD display, you will get instantaneous position readouts — provided you can interpret them. But an easier way to cut down on unwanted lag might be to shorten up those sampling intervals for high-speed operation. (Keep in mind that a very short sampling interval will decrease your accuracy at trolling speeds.)

ETA AND VMG

By using range, bearing, and speed calculations, your loran can perform a couple of additional tricks that you may find useful at some point. Estimated time of arrival (ETA) is exactly what it sounds like. The loran looks at your speed and course to the desired destination, then calculates how long it will take you to get there if you maintain your present speed.

Velocity made good (VMG) is a function fishermen may or may not find useful. Sailboat captains, especially racers, find it almost invaluable. The VMG function remembers your

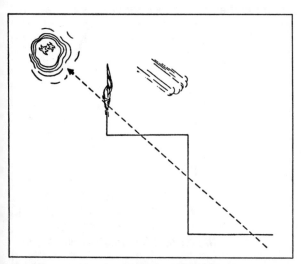

A sailboat uses the Velocity Made Good setting to keep track of its progress to its destination.

starting point and your destination, and updates you as to how far you have traveled in the direction of your destination.

If you were to punch in a destination waypoint 10 miles due east of the harbor, then motor only one mile east and spend the rest of the day trolling north and south, your VMG function wouldn't concern itself with your north/south wanderings, and would keep track of how far you still have to go to get to your original waypoint. Sailboat skippers who have to zig-zag at right angles to work their way into the wind often use VMG to keep track of their progress toward their upwind goal.

ASF

Earlier, we mentioned that loran works on the principle that radio waves travel at a constant speed. The truth is that the signals' speed over water and the speed over land are slightly different, which can have an effect on the accuracy of a loran fix. Several years ago, the Coast Guard began calculating the variances in loran signals created by various land masses. These corrections are known as Automatic Secondary Factors (ASF), and they represent the calculated differences between theoretical and actual TD positions when the distortion caused by land is added in.

Most new machines have ASF corrections built into the memory, while older units don't. A lot of boaters will never be aware of these corrections and couldn't care less. The most common problem resulting from ASF corrections comes from the fisherman who trades his old loran in for a new one. He may suddenly find that his fancy new machine can't find a lot of his favorite fishing spots.

Attacking the machine with profanity or a hammer is not the solution. In many such cases, the problem is that the old loran didn't have ASF corrections built in, and the fisherman's numbers were based on uncorrected machine readings. Since the new loran will automatically add in those corrections, it will take the boater to a slightly different location using the same coordinates.

If you have such a problem, the solution is to turn off the new loran's ASF correction program and take yourself to the fishing spot using your old numbers. Once you have found your place, switch the ASF back on and make a note of the new coordinates based on the machine's correction.

Remember, too, that all the coordinates printed in this publication were found with the ASF in the OFF position.

CROSS TRACK ERROR

The cross track error function (XTE, CTE, or CT) is a helpful feature for holding a course. The range and bearing mode tells you where to go and how far away you are, but it is the cross track that will help you steer a straight course to your destination. It does this by telling you if you are holding to that course line or if you are steering off to one side or another, which is your cross track error.

To understand the importance of knowing your cross track, let's look at a skipper who doesn't use it. Our captain has a very slow boat that he likes to run to a secluded island. Every trip, he punches the location of the island into his loran, and his range and bearing tell him to steer due east for 40 miles. Since his boat only does 10 knots, he figures it's okay to check the course every hour or so. He sets the autopilot and relaxes.

After making the same trip several times, our man begins to wonder why the loran always begins by telling him to steer 90 degrees, then 85 degrees the second hour, 40 degrees the third hour, and due north the fourth hour. He always ends up coming to the island from the south instead of from the west.

From an overhead vantage point, we can see what the skipper doesn't. The water between his home port and the island has a six-knot current flowing due south. As our captain steers in the direction of the island, he is pushed south by the current and has to make bigger and bigger corrections as he approaches his destination. The obvious solution, we would say, would be to "crab" into the current by steering a bit north of the island.

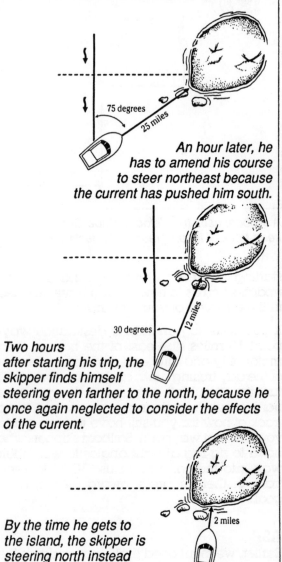

Starting from the marina, the skipper checks range and bearing on his loran and steers due east to the island, not aware of the southerly current drift.

An hour later, he has to amend his course to steer northeast because the current has pushed him south.

Two hours after starting his trip, the skipper finds himself steering even farther to the north, because he once again neglected to consider the effects of the current.

By the time he gets to the island, the skipper is steering north instead of east.

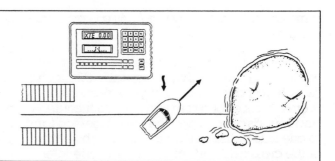

By setting his machine on the Cross Track Error setting, our skipper can run a straight course to the island. To him, it may seem as though he's heading northeast, but he is really only crabbing into the current to produce an easterly course.

Simple enough from a crow's vantage point, right? But not so obvious when you are on the water. That's when the loran's cross track error indicator becomes useful. If our friend had set his machine in the CTE mode and paid attention, it would have warned him when he first began to drift off to the south.

Most lorans do this by displaying the distance the boat has moved to one side or the other of the desired course. Current and wind drift can be compensated for by simply adjusting the boat's heading to keep it centered on the loran's display. Remember that a loran doesn't have any idea which way the nose of the boat is pointed; it only knows the direction to the destination and the true course you are running across the ocean bottom.

Thus, to those not aware of drift and the necessary correction angle, it may seem strange that the boat has to steer 80 degrees to reach a destination due east (90 degrees). But by following the loran's XTE display, a skipper will maintain the straightest course possible.

Note that the error away from the course line is usually displayed in hundredths of a nautical mile. A hundredth of a nautical mile is only 60 feet, a couple of boat lengths. If you have a cross track error of .02, that's only 120 feet. What that means is that you should not make large helm corrections to get back on course.

A distance of 120 feet isn't much error in the ocean and a small, gradual helm movement will get you back on course, while a large correction will probably send you too far on the other side of your desired heading. If you get way off your original course line you might want to reset the cross track error from your new position instead of steering way off course to get back to the old line.

CAUSE FOR ALARM

The additional features built into most new lorans include several useful alarm functions, including an anchor watch alarm, destination alarm, and cross track error alarm. The anchor watch does what the name implies. The machine keeps track of your anchored position and sounds an alarm if the boat drifts outside the limits you have set (a quarter mile, a half mile, or whatever). Setting a limit for the alarm allows you to swing at anchor without disturbance but alerts you in the event of a major position shift that signals a dragging anchor.

A destination alarm simply lets you know where you are within a certain distance (which you can specify) of your destination. A cross track error alarm monitors your course, and sounds a warning when you steer too far to one side or the other. You can set the limits of the cross track alarm so the machine tolerates the minor helm swings and only warns you when there is a major change in heading.

ROOM FOR ERROR

Once a skipper masters the basics of loran navigation, there is a temptation to let the machine do all the work. For example, let's follow a skipper as he leaves the Port Everglades channel in Fort Lauderdale, Florida, and heads north to Saint Mary's, Georgia. He punches in latitude and longitude for the sea buoy eight miles out of Saint Mary's (30.42.70, 81.19.00), hits his GOTO, and lets the machine guide him there, using range and bearing, cross track error, and all the other functions we've talked about.

First off, let's hope he checked a chart to make sure there are no islands or sandbars in his path. Second, let's hope he double-checked his coordinates before he entered them. If he hit an 80 instead of an 81 for his longitude, he'll be hunting for the sea buoy somewhere way to the east of the continental shelf.

But he's in luck this time. He entered the numbers correctly, and he looked a chart over to familiarize himself with the course he will be running. In other words, he is practicing good basic seamanship, using the loran as an aid to navigation instead of relying on it as his sole source of information.

After a long run up the coast, he finds himself at what his loran says is his destination, and there is no sea buoy there! After a few minutes of searching, his mate gives a yell and points to a shape on the horizon. The sea buoy is almost a mile away.

Loran is supposed to be accurate; what happened? It could have been one of a number of things (which we'll describe in more detail in the "Sources of Error" section). Maybe the ASF correction wasn't 100 percent. Maybe the sea buoy was moved. Buoys and channel markers are sometimes changed, and to stay updated on these changes, skippers should read the Coast Guard's *Notice to Mariners* and note such changes on their charts and logs.

Perhaps the TD lines our friend used gave a poor crossing angle, in which case he should switch to the stations with TD lines crossing as near 90 degrees as possible. Base line extension and poor crossover angles aren't a problem in Georgia, but in some areas on the fringes of loran coverage (like the Bahamas), poor crossover angles can reduce loran accuracy to a mile or more.

The point is, loran accuracy and repeatability is quite good, but you shouldn't trust your machine as the absolute authority on your position. Loran navigation should be backed up by a solid understanding of plotting and charting techniques and by good solid seamanship.

By the way, it might be a good thing that our

friend's loran didn't send him straight to the buoy. Improbable as it may seem, there are cases on record of skippers who entered the coordinates of a marker on their machine and ran, literally, right up on top of it. Such embarrassing and potentially dangerous collisions are rare, but you should still make a habit of slowing down the last half mile or so before reaching waypoint destinations set close to shore, shoals, or other hard objects.

A MATTER OF RECORD

Before we leave our friend to tie up at the Saint Mary's dock, there is one more piece of business that needs to be taken care of. After checking his *Notice to Mariners* to make sure the sea buoy wasn't moved by the Coast Guard, our skipper should enter the corrected loran coordinates for the buoy in his loran log book. That way, he will have the right numbers for his particular loran to refer to the next time he comes north.

All loran users should keep permanent written records of such corrections, as well as numbers for favorite fishing spots, harbor entrances, navigation hazards, and all waypoints that might by reused. Many lorans will store up to several hundred waypoints in the memory, but it would be unwise to trust the machine to remember everything without a backup. More than one skipper has had a lightning bolt, voltage jump, or simple machine failure wipe out years of valuable coordinates because he didn't back the machine's memory up with a written record.

FINDING A DIFFICULT WAYPOINT

Here's a little problem that you may have run into: you were out fishing one day and found a fantastic piece of bottom. You saved it in

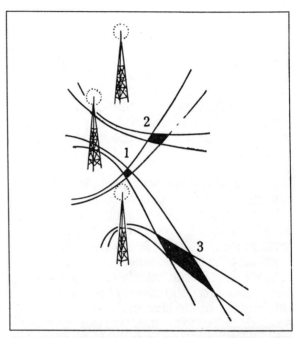

The double lines indicate the .1 TD margin of accuracy which loran can give us. Notice that in some areas where TDs intersect at nearly right angles (point 1), the area of uncertainty is relatively small, while the area increases as the angles become more acute (points 2 and 3).

the loran's memory as a waypoint, but when you tried to run back to the same spot on another trip, you couldn't find the bottom.

In a case like this, it might be the loran system itself that is causing you trouble, and an understanding of the system might help you find that bottom. If you know the TD coordinates for that spot, look on the chart and check the angle the lines cross at and the width between the TD lines. In areas along the curve where lines are spread and intersect at wide angles, there will be more surface area inside the TD grid.

The grid is the minimum time delay difference your machine can recognize. Newer machines can work in hundredths of TD units (although they may still display it in tenths), while older machines work in tenths. All points inside that grid will have the same TD coordinates.

If your machine is operating in latitude/longitude, the best it can do is to put you somewhere in that grid. By switching the machine to a TD readout, you can use a little trick to gain more accuracy. Begin by looking at a loran chart and figure which of your two slave stations has TD lines bunched closer together. Next, steer to a point along that narrower line and run down the line until you intersect the second TD. By doing this, you put yourself on a track that might be only 100 feet wide, while the track following the other TD line might be as wide as 500 or 600 feet.

ANCHORING ON A REEF

Finding a likely piece of structure isn't always enough. For bottom or drift fishing, you might want to anchor and leave yourself right above a particular spot. Instead of estimating wind and current drift and setting the anchor by guessing, you can use your loran to calculate exactly where to drop the hook so you can drift back to your spot.

To do this, put the boat right over the desired piece of bottom and enter this spot as a destination on your loran. Now, switch the machine to range and bearing mode and let the boat drift with the current for a few minutes.

For the sake of example, let's suppose you are in 100 feet of water and you plan to put out about 500 feet of anchor line. If you remember that each .01 of a nautical mile is 60 feet, you can figure that 500 feet is .08 nautical miles.

With this in mind, let the boat drift for awhile and then steer back on the bearing your loran tells you to. Continue past the destination on the same heading for about .08 nautical miles, plus a little extra to give the anchor time to sink. Then drop the hook. This will automatically put you upwind and upcurrent of your destination, and when your 500 feet of line is out, you will have drifted back.

By the way, if there is much current, your fishing lines won't go straight down, but will drift back behind the boat. If the current is much stronger than one knot, you should anchor even farther upcurrent so your lines will be over the structure when they drift back.

WARNING

Loran C is one of many aids to navigation. The prudent mariner should never depend on any single source of navigation information to the exclusion of others. You should also regularly plot and log loran C fixes during open-water navigation.

While your loran C set can tell you the direct course to steer to any given waypoint, it cannot tell you whether this is a safe course to follow. It doesn't tell you whether there is land or a dangerous reef in the way. You should always plot courses on a nautical chart before following the loran's recommended course.

SOURCES OF ERROR

This section is not intended to be a basic course in loran installation and operation, but is a troubleshooting guide for boaters who are already familiar with the operation of their particular machines. So we'll assume that you had your loran installed by a qualified dealer, who mounted it properly and adjusted everything correctly, and that you paid attention while he thoroughly explained the machine (as any reputable dealer should take the time to do).

We can call the first group of errors built-in errors, since they are inherent to the way loran works. There is really nothing you can do about system errors except understand them and try to minimize their effects.

The first, cross angle error, isn't really something that will show up on the screen as a bad number, but not understanding it could keep you from finding a waypoint. To explain cross angle errors, we need to remember how a loran receiver finds a position as the intersection of two TD lines, with the width of those lines being the minimum time delay distance your receiver can calculate. Again, these crossover lines are most accurate when they are nearest the base line, and when they intersect at close to a 90-degree angle. You begin to run into trouble when you use lines that are way out on a TD curve, or when two TD curves overlap at a large angle.

TD lines are measurable to within a tenth, and system accuracy is within plus or minus one-tenth. If you choose your time delay so that crossover angles are good, you'll have a repeatability of within 50 to 100 feet. If that seems like a big area to you, keep in mind that it is really only three or four boat lengths, and you couldn't stop that quickly if you were running at speed.

But you don't always have the best possible crossover angle, and you may find yourself above a rock pile with a TD intersection that is 100 feet in one direction, but 600 feet the other way. In such a case, you can use a little trick to increase your repeatability when you come back. Run up the narrower TD line, and cut your throttles as the wider number comes onto your screen.

Signal strength is a system variable that can shut your machine down. The most common cause of a weak signal is distance; the transmitter is just too far away. The best way to deal with weak signals is to avoid them by switching to a closer transmitter. For example, anyone looking at loran charts in Ft. Myers, Florida, might pick the Raymondville, Texas, and Jupiter, Florida, transmitters because the crossing angles look best. But the Texas transmitter is so far away that weak signals will disrupt operation from time to time. You would be better off using the stronger and closer transmitter in Grangeville, Louisiana, even though the crossover angles aren't as good.

Also, loran signals lag as they cross over land, so be aware of this if you are navigating in an area with a large landmass between you and the transmitter. For example, the Florida mainland lies between the Keys and all the transmitters in the southern chain. This can cause discrepancies of up to one mile on a loran fix. But this isn't really that bad, as this lag is fairly consistent and affects accuracy, but not repeatability in most cases.

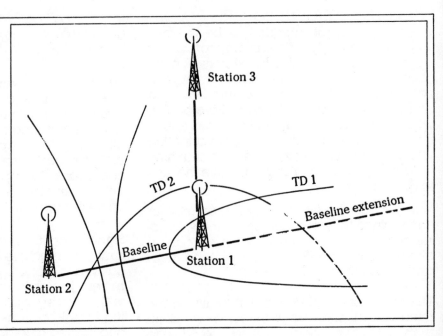

Base line extension error can occur when TD lines are very close to the transmitter. The steep curve made by transmitters 1 and 2 (TD 1) begins close to transmitter 1 and curves sharply behind it, where it is intersected by the transmitter 1 and 3 TD line (TD 2) in two distinct places. A loran receiver cannot tell the difference, and will give the same TD position for both places.

This means locals who already know where they are going have no problem. But transient boaters who are using the loran to steer a course by the charts might be in for a surprise.

Chart accuracy is something we too often take for granted. Just because a chart says a buoy is in a certain place doesn't mean it is always there. Check your *Notice to Mariners* for corrections, and generally be aware of discrepancies in the chart. For places you run to frequently, you might want to keep a corrections log that shows the difference in your reading and the chart numbers. In the end, if repeatability is our goal, we shouldn't worry about where a thing is as much as we should about how to get back there again. When accuracy is required, however, the skipper must leave a margin for error.

Base line extension is the final system fluke we will mention. A base line extension is an imaginary line that runs on beyond the two transmitters in a series. The closer you get to the base line extension, the less accurate your readings get. With TD lines very close to the extension, there is a possibility of duplicate readings (there are two places with the same loran number). Keep this in mind when you are traveling through these affected areas, and don't trust your navigation or autopilot when the numbers are close to the base line extension.

EQUIPMENT RELIABILITY

One of the biggest physical problems facing loran receivers is moisture. Unless your unit specifically says it is waterproof, don't assume that it is. Mount your loran in an enclosed area where spray and sea air can't get at it.

The next most common problem that affects receivers is poor power supply. If the loran is hooked into the same line as the starter battery, starting an engine or otherwise drawing a large surge of power can lock up the loran. The solution is to incorporate a second power supply just for the electronics.

Transmitter malfunctions are another source of potential error. Most transmitters have a back-up system, but lightning, power outages, or maintenance can take a station off the air for a while. To make sure your stations are working, check the SNR (signal-to-noise ratio) and look at each station to make sure they all read. If a station is off the air, switch to another. If the master is down, you may just have to wait.

ENVIRONMENTAL ERRORS

The third group of errors we can look at are environmental errors, which include things both inside and outside of the boat.

Weather can affect loran reception. If there is a cold front moving between you and a transmitter, you will lose half to three-quarters of your signal strength. There's really nothing you can do about a cold front, other than to be aware of it, and maybe try to find an unaffected transmitter. Local systems such as squalls can also affect reception.

The lightning that comes with a squall line doesn't affect the receiver (unless you get a direct hit), but the static buildup in the air will. If you start to notice a buzzing or humming sound, lay the antenna down and shut the loran off to protect the machine.

Antenna location can have a lot to do with loran reception. If your loran antenna is in the shadow of a larger VHF whip, you will lose reception. Try to set your antennas as far apart as possible, and use an extension on the loran antenna to get it up to the same height as the VHF.

Electronic noise is a problem for lorans. Alternators are a common culprit, but each vessel is different. To locate the source of any disruptive noise, turn on the SNR function, then start turning on different ship's systems until you locate the problem. Noise must be dealt with at the source, and you will have to depend on your electronics dealer to install the right filters to eliminate noise.

One common loran failure occurs in bad weather when windshield wipers are turned on. Not many people think to try the windshield wipers when they are checking the system back at the dock in good weather. The moral is, try to think of all possible sources of noise, as it could save you trouble later.

Noise in the local environment can disrupt a loran. If you have ruled out other possible sources of malfunction, pay attention to the area where the loran is located. Excessive heat build-up can make your electronics malfunction. To prevent this, make sure your receiver is adequately ventilated. Sometimes sunlight coming through a windshield can have a "greenhouse effect," so make sure your loran is not in direct sunlight.

Humidity is another cause of malfunction that may disappear once the machine dries out.

More than one irate loran owner has disconnected his inoperative system and carted it down to the dealer . . . where it worked perfectly. (It probably dried out on the way to the shop.) The best thing for you to do when a malfunction occurs is to be observant.

OPERATOR ERRORS

Lack of navigational skills has gotten more than one loran user in trouble. It's not enough simply to punch in numbers and go. You need to have an idea of how those numbers came about and where they are in relation to the rest of the ocean.

Carelessness is another source of problems. If you put the wrong numbers into the machine, it will send you to the wrong place. Take a little extra time to check your numbers before saving them.

Lack of system understanding is something you can't blame on the machine or anyone else. If you bought a used loran, or didn't get adequate instructions from your dealer, make the effort to learn your machine thoroughly. Read the manual, get a friend with a similar system to go over it with you, or take it to a dealer who has the time to explain things properly. Your loran can do a lot for you, but only if you know how to use it.

MORE ABOUT LORAN
by Rod and Susie Stebbins

Much has been written about the loran system, and for whose who would like to delve a bit more into the technical details, good books are available. Two of the best, because they are easy to understand, are *The Loran-C User's Guide* by Bonnie Dahl (Richardson's Marine Publishing, Inc., 1986), and *The Complete Loran-C Handbook* by Luke Melton (International Marine Publishing Company, 1986). The goals in the paragraphs that follow are to set straight one or two common misconceptions and to offer some common-sense advice on using the coordinates in this book to best advantage.

We have had the pleasure of having aboard our Sancho several brands of loran receivers to use for verification of coordinates, and we have yet to see much difference among them when reading TDs. Currently, we have four loran units aboard, and except for the time it takes each of them to settle down after a change in speed or direction has been initiated, they all agree consistently in the TD mode. Thus, we suggest in this book that reefs, wrecks, rocks, ledges, and the like ought to be located using TDs with the loran's ASF (Automated Secondary Factor) disabled. At least this way all of us will be using the same measurements in our searches. Please note, however, that when your destination is a charted aid to navigation, you should input the Lat/Lon rather than the TD coordinates as a waypoint in your loran, but only after "squaring" the loran receiver with the real world as described below. This applies to all the coordinates listed in Chapter 6 on "passes," and you'll find an explanation in the introduction to that chapter.

Why must the loran be reconciled to local geography? Because, while all lorans are consistent when displaying TDs at a given location, the same machines at the same location when asked to display latitudes and longitudes will not agree at all. This is true whether or not the ASFs provided by the factory are in operation; the root cause is in the software and the arithmetic conversions from TDs to Lat/Lons.

To help you understand loran's local limitations, we suggest you conduct the following exercises on one of those wonderful weekends when the weather is peaches and cream, and that you duplicate the test when the weather is less than nice. Also, verify a position or a range and bearing frequently — say, on the same day of each month — and save all your findings for the year. Not only will you know the local limitations, you will also know in subsequent years when the object of your affection is becoming a candidate for the shop or the scrap pile.

1. Initializing (seeding) your loran:

- *At a wet slip.* Determine the latitude and longitude of your slip as accurately as you possibly can and initialize (seed) your loran. This procedure is necessary with all lorans; using this "seed" your loran will subsequently pick the best loran transmitting chain and the two strongest slave or secondary stations within that chain. Based on local knowledge, change your secondary selection using manual override when advisable. Turn the loran on, seed it, and once it has settled down and is providing your present-position information, write down your position in TDs and Lat/Lon. We call this position "home," and we store the Lat/Lon into memory position 98 (loran capacity of 100) or 198 (loran capacity of 200). If you are able to determine a very accurate Lat/Lon position of "home" from the chart or an actual survey benchmark, note the difference your loran offers and save that information.
- *On a trailer.* Do the same as above, choosing for the site at which you enter your "seed" the place where you launch your boat regularly. Save that Lat/Lon coordinate.

2. Selecting test coordinates:

Select five or six permanent navigational markers that are not likely to move or be moved and/or some geographical objects from a NOAA chart that are easy to get right next to in a boat. We use a coastal chart (scale of 1:40,000). Make sure you have the most recent edition of the chart. Scale as accurately as you can the Lat/Lons of each buoy or landmark, and list these coordinates on a piece of paper.

3. Verifying your loran's ability:

- Get underway to the first selected location. Position your boat just as close to the marker or object as you can get with bow and stern anchors.
- Once the loran has settled down for, say, 10 or 20 minutes, read the TDs and the Lat/Lons and record each of them as loran readings. Enter the TDs into the loran's waypoint memory so that you will have them available throughout the year. Note the difference between the loran's Lat/Lon and the Lat/Lon taken from the NOAA chart.
- You now know how far your loran's Lat/Lon deviates from the real world and the chart. In Sancho, we have tied ourselves

to a marker so that our loran antenna was just a few feet from it, only to be informed by our loran that we were as much as 0.08 nautical mile away. Eight one-hundredths of a nautical mile is only about 438 feet: close enough to see the marker, but no cigar.
- Still at the first location, check whether your loran will accept additional corrections; depending on the unit, this may be done by modifying the ASF, inserting "Additional Correction Factors," or inserting a "Current Position." If your loran has this capability, then your choice of a receiver was a wise one. If it does not, commit to memory how far "off position" you are and what you have to do to correct the error. (We are not aware of lorans on the market today that lack all ability to accept corrections.)
- With the correction factors in place, you should have a loran that is reconciled to the real world. All that is left is to verify that fact. Weigh your anchors and visit the next of the locations you have chosen. Be sure to set yourself up as you did at location #1. Allowing 10 to 20 minutes to settle down, record the TDs and Lat/Lons as before; you should find that the Lat/Lons are very close or identical to the coordinates you have measured from the chart.
- If you discover any difference, doublecheck your chart measurement for accuracy. We ought to be nearly splitting hairs, and you will probably find that you are as close as you are able to measure and interpolate to the coordinates you have taken from the chart.
- Verify each test location in turn and enter the proper coordinates into your loran. Note what has happened to your TDs as well.

4. Establishing your own benchmark:

- As soon as you have completed correcting your loran, return to port and secure your boat at a location that is easily accessed and will not likely be subject to change. This might be a gas dock, your wet slip (provided your wet slip is not covered or jammed in among buildings, masts, hills, etc.), a piling, or a floating dock that might be well out of the way.
- Note the exact location and record its TDs and Lat/Lon.
- Check this reference location often. Keep records of your findings, as you are likely to see slight variations each time. There is no reason for alarm; the loran system is simply "floating" about naturally. "Loran system float" is due to a multitude of factors, which include electronic interference "noises" on your boat or in the atmosphere, degree of humidity, condition of foliage and vegetation, etc. But these variations should be minor. As long as we remain in the TD mode and ignore the Lat/Lon, the loran will take us back to the same spot over and over again with uncanny accuracy.

The only time we seem to get confused or in trouble is when we try to make the loran geographically correct and agree with the local charting. The loran can accomplish this feat only by calculating the Lat/Lons from the TDs it sees. This is why we went through the exercises above, and why we entered in those additional corrections for the loran to use in its calculations.

CHAPTER 4
BOATING BUDDIES

Welcome to the world of loran owners, sailors, and boaters! Whether you are a seasoned salt or a novice, we are sure you will appreciate loran more as you discover the joys of boating and cruising it unlocks.

When we first started boating, we thought that a 10- to 20- mile trip was exciting, and when enroute, we were never quite sure we'd be able to survive the trip, since we didn't know what we were doing. We used to dream about taking vacations on a small boat. We would try to imagine just how we would make a three-week vacation on a 22-foot Glastron boat with a "cuddly" cuddy cabin work.

It seemed that we almost never had enough room, and over the years we kept buying bigger boats, with the same end result. No matter how large the boat, we never seemed to have quite enough room to take all the things we just knew we would be lost without!

It also seemed that the size of our boats increased with the scope of our abilities. Our first 22-foot boat was great for running around in small circles fast. There always seemed to be enough room for swimming suits, towels, lunch, and a small cooler. Then we started fishing, and when we added tackle for two, we needed a bigger boat. And so we bought a 24-foot Sea Ray with an aft stateroom (bedroom) for Christmas.

By the time the next fall arrived, we were armed with scuba certificates, and what with our diving gear, there was no continuing without an even larger boat soon. We justified it because we had just taken a couple of long trips. The first consisted of 350 miles and the second was a 980-miler over a three-week vacation. We soon found that traveling by small boat is very practical and quite easily done, even with the most modest of means.

But a friend of ours had that bigger boat, and every time we looked at it, we just knew it was the perfect boat for us. It was a twin-engine 27-foot Sea Ray, fully loaded with almost all the toys, including air conditioning and a custom-made livewell, which he used to keep live lobster in until dinner time.

Our friend's boat went up on the block, and within a couple of weeks, Sancho number three was ours. We settled down for awhile, knowing that we had arrived at the perfect size and that we were adequately equipped to do whatever we wanted to.

Then came the two-week trips, the six-week trips, the three months in the Bahamas, and the four and a half months in the Florida Keys.

One night on the way home to Tampa, we were cruising about 35 miles offshore when

---

HELPFUL HINT

Use your VHF radio for essential calls and remember that VHF Channel 16 is for emergencies only, not for radio checks, finding out how the fishing is, and general chatting. Once you have made contact with your party, go to another channel approved for general use. Your consideration will be greatly appreciated by all, including the Feds!

the skies clouded over and the rain came. The seas built, our windows were covered with salt spray, and we couldn't see anything but black outside. Though not in any real danger that night, we suddenly found ourselves in what seemed to be an unusually small boat.

That next Christmas we took delivery of our fourth Sancho and marveled at how big this 30-foot Sea Ray was, with its full 11-foot-wide beam. At last, a roller skating rink that floats! This was it — a generator and all the toys, including a radar. Happiness at last, right? Wrong.

DAFFYNITION

First Mate: (1) Wife and usually 50-percent owner of the vessel and accompanying debt. (2) The hardest-working member of the crew. (3) The only member of the crew that knows where anything is, as evidenced by the "get me" commands. (4) The person on the vessel who gets yelled at most of the time. (5) A multipurpose person capable of cooking, washing windows, polishing, looking for "things," getting "things," and knowing what the Captain is trying to say, all the while pretending that boating is great fun. (6) Kid tender. (7) Guest tender. (8) The only responsible person on the vessel, yet seldom allowed to drive. (9) Honey dearest. (10) Girlfriend or fiance. (11) Any person not at the helm. (12) The only person who can get even with the Captain and get away with it and always wins all of the arguments (one way or the other).

Within the first year, Susie was already wishing for the boat of her dreams, a 36-foot Sea Ray with inboard engines and a football field for a cockpit. As of this printing, we have just taken delivery and will soon be out on the water. We are positive that this boat will have enough room . . . for now.

OUR FAVORITE THINGS

For us to define boating would require a lot of paper, because boating is as diverse as life itself. There are so many different aspects and facets of boating that it simply isn't possible to write about them all in one small volume.

Boat owners range from those who are casual about their pastime to the ardent "aficionados" who spend much of their lives reading, living, and breathing boating at every salty opportunity. We sincerely hope that by reading some of our text, you'll find for yourself some of the things that have become dear to our hearts. We will try to ring that certain bell or spark up the proverbial idea light that just might start a new hobby.

Just run your fingers down the list of destinations in this book, imagine the wrecks and the reefs, the many havens and endless ports that are not even listed, then close your eyes and drift off into that magic land called imagination to dream of trips that you will be taking... one of these days.

SNORKELING

The sport of snorkeling is something that can be done at one's own speed. When left to myself, I can actually fall asleep while floating and looking! Snorkeling is a very personal sport that is filled with colors and curiously shaped things that often defy the imagination.

Snorkeling can be done in water that is as shallow as six inches to a foot deep, depending on how fat you are. Susie can snorkel right up to the beach, but I have to snorkel out where the water is at least knee-deep, or else I'll wear part of my stomach off.

It isn't hard to learn how to snorkel. Just learn how to breathe through a tube without inhaling salt water. If you are hunting shells or treasure, it's a lot easier to float and kick with a mask and snorkel than it is to walk down the beach and bend over to pick up the same object.

Equipment needed: Snorkel, net-type bag, mask, and fins.

SCUBA DIVING

Scuba diving and boating are natural partners. We keep a couple of air tanks and our scuba gear on the boat at all times. We use this equipment to identify reefs, ledges, and wrecks, and find it useful for cleaning the bottom of the boat and inspecting the zinc anodes, trim tabs, and engine shafts. We use the equipment for hunting for something to eat, something to photograph, something to watch, and something to collect.

There are classes in scuba diving just about everywhere you turn. Equipment can be purchased new from dealers or used from the classified ads in the newspapers. Scuba diving used to be very expensive, but now just about anyone can afford the sport in varying degrees.

There are books that have been written to address just about every facet of diving, from beginning techniques to the very special advanced disciplines.

Scuba is a very natural addition to the boater's learned skills. If you don't wish to participate in the sport, you can be assured of missing out on about 80 percent of what the seas have to offer. Scuba diving is open to persons of almost any age. The young and bold dive deep and long, but even older folks can enjoy much of the underwater world if skill is tempered with good judgment.

We seldom dive deeper than about 45 to 50 feet unless the water is crystal-clear. Most of the colors of the spectrum disappear below about 30 feet, and since we dive to see the colors, we are usually in shallow water diving around the live coral reefs.

But we also like the excitement of new adventure, such as exploring a new wreck or something of that sort, too, and, properly tempted, we have made some rather exciting and (we later felt) risky dives as well.

Equipment needed: Certification and about 300 pounds of diving equipment per diver.

CAMPING

Camping on the beaches is full of romance and fun. The campfires at the water's edge and the sing-alongs make for great fun. We used to camp with a tent and the works until we got our "bigger boat." Now we have the best of both worlds. We sleep in beds with sheets on them and slap the bugs with everyone else at the campfire.

We always keep a case or two of beer available for these events and never pass up the opportunity to share a case by the fire. We have met some of the nicest people camping, usually young and in love and full of life, adventure, and hopes for the future.

The feelings are contagious and we love to be near people going places, sharing sea stories and information of wonderful things gone by.

Beaches have a certain charm that invites people everywhere to remember their childhoods. Where else can you find all sorts of people prodding the sand, building sand castles, digging moats, basking, swimming, running, tossing and riding toys, and — oh my — wearing all of those tiny swimming suits? Susie has as much fun as I looking at all of the shapes of humanity, all clad in their least and some strutting their most.

There is nothing quite like a beach full of boaters with their boats anchored to and fro, parked side by side, each having its own story to tell.

Beaches are grand places for dreamers, but we have found that some are not the best for overnighting. Some beaches are quite tame through most of the tides, but some can be quite bumpy with a bit of wind.

This brings up learning from experience. We now lay out lots of anchor line when we are anticipating spending the night. We make sure that the stern anchor is going to stay put. By the way, our stern anchor is the same size as our bow anchor, thereby serving as a spare anchor as well.

We very often raft with other boats. We have discovered that one anchor will hold several boats quite well provided the current isn't too strong during the change of tides.

Once, while rafted up, we thought we would be safer with two anchors down. By morning the two anchor lines were fairly well braided, so we don't do that much anymore without well-placed stern anchors to keep the rafted boats from turning about themselves. We have not had the problem with one anchor that we have had with several. The number of anchors a rafting party should consider using is a judgment call.

When we are in doubt, we don't raft up; instead, we set our own anchor. Rafting boats together where there is the possibility of waves should be done with great care. Sailboats probably should never raft side by side lest their rigging get caught by some uncaring power yacht throwing a three-foot wake in passing. We have seen this happen, and the noise of masts colliding is heart-breaking.

When rafting power boats, large fenders at least 12 inches in diameter should be used, and the boats must be lashed together as tightly as possible. When boats are improperly lashed together with the wrong fenders, you can just about bank on damages.

Equipment needed: Friends and a case of beer.

BOATING

Boating to us encompasses many categories: cruising, fishing, water skiing, camping, cooking, social events, boating clubs, dining out along the waterways, powerboat races, watching or participating in sailing regattas, entertaining friends and business associates, using the boat as a summer cottage, and last, but in no way least, just plain putt-putting. It's great to travel fast or slowly and go nowhere as quickly or as slowly as one can.

Owning a boat is a unique kind of experience. We have not been able to figure out why we think that something that simply floats is so neat.

Susie and I were discussing this phenomenon. When I said, "I just don't know why we love it so much; you figure it out," she countered with, "It is easy to understand. If I can love you and not understand why, then you can love the boat and not understand it, too!" I guess she has it straight in her mind, so it must be okay.

Better than 50 percent of the pleasure of owning a boat is having your mate enjoy it as much or more than you do. We have just such a circumstance and enjoy all of the activities we've mentioned here during the course of the year. Our favorites are fishing, cruising, scuba diving, camping at our favorite gunkhole while rafted with dear friends, and looking forward to the next time we are going out — which is just about every week.

We first thought that cruising was a bit risky and truly an adventure. Now that we have taken many several-hundred-mile trips, we have come to the conclusion that cruising long distances is little more than a whole lot of little trips put together into one big journey.

Sometimes we make major crossings of large bodies of water when we can't see land for hours. But even then, we are rarely more than 35 miles from land and we are always well prepared. Sancho will have plenty of fuel, we will have plenty of supplies for meals, and we'll stock lots of water, soft drinks, and bait for fishing. Sancho has never let us down to date, but we are always prepared.

Preventive maintenance is the real answer to keeping the boat going. We change the oil and oil filters every 25 hours of running, we change the fuel/water separator filters every 50 hours, and we have a major tune-up every change of the season or no less than four times a year. The major tune-up includes checking ignition wiring, plugs, coils, condensers, rotors, and rotor caps. Now that we have an electronic ignition, we carry an extra unit on board.

Other spare parts that we keep on board include: a full set of fuses, a set of hand tools, a handful of wire connectors, a few feet of extra electrical wire (various sizes), two sets of fan belts, extra props, and extra prop nuts (we have lost the nuts while changing the props and a prop without nuts is embarrassing and impossible). A wrench to remove the prop nut is also a handy thing to have available. We carry containers with the proper hydraulic oil and engine oil. We always have enough engine oil to change the oil in one engine, at least. A couple of extra oil and separator filters make up the rest of the spares we have found necessary.

Cruising with loran and all the other little toys made for boats is neat and not at all confusing. Many of the electronic devices have multiple purposes, offering a certain redundancy that provides us with extra security. For example, the white line doubles as a depth finder, the radar doubles as a limited range finder, the loran doubles as a knot meter and a compass, the VHF doubles as a weather station/advisory, and the depth indicator doubles as a "passifier."

We think of our compass as the main instrument, and we like to imagine that the dial is similar to the doggie statue in the back window of a "Mexican taxi," with his head lazily moving about left to right, fore and aft. We're sure he's quietly thinking, "Ole, ole, ole."

We enjoy cruising at night while watching the shore lights. We have romantic moons, good wine, and soft music, without the threat of a midnight wrestling session with a crab trap line and float that are fouled in the props. We are either very lucky or the crabbers take their traps in at night. In the daytime, it's a different story.

We love to take long walks along the beaches while combing for meaningless treasure, and we have been tempted to buy an electronic metal detector so that we could have something else to carry in the boat. We will get that when we get our bigger boat . . . after our next bigger boat.

At anchor, we can usually be found swimming about, basking in the sun, or cleaning the water line and inspecting Sancho's bottom. There are plenty of things to do to the boat when cruising, such as checking the engine's various types of juices, including battery water levels and hydraulic reservoirs, soaping down bilges, wiping the engines down, cleaning those mysterious white spots from the Bimini top, scrubbing windows, polishing bright work, oiling the teak, greasing the zerks of the steering and the outdrives, greasing the underwater zerks on the outdrives, polishing the boat, flushing the sand from the rope locker, washing down the fishing poles and diving gear, spraying the metal parts with silicone lubricant . . . And then there is the constant challenge of getting Susie to do all this while I do something "very important" that can't be interrupted even for a minute.

Susie always wants to know why it is that just when she finishes washing and polishing the windshields and gets her supplies put away, the largest bird in the county suddenly deposits its signature for everyone to see. I guess the only response to her dilemma is that she ought to be grateful that cows can't fly.

On any quiet evening at anchor, there is no serenity quite like that found while holding that special person and watching a sunset that brings on songs of eternal love and commitment. It seems Susie and I have more of these moments on the boat than at home. I guess this is why Sancho figures into our plans so often.

You don't have to have an expensive boat to discover all those special feelings and experiences. It doesn't matter if you're aboard a motoryacht, a sailboat, or a rowboat. With a

---

WIT & WISDOM
A displacement hull can best be described as a sea plow.

little imagination and planning, the sunset will do the rest.

People who say that a boat is a hole in the water probably don't have a mate who shares the experiences of boating with them.

The sea has fed us emotionally as well as figuratively and when we have least expected it, it has provided splendid food for the table.

Now, let us try to summarize BOAT. It is a platform and vehicle for romance, beauty, togetherness, travel, excitement, and nourishment, and we doubt that many hobbies can offer quite that much. I often wonder what else there is worth having that Sancho is not already a part of providing.

Equipment needed. A boat and a bucket of money.

CHAPTER 5

THE LOWDOWN ON DIVING

Diving in the oceans and gulfs of the world requires proper training, including instruction in open-water diving skills. Deep dives are always hazardous and should be attempted only by those who are experienced and physically ready. Dives deeper than 25 feet in open seas should be planned carefully and attempted only with someone who has already made that particular dive.

Smart divers keep a knife handy and consider it a tool rather than a weapon. There is no telling when a diver may encounter the remains of some type of rope, net, or very stout monofilament fishing line that is impossible to cut or break by hand and often too stout to bite. If you become entangled, stay calm and use your knife to free yourself.

When tides change, so does the flow of water. Remember to check on whether the present water flow will remain the same throughout the duration of your dive or whether it will shift, leaving you with a long swim upcurrent. Swimming against currents and tides when you are tired after a fun dive can be very risky, if not impossible, especially if the current takes the boat and diver out of each other's sight.

Those new to saltwater and open-water diving are advised to contact a dive shop in the area they plan to dive to learn the area's potential hazards and make sure they have the necessary skills. We urge everyone to know all there is to know about a dive before venturing into the water.

Always keep someone who can navigate, drive, and anchor the boat aboard when divers are in the water. If there is no one left topside to deal with unforeseen circumstances, the boat might not be there when you surface. The newspapers sometimes report a boat found drifting with nobody aboard.

The "boat keeper" should know the exact coordinates the divers entered the water, and he or she should monitor the boat's location with the loran to make sure it hasn't slipped anchor and departed the scene. The tender should also know when the divers are scheduled to surface and the maximum amount of time each diver can spend underwater.

When currents make it difficult for divers to stay near the boat, we always run a line from the stern on a float, and drop a second anchor at the stern so that it almost reaches the bottom (it's usually within a foot or two). We call this our story pole. We attach a 40-foot line to our wrists and tie the other end to the story pole line with a large stainless steel snap. We have found this method best when diving in limited visibility and currents that are too strong to swim against easily.

On Sancho, we have a freshwater faucet in the cockpit, with a 25-foot hose attached for washing ourselves and our diving gear when we are done for the day. We also keep a spray can of silicone lubricant around to spray all of the metal pieces of our regulator and other diving equipment.

We have power heads (cartridge spear heads) we use as a precaution against aggressive fish (sharks). We disassemble them at the end of every dive and wash the pieces in fresh water and spray the parts before assembling them again.

Susie paints the cartridge firing caps and the perimeter of the bullet where it meets the cartridge with fingernail polish. This helps keep the powder dry. We use a powerhead that will accept both .357 Magnum and .38 Special rounds.

Last, when we are underway and the boat is bouncing about, we tie all of the tanks together with a line and lay them down. This keeps them from rolling about the cockpit and endangering life, limb, and the all-important pursuit of happiness.

CHAPTER 6

MAKING PASSES

This chapter works differently from those that follow, so a few words of explanation are in order. Beginning with Chapter 7, our chief business is life, liberty, and the pursuit of happiness — specifically, we'll be looking for fine anchorages and great spots for fishing and diving. Here in Chapter 6, however, we're pursuing aids to navigation — sea buoys, channel buoys, midchannel buoys, and primary and secondary lights — and this is serious business indeed. The Coast Guard fixes and records the locations of navaids not by TDs but by latitude and longitude, and so must we. If you should ever have to make an emergency call to the Coast Guard they will want to know your position, not in TDs but in degrees of latitude and longitude, and if you want help promptly you'd best know the answer.

Thus the controlling coordinates in this chapter are latitude and longitude, and from these the associated TDs have been calculated for your convenience using standard algorithms to which *no* ASF corrections have been applied. We have taken great care to ensure the accuracy of each latitude and longitude, but we cannot guarantee the same degree of accuracy for the TDs due to two mitigating factors: (1) The algorithms used to convert TDs to Lat/Lons or vice versa are not uniformly precise; and (2) the TDs overprinted on government charts are calculated not with the use of algorithms, but rather using theoretical rates of propagation of radio waves from loran transmitter locations. We do well always to remember that loran was conceived as an *approximate* position-fixing aid — as a means of finding the haystack in the field, not the needle in the haystack. With smarter, more sensitive machines and a growing database to work with, loran's users can now coax a level of performance from the system far beyond anything its originators conceived of. But we must be mindful, in doing so, of the limitations we sidestep but cannot eliminate. Loran supplements but does not replace chartwork, dead reckoning, and a navigator's care and skill.

For this chapter, proceed as follows: Initialize your loran receiver and "align" it with local geography as described near the end of Chapter 3. Then, when using the waypoints listed in this chapter, input latitudes and longitudes, *not* TDs. You may or may not want the ASF function enabled, depending on the model and its method of receiving additional local corrections from you, the user (as outlined in Chapter 3). Consult the manufacturer's instructions, and you should have no problem. When chartering or operating your own boat in unfamiliar waters, you may use the TDs as waypoints (again, with the ASF function disabled), but do so cautiously.

Please note that the convoluted coastlines along British Columbia's borders with Alaska and Washington led us to include some British Columbia coordinates with those of Alaska and Washington. They are so noted. Also, coordinates designated "Aleutians" include the Alaska Peninsula.

This chapter eliminates the need to search for charts, to measure, and then to interpolate coordinates. If your favorite pass and its markers are not found in this chapter, please understand that we did not omit it intentionally; we probably just haven't made it there yet! If you have an immediate need to see your coordinates printed in this book, turn your loran on, your ASF off, take the readings, and send them to us. We will make the entries and include the changes in the next printing.

No effort will be made by us to issue errata for pass buoys or markers that have been moved for whatever reason. We sincerely hope that each boater remains responsible enough to search throughout the volumes that contain "Notice to Mariners" when planning trips. Probably the only time that the cheese really gets binding is when we are approaching a new pass or a pass we have not been to for some time and it is dark, foggy, and the radar decides to take a vacation.

That is when Susie will always ask, "Honey, did you check to see if the buoy has been moved?" Like any good husband who doesn't want to alarm his mate or get into trouble with her (whichever the case may be), I respond, "Yes, dearest darling," while I maintain a 100 percent pucker.

DIVING IN
Hey, divers! Remember, it might be a good idea to look below at the manmade tripod structures and markers found near and in passes. Sometimes large meals can be found at the markers. Sometimes other types of treasures, such as fishing poles, tackle, and anchors, can be found nearby. Watch out for boaters, and be advised that a red flag in the channel might invite a "matador" instead of informing the oncoming boater that there is a precious person underwater.

Believe it or not, there are boaters out there who do not know the rules of the road and there are many who really don't care either.

They'll just plow right on through where you are, so floating a diving flag is no insurance against propeller damage and/or serious injury.

We have learned to tie a floating flag to a line that is surrounded by an innertube painted bright red. Then, when we surface, we surface at the tube. We never dive, swim, or water ski in tight channels that boaters use for navigation.

Even with all of these precautions, beware of passes and areas that have markers, for you can be sure that there will be a boater coming along soon enough.

Sea buoys are fun to dive, as they very often will attract many kinds of fish. Diving these structures is easy. The dives are seldom deep, and always hold a mystery that's fun to solve, so be sure to take your camera and spear gun (where allowed). Also, blue crabs can easily be caught along the pilings and up the chains.

Remember that seldom are boaters allowed to tie boats and equipment directly to a buoy or buoy structure. Anchoring to the buoy may invite a not-so-welcome visit from the state police and/or Coast Guard.

We also have learned to have a boat watch aboard when everyone else is in the water. The boat watch will assure us we will not have to walk home.

TIDAL TIPS
Here's another important thing we discovered the hard way about traversing passes when

the tides are running strong: Where there is a narrow pass or inlet, it is possible to run into water conditions that would chill the heart of Neptune himself. Fast running tides through a pass or inlet, coupled with a strong seasonal wind in the right direction, can make for impossible conditions.

We went sideways (broached) once and thought for a minute we were going to go swimming. Check local conditions before taking on a pass during strong tidal conditions. Be prepared to go somewhere else instead of following the desire to get through. It's always better to be safe than sorry.

UNCOMMON COURTESY

Arriving at passes is always something of an event on our boat. It seems we arrive at just about the same time as all the "redneck boaters" do. A "redneck boater" is a boater who has not read the book (and probably can't read), has no idea what consideration is, and is intent upon arriving at the dock in time to make life just a bit nervy. We are sure there are only a few of these peculiar breeds around. They could easily be spotted if given an IQ test because they'd flunk spectacularly.

Please remember that courtesy is probably the only thing boaters ought to have in common. We try to be courteous to all boaters, but it sure is hard to be nice in a gaggle of "redneck boaters." As a matter of fact, it is hard not to act just like them when faced with a lack of consideration.

PASSES

STATE/COUNTRY	COUNTY/PROV	NAME	LAT	LON	TD#1	TD#2	CHART NO
AK		VALDEZ BOAT HARBOR NO 2	61-27.40	146-21.10	14754.92	32405.37	16700
AK		POINT MACKENZIE RANGE LIGHT	61-14.40	149-59.30	13822.78	32412.79	16660
AK		POINT MACKENZIE LIGHT NO 11	61-14.30	149-59.10	13822.52	32412.13	16660
AK		POINT WORONZOF LIGHT NO 10	61-12.30	150-00.80	13797.84	32400.85	16660
AK		KNIK ARM SHOAL BUOY NO 7	61-12.20	150-05.20	13782.00	32401.73	16660
AK		POINT WORONZOF RANGE LIGHT	61-12.20	150-01.20	13795.53	32400.40	16660
AK		FIRE ISLAND RANGE LIGHT	61-10.40	150-11.90	13742.42	32393.41	16660
AK		RACE POINT LIGHT	61-10.10	150-13.40	13734.57	32392.17	16660
AK		RACE POINT RANGE LIGHT	61-09.90	150-13.50	13732.34	32391.03	16660
AK		COOK INLET BUOY NO 5	61-08.30	150-20.80	13692.92	32384.21	16660
AK		FIRE ISLAND LIGHT NO 6	61-07.60	150-16.80	13699.49	32378.73	16660
AK		PORT VALDEZ LIGHT NO 15	61-07.40	146-33.90	14515.06	32256.47	16700
AK		VALDEZ BOAT HARBOR NO 3	61-07.40	146-21.20	14562.93	32245.50	16700
AK		PORT VALDEZ ROCK BUOY	61-05.40	146-24.60	14530.89	32232.46	16700
AK		PORT VALDEZ BRKWTR LIGHT	61-05.20	146-23.30	14533.86	32229.68	16700
AK		PORT VALDEZ ENTR ISLAND NO 14	61-05.10	146-36.70	14482.38	32240.66	16700
AK		MIDDLE ROCK LIGHT NO 13	61-04.90	146-39.00	14471.75	32241.03	16700
AK		ENTRANCE POINT LIGHT NO 12	61-03.80	146-39.60	14458.91	32232.88	16700
AK		POTATO POINT LIGHT NO 11	61-03.40	146-41.70	14447.12	32231.53	16700
AK		VALDEZ NARROWS BUOY NO 11A	61-03.30	146-41.50	14446.92	32230.57	16700
AK		POINT POSSESSION LIGHT	61-02.10	150-24.20	13622.47	32349.35	16660
AK		COOK INLET BUOY NO 3	60-59.20	150-52.10	13505.19	32343.41	16660
AK		MOOSE POINT LIGHT	60-57.40	150-41.00	13522.87	32328.77	16660
AK		ROCKY POINT LIGHT NO 10	60-57.10	146-46.00	14370.24	32185.91	16700
AK		BUSBY ISLAND LIGHT	60-53.80	146-48.90	14327.49	32162.75	16700
AK		ELLAMAR ENTRANCE BUOY NO 2	60-53.70	146-43.20	14348.09	32156.63	16700
AK		VALDEZ ARM BUOY NO 9	60-52.60	146-52.60	14301.92	32156.82	16700
AK		GLACIER ISLAND LIGHT	60-52.40	147-05.40	14251.40	32166.81	16700
AK		BLIGH REEF BUOY NO 6	60-50.50	146-54.30	14275.24	32142.08	16700
AK		TRINITY POINT LIGHT	60-48.40	148-34.00	13878.11	32205.81	16700
AK		DECISION POINT LIGHT	60-48.40	148-27.20	13903.42	32201.20	16700
AK		POINT PIGOT LIGHT	60-48.10	148-21.30	13922.56	32195.03	16700
AK		POINT ESTHER LIGHT	60-47.20	148-05.80	13972.00	32177.48	16700
AK		WHITTIER BRKWTR LIGHT NO 1	60-46.80	148-41.50	13834.79	32199.96	16700
AK		CULROSS ISLAND LIGHT	60-44.90	148-06.70	13946.42	32161.85	16700
AK		EAST FORELAND LIGHT	60-43.20	151-24.30	13252.27	32267.16	16660
AK		GOOSE ISLAND LIGHT	60-42.80	146-43.50	14241.98	32071.02	16700
AK		KENAI PIPE LINE DOCK N LIGHT	60-41.10	151-23.90	13232.79	32255.28	16660
AK		KENAI PIPE LINE DOCK S LIGHT	60-40.90	151-23.70	13231.41	32254.07	16660
AK		KNOWLES HEAD SHOAL BUOY NO 4	60-40.50	146-44.00	14217.95	32053.40	16700
AK		RED HEAD LIGHT	60-40.30	146-30.10	14268.49	32036.44	16700
AK		PERRY ISLAND LIGHT	60-39.30	147-55.80	13933.39	32113.01	16700
AK		LONE ISLAND SHOAL NO 2	60-38.30	147-47.20	13956.35	32098.32	16700
AK		ORCA BAY LIGHT NO 9	60-38.00	145-45.00	14413.89	31961.22	16700

PASSES

STATE/COUNTRY	COUNTY/PROV	NAME	LAT	LON	TD#1	TD#2	CHART NO
AK		NORTH ISLAND ROCK LIGHT NO 10	60-37.70	145-42.60	14419.77	31955.39	16700
AK		ORCA INLET CHANNEL BUOY NO 12	60-37.50	145-41.40	14422.23	31952.03	16700
AK		GRAVINA POINT LIGHT NO 3	60-37.40	146-15.10	14296.88	31995.23	16700
AK		ORCA INLET W CHANNEL LIGHT NO 2	60-36.90	145-45.50	14401.53	31952.61	16700
AK		ORCA INLET CHANNEL BUOY NO 14	60-36.90	145-41.80	14415.03	31947.49	16700
AK		ORCA INLET CHANNEL BUOY NO 15	60-36.80	145-41.50	14415.16	31946.22	16700
AK		CHANNEL ISLAND ROCK NO 7	60-36.50	145-48.70	14385.99	31953.61	16700
AK		THE NARROWS LIGHT NO 8	60-36.20	145-47.40	14387.88	31949.31	16700
AK		HANKS ISLAND ROCK BOUY NO 5	60-36.00	145-59.40	14341.81	31963.73	16700
AK		PORT NELLIE JUAN LIGHT	60-35.90	148-06.00	13861.79	32097.31	16700
AK		ORCA INLET CHANNEL BUOY NO 16	60-35.90	145-42.50	14402.91	31939.98	16700
AK		POINT ELEANOR LIGHT	60-34.90	147-33.70	13974.86	32060.90	16700
AK		ORCA INLET W CHANNEL NO 3	60-34.90	145-45.20	14383.50	31935.29	16700
AK		ORCA INLET W CHANNEL NO 4	60-34.70	145-45.60	14380.13	31934.16	16700
AK		ORCA INLET CHANNEL BUOY NO 18	60-34.60	145-44.70	14382.46	31932.06	16700
AK		ORCA INLET JUNCTION BUOY OI	60-34.00	145-45.50	14373.80	31928.11	16700
AK		KENAI RIVER RANGE LIGHT	60-33.00	151-15.80	13176.42	32205.67	16660
AK		SPIKE ISLAND LIGHT	60-33.00	145-46.10	14362.06	31920.51	16700
AK		CORDOVA BOAT HARBOR LIGHT NO 2	60-32.80	145-46.00	14360.51	31918.68	16700
AK		MIDDLE GROUND SHOAL BUOY NO 2	60-32.50	146-22.00	14224.08	31963.91	16723
AK		ODIAK PHAROS LIGHT	60-32.30	145-45.70	14356.84	31914.04	16700
AK		SMITH ISLAND BELL NO 1	60-32.10	147-17.10	14011.18	32023.38	16700
AK		KENAI ENTRANCE CHANNEL NO 1KE	60-31.30	151-20.50	13145.65	32198.58	16660
AK		CRAFTON ISLAND LIGHT	60-30.70	147-55.90	13849.64	32051.00	16700
AK		KALGIN ISLAND LIGHT	60-29.00	151-50.50	13038.19	32201.72	16660
AK		JOHNSTONE POINT LIGHT	60-29.00	146-36.70	14135.14	31953.90	16700
AK		MUMMY ISLAND LIGHT NO 5	60-27.80	145-59.20	14264.25	31895.32	16723
AK		KALGIN ISLAND W CHANNEL NO 2	60-26.90	152-06.50	12975.02	32198.67	16660
AK		PENNSYLVANIA ROCK BUOY NO 2	60-26.80	147-24.00	13933.72	31990.58	16700
AK		SEAL ISLAND LIGHT	60-25.80	147-24.90	13920.64	31984.02	16700
AK		HARRIET POINT LIGHT	60-23.70	152-14.40	12923.08	32185.66	16660
AK		KASILOF ENTRANCE CHANNEL NO 1	60-23.40	151-23.50	13057.82	32155.59	16660
AK		BEAR CAPE LIGHT NO 2	60-23.40	146-43.70	14055.02	31918.13	16700
AK		EGG ISLAND LIGHT E	60-22.30	145-44.70	14265.52	31828.32	16723
AK		EGG ISLAND LIGHT E	60-22.20	145-44.70	14264.58	31827.48	16013
AK		APPLEGATE SHOALS LIGHT	60-21.30	147-23.50	13882.68	31948.64	16700
AK		KALGIN ISLAND S LIGHT	60-20.80	152-04.50	12919.26	32164.65	16660
AK		POINT BENTINCK LIGHT NO 1	60-19.40	145-59.70	14182.70	31826.43	16723
AK		NEW YEAR ISLANDS LIGHT	60-18.70	147-55.00	13736.75	31963.18	16700
AK		PETER DAHL BAR CHANNEL P	60-18.50	145-29.70	14284.42	31772.68	16723
AK		SCHOONER ROCK LIGHT NO 1	60-18.40	146-54.30	13966.84	31892.10	16700
AK		EGG ISLAND WHISTLE EI	60-17.40	145-43.10	14225.19	31784.65	16013
AK		EGG ISLAND WHISTLE EI	60-17.40	145-43.10	14225.19	31784.65	16723
AK		GRASS ISLAND BAR LIGHT G	60-14.80	145-16.90	14295.92	31719.65	16723

PASSES

STATE/COUNTRY	COUNTY/PROV	NAME	LAT	LON	TD#1	TD#2	CHART NO
AK		PLEIADES LIGHT	60-14.40	148-00.50	13674.02	31937.81	16700
AK		CAPE HINCHINBROOK LIGHT	60-14.30	146-38.70	13987.41	31839.77	16013
AK		SOFTUK BAR CHANNEL LIGHT NO 5	60-13.80	144-57.00	14357.13	31675.73	16723
AK		KOKENHENIC BAR CHANNEL LIGHT K	60-13.60	145-08.60	14314.36	31694.84	16723
AK		SEAL ROCKS SHOAL NO 1	60-10.00	146-44.80	13923.36	31814.09	16013
AK		SEAL ROCKS SHOAL NO 1	60-10.00	146-44.80	13923.36	31814.09	16700
AK		MARTIN ISLANDS LIGHT	60-09.90	144-36.20	14393.12	31601.79	16723
AK		SEAL ROCKS LIGHT	60-09.80	146-50.20	13900.75	31819.77	16013
AK		SEAL ROCKS LIGHT	60-09.80	146-50.20	13900.75	31819.77	16700
AK		POINT HELEN LIGHT	60-09.20	147-45.80	13680.42	31883.86	16700
AK		SEWARD E BRKWTR LIGHT NO 2	60-06.00	149-26.40	13268.64	31963.69	16680
AK		CHISIK ISLAND LIGHT	60-05.70	152-33.60	12696.39	32100.80	16640
AK		FOURTH OF JULY S BRKWTR LIGHT	60-05.10	149-21.50	13277.58	31953.33	16680
AK		LOWER COOK INLET BUOY CI	60-04.70	152-09.70	12743.28	32080.31	16640
AK		CRAB BAY DAYBEACON NO 2	60-04.10	148-00.40	13574.86	31863.43	16700
AK		NINILCHIK ROCK SILL N MARKER	60-03.30	151-39.70	12807.77	32052.44	16640
AK		NINILCHIK CHANNEL ENTRANCE LIGHT	60-03.30	151-39.60	12808.05	32052.37	16640
AK		SAWMILL BAY LIGHT NO 3	60-03.30	148-02.10	13560.57	31859.60	16700
AK		SAWMILL BAY BUOY NO 1	60-03.20	148-01.20	13563.09	31857.86	16700
AK		SAWMILL BAY BUOY NO 6	60-03.10	148-03.60	13552.84	31859.87	16700
AK		SAWMILL BAY BUOY NO 5	60-03.10	148-03.10	13554.78	31859.30	16700
AK		PORT SAN JUAN BUOY	60-03.00	148-03.60	13551.88	31859.16	16700
AK		ELRINGTON PASSAGE LIGHT	60-02.80	148-00.50	13561.94	31854.17	16700
AK		THUMB COVE LIGHT	60-00.40	149-19.90	13236.74	31920.89	16680
AK		EVANS ISLAND LIGHT	59-59.20	148-07.30	13500.90	31836.17	16700
AK		CAINES HEAD LIGHT	59-59.00	149-23.10	13211.04	31914.76	16680
AK		LONETREE POINT LIGHT	59-59.00	148-11.90	13481.14	31840.04	16700
AK		POINT ELRINGTON LIGHT	59-56.20	148-14.90	13442.49	31823.62	16700
AK		HIVE ISLAND LIGHT	59-53.40	149-22.10	13159.06	31876.98	16680
AK		RUGGED ISLAND LIGHT	59-50.30	149-22.30	13127.53	31856.80	16013
AK		RUGGED ISLAND LIGHT	59-50.30	149-22.30	13127.53	31856.80	16680
AK		CAPE ST ELIAS LIGHT	59-47.90	144-35.80	14196.33	31407.24	16013
AK		WESSELS REEF WHISTLE NO 1	59-47.80	146-06.00	13865.38	31578.05	16013
AK		ANCHOR POINT LIGHT	59-46.20	151-51.90	12598.14	31965.49	16640
AK		CAPE ST ELIAS NO 2	59-44.80	144-37.90	14161.67	31384.75	16013
AK		PILOT ROCK LIGHT	59-44.60	149-28.10	13049.30	31825.49	16013
AK		YAKUTAT BUOY NO 6	59-42.60	139-41.80	14946.56	30508.70	16760
AK		YAKUTAT BUOY NO 8	59-41.40	139-38.50	14944.25	30485.34	16760
AK		USCOE RESEARCH BUOY NO 2	59-36.40	151-32.40	12548.99	31894.00	16640
AK		HOMER BRKWTR LIGHT NO 2	59-36.30	151-24.80	12569.80	31886.78	16640
AK		HOMER FUEL DOCK S LIGHT	59-36.20	151-24.90	12568.46	31886.29	16640
AK		HALIBUT COVE LIGHT NO 2	59-36.10	151-12.80	12603.42	31874.92	16640
AK		YAKUTAT BAY WHISTLE NO 4	59-35.60	139-51.10	14877.69	30473.49	16760
AK		ARCHIMANDRITOF SHOALS BUOY NO 3	59-35.50	151-26.10	12557.64	31883.32	16640

PASSES

STATE/COUNTRY	COUNTY/PROV	NAME	LAT	LON	TD#1	TD#2	CHART NO
AK		GULL ISLAND LIGHT NO 2	59-35.10	151-19.60	12572.55	31875.22	16640
AK		USCOE RESEARCH BUOY NO 1	59-34.50	151-58.70	12458.12	31905.75	16640
AK		YAKUTAT ROADS LIGHT NO 2	59-34.10	139-44.70	14879.76	30436.42	16760
AK		KHANTAAK ISLAND LIGHT	59-33.60	139-46.90	14871.76	30439.36	16760
AK		YAKUTAT ROADS LIGHT NO 1	59-33.40	139-45.80	14872.54	30433.54	16760
AK		COHEN ISLAND ROCK LIGHT	59-33.00	151-27.90	12526.20	31870.54	16640
AK		OCEAN CAPE LIGHT	59-32.10	139-51.30	14852.10	30440.37	16016
AK		OCEAN CAPE LIGHT	59-32.10	139-51.30	14852.10	30440.37	16760
AK		YAKUTAT BAY ENTR NO 2	59-31.90	139-57.10	14838.74	30458.80	16016
AK		YAKUTAT BAY ENTR BUOY NO 2	59-31.90	139-57.10	14838.74	30458.80	16760
AK		SEAL ROCKS LIGHT	59-31.30	149-37.70	12881.18	31749.61	16013
AK		McARTHUR PASS LIGHT	59-27.80	150-20.10	12690.99	31773.66	16680
AK		SELDOVIA BAY ENTRANCE LIGHT	59-27.20	151-43.20	12422.09	31851.26	16640
AK		SELDOVIA BAY BUOY NO 1	59-26.90	151-43.30	12418.64	31849.65	16640
AK		SKAGWAY BRKWTR LIGHT NO 2	59-26.90	135-19.20	15235.97	29384.70	17300
AK		SELDOVIA BAY BUOY NO 2	59-26.80	151-43.30	12417.58	31849.09	16640
AK		TAIYA INLET LIGHT	59-26.80	135-21.60	15232.71	29392.34	17300
AK		SELDOVIA BAY LIGHT NO 3	59-26.60	151-43.20	12415.74	31847.87	16640
AK		SELDOVIA BUOY NO 4	59-26.50	151-43.40	12414.14	31847.48	16640
AK		SELDOVIA DOCK LIGHTS	59-26.50	151-43.10	12414.96	31847.21	16640
AK		SELDOVIA BRKWTR LIGHT NO 5	59-26.40	151-43.10	12413.91	31846.64	16640
AK		POINT POGIBSHI LIGHT	59-25.50	151-53.10	12377.65	31850.63	16640
AK		PORT GRAHAM ENTRANCE SHOAL NO 1	59-22.80	151-54.10	12346.44	31836.42	16640
AK		PORT GRAHAM ENTRANCE LIGHT	59-22.40	151-53.00	12345.07	31833.18	16640
AK		PORT GRAHAM BUOY NO 3	59-22.40	151-52.50	12346.38	31832.72	16640
AK		FLAT ISLAND LIGHT	59-19.90	151-59.60	12301.54	31825.29	16640
AK		INDIAN ROCK LIGHT	59-16.40	135-23.90	15174.35	29295.40	17300
AK		NUKDIK POINT BUOY NO 1	59-14.70	135-25.10	15163.83	29282.56	17300
AK		HAINES SMALL BOAT HARBOR NO 2	59-14.00	135-26.20	15158.74	29279.49	17300
AK		PORT CHATHAM ENTRANCE LIGHT	59-12.60	151-46.40	12258.39	31771.83	16640
AK		BATTERY POINT LIGHT	59-12.60	135-21.80	15156.67	29249.26	17300
AK		CHUGACH PASSAGE BUOY NO 3	59-10.90	151-47.40	12237.54	31763.25	16640
AK		LETNIKOF COVE LIGHT NO 2	59-10.40	135-23.90	15142.39	29234.64	17300
AK		CAPE ELIZABETH LIGHT	59-08.90	151-52.50	12202.54	31757.09	16640
AK		PERL ISLAND LIGHT NO 1	59-07.10	151-38.30	12222.19	31732.57	16640
AK		EAST CHUGACH LIGHT	59-06.40	151-26.50	12249.21	31716.28	16013
AK		EAST CHUGACH LIGHT	59-06.40	151-26.50	12249.21	31716.28	16640
AK		KENNEDY ENTRANCE BUOY KE	59-06.40	151-26.50	12249.21	31716.28	16640
AK		PERL ROCK LIGHT	59-05.40	151-41.50	12195.00	31726.23	16640
AK		TALSANI ISLAND LIGHT	59-04.70	135-16.30	15121.76	29149.09	17300
AK		CHILKOOT INLET EAST LIGHT	59-01.00	135-11.70	15108.21	29094.74	17300
AK		ELDRED ROCK LIGHT	58-58.30	135-13.20	15092.25	29072.79	17300
AK		SULLIVAN ISLAND DAYBEACON NO 2	58-58.00	135-21.20	15080.36	29099.13	17300
AK		EAST AMATULI ISLAND LIGHT	58-55.00	151-57.00	12041.43	31684.16	16013

PASSES

STATE/COUNTRY	COUNTY/PROV	NAME	LAT	LON	TD#1	TD#2	CHART NO
AK		EAST AMATULI ISLAND LIGHT	58-55.00	151-57.00	12041.43	31684.16	16640
AK		SULLIVAN ISLAND LIGHT	58-53.90	135-18.10	15063.00	29046.17	17300
AK		POINT SHERMAN LIGHT	58-51.30	135-09.00	15061.47	28986.30	17300
AK		LATAX ROCKS LIGHT	58-41.40	152-28.90	11820.63	31644.02	16013
AK		LATAX ROCKS LIGHT	58-41.40	152-28.90	11820.63	31644.02	16580
AK		LITUYA BAY ENTR RANGE LIGHT	58-37.60	137-39.40	14752.99	29427.00	16760
AK		VANDERBILT REEF LIGHT	58-35.50	135-01.00	14991.81	28796.31	17300
AK		SENTINEL ISLAND LIGHT	58-32.80	134-55.30	14986.08	28747.77	17300
AK		LITTLE ISLAND LIGHT	58-32.40	135-02.70	14973.91	28771.19	17300
AK		POUNDSTONE ROCK BUOY PR	58-31.70	134-55.90	14979.79	28738.82	17300
AK		LIGHT HOUSE POINT LIGHT	58-29.00	152-39.00	11667.74	31588.99	16580
AK		ALLIGATOR ISLAND LIGHT	58-28.50	152-47.10	11649.90	31595.41	16580
AK		AARON ISLAND LIGHT NO 2	58-26.30	134-49.50	14961.86	28660.18	17300
AK		COHEN REEF DAYBEACON CR	58-25.90	134-48.10	14961.83	28650.92	17300
AK		TEE HARBOR LIGHT	58-25.70	134-45.90	14963.88	28640.75	17300
AK		POINT STEPHENS ROCK NO 2	58-25.40	134-46.10	14962.13	28638.43	17300
AK		FAUST ROCK BUOY	58-25.10	134-55.60	14947.46	28670.70	17300
AK		TEE HARBOR CONTROL BUOY	58-24.80	134-45.50	14960.02	28630.10	17300
AK		POINT RETREAT LIGHT	58-24.70	134-57.20	14943.24	28672.64	17300
AK		GUSTAVUS BUOY NO 1	58-23.30	135-44.80	14866.17	28840.33	117300
AK		ICY PASSAGE LIGHT NO 2	58-23.20	135-37.60	14876.65	28811.46	117300
AK		AUKE BAY BOAT HARBOR NO 2	58-23.00	134-39.20	14959.91	28588.48	17300
AK		AUKE BAY BRKWTR LIGHTS	58-23.00	134-38.90	14960.32	28587.37	17300
AK		FAVORITE REEF LIGHT NO 2	58-22.80	134-51.60	14941.74	28632.44	17300
AK		SHELTER ISLAND LIGHT	58-22.60	134-48.40	14945.23	28618.48	17300
AK		ANCON ROCK BUOY NO 2	58-22.40	135-55.80	14844.42	28874.28	117300
AK		FALSE POINT RETREAT LIGHT NO 4	58-22.20	134-58.10	14929.61	28650.71	17300
AK		COGHLAN ISLAND BUOY NO 1	58-21.90	134-41.70	14951.12	28586.48	17300
AK		TONKI CAPE LIGHT	58-21.20	151-59.10	11668.58	31499.94	16013
AK		PORTLAND ISLAND LIGHT	58-21.20	134-45.40	14942.58	28593.09	17300
AK		MENDENHALL BAR CHANNEL NO 14	58-20.80	134-32.20	14958.85	28540.25	17300
AK		MENDENHALL BAR CHANNEL NO 17	58-20.60	134-34.10	14955.29	28545.19	17300
AK		MENDENHALL BAR CHANNEL NO 19	58-20.40	134-35.60	14952.27	28548.66	17300
AK		LYNN CANAL SOUTHWEST LIGHT	58-20.10	135-02.80	14912.51	28647.25	17300
AK		MENDENHALL BAR CHANNEL NO 21	58-19.90	134-36.80	14948.20	28547.97	17300
AK		GIBBY ROCK LIGHT NO 2	58-19.60	134-41.20	14940.66	28561.21	17300
AK		MENDENHALL BAR CHANNEL NO 7	58-19.50	134-27.90	14958.47	28511.19	17300
AK		MENDENHALL BAR CHANNEL NO 5	58-19.50	134-27.90	14958.47	28511.19	17300
AK		LEMESURIER ISLAND LIGHT	58-19.20	136-02.30	14817.45	28868.38	117300
AK		GEORGE ROCK LIGHT	58-18.90	134-41.90	14936.29	28556.67	17300
AK		AURORA BASIN LIGHT 1B	58-18.50	134-26.30	14955.87	28495.09	17300
AK		PLEASANT ISLAND BUOY NO 11	58-18.40	135-39.20	14849.67	28770.14	117300
AK		AURORA BASIN LIGHT 1A	58-18.30	134-25.90	14955.46	28491.58	17300
AK		HARRIS HARBOR LIGHT 1H	58-18.10	134-25.70	14954.78	28488.80	17300

PASSES

STATE/COUNTRY	COUNTY/PROV	NAME	LAT	LON	TD#1	TD#2	CHART NO
AK		GASTINEAU CHANNEL LIGHT NO 4	58-17.80	134-25.30	14953.89	28484.26	17300
AK		SUGARLOAF ISLAND SHOAL NO 2	58-17.40	136-53.20	14722.19	29052.67	16016
AK		LAWSON CREEK BAR LIGHT NO 3	58-17.30	134-24.30	14952.87	28475.47	17300
AK		GRAVES HARBOR DAYBEACON NO 2	58-17.20	136-41.50	14741.56	29004.19	17300
AK		POINT ADOLPHUS LIGHT	58-17.20	135-46.90	14831.55	28788.37	117300
AK		ROCK DUMP BUOY NO 2A	58-17.20	134-23.70	14953.21	28472.26	17300
AK		DOUGLAS BOAT HARBOR NO 10	58-16.60	134-23.10	14951.18	28463.91	17300
AK		JUNEAU ISLE LIGHT	58-16.60	134-23.00	14951.32	28463.55	17300
AK		LIBBY ISLAND LIGHT	58-16.40	136-46.30	14728.91	29015.66	16016
AK		NORTH INIAN PASS LIGHT	58-16.30	136-24.00	14766.60	28925.98	117300
AK		SOUTH PASSAGE LIGHT	58-15.60	136-06.80	14791.42	28851.04	117300
AK		SHEEP CREEK LIGHT NO 2	58-15.50	134-19.70	14950.59	28440.23	17300
AK		NAKED ISLAND LIGHT	58-15.40	134-56.70	14898.21	28576.77	17300
AK		HORSE SHOAL LIGHT NO 1	58-15.30	134-42.10	14918.60	28520.80	17300
AK		SOUTH PASSAGE LIGHT NO 8	58-14.90	135-54.30	14808.01	28794.88	117300
AK		MIDDLE POINT LIGHT	58-14.90	134-37.60	14923.01	28499.96	17300
AK		FUNTER BAY ENTRANCE LIGHT NO 1	58-14.60	134-54.90	14896.91	28561.88	17300
AK		SOUTH INDIAN PASS BUOY NO 6	58-13.90	136-15.30	14768.54	28868.27	117300
AK		INNER POINT DAYBEACON	58-13.90	134-35.30	14921.44	28481.22	17300
AK		POINT LAVINIA LIGHT	58-13.40	136-21.20	14756.03	28886.92	117300
AK		SWANSON HARBOR CHANNEL STAKES	58-13.10	135-07.00	14871.84	28592.94	117300
AK		POINT HILDA LIGHT	58-13.10	134-30.30	14924.61	28454.53	17300
AK		GEORGE ISLAND LIGHT NO 2	58-12.70	136-22.80	14749.66	28886.57	117300
AK		CAPE SPENCER LIGHT	58-11.90	136-38.30	14718.80	28940.83	16016
AK		CAPE SPENCER LIGHT	58-11.90	136-38.30	14718.80	28940.83	117300
AK		MORMION ISLAND LIGHT	58-11.90	134-15.30	14939.63	28387.19	17300
AK		ELFIN COVE OUTER LIGHT	58-11.80	136-20.90	14748.15	28870.34	117300
AK		ELFIN COVE ENTRANCE LIGHT NO 2	58-11.70	136-21.00	14747.46	28869.78	117300
AK		SWANSON HARBOR ENTRANCE NO 2	58-11.60	135-04.60	14868.04	28568.71	117300
AK		ROCKY ISLAND LIGHT NO 13	58-10.70	135-03.00	14866.01	28553.56	117300
AK		THE SISTERS LIGHT	58-10.30	135-15.40	14845.44	28597.40	117300
AK		ALTHORP ROCK LIGHT NO 3	58-10.10	136-21.40	14738.41	28856.02	117300
AK		PINTA ROCK BUOY NO 2	58-10.00	135-27.10	14826.02	28639.97	117300
AK		RASPBERRY STRAIT LIGHT	58-09.60	153-13.30	11428.54	31527.31	16580
AK		POINT ARDEN LIGHT	58-09.60	134-10.60	14935.29	28346.44	17300
AK		THREE HILL ISLAND LIGHT	58-09.20	136-22.90	14731.16	28853.40	117300
AK		PORT FREDERICK LIGHT NO 3	58-07.90	135-27.80	14814.47	28621.99	117300
AK		SPASSKI ISLAND LIGHT NO 12	58-07.90	135-16.10	14832.54	28576.27	117300
AK		HANUS REEF LIGHT	58-07.90	134-59.80	14857.11	28513.23	117300
AK		COLUMN POINT BUOY NO 1	58-06.90	136-27.60	14711.05	28850.29	117300
AK		HOONAH BRKWTR LIGHT NO 2	58-06.50	135-26.90	14808.92	28604.68	117300
AK		DOLPHIN POINT LIGHT NO 3	58-06.40	153-08.90	11398.13	31505.84	16580
AK		HOONAH BRKWTR LIGHT NO 3	58-06.40	135-26.80	14808.58	28603.29	117300
AK		HAWK INLET EAST SHOAL NO 2	58-06.20	134-46.30	14868.81	28444.53	17300

PASSES

STATE/COUNTRY	COUNTY/PROV	NAME	LAT	LON	TD#1	TD#2	CHART NO
AK		GRAND ISLAND LIGHT	58-06.00	134-06.40	14924.31	28294.09	17300
AK		LISIANSKI INLET LIGHT	58-05.90	136-27.90	14705.31	28841.99	17300
AK		HAWK INLET ENTRANCE NO 1	58-05.50	134-46.70	14864.88	28439.00	17300
AK		LISIANSKI INLET LIGHT NO 2	58-04.20	136-25.80	14700.11	28817.37	17300
AK		GRAVE POINT LIGHT	58-03.80	134-03.00	14918.83	28259.07	17300
AK		CHATHAM STRAIT LIGHT NO 20	58-02.80	134-48.50	14849.31	28418.71	17300
AK		MALINA POINT LIGHT	58-02.40	153-21.80	11357.78	31500.73	16580
AK		POINT AUGUSTA LIGHT	58-02.30	134-56.80	14834.53	28445.65	17300
AK		LISIANSKI INLET BUOY NO 4	58-02.10	136-21.80	14696.19	28781.28	17300
AK		LISIANSKI INLET LIGHT NO 5	58-01.70	136-19.90	14697.42	28769.80	17300
AK		SKIPWITH REEFS BUOY NO 2	58-00.70	152-39.20	11359.66	31440.22	16580
AK		HOG ISLAND LIGHT	58-00.20	152-41.20	11351.99	31440.12	16580
AK		LISIANSKI STRAIT LIGHT NO 8	58-00.20	136-21.10	14687.62	28760.42	17300
AK		JUNCTION ISLAND LIGHT J	57-59.90	136-18.90	14689.90	28748.67	17300
AK		UGANIK BAY BUOY K	57-59.60	153-10.60	11330.85	31473.22	16580
AK		LISIANSKI STRAIT LIGHT NO 6	57-59.40	136-22.10	14681.76	28756.89	17300
AK		LISIANSKI STRAIT DAYBEACON 5	57-59.20	136-22.60	14679.86	28757.03	17300
AK		LAST TIMBER POINT LIGHT NO 6	57-58.70	152-58.90	11324.07	31454.36	16580
AK		SURGE BAY ENTR LIGHT	57-58.60	136-33.50	14657.50	28795.64	16016
AK		DRY SPRUCE ISLAND ROCK NO 7	57-57.90	153-04.10	11314.84	31456.65	16580
AK		DRY SPRUCE BAY ENTRANCE LIGHT	57-57.40	153-06.10	11309.74	31456.55	16580
AK		PELICAN ENTRANCE LIGHT	57-57.30	136-13.60	14685.81	28702.52	17300
AK		DEER HARBOR BUOY NO 1	57-56.20	136-34.50	14643.29	28777.22	16016
AK		LISIANSKI STRAIT LIGHT NO 4	57-56.10	136-21.60	14665.73	28723.70	17300
AK		NOISY ISLANDS LIGHT	57-56.00	153-33.60	11304.13	31482.61	16580
AK		KONIUJI ISLAND LIGHT NO 5	57-55.80	152-50.20	11298.05	31428.60	16580
AK		SHAKMANOF POINT LIGHT	57-55.60	152-35.20	11308.88	31408.47	16580
AK		THREE BROTHERS LIGHT NO 8	57-55.50	152-33.10	11310.50	31405.24	16580
AK		ILKOGNAK ROCK LIGHT NO 1	57-54.90	152-46.90	11290.55	31419.78	16580
AK		ENTRANCE POINT SHOAL NO 5	57-54.80	152-31.50	11305.00	31399.50	16580
AK		PROKODA ISLAND LIGHT NO 2	57-54.70	152-30.20	11305.80	31397.29	16580
AK		TONKI CAPE LIGHT	57-54.70	152-30.20	11305.80	31397.29	16580
AK		FRESHWATER BAY DAYBEACON NO 5	57-54.30	135-07.90	14779.07	28409.69	17300
AK		SETTLERS COVE BRKWTR LIGHT 2	57-52.40	152-51.70	11262.46	31412.98	16580
AK		SETTLERS COVE DAYBEACON NO 1	57-52.20	152-51.40	11260.52	31411.57	16580
AK		PORT WAKEFIELD BUOY NO 2	57-51.60	152-51.40	11254.42	31408.48	16580
AK		GREENTOP ISLAND LIGHT	57-51.30	136-29.00	14628.05	28708.96	16016
AK		KODIAK ISLAND WHISTLE NO 3	57-50.90	152-13.60	11296.75	31355.24	16580
AK		LISIANSKI STRAIT LIGHT NO 2	57-50.70	136-26.00	14630.39	28691.06	16016
AK		LISIANSKI STRAIT LIGHT NO 2	57-50.70	136-26.00	14630.39	28691.06	17300
AK		WILLIAMS REEF WHISTLE NO 1	57-50.30	152-09.30	11301.79	31346.23	16013
AK		WILLIAMS REEF WHISTLE NO 1	57-50.30	152-09.30	11301.79	31346.23	16580
AK		MIDWAY ISLANDS LIGHT	57-50.20	133-48.70	14876.93	28066.67	17300
AK		HANIN ROCK LIGHT	57-50.10	152-18.70	11275.64	31357.87	16580

PASSES

STATE/COUNTRY	COUNTY/PROV	NAME	LAT	LON	TD#1	TD#2	CHART NO
AK		TENAKEE DAYBEACON T	57-50.10	135-24.80	14731.90	28436.07	17300
AK		STAR ROCK BUOY	57-49.80	136-28.00	14622.22	28690.89	16016
AK		SPRUCE CAPE LIGHT	57-49.40	152-19.40	11266.29	31355.12	16580
AK		KODIAK ISLAND CHANNEL WHISTLE 5	57-49.40	152-17.90	11269.63	31353.10	16580
AK		TRACY ARM DAYBEACON	57-49.30	133-34.40	14892.64	28006.13	17360
AK		KODIAK N ENTR CHANNEL NO 8	57-48.80	152-19.40	11259.58	31351.95	16580
AK		KODIAK N CHANNEL NO 10	57-48.20	152-20.60	11250.32	31350.40	16580
AK		KODIAK N CHANNEL BELL KH	57-47.80	152-21.40	11244.20	31349.38	16580
AK		WOODY ISLAND LIGHT	57-47.80	152-20.20	11246.68	31347.76	16580
AK		CYANE ROCK BUOY NO 15	57-47.50	152-23.10	11237.53	31350.09	16580
AK		KODIAK BOAT HARBOR NO 2	57-47.20	152-24.40	11231.80	31350.26	16580
AK		WOODY ISLAND CHANNEL NO 2	57-47.20	152-21.60	11237.09	31346.49	16580
AK		NORTHEAST ARM LIGHT NO 1	57-47.10	153-27.10	11226.47	31430.47	16580
AK		KODIAK BOAT HARBOR LIGHT NO 1	57-47.10	152-24.50	11230.50	31349.87	16580
AK		KODIAK HARBOR ENTRANCE NO 16	57-47.10	152-24.40	11230.68	31349.74	16580
AK		DOG BAY N ENTRANCE LIGHT NO 2	57-47.00	152-24.40	11229.56	31349.21	16580
AK		DOG BAY N ENTRANCE LIGHT NO 1	57-47.00	152-24.40	11229.56	31349.21	16580
AK		GULL ISLAND BUOY NO 10	57-46.90	152-25.10	11227.22	31349.63	16580
AK		GULL ISLAND BUOY GI	57-46.80	152-25.90	11224.77	31350.18	16580
AK		DOG BAY S ENTRANCE LIGHT NO 4	57-46.70	152-24.80	11225.51	31348.18	16580
AK		DOG BAY S ENTR DAYBEACON NO 3	57-46.70	152-24.80	11225.51	31348.18	16580
AK		DOG BAY S APPROACH BUOY NO 1	57-46.50	152-25.20	11222.59	31347.67	16580
AK		TENAKEE INLET LIGHT NO 4	57-46.50	135-11.80	14735.60	28348.85	17300
AK		TENAKEE ENTRANCE NO 1	57-46.40	134-56.00	14760.14	28284.79	17300
AK		TENAKEE REEF LIGHT	57-46.20	135-13.50	14731.44	28352.77	17300
AK		HOLKHAM BAY RANGE DAYBEACON	57-46.10	133-38.50	14872.89	27987.36	17360
AK		WOODY ISLAND CHANNEL NO 5	57-45.60	152-22.20	11217.99	31338.89	16580
AK		STARR POINT LIGHT NO 3	57-45.40	153-22.00	11208.91	31415.67	16580
AK		ST PAUL HARBOR WHISTLE NO 3	57-44.50	152-25.40	11199.93	31337.46	16580
AK		ST PAUL HARBOR ENTRANCE LIGHT	57-44.40	152-25.70	11198.32	31337.35	16580
AK		WOOD SPIT LIGHT	57-44.30	133-34.50	14870.52	27954.31	17360
AK		ST PAUL HARBOR WHISTLE SP	57-44.10	152-24.20	11197.49	31333.74	16580
AK		WOMENS BAY MIDDLE SHOAL NO 19	57-43.80	152-31.00	11184.52	31341.37	16580
AK		HILL ISLAND LIGHT	57-43.70	136-16.50	14612.20	28586.78	16016
AK		HILL ISLAND LIGHT	57-43.70	136-16.50	14612.20	28586.78	17320
AK		WOMENS BAY CHANNEL NO 11	57-43.50	152-29.20	11183.32	31337.38	16580
AK		WOMENS BAY RANGE LIGHT	57-43.40	152-28.70	11182.85	31336.19	16580
AK		WOMENS BAY CHANNEL NO 13	57-43.20	152-30.00	11179.05	31336.90	16580
AK		MINNIE REEF DAYBEACON NO 5	57-43.20	136-10.20	14620.95	28556.06	17320
AK		HUMPBACK ROCK WHISTLE NO 1	57-42.80	152-14.10	11205.79	31313.05	16013
AK		HUMPBACK ROCK WHISTLE NO 1	57-42.80	152-14.10	11205.79	31313.05	16580
AK		BLACK BAY ROCKS DAYBEACON NO 4	57-42.40	136-09.20	14618.77	28544.47	17320
AK		HARVESTER ISLAND SPIT LIGHT 2	57-38.30	153-59.50	11197.73	31427.03	16580
AK		SNIPE ROCK DAYBEACON NO 1	57-38.30	136-10.60	14596.04	28512.28	17320

PASSES

STATE/COUNTRY	COUNTY/PROV	NAME	LAT	LON	TD#1	TD#2	CHART NO
AK		CAPE CHINIAK LIGHT	57-37.70	152-09.10	11166.92	31279.14	16013
AK		POINT HUGH LIGHT	57-37.20	133-48.30	14819.86	27931.11	17360
AK		KLAG ISLAND DAYBEACON B	57-37.10	136-05.90	14598.57	28481.60	17320
AK		BROAD ISLAND LIGHT	57-35.20	135-23.50	14662.81	28287.77	17320
AK		ELOVOI ISLAND LIGHT NO 26	57-34.90	135-27.90	14653.98	28303.09	17320
AK		COZIAN REEF BUOY NO 3	57-34.10	135-25.50	14654.25	28285.60	17320
AK		OTSTOIA ISLAND LIGHT	57-33.70	135-26.90	14650.00	28287.61	17320
AK		WINDHAM BAY ENTRANCE LIGHT	57-33.70	133-32.50	14827.17	27836.89	17360
AK		LARSEN BAY RANGE LIGHT	57-32.80	154-00.10	11166.54	31401.30	16580
AK		LARSEN BAY ENTRANCE ROCK NO 1	57-32.70	153-58.50	11164.05	31398.84	16580
AK		PESCHANI POINT LIGHT	57-32.30	135-19.20	14656.36	28242.48	17320
AK		KHAZ BREAKER WHISTLE NO 2	57-31.20	136-07.70	14566.61	28434.91	17320
AK		DANGER POINT LIGHT	57-30.90	134-36.30	14719.53	28053.88	17320
AK		POVOROTNI ISLAND LIGHT	57-30.80	135-33.20	14625.56	28286.51	17320
AK		KOOTZNAHOO INLET LIGHT NO 2	57-30.30	134-34.80	14719.17	28041.97	17320
AK		KOOTZNAHOO INLET DAYBEACON NO 2	57-30.10	134-34.60	14718.58	28039.21	17320
AK		KENASNOW ROCK NO 2	57-30.00	134-36.20	14715.61	28044.66	17320
AK		KOOTZNAHOO INLET BUOY NO 6	57-29.90	134-34.00	14718.62	28034.83	17320
AK		PERIL STRAIT LIGHT NO 22	57-29.50	135-32.40	14620.80	28271.01	17320
AK		POINT BENHAM LIGHT	57-29.00	135-11.70	14653.52	28180.13	17320
AK		KILLISNOO HARBOR LIGHT NO 7	57-28.30	134-34.00	14711.41	28019.15	17320
AK		KILLISNOO HARBOR LIGHT NO 6	57-28.30	134-33.60	14712.04	28017.54	17320
AK		KILLISNOO HARBOR LIGHT NO 3	57-27.90	134-33.80	14709.93	28014.44	17320
AK		LONE ROCK DAYBEACON NO 4	57-27.90	134-33.40	14710.56	28012.83	17320
AK		GAMBIER BAY ENTRANCE NO 2	57-27.90	133-55.10	14769.17	27861.91	17360
AK		POINT CRAVEN LIGHT	57-27.80	134-51.90	14680.54	28087.05	17320
AK		KILLISNOO HARBOR ENTRANCE NO 2	57-27.70	134-34.50	14707.92	28015.30	17320
AK		BIG ROSE ISLAND LIGHT NO 21	57-27.50	135-32.30	14611.57	28251.93	17320
AK		ROSE ISLAND ROCK LIGHT NO 19	57-27.30	135-32.30	14610.63	28250.07	17320
AK		McCLELLAN ROCK LIGHT	57-27.20	135-01.50	14662.12	28120.80	17320
AK		YELLOW POINT LIGHT NO 16	57-26.90	135-33.60	14606.50	28251.80	17320
AK		FAIRWAY ISLAND LIGHT NO 32	57-26.60	134-52.20	14674.59	28076.74	17320
AK		MIDDLE POINT LIGHT NO 14	57-26.40	135-34.40	14602.77	28250.53	17320
AK		POINT GAMBIER LIGHT	57-26.10	133-50.30	14768.46	27825.28	17360
AK		POINT SIROI ISLAND NO 12	57-25.20	135-35.20	14595.75	28242.78	17320
AK		SERGIUS NARROWS LIGHT NO 9	57-24.50	135-37.80	14587.92	28247.29	17320
AK		WEST FRANCIS ROCK BUOY NO 6	57-24.30	135-38.30	14586.11	28247.55	17320
AK		KLOKACHEF ISLAND LIGHT	57-24.20	135-54.20	14557.41	28314.01	16016
AK		KLOKACHEF ISLAND LIGHT	57-24.20	135-54.20	14557.41	28314.01	17320
AK		HOBART BAY LIGHT NO 2	57-23.90	133-27.90	14791.74	27718.57	17360
AK		SULOIA POINT LIGHT NO 5	57-23.40	135-38.90	14580.84	28241.81	17320
AK		KAKUL NARROWS LIGHT NO 4	57-22.50	135-40.90	14573.09	28242.03	17320
AK		BRAD ROCK BUOY NO 3	57-22.40	135-41.30	14571.92	28242.81	17320
AK		FALSE POINT PYBUS DAYBEACON	57-21.10	133-52.40	14743.68	27782.82	17360

PASSES

STATE/COUNTRY	COUNTY/PROV	NAME	LAT	LON	TD#1	TD#2	CHART N
AK		KANE ISLANDS LIGHT NO 25	57-19.40	135-39.70	14560.74	28208.59	17320
AK		POINT LULL LIGHT	57-18.60	134-48.30	14644.83	27984.11	17320
AK		ENTRANCE ISLAND LIGHT NO 24	57-17.50	135-36.20	14558.12	28176.34	17320
AK		HIGHWATER ISLAND SHOAL NO 23	57-16.90	135-36.00	14555.70	28170.02	17320
AK		WYVILLE REEF BUOY NO 22	57-16.30	135-35.40	14553.99	28162.00	17320
AK		FIVE FINGER LIGHT	57-16.30	133-37.80	14744.98	27677.91	17360
AK		GRAVE ISLAND LIGHT	57-16.00	134-04.90	14702.58	27781.27	17360
AK		NEVA STRAIT NO 20	57-15.80	135-34.80	14552.74	28154.89	17320
AK		ROUND ROCK LIGHT	57-15.60	133-56.10	14714.40	27742.24	17360
AK		WHITESTONE CHANNEL RANGE LIGHT	57-15.20	135-34.00	14551.40	28146.02	17320
AK		BILL POINT LIGHT	57-15.10	133-32.50	14747.76	27645.45	17360
AK		WHITESTONE CHANNEL NO 17	57-14.90	135-33.90	14550.19	28142.86	17320
AK		WHITESTONE CHANNEL NO 15	57-14.80	135-33.80	14549.91	28141.52	17320
AK		WHITESTONE POINT LIGHT NO 14	57-14.70	135-33.60	14549.81	28139.76	17320
AK		NEVA POINT REEF LIGHT NO 12	57-14.10	135-33.00	14548.11	28131.75	17320
AK		OLGA STRAIT LIGHT NO 11	57-13.80	135-32.00	14548.50	28124.73	17320
AK		BUSH POINT LIGHT NO 2	57-13.20	153-12.90	11025.31	31243.97	16580
AK		DUCK POINT LIGHT	57-12.70	133-30.90	14740.04	27614.89	17360
AK		SITKALIDAK PASSAGE LIGHT NO 4	57-12.60	153-16.40	11027.62	31245.89	16580
AK		OLGA STRAIT BUOY NO 9	57-12.60	135-29.60	14547.26	28103.54	17320
AK		BIRD ROCK LIGHT NO 2	57-12.50	133-35.30	14732.65	27629.74	17360
AK		NUT ISLAND LIGHT N	57-12.30	153-09.50	11019.89	31234.78	16580
AK		TABLE ISLAND LIGHT	57-11.40	152-55.10	11006.48	31209.89	16580
AK		OLGA STRAIT LIGHT NO 5	57-11.40	135-27.90	14544.79	28085.36	17320
AK		CAPE FANSHAW LIGHT	57-11.10	133-34.30	14728.25	27611.70	17360
AK		DEEPWATER POINT LIGHT	57-10.30	134-14.10	14663.53	27762.84	17320
AK		LISIANSKI POINT LIGHT NO 4	57-09.00	135-24.40	14540.07	28048.57	17320
AK		BIG GAVANSKI ISLAND LIGHT NO 3	57-08.50	135-24.90	14536.93	28046.22	17320
AK		TURNABOUT ISLAND LIGHT	57-07.90	133-59.20	14676.69	27678.56	17320
AK		OLD SITKA ROCKS LIGHT NO 2	57-06.90	135-24.60	14530.23	28030.53	17320
AK		EAST PINTA ROCKS NO 1	57-05.60	133-58.40	14668.17	27652.79	17320
AK		GRAND POINT LIGHT	57-05.50	133-11.10	14739.36	27466.27	17360
AK		KASIANA ISLAND SHOAL NO 1	57-05.40	135-24.30	14524.01	28015.79	17320
AK		WEST PINTA ROCKS LIGHT	57-05.20	134-00.60	14663.02	27657.89	17320
AK		WARM SPRING BAY LIGHT	57-04.80	134-46.40	14586.84	27846.49	17320
AK		CHANNEL ROCK BUOY NO 7	57-03.80	135-21.80	14521.27	27990.59	17320
AK		BATTERY ISLAND LIGHT NO 6	57-03.60	135-22.80	14518.60	27993.17	17320
AK		CHANNEL ROCK LIGHT NO 8	57-03.60	135-22.10	14519.84	27990.12	17320
AK		SITKA HARBOR CHANNEL BUOY NO 11	57-03.20	135-20.90	14520.18	27981.31	17320
AK		USHER ROCK SHOAL NO 5	57-03.10	135-23.70	14514.76	27992.65	17320
AK		SIGNAL ISLAND LIGHT NO 4	57-03.10	135-23.70	14514.76	27992.65	17320
AK		CRESCENT HARBOR E BRKWTR NO 4	57-03.00	135-19.70	14521.41	27974.29	17320
AK		JAPONSKI HARBOR DAYBEACON NO 7	57-02.90	135-20.80	14519.02	27978.20	17320
AK		JAPONSKI HARBOR ENTR NO 6	57-02.90	135-20.70	14519.20	27977.76	17320

PASSES

STATE/COUNTRY	COUNTY/PROV	NAME	LAT	LON	TD#1	TD#2	CHART NO
AK		JAPONSKI HARBOR ENTRANCE NO 5	57-02.80	135-20.70	14518.75	27976.87	17320
AK		ALEUTSKI PASS DAYBEACON NO 4	57-02.80	135-20.50	14519.10	27975.99	17320
AK		ALEUTSKI PASS DAYBEACON NO 2	57-02.80	135-20.40	14519.28	27975.56	17320
AK		TURNING ISLAND LIGHT NO 11	57-02.60	135-20.10	14518.92	27972.46	17320
AK		MAKHNATI ROCK WHISTLE NO 2	57-02.20	135-23.70	14510.73	27984.65	17320
AK		ROCKWELL LIGHT	57-02.20	135-19.90	14517.49	27968.03	17320
AK		THE TWINS LIGHT NO 9	57-02.10	135-18.70	14519.17	27961.89	17320
AK		ENTRY POINT LIGHT NO 1	57-02.00	135-14.90	14525.44	27944.39	17320
AK		ROCKY PATCH BUOY RP	57-01.70	135-18.30	14518.10	27956.57	17320
AK		POINT MACARTNEY LIGHT	57-01.50	134-03.40	14642.92	27633.59	17320
AK		TSARITSA ROCK BUOY NO 7	57-01.30	135-19.40	14514.37	27957.83	17320
AK		SIMPSON ROCK BUOY NO 5	57-01.20	135-20.60	14511.79	27962.20	17320
AK		THE ECKHOLMS LIGHT	57-00.60	135-21.40	14507.70	27960.38	17320
AK		POINT GARDNER LIGHT	57-00.60	134-36.80	14584.66	27766.40	17320
AK		PORTAGE BAY DAYBEACON NO 2	57-00.50	133-19.50	14706.46	27447.04	17360
AK		PORTAGE BAY LIGHT NO 3	57-00.30	133-19.30	14705.94	27444.24	17360
AK		VITSKARI ISLAND LIGHT	56-60.00	135-32.60	14484.88	28004.32	17320
AK		KULICHKOF ROCK BUOY NO 2	56-60.00	135-26.90	14495.17	27979.24	17320
AK		CAPE EDGECUMBE LIGHT	56-59.90	135-51.30	14450.05	28085.88	16016
AK		CAPE EDGECUMBE LIGHT	56-59.90	135-51.30	14450.05	28085.88	17320
AK		CAPE STRAIT LIGHT	56-59.90	133-05.50	14724.77	27387.58	17360
AK		THOMAS BAY NO 4	56-59.90	132-57.60	14736.31	27358.31	17360
AK		THOMAS BAY ENTRANCE NO 1	56-59.30	132-58.20	14733.02	27354.27	17360
AK		KAKE ENTRANCE LIGHT NO 2	56-59.10	134-01.30	14636.14	27601.75	17360
AK		THOMAS BAY ENTRANCE NO 2	56-59.10	132-57.80	14732.80	27350.72	17360
AK		YASHA ISLAND SHOAL NO 2	56-58.90	134-34.50	14581.17	27740.77	17320
AK		MOSER BAY LIGHT NO 2	56-58.40	154-06.30	11046.90	31246.46	16580
AK		KAKE HARBOR DAYBEACON NO 9	56-58.40	133-56.70	14640.50	27575.86	17360
AK		KAKE HARBOR LIGHT NO 5	56-58.30	133-56.90	14639.77	27575.73	17360
AK		KAKE FLATS BUOY NO 3	56-58.20	133-57.20	14638.88	27576.01	17360
AK		KAKE SALMON PEN LIGHT	56-58.00	133-55.70	14640.41	27567.85	17360
AK		KAKE CANNERY FLATS BO 7	56-57.90	133-56.10	14639.36	27568.54	17360
AK		KAKE HARBOR LIGHT	56-57.60	133-57.00	14636.68	27569.40	17360
AK		PORTAGE PASS LIGHT NO 2	56-57.40	133-55.30	14638.54	27560.39	17360
AK		PORTAGE PASS DAYBEACON NO 3	56-57.10	133-54.30	14638.87	27553.34	17360
AK		PORTAGE PASS LIGHT	56-56.80	133-53.90	14638.25	27548.78	17360
AK		BEACON POINT DAYBEACON BP	56-56.40	132-59.60	14719.33	27329.39	17360
AK		CORNWALLIS POINT LIGHT	56-55.90	134-16.30	14598.45	27634.74	17320
AK		KOKA ISLAND PASSAGE NO 1	56-54.90	135-23.60	14478.49	27920.02	17320
AK		AKHOIK REEF BUOY NO 1	56-54.80	154-07.70	11040.93	31231.60	16580
AK		SUKOI ISLETS LIGHT	56-53.80	132-56.50	14713.48	27290.95	17360
AK		LAZY BAY LIGHT NO 2	56-53.50	154-12.90	11043.26	31232.67	16580
AK		SECURITY BAY LIGHT NO 1	56-52.40	134-22.30	14573.78	27628.04	17320
AK		SALT POINT LIGHT	56-50.70	133-51.90	14616.13	27481.88	17360

P A S S E S

STATE/COUNTRY	COUNTY/PROV	NAME	LAT	LON	TD#1	TD#2	CHART NO
AK		CAPE ALITAK LIGHT	56-50.60	154-18.30	11042.75	31226.65	16580
AK		KINGSMILL POINT LIGHT	56-50.60	134-25.10	14561.52	27623.69	17320
AK		WRANGELL NARROWS N ENTR WN	56-49.80	132-55.70	14698.75	27246.68	17360
AK		WRANGELL NARROWS CHANN NO 62	56-49.60	132-56.00	14697.52	27245.76	17360
AK		WRANGELL NARROWS CHANN NO 61	56-49.50	132-56.00	14697.12	27244.73	17360
AK		ELOVOI ROCK DAYBEACON NO 1	56-49.30	135-22.60	14455.73	27867.19	17320
AK		WRANGELL NARROWS CHANN NO 60	56-49.10	132-57.40	14693.46	27245.94	17360
AK		WRANGELL NARROWS CHANN NO 59	56-48.90	132-57.90	14691.93	27245.79	17360
AK		PETERSBURG CREEK RANGE LIGHT	56-48.50	132-59.20	14688.41	27246.67	17360
AK		MARINE HIGHWAY TERMINAL	56-48.50	132-58.50	14689.45	27243.99	17360
AK		WRANGELL NARROWS CHANN NO 53	56-48.00	132-59.10	14686.58	27241.18	17360
AK		WRANGELL NARROWS CHANN NO 52	56-46.90	132-58.80	14682.67	27228.80	17360
AK		HOGGATT BAY LIGHT	56-45.90	134-39.20	14517.80	27643.55	17320
AK		WRANGELL NARROWS CHANN NO 51	56-44.30	132-57.30	14674.65	27196.52	17360
AK		AIAKTALIK ISLAND LIGHT NO 5	56-43.90	154-02.90	11020.31	31174.42	16580
AK		WASHINGTON BAY LIGHT	56-42.90	134-23.20	14532.46	27545.64	17320
AK		TONKA TIMBER LOG BOOM LIGHTS	56-42.70	132-57.00	14668.81	27179.11	17360
AK		WRANGELL NARROWS CHANN NO 50	56-42.30	132-56.80	14667.54	27174.27	17360
AK		WRANGELL NARROWS CHANN NO 49	56-42.10	132-56.90	14666.60	27172.64	17360
AK		WRANGELL NARROWS CHANN NO 48	56-41.70	132-56.90	14665.04	27168.59	17360
AK		WRANGELL NARROWS CHANN NO 47	56-41.60	132-57.00	14664.49	27167.96	17360
AK		WRANGELL NARROWS CHANN NO 46	56-41.50	132-56.90	14664.25	27166.56	17360
AK		WRANGELL NARROWS CHANN NO 44	56-41.10	132-56.50	14663.29	27160.95	17360
AK		WRANGELL NARROWS CHANN NO 43	56-41.00	132-56.60	13227.34	26410.92	17360
AK		WRANGELL NARROWS CHANN NO 42	56-40.40	132-56.10	14661.15	27152.30	17360
AK		WRANGELL NARROWS CHANN NO 40	56-40.30	132-56.00	14660.91	27150.89	17360
AK		WRANGELL NARROWS CHANN NO 39	56-40.10	132-56.00	14660.13	27148.88	17360
AK		WRANGELL NARROWS CHANN NO 37	56-40.00	132-55.80	14660.03	27147.08	17360
AK		WRANGELL NARROWS CHANN NO 36	56-39.90	132-55.70	14659.79	27145.67	17360
AK		WRANGELL NARROWS CHANN NO 34	56-39.70	132-55.60	14659.16	27143.26	17360
AK		WRANGELL NARROWS CHANN NO 32A	56-39.60	132-55.50	14658.92	27141.86	17360
AK		WRANGELL NARROWS CHANN NO 33	56-39.50	132-55.60	14658.38	27141.24	17360
AK		WRANGELL NARROWS CHANN NO 32	56-39.40	132-55.40	14658.29	27139.45	17360
AK		WRANGELL NARROWS CHANN NO 31	56-39.40	132-55.40	14658.29	27139.45	17360
AK		TOW CHANNEL BUOY 7TC	56-39.30	132-55.30	14658.05	27138.04	17360
AK		WRANGELL NARROWS CHANN NO 29	56-39.20	132-55.20	14657.81	27136.64	17360
AK		WRANGELL NARROWS CHANN NO 28	56-39.10	132-55.10	14657.57	27135.24	17360
AK		WRANGELL NARROWS CHANN NO 27	56-38.90	132-55.20	14656.64	27133.61	17360
AK		TOW CHANNEL BUOY 5TC	56-38.80	132-55.50	14655.80	27133.78	17360
AK		WRANGELL NARROWS CHANN NO 25	56-38.80	132-55.20	14656.25	27132.60	17360
AK		WRANGELL NARROWS CHANN NO 26	56-38.80	132-55.10	14656.40	27132.20	17360
AK		DUNCAN CANAL BUOY NO 8	56-38.60	133-06.30	14638.62	27175.04	17360
AK		BLIND POINT RANGE LIGHT NO 24	56-38.60	132-55.30	14655.32	27130.98	17360
AK		WRANGELL NARROWS CHANN NO 21	56-38.40	132-55.90	14653.63	27131.33	17360

PASSES

STATE/COUNTRY	COUNTY/PROV	NAME	LAT	LON	TD#1	TD#2	CHART NO
AK		DRY STRAIT LIGHT NO 5	56-38.20	132-36.70	14681.47	27055.54	17360
AK		WRANGELL NARROWS CHANN NO 19	56-38.00	132-56.70	14650.87	27130.48	17360
AK		BUSH TOP ISLAND RANGE LIGHT	56-37.90	132-57.00	14650.03	27130.67	17360
AK		WRANGELL NARROWS CHANN NO 18	56-37.90	132-56.80	14650.33	27129.87	17360
AK		WRANGELL NARROWS CHANN NO 17	56-37.70	132-57.20	14648.94	27129.46	17360
AK		WRANGELL NARROWS CHANN NO 15	56-37.40	132-57.60	14647.17	27128.05	17360
AK		WRANGELL NARROWS CHANN NO 16	56-37.40	132-57.40	14647.47	27127.25	17360
AK		WHIRLPOOL POINT LIGHT	56-37.00	154-05.50	11014.73	31146.35	16013
AK		WHIRLPOOL POINT LIGHT	56-37.00	154-05.50	11014.73	31146.35	16580
AK		WRANGELL NARROWS CHANN NO 13A	56-36.70	132-58.30	14643.38	27123.85	17360
AK		WRANGELL NARROWS CHANN NO 14	56-36.70	132-58.10	14643.68	27123.05	17360
AK		WRANGELL NARROWS CHANN NO 13	56-36.60	132-58.30	14642.99	27122.85	17360
AK		WRANGELL NARROWS CHANN NO 11	56-36.50	132-58.20	14642.75	27121.45	17360
AK		DRY STRAIT DAYBEACON NO 3	56-36.50	132-33.00	14680.38	27024.14	17360
AK		BURNT ISLAND RANGE LIGHT	56-36.40	132-58.50	14641.91	27121.66	17360
AK		HOMER SPIT LIGHT	56-36.10	151-24.50	11206.82	30886.62	16640
AK		WRANGELL NARROWS CHANN NO 10	56-36.10	132-58.40	14640.89	27118.27	17360
AK		WRANGELL NARROWS CHANNEL NO 9	56-35.90	132-58.50	14639.96	27116.67	17360
AK		WRANGELL NARROWS CHANN NO 8	56-35.70	132-58.40	14639.33	27114.28	17360
AK		DRY STRAIT LIGHT NO 1	56-35.10	132-32.60	14675.61	27008.09	17360
AK		WRANGELL NARROWS CHANN NO 5	56-34.90	132-58.50	14636.07	27106.72	17360
AK		BEECHER PASS LIGHT NO 6	56-34.80	133-04.40	14626.66	27129.79	17360
AK		TOW CHANNEL BUOY 4TC	56-34.70	132-58.30	14635.60	27103.93	17360
AK		WRANGELL NARROWS CHANN NO 3A	56-34.60	132-58.50	14634.90	27103.74	17360
AK		TOW CHANNEL BUOY 3TC	56-34.60	132-58.10	14635.51	27102.13	17360
AK		DUNCAN CANAL BUOY NO 5	56-34.50	133-05.30	14624.10	27130.55	17360
AK		DUNCAN CANAL LIGHT NO 3	56-34.50	133-05.30	14624.10	27130.55	17360
AK		WRANGELL NARROWS CHANN NO 4	56-34.50	132-58.40	14634.67	27102.35	17360
AK		WRANGELL NARROWS CHANN NO 3	56-34.30	132-58.40	14633.89	27100.36	17360
AK		WRANGELL NARROWS CHANN NO 2	56-34.10	132-58.10	14633.57	27097.16	17360
AK		POINT ELLIS LIGHT	56-34.00	134-19.90	14501.36	27452.20	17320
AK		WRANGELL NARROWS CHANN NO 1	56-34.00	132-58.00	14633.34	27095.76	17360
AK		CAPE ULITKA LIGHT	56-33.80	133-43.60	14560.86	27287.79	16016
AK		DUNCAN CANAL BUOY NO 4	56-33.80	133-05.00	14621.83	27122.45	17360
AK		POINT LOCKWOOD LIGHT PL	56-33.40	132-57.70	14631.47	27088.59	17360
AK		DECEMBER POINT LIGHT DP	56-32.90	132-57.60	14629.68	27083.23	17360
AK		PATTERSON POINT LIGHT	56-32.40	134-38.20	14463.20	27521.97	17320
AK		TOW CHANNEL BUOY 1TC	56-32.40	132-57.90	14627.29	27079.52	17360
AK		BUTTERWORTH ISLAND LIGHT NO 2	56-32.20	133-04.40	14616.53	27104.33	17360
AK		MIDWAY ROCK LIGHT MR	56-31.80	132-57.80	14625.12	27073.18	17360
AK		POINT ALEXANDER LIGHT	56-30.60	132-56.90	14621.86	27057.67	17360
AK		FOREMOST ROCK DAYBEACON	56-30.10	133-00.30	14614.71	27066.80	17360
AK		STATION ISLAND LIGHT	56-29.70	132-45.70	14635.44	27003.35	17360
AK		TWO TREE ISLAND LIGHT	56-29.70	132-38.00	14647.01	26972.99	17360

PASSES

STATE/COUNTRY	COUNTY/PROV	NAME	LAT	LON	TD#1	TD#2	CHART NO
AK		EASTERN PASSAGE LIGHT	56-29.70	132-22.10	14670.55	26913.10	17360
AK		POINT HIGHFIELD REEF	56-28.90	132-23.60	14665.33	26910.20	17360
AK		FIVE MILE ISLAND LIGHT	56-28.30	132-30.60	14652.73	26930.17	17360
AK		WRANGELL HARBOR BRKWTR NO 2	56-28.00	132-23.00	14662.83	26898.60	17360
AK		WRANGELL HARBOR NO 5	56-27.90	132-22.70	14662.89	26896.44	17360
AK		WRANGELL HARBOR NO 4	56-27.90	132-22.70	14662.89	26896.44	17360
AK		WRANGELL HARBOR NO 8	56-27.90	132-22.60	14663.04	26896.07	17360
AK		WRANGELL HARBOR NO 7	56-27.90	132-22.60	14663.04	26896.07	17360
AK		WRANGELL HARBOR NO 6	56-27.90	132-22.60	14663.04	26896.07	17360
AK		LOW POINT DAYBEACON	56-27.50	132-55.40	14612.24	27021.05	17360
AK		CRAIG POINT LIGHT	56-27.40	132-42.90	14630.89	26969.08	17360
AK		LEVEL ISLAND BUOY NO 11	56-27.10	133-02.40	14599.90	27046.49	17360
AK		TEBENKOF BAY LIGHT NO 1	56-27.00	134-08.20	14492.88	27338.18	17320
AK		VANK ISLAND LIGHT	56-26.90	132-35.90	14639.53	26936.32	17360
AK		WORONKOFSKI POINT DAYBEACON	56-26.40	132-28.70	14648.38	26903.38	17360
AK		VICHNEFSKI ROCK LIGHT	56-26.30	133-00.80	14599.30	27032.01	17360
AK		MITCHELL POINT BUOY NO 9	56-25.40	133-10.70	14580.38	27065.83	17360
AK		SHOEMAKER BAY DAYBEACON NO 1	56-25.10	132-21.10	14654.76	26861.32	17360
AK		SMALL BOAT HARBOR NO 3	56-25.10	132-21.00	14654.90	26860.95	17360
AK		SMALL BOAT HARBOR LIGHT NO 2	56-25.10	132-21.00	14654.53	26859.90	17360
AK		POINT ANCON LIGHT	56-24.30	132-33.20	14633.76	26899.35	17360
AK		McARTHUR REEF BUOY	56-23.70	133-10.60	14573.99	27049.44	17360
AK		SOUTH CRAIG POINT LIGHT	56-23.40	132-37.30	14624.21	26906.55	17360
AK		PORT WALTER LIGHT	56-23.30	134-38.10	14426.17	27445.92	17320
AK		THE EYE OPENER LIGHT	56-23.10	133-16.40	14562.49	27069.33	17360
AK		HAT ISLAND LIGHT	56-22.50	132-25.50	14638.52	26851.05	17360
AK		STRAIT ISLAND BUOY NO 7	56-22.40	133-41.90	14518.53	27177.73	17360
AK		HELM ROCK BUOY NO 8	56-22.20	133-38.40	14523.49	27160.01	17360
AK		EASTERN PASSAGE NO 5	56-22.20	132-10.20	14659.97	26791.23	17360
AK		THE NARROWS BUOY NO 3	56-21.80	132-06.60	14663.74	26774.30	17360
AK		FIVE FATHOM SHOAL BUOY	56-21.70	133-13.90	14561.07	27045.36	17360
AK		POINT BAKER LIGHT	56-21.60	133-37.00	14523.44	27148.33	17360
AK		POINT BAKER LIGHT	56-21.60	133-37.00	14523.44	27148.33	17360
AK		WEST ROCK LIGHT	56-21.20	133-38.10	14520.08	27149.83	17360
AK		PORT PROTECTION DAYBEACON	56-20.30	133-38.00	14516.74	27141.47	17360
AK		POINT COLPOYS LIGHT	56-20.20	133-11.80	14558.64	27022.24	17360
AK		BAY POINT DAYBEACON BP	56-20.20	133-09.70	13179.13	26434.61	17420
AK		PORT PROTECTION LIGHT	56-19.60	133-36.70	14516.15	27129.39	17360
AK		SNOW PASSAGE BUOY SP	56-19.20	133-05.20	14565.25	26983.82	17420
AK		ROOKERY ISLAND LIGHT	56-18.90	133-06.30	14562.38	26985.89	17420
AK		LITTLE BRANCH BAY LIGHT	56-18.30	134-50.60	14383.52	27464.74	17320
AK		NOAA BUOY 46001	56-18.00	148-18.00	11928.91	30411.30	531
AK		POINT HARRIS LIGHT	56-17.40	134-17.90	14437.93	27303.07	17320
AK		ROUND POINT LIGHT	56-16.70	132-39.40	14595.87	26848.90	17360

PASSES

STATE/COUNTRY	COUNTY/PROV	NAME	LAT	LON	TD#1	TD#2	CHART NO
AK		BUSHY ISLAND LIGHT	56-16.60	132-57.50	14567.48	26925.74	17420
AK		SNOW PASSAGE BUOY NO 4	56-16.20	132-56.50	14567.54	26917.62	17420
AK		CALDER ROCKS WHISTLE NO 6	56-15.50	133-43.30	14489.32	27124.67	17360
AK		BEAUCLERC ISLAND LIGHT	56-15.40	133-51.00	14476.05	27159.91	17360
AK		PORT ALEXANDER RANGE LIGHT	56-14.70	134-39.00	14389.95	27381.60	17320
AK		PORT ALEXANDER LIGHT	56-14.40	134-38.90	14388.93	27378.78	17320
AK		STEAMER POINT LIGHT	56-13.40	132-42.70	14578.49	26831.14	17360
AK		NESBITT REEF LIGHT	56-13.20	132-51.70	14563.77	26868.54	17420
AK		VILLAGE ISLANDS ROCK NO 15	56-13.20	132-18.90	14613.95	26730.47	17360
AK		KASHEVAROF PASSAGE NO 2	56-12.90	133-01.20	14547.70	26908.14	17420
AK		VILLAGE ROCK DAYBEACON NO 12	56-12.90	132-17.50	14614.94	26721.90	17360
AK		VILLAGE ISLANDS LIGHT NO 13	56-12.80	132-18.00	14613.83	26722.85	17360
AK		BLAKE CHANNEL NO 1	56-12.70	131-55.30	14646.98	26637.97	17360
AK		BARRIER ISLAND BUOY NO 4	56-12.60	133-42.00	14480.28	27094.20	17360
AK		MIDCHANNEL ROCK DAYBEACON	56-12.20	132-16.20	14614.33	26709.68	17360
AK		DOUBLE DAY DAYBEACON NO 8	56-12.20	132-15.40	14615.52	26706.54	17360
AK		BUTTON ISLAND SHOAL NO 5	56-12.10	132-14.80	14616.05	26703.18	17360
AK		ZIMOVIA STRAIT BUOY NO 10	56-11.90	132-15.50	14614.27	26703.88	17360
AK		ZIMOVIA STRAIT BUOY NO 9	56-11.90	132-15.50	14614.27	26703.88	17360
AK		ZIMOVIA STRAIT LIGHT NO 6	56-11.90	132-15.50	14614.27	26703.88	17360
AK		TRAP ROCK BUOY NO 3	56-11.30	132-13.30	14615.37	26689.16	17360
AK		FOUND ISLAND ROCK NO 2	56-11.10	132-12.70	14615.54	26684.78	17360
AK		KASHEVAROF PASSAGE LIGHT	56-10.80	133-01.20	14539.81	26889.19	17420
AK		AMELIUS ISLAND SHOAL A	56-10.20	133-49.60	14458.27	27110.44	17360
AK		DRY PASS DAYBEACON NO 13	56-09.90	133-25.60	14497.06	26994.32	17400
AK		DRY PASS DAYBEACON NO 11	56-09.90	133-25.40	14497.39	26993.39	17400
AK		DRY PASS DAYBEACON NO 9	56-09.90	133-25.10	14497.88	26991.97	17400
AK		DRY PASS DAYBEACON NO 6	56-09.90	133-24.60	14498.70	26989.63	17400
AK		DRY PASS DAYBEACON NO 16	56-09.80	133-26.10	14495.86	26995.83	17400
AK		DRY PASS DAYBEACON NO 15	56-09.80	133-25.90	14496.19	26994.89	17400
AK		DRY PASS DAYBEACON NO 14	56-09.80	133-25.80	14496.35	26994.42	17400
AK		DRY PASS DAYBEACON NO 7	56-09.80	133-24.60	14498.32	26988.78	17400
AK		DRY PASS DAYBEACON NO 18	56-09.70	133-26.30	14495.15	26995.93	17400
AK		DRY PASS DAYBEACON NO 17	56-09.70	133-26.10	14495.48	26994.98	17400
AK		DRY PASS DAYBEACON NO 5A	56-09.70	133-24.00	14498.92	26985.12	17400
AK		CAPE OMMANEY LIGHT	56-09.60	134-39.60	14368.59	27345.23	17320
AK		CAPE OMMANEY LIGHT	56-09.60	134-39.60	14368.59	27345.23	16016
AK		DRY PASS DAYBEACON NO 20	56-09.60	133-26.60	14494.28	26996.49	17400
AK		DRY PASS DAYBEACON NO 19	56-09.60	133-26.40	14494.61	26995.55	17400
AK		DRY PASS DAYBEACON NO 5	56-09.60	133-23.30	14499.69	26980.98	17400
AK		DRY PASS DAYBEACON NO 4	56-09.60	133-23.20	14499.85	26980.51	17400
AK		KEY REEF LIGHT	56-09.60	132-49.80	14553.30	26826.84	17420
AK		DRY PASS DAYBEACON NO 22	56-09.50	133-27.10	14493.08	26998.00	17400
AK		DRY PASS DAYBEACON NO 23	56-09.50	133-27.00	14493.24	26997.53	17400

PASSES

STATE/COUNTRY	COUNTY/PROV	NAME	LAT	LON	TD#1	TD#2	CHART NO
AK		DRY PASS DAYBEACON NO 21	56-09.50	133-26.80	14493.57	26996.59	17400
AK		DRY PASS DAYBEACON NO 3	56-09.50	133-22.80	14500.13	26977.78	17400
AK		DRY PASS DAYBEACON NO 2	56-09.50	133-22.80	14500.13	26977.78	17400
AK		DRY PASS DAYBEACON NO 25	56-09.40	133-27.10	14492.70	26997.16	17400
AK		DRY PASS DAYBEACON NO 26	56-09.30	133-27.30	14491.99	26997.26	17400
AK		DRY PASS BUOY NO 28	56-09.20	133-27.60	14491.12	26997.84	17400
AK		SHAKAN BAY LIGHT	56-09.00	133-37.50	14473.96	27043.05	17360
AK		SHAKAN STRAIT DAYBEACON	56-07.80	133-30.20	14481.51	26998.47	17360
AK		POINT CROWLEY LIGHT	56-07.20	134-15.40	14402.22	27210.48	17320
AK		HAMILTON ISLAND DAYBEACON	56-06.90	133-34.20	14471.46	27010.11	17360
AK		FOUND ISLAND ROCK DAYBEACON	56-06.80	132-04.30	14612.46	26608.22	17360
AK		FOUND ISLAND LIGHT	56-06.20	132-04.70	14609.70	26603.57	17420
AK		POINT ST ALBANS BUOY NO 3	56-05.20	133-54.50	14430.71	27094.08	17360
AK		LEMON POINT ROCK LIGHT	56-04.40	134-06.60	14406.75	27146.47	17360
AK		BURNETT INLET BUOY NO 2	56-03.90	132-28.20	14565.84	26678.12	17420
AK		LINCOLN ROCK WEST LIGHT	56-03.40	132-41.80	14542.93	26734.34	17420
AK		BLAKE CHANNEL NO 2	56-02.80	132-00.30	14604.05	26551.64	17360
AK		POINT HARRINGTON BUOY NO 4	56-01.70	132-44.30	13198.84	26399.09	17420
AK		SOUTH NIBLACK ISLANDS LIGHT	56-00.40	132-05.30	14588.01	26547.07	17420
AK		POINT STANHOPE BUOY NO 2	56-00.20	132-36.90	14538.90	26683.21	17420
AK		CAPE DECISION LIGHT	56-00.10	134-08.10	14387.62	27121.41	16016
AK		CAPE DECISION LIGHT	56-00.10	134-08.10	14387.62	27121.41	17360
AK		SPANISH ISLANDS LIGHT	55-59.20	134-06.20	14387.51	27105.46	17360
AK		FISHERMAN'S HARBOR NO 1	55-58.50	133-47.80	14416.68	27010.05	17360
AK		BURNT ISLAND LIGHT NO 5	55-58.50	133-17.60	14467.38	26862.44	17400
AK		FISHERMAN'S HARBOR LIGHT	55-58.10	133-47.60	14415.52	27006.06	17360
AK		EDNA BAY SHOAL BUOYS	55-57.80	133-37.30	14431.90	26953.26	17400
AK		EDNA BAY N DAYBEACON NO E	55-57.70	133-37.30	14431.53	26952.50	17400
AK		EDNA BAY LIGHT NO 3	55-56.50	133-39.40	14423.47	26953.75	17400
AK		EDNA BAY BUOY NO 2	55-56.50	133-38.90	14424.32	26951.29	17400
AK		HUB ROCK DAYBEACON NO 3	55-56.50	133-17.70	14459.80	26847.19	17400
AK		EDNA BAY ENTRANCE LIGHT	55-56.40	133-36.90	14427.33	26940.70	17400
AK		TOKEEN HARBOR ENTRANCE LIGHT	55-56.20	133-19.80	14455.21	26855.14	17400
AK		BROWNSON ISLAND ROCKS BI	55-56.00	132-06.70	14570.23	26509.62	17420
AK		EL CAPITAN PASSAGE NO 1	55-55.70	133-18.20	14456.01	26843.42	17400
AK		SNIPE POINT LIGHT	55-55.60	131-36.80	14613.26	26391.31	17420
Canada	B Columbia	STEWART DOLPHIN WEST LIGHT	55-54.80	130-00.10	14743.98	26318.48	17420
AK		SALMON RIVER SHOAL NO 3	55-54.50	130-00.20	14742.86	26315.88	17420
AK		HYDER HARBOR ENTRANCE NO 1	55-54.30	130-00.50	14741.82	26313.93	17420
AK		AIKENS ROCK DAYBEACON NO 3	55-54.10	133-15.60	14454.41	26818.30	17400
AK		EASTERLY ISLAND LIGHT	55-53.80	132-05.30	14564.55	26482.44	17420
AK		VILLAGE ROCK DAYBEACON VR	55-53.50	133-15.30	14452.69	26812.23	17400
AK		RATZ HARBOR ENTRANCE LIGHT	55-53.30	132-35.80	14515.67	26618.04	17420
AK		BLUFF POINT LIGHT	55-53.10	131-44.70	14592.93	26391.90	17420

PASSES

STATE/COUNTRY	COUNTY/PROV	NAME	LAT	LON	TD#1	TD#2	CHART NO
AK		SURF POINT LIGHT	55-50.00	133-37.90	14401.83	26898.79	17400
AK		HELM POINT LIGHT	55-49.60	134-16.10	14333.57	27086.31	16016
AK		HELM POINT LIGHT	55-49.60	134-16.10	14333.57	27086.31	17360
AK		PEEP ROCK LIGHT	55-49.20	133-19.80	14429.44	26802.58	17400
AK		KARHEEN PASSAGE BUOY NO 8	55-48.50	133-18.90	14428.38	26793.01	17400
AK		CHAPIN ISLAND RANGE DAYBEACON	55-47.80	133-18.60	14426.33	26786.46	17400
AK		KARHEEN PASSAGE DAYBEACON NO 6	55-47.80	133-18.30	14426.83	26784.96	17400
AK		STEWART LIGHT	55-47.70	129-59.40	14721.72	26261.69	17420
AK		NARROW POINT LIGHT	55-47.50	132-28.50	14506.43	26534.74	17420
AK		KARHEEN PASSAGE BUOY NO 5	55-47.20	133-17.30	14426.31	26775.65	17400
AK		CAPE LYNCH LIGHT	55-46.90	133-42.00	14383.35	26897.66	17400
AK		KARHEEN PASSAGE BUOY NO 4	55-46.90	133-16.90	14425.89	26771.50	17400
AK		McHENRY LEDGE BUOY NO 2	55-46.80	132-18.20	14520.04	26478.94	17420
AK		KARHEEN PASSAGE BUOY NO 3	55-46.50	133-17.90	14422.76	26773.69	17400
AK		KARHEEN PASSAGE DAYBEACON NO 1	55-46.30	133-19.30	14419.69	26779.33	17400
AK		POINT SWIFT SHOAL NO 2	55-46.30	133-18.80	14420.53	26776.81	17400
AK		TONOWEK NARROWS DAYBEACON 2T	55-45.30	133-20.40	14414.21	26777.87	17400
AK		MISERY ISLAND DAYBEACON NO 1	55-44.70	132-16.50	14515.30	26453.31	17420
AK		MEYERS CHUCK BUOY NO 3	55-44.60	132-15.70	14516.19	26448.58	17420
AK		MEYERS CHUCK BUOY NO 1	55-44.60	132-15.70	14516.19	26448.58	17420
AK		EMERALD ISLAND BUOY NO 9	55-44.50	133-40.10	14377.80	26871.79	17400
AK		MEYERS CHUCK BUOY NO 4	55-44.50	132-15.70	14515.84	26447.76	17420
AK		WHITE CLIFF BUOY NO 12	55-43.90	133-39.60	14376.46	26865.25	17400
AK		BUSHY POINT LIGHT	55-43.90	131-43.80	14562.39	26294.59	17420
AK		DESCONOCIDA REEF BUOY NO 10	55-41.30	133-31.40	14381.04	26806.54	17400
AK		THORNE BAY ENTRANCE NO 2	55-40.80	132-27.40	14484.51	26477.35	17420
AK		CURACAO REEF BUOY NO 8	55-39.30	133-28.20	14379.25	26777.29	17400
AK		SHIP ISLAND LIGHT	55-36.00	132-12.10	14491.87	26364.56	17420
AK		LARZATITA ISLAND REEF LIGHT	55-35.10	133-19.60	14378.79	26706.93	17400
AK		HELM BAY LIGHT	55-34.90	131-55.60	14513.64	26272.05	17420
AK		SAN CHRISTOVAL 3 FATHOM BUOY	55-34.60	133-18.90	14378.20	26700.28	17400
AK		HERMANOS ISLAND RANGE MARKER	55-34.30	133-17.80	14378.99	26692.80	17400
AK		CAPE ULITKA LIGHT	55-33.80	133-43.60	14332.81	26821.70	17400
AK		HERMANOS ISLANDS REEF NO 8	55-33.80	133-17.70	14377.38	26689.26	17400
AK		PIEDRAS ISLAND REEF NO 9	55-33.70	133-17.80	14376.85	26689.17	17400
AK		WADLEIGH ISLAND BUOY NO 9	55-33.70	133-06.90	14395.20	26633.07	17400
AK		HIGHWATER ROCK DAYBEACON NO 1	55-33.60	133-06.20	14396.02	26628.85	17400
AK		KLAWOCK HARBOR ENTRANCE NO 2	55-33.50	133-06.20	14395.67	26628.24	17400
AK		KLAWOCK LEDGE DAYBEACON NO 3	55-33.40	133-06.10	14395.48	26627.11	17400
AK		POINT INCARNATION LIGHT	55-33.30	133-37.30	14341.98	26786.63	17400
AK		GRANT ISLAND LIGHT	55-33.30	131-43.60	14526.50	26199.02	17420
AK		NIBLACK POINT DAYBEACON	55-33.00	132-07.10	14489.34	26318.05	17420
AK		KLAWOCK INLET SHOAL NO 8	55-32.60	133-07.00	14391.14	26626.95	17400
AK		SAN ALBERTO BAY NO 7	55-32.30	133-15.00	14376.62	26666.40	17400

PASSES

STATE/COUNTRY	COUNTY/PROV	NAME	LAT	LON	TD#1	TD#2	CHART NO
AK		KASAAN LIGHT	55-32.10	132-23.70	14460.10	26398.93	17420
AK		HUMP ISLAND DAYBEACON	55-31.10	131-45.30	14516.47	26191.60	17420
AK		KLAWOCK REEF BUOY NO 1	55-30.60	133-11.10	14377.19	26636.35	17400
AK		KLAWOCK REEF BUOY NO 3	55-30.50	133-10.40	14378.02	26632.17	17400
AK		KLAWOCK REEF BUOY NO 2	55-30.40	133-11.10	14376.48	26635.20	17400
AK		KLAWOCK JUNCTION BUOY KL	55-30.40	133-10.40	14377.66	26631.59	17400
AK		KLAWOCK INLET BUOY NO 6	55-30.40	133-09.60	14379.01	26627.46	17400
AK		KLAWOCK TOW CHANNEL 4TC	55-30.30	133-10.30	14377.48	26630.49	17400
AK		KLAWOCK TOW CHANNEL 3TC	55-30.20	133-10.80	14376.29	26632.50	17400
AK		PARIDA ISLAND SOUTH REEF NO 5	55-30.10	133-13.30	14371.71	26644.82	17400
AK		KLAWOCK TOW CHANNEL ENTR 2TC	55-29.90	133-11.50	14374.04	26634.39	17400
AK		CAAMANO POINT LIGHT	55-29.90	131-58.90	14491.51	26255.14	17420
AK		CLARK BAY DAYBEACON	55-29.30	132-37.00	14429.04	26451.76	17420
AK		CRAIG SHOAL NO 7	55-29.20	133-08.70	14376.30	26615.96	17400
AK		FERN REEF BUOY NO 3A	55-29.10	133-15.80	14363.94	26652.03	17400
AK		SALTERY POINT SHOAL NO 6	55-28.90	133-08.70	14375.25	26614.26	17400
AK		CRAIG BUOY NO 4	55-28.90	133-08.70	14375.25	26614.26	17400
AK		CLOVER PASSAGE ENTRANCE LIGHT	55-28.70	131-48.70	14503.18	26193.90	17420
AK		BALANDRA SHOAL NO 3	55-28.60	133-13.70	14365.74	26638.40	17400
AK		CLOVER PASSAGE DAYBEACON CP	55-28.60	131-47.90	14504.06	26189.06	17420
AK		FISH EGG REEF BUOY NO 3	55-28.50	133-09.50	14372.49	26616.15	17400
AK		SHELTER COVE RANGE DAYBEACON	55-28.50	133-08.40	14374.35	26610.47	17400
AK		SHELTER COVE BRKWTR NO 2	55-28.40	133-08.50	14373.83	26610.43	17400
AK		KNUDSON COVE DAYBEACON	55-28.40	131-47.70	14503.70	26186.80	17420
AK		BALLENA ISLAND SHOAL NO 2	55-28.30	133-13.10	14365.70	26633.62	17400
AK		GUARD ISLANDS LIGHT	55-26.80	131-52.80	14490.46	26204.78	17420
AK		POND REEF NO 16	55-26.30	131-48.80	14494.94	26180.83	17420
AK		VALLENAR POINT BUOY NO 17	55-25.80	131-50.40	14490.80	26186.75	17420
AK		ST IGNACE ROCK LIGHT	55-25.70	133-23.60	14338.63	26673.49	17400
AK		SKOWL POINT LIGHT	55-25.70	132-16.10	14450.23	26322.25	17420
AK		SOLA ROCK DAYBEACON SR	55-25.60	133-28.40	14329.30	26699.63	17400
AK		ROSA REEF NO 15	55-24.80	131-48.10	14490.99	26169.56	17420
AK		REFUGE COVE DAYBEACON NO 5	55-24.30	131-44.70	14494.54	26149.19	17420
AK		HIGH ISLAND LIGHT	55-24.10	132-09.80	14454.78	26280.96	17420
AK		REFUGE COVE DAYBEACON NO 3	55-24.10	131-44.90	14493.56	26149.35	17420
AK		REFUGE COVE ENTRANCE NO 2	55-24.00	131-44.90	14493.23	26148.90	17420
AK		OHIO ROCK BUOY	55-23.80	131-46.20	14490.56	26154.89	17420
AK		CHANNEL ISLAND NO 14	55-23.70	131-45.80	14490.85	26152.34	17420
AK		PENINSULA POINT REEF NO 2	55-23.10	131-44.30	14491.15	26141.89	17420
AK		LEWIS REEF LIGHT NO 11	55-22.50	131-44.20	14489.30	26138.97	17420
AK		TONGASS NARROWS NO 10	55-22.40	131-43.50	14490.04	26134.93	17420
AK		CAPE FLORES BUOY NO 2	55-21.40	133-17.60	14333.88	26620.47	17400
AK		TONGASS NARROWS NO 9	55-21.30	131-43.10	14487.00	26128.87	17420
AK		BAR HARBOR N ENTRANCE NO 2N	55-21.10	131-41.30	14489.10	26118.95	17420

PASSES

STATE/COUNTRY	COUNTY/PROV	NAME	LAT	LON	TD#1	TD#2	CHART NO
AK		BAR HARBOR ENTRANCE NO 2	55-21.00	131-41.00	14489.22	26117.09	17420
AK		BAR HARBOR ENTRANCE NO 3	55-21.00	131-41.00	14489.22	26117.09	17420
AK		IDAHO ROCK BUOY NO 4	55-20.90	131-41.00	14488.89	26116.78	17420
AK		BAR HARBOR S ENTRANCE NO 2S	55-20.90	131-40.60	14489.51	26114.73	17420
AK		BAR HARBOR S ENTRANCE NO 3S	55-20.90	131-40.60	14489.51	26114.73	17420
AK		EAST CLUMP NO 7	55-20.70	131-41.20	14487.92	26117.18	17420
AK		TONGASS NARROWS E CHAN NO 4A	55-20.40	131-38.90	14490.45	26104.65	17420
AK		PENNOCK ISLAND REEF PR	55-20.30	131-40.00	14488.44	26109.90	17420
AK		THOMAS BASIN ENTRANCE NO 2	55-20.30	131-38.50	14490.73	26102.36	17420
AK		THOMAS BASIN ENTRANCE NO 3	55-20.30	131-38.50	14490.73	26102.36	17420
AK		POINT ARBOLEDA LIGHT	55-19.30	133-28.30	14308.07	26664.93	17400
AK		TONGASS NARROWS W CHANNEL NO 4	55-19.20	131-38.50	14487.10	26099.57	17420
AK		CALIFORNIA ROCK BUOY NO 3	55-18.90	131-36.10	14489.78	26087.27	17420
AK		SAXMAN BRKWTR LIGHT	55-18.90	131-35.70	14490.39	26085.36	17420
AK		TONGASS NARROWS E CHANNEL NO 2	55-18.60	131-35.20	14490.16	26082.42	17420
AK		TONGASS NARROWS W CHANNEL NO 5	55-18.20	131-38.80	14483.33	26098.81	17420
AK		SKIN ISLAND LIGHT	55-18.10	132-04.30	14443.29	26226.82	17420
AK		POTTER ROCK BUOY	55-18.10	131-34.50	14489.59	26078.31	17420
AK		TONGASS NARROWS W CHANNEL NO 2	55-18.00	131-36.20	14486.66	26086.06	17420
AK		MOUNTAIN POINT LIGHT	55-17.70	131-32.80	14490.86	26070.01	17420
AK		CUTTER ROCKS DAYBEACON CR	55-17.40	131-31.40	14492.01	26063.50	17420
Canada	B Columbia	HATTIE ISLAND LIGHT	55-17.20	129-58.40	14625.89	26084.32	17420
AK		MEARES ISLAND LIGHT	55-16.40	133-10.50	14328.71	26560.42	17400
AK		WALDEN ROCK LIGHT WR	55-16.30	131-36.60	14480.45	26085.27	17420
AK		SPIRE ISLAND REEF LIGHT SI	55-16.10	131-29.90	14490.03	26056.28	17420
AK		TLEVAK NARROWS BUOY NO 4	55-16.00	133-08.10	14331.43	26546.37	17400
AK		BLANK ISLAND LIGHT	55-16.00	131-38.30	14476.85	26092.57	17420
AK		TLEVAK NARROWS LIGHT NO 2	55-15.80	133-06.90	14332.79	26539.35	17400
AK		MASTIC ROCK DAYBEACON	55-15.50	131-23.90	14497.18	26034.17	17420
AK		BAILEY ROCK DAYBEACON BR	55-15.40	131-35.90	14478.56	26081.06	17420
AK		ANGLE POINT LIGHT	55-14.30	131-25.50	14490.84	26039.84	17420
AK		CAPE BARTOLOME LIGHT	55-13.90	133-36.80	14274.40	26682.87	16016
AK		CAPE BARTOLOME LIGHT	55-13.90	133-36.80	14274.40	26682.87	17400
AK		LIVELY ISLANDS LIGHT	55-13.70	133-05.00	14328.83	26520.65	17400
AK		SUKKWAN NARROWS BUOY NO 4	55-12.30	132-50.20	14349.06	26439.76	17400
AK		SUKKWAN NARROWS LIGHT	55-12.10	132-50.40	14348.05	26440.01	17400
AK		HYDABURG BUOY NO 2A	55-12.10	132-49.50	14349.56	26435.44	17400
AK		SUKKWAN STRAIT OBSTRUCTION BUOY	55-12.00	132-49.70	14348.89	26436.08	17400
AK		HYDABURG BUOY NO 2	55-11.70	132-49.00	14349.04	26431.39	17400
AK		SOUTH PASSAGE BUOY NO 3	55-11.60	132-51.20	14345.02	26442.16	17400
AK		SUKKWAN NARROWS BUOY NO 1	55-11.60	132-51.20	14345.02	26442.16	17400
AK		SCRAG ISLAND LEDGE BUOY NO 5	55-11.30	132-51.50	14343.50	26442.54	17400
AK		DIVER ISLANDS LIGHT	55-10.70	133-15.80	14300.07	26563.03	16016
AK		DIVER ISLANDS LIGHT	55-10.70	133-15.80	14300.07	26563.03	17400

PASSES

STATE/COUNTRY	COUNTY/PROV	NAME	LAT	LON	TD#1	TD#2	CHART NO
AK		HOG ROCKS LIGHT	55-10.70	131-16.90	14492.19	26019.31	17420
AK		DRIEST POINT LIGHT NO 4	55-10.60	131-36.30	14462.26	26079.32	17420
AK		GOAT ISLAND LIGHT	55-10.10	132-53.50	14336.08	26448.17	17400
AK		TURN BACK DAYBEACON	55-10.00	132-54.80	14333.55	26454.35	17400
AK		KELP ROCKS NO 1	55-09.50	131-37.80	14456.36	26084.77	17420
AK		LIVELY ROCK BUOY NO 9	55-09.50	131-35.10	14460.53	26074.38	17420
AK		EAST CHANNEL NO 2	55-09.30	131-36.30	14458.02	26078.88	17420
AK		POINT McCARTEY NO 2	55-08.80	131-39.60	14451.29	26091.57	17420
AK		TWIN ISLANDS LIGHT TI	55-08.60	131-12.90	14491.46	26014.04	17420
AK		SCRUB ISLAND BUOY NO 7	55-08.50	131-33.80	14459.29	26069.51	17420
AK		EEK POINT LIGHT	55-08.30	132-39.90	14352.79	26373.74	17400
AK		GULL ISLAND LIGHT GI	55-08.30	131-36.30	14454.77	26078.67	17420
AK		SCRUB ISLAND BUOY NO 5	55-08.30	131-34.30	14457.86	26071.31	17420
AK		WARBURTON ISLAND LIGHT	55-07.90	131-37.90	14451.00	26084.62	17420
AK		METLAKATLA BOAT HARBOR NO 2	55-07.90	131-35.00	14455.49	26073.83	17420
AK		METLAKATLA INNER HARBOR NO 3	55-07.90	131-35.00	14455.49	26073.83	17420
AK		VILLAGE POINT LIGHT NO 4	55-07.90	131-34.60	14456.10	26072.38	17420
AK		METLAKATLA INNER HARBOR NO 5	55-07.80	131-35.10	14455.01	26074.19	17420
AK		METLAKATLA INNER HARBOR NO 7	55-07.80	131-35.00	14455.16	26073.82	17420
AK		METLAKATLA BRKWTR LIGHT NO 1	55-07.80	131-34.10	14456.55	26070.59	17420
AK		POINT McCARTEY LIGHT	55-06.90	131-42.20	14441.06	26100.97	17420
AK		POINT McCARTEY BUOY NO 1	55-06.70	131-41.70	14441.20	26098.91	17420
AK		MAY ISLAND LIGHT	55-06.00	131-10.90	14486.15	26013.32	17420
AK		SLATE ISLANDS LIGHT	55-05.30	131-03.10	14495.63	26005.64	17420
AK		MOIRA ROCK LIGHT	55-05.00	131-59.80	14407.13	26173.77	17420
AK		REEF ISLAND LIGHT	55-04.80	130-12.10	14568.26	26030.01	17420
AK		HID REEF WHISTLE NO 2	55-04.20	131-40.40	14435.12	26093.24	17420
AK		VIEW COVE ENTRANCE LIGHT	55-03.20	132-57.80	14305.61	26446.02	17400
AK		TAMGAS HARBOR BUOY NO 1	55-02.10	131-31.20	14442.66	26062.59	17420
AK		INDIAN ROCK NO 6	55-01.80	131-20.70	14457.86	26035.01	17420
AK		MELLEN ROCK LIGHT	55-01.60	132-39.90	14330.49	26354.26	17400
AK		BLACK ROCK LIGHT	55-01.40	131-03.50	14482.67	26008.44	17420
AK		TAMGAS HARBOR ENTRANCE LIGHT	55-01.30	131-30.80	14440.71	26061.77	17420
AK		SNIPE ISLAND LIGHT NO 5	55-00.30	131-23.20	14449.25	26042.00	17420
AK		HARRIS ISLAND LIGHT NO 2	55-00.20	131-32.00	14435.34	26065.87	17420
AK		AJAX REEF LIGHT NO 3	55-00.10	131-27.60	14441.83	26053.38	17420
AK		POINT DAVIDSON LIGHT	54-59.70	131-36.80	14426.26	26081.06	17420
Canada	B Columbia	RAMSDEN POINT LIGHT	54-59.00	130-06.20	14558.77	26025.70	17420
AK		SHOE ISLAND SHOAL BUOY NO 2	54-57.40	132-45.40	14307.39	26369.99	17400
AK		SHOE ISLAND LIGHT	54-57.10	132-44.60	14307.76	26365.50	17400
AK		FOGGY POINT LIGHT	54-55.50	130-58.50	14471.65	26008.00	17420
AK		EAST ISLAND LIGHT	54-52.20	131-11.60	14441.47	26026.00	17420
AK		LOWRIE ISLAND LIGHT	54-51.60	133-31.80	14207.64	26575.26	16016
AK		WALLACE ROCK BUOY NO 2	54-51.10	132-26.90	14317.84	26273.68	17400

PASSES

STATE/COUNTRY	COUNTY/PROV	NAME	LAT	LON	TD#1	TD#2	CHART NO
Canada	B Columbia	LIZARD POINT LIGHT	54-50.00	130-16.50	14516.62	26007.55	17420
AK		GUIDE ROCKS DAYBEACON NO 4	54-49.60	132-21.40	14322.13	26248.20	17400
AK		CENTER ISLAND REEF NO 3	54-48.20	132-22.90	14315.15	26252.96	17400
AK		TREE POINT LIGHT	54-48.20	130-55.90	14452.90	26010.39	17420
AK		McLEAN POINT LIGHT	54-47.50	131-57.30	14354.82	26152.18	17420
AK		TONGASS REEF DAYBEACON	54-47.20	130-44.60	14466.80	26004.10	17420
AK		PEARSE CANAL ISLAND LIGHT	54-47.10	130-36.50	14478.54	26002.17	17420
AK		EUREKA CHANNEL DAYBEACON NO 1	54-46.90	132-23.20	14310.48	26252.83	17400
AK		BOAT ROCK LIGHT	54-46.80	130-47.90	14460.63	26005.76	17420
AK		ROUND ISLANDS LIGHT	54-46.70	132-30.40	14297.83	26282.92	17400
AK		BARREN ISLAND LIGHT	54-44.70	131-20.90	14403.74	26049.23	17420
AK		LORD ROCK LIGHT	54-43.60	130-49.10	14449.04	26008.01	17420
AK		POINT MARSH LIGHT	54-42.70	132-17.60	14306.39	26226.66	17420
AK		POINT MARSH LIGHT	54-42.70	132-17.60	14306.39	26226.66	17400
AK		POINT CORNWALLIS LIGHT	54-42.20	132-52.30	14246.19	26371.19	16016
AK		NICHOLS BAY ENTRANCE DAYBEACON	54-42.10	132-05.30	14324.75	26179.94	17400
AK		CAPE CHACON LIGHT	54-41.50	132-00.90	14330.04	26164.20	17420
AK		CAPE MUZON LIGHT	54-39.90	132-41.40	14257.49	26321.02	17400
AK		CAPE MUZON LIGHT	54-39.90	132-41.40	14257.49	26321.02	16016
AK	ALEUTIANS	EGEGIK ENTRANCE BUOY NO 1	58-15.50	157-42.00	18746.46	45162.67	16006
AK	ALEUTIANS	RED BLUFF DAYBEACON	58-14.20	157-29.00	18746.09	45077.70	16006
AK	ALEUTIANS	UGASHIK RIVER ENTRANCE UR	57-37.50	157-52.30	18732.68	45205.11	16006
AK	ALEUTIANS	SMOKY POINT LIGHT	57-37.50	157-41.50	18732.61	45133.36	16006
AK	ALEUTIANS	CHIGNIK SPIT LIGHT	56-18.60	158-22.90	18658.34	45441.71	16011
AK	ALEUTIANS	WALRUS ISLAND LIGHT	56-01.80	160-49.70	18616.95	46419.42	16011
AK	ALEUTIANS	NELSON LAGOON LIGHT	56-00.90	161-06.70	18612.91	46531.68	16011
AK	ALEUTIANS	PORT MOLLER ENTRANCE NO 2	55-60.00	160-39.10	18615.11	46350.54	16011
AK	ALEUTIANS	PORT MOLLER ENTRANCE NO 3	55-59.40	160-36.70	18614.35	46335.06	16011
AK	ALEUTIANS	PORT MOLLER LIGHT NO 5	55-58.60	160-34.60	18613.19	46321.68	16011
AK	ALEUTIANS	HAGUE CHANNEL BUOY NO 6	55-58.10	160-39.40	18611.58	46353.43	16011
AK	ALEUTIANS	HAGUE CHANNEL BUOY NO 5	55-57.90	160-38.50	18611.34	46347.61	16011
AK	ALEUTIANS	HAGUE CHANNEL BUOY NO 8	55-56.20	160-42.50	18607.59	46374.67	16011
AK	ALEUTIANS	HAGUE CHANNEL BUOY NO 7	55-55.90	160-41.70	18607.15	46369.57	16011
AK	ALEUTIANS	HARBOR SPIT LIGHT	55-54.90	160-34.60	18606.36	46323.54	16011
AK	ALEUTIANS	HAGUE CHANNEL BUOY NO 10	55-54.00	160-47.00	18602.73	46405.18	16011
AK	ALEUTIANS	HAGUE CHANNEL BUOY NO 9	55-53.60	160-47.10	18601.94	46406.01	16011
AK	ALEUTIANS	JOHNSTON CHANNEL BUOY NO 1J	55-53.10	160-48.40	18600.77	46414.75	16011
AK	ALEUTIANS	JOHNSTON CHANNEL BUOY NO 2J	55-52.80	160-48.50	18600.18	46415.54	16011
AK	ALEUTIANS	JOHNSTON CHANNEL BUOY NO 3	55-52.40	160-48.10	18599.47	46413.10	16011
AK	ALEUTIANS	JOHNSTON CHANNEL BUOY NO 5	55-51.50	160-47.70	18597.79	46410.89	16011
AK	ALEUTIANS	JOHNSTON CHANNEL BUOY NO 6	55-51.40	160-47.60	18597.61	46410.28	16011
AK	ALEUTIANS	JOHNSTON CHANNEL BUOY NO 7	55-49.20	160-46.60	18593.49	46404.75	16011
AK	ALEUTIANS	JOHNSTON CHANNEL BUOY NO 8	55-48.80	160-46.80	18592.66	46406.25	16011
AK	ALEUTIANS	JOHNSTON CHANNEL BUOY NO 10	55-47.40	160-47.40	18589.79	46410.80	16011

PASSES

STATE/COUNTRY	COUNTY/PROV	NAME	LAT	LON	TD#1	TD#2	CHART NO
AK	ALEUTIANS	JOHNSTON CHANNEL BUOY NO 9	55-47.40	160-47.10	18589.84	46408.84	16011
AK	ALEUTIANS	CROW REEF BUOY NO CR	55-45.60	160-43.40	18586.94	46385.59	16011
AK	ALEUTIANS	UNGA SPIT LIGHT	55-24.50	160-43.50	18542.67	46396.45	16011
AK	ALEUTIANS	PIRATE COVE DAYBEACON	55-21.80	160-21.60	18542.46	46258.11	16011
AK	ALEUTIANS	SAND POINT OUTFALL BUOYS	55-21.60	160-28.80	18540.16	46304.11	16011
AK	ALEUTIANS	POPOF STRAIT ENTR LIGHT NO 1	55-21.40	160-30.30	18539.33	46313.78	16011
AK	ALEUTIANS	SEAL CAPE LIGHT	55-21.00	161-15.10	18526.01	46599.88	16011
AK	ALEUTIANS	POPOF STRAIT BUOY NO 3	55-20.80	160-30.90	18537.86	46317.95	16011
AK	ALEUTIANS	ANDRONICA ISLAND LIGHT	55-20.80	160-03.60	18544.92	46144.28	16011
AK	ALEUTIANS	HUMBOLDT HARBOR LIGHT NO 2	55-20.00	160-30.10	18536.32	46313.30	16011
AK	ALEUTIANS	HUMBOLDT HARBOR BRKWTR NO 3	55-20.00	160-29.90	18536.38	46312.03	16011
AK	ALEUTIANS	SAND POINT LIGHT NO 7	55-19.20	160-31.60	18534.16	46323.29	16011
AK	ALEUTIANS	CAPE WEDGE LIGHT	55-17.50	159-52.80	18540.78	46078.36	16011
AK	ALEUTIANS	UKOLNOI ISLAND LIGHT	55-14.70	161-39.50	18502.99	46756.82	16011
AK	ALEUTIANS	BARALOF BAY LIGHT	55-14.50	160-32.10	18523.56	46329.10	16011
AK	ALEUTIANS	ARCH POINT LIGHT	55-12.40	161-54.30	18491.92	46851.02	16011
AK	ALEUTIANS	DELTA POINT LIGHT	55-11.60	162-38.50	18472.70	47130.83	16011
AK	ALEUTIANS	BLUFF POINT SHOAL NO 1	55-11.50	161-52.30	18490.30	46838.40	16011
AK	ALEUTIANS	COLD BAY CHANNEL NO 4	55-07.20	162-31.50	18463.13	47085.80	16011
AK	ALEUTIANS	MOSS CAPE LIGHT NO 4	55-07.10	161-56.20	18477.22	46863.30	16011
AK	ALEUTIANS	COLD BAY CHANNEL NO 3	55-06.70	162-31.90	18461.54	47088.22	16011
AK	ALEUTIANS	GOLOI SANDSPIT LIGHT NO 3	55-06.70	161-55.40	18476.46	46858.27	16011
AK	ALEUTIANS	KASLOKAN POINT LIGHT NO 2	55-06.40	162-31.50	18460.85	47085.65	16011
AK	ALEUTIANS	BECHEVIN BAY ENTRANCE BB	55-06.20	163-28.60	18433.38	47443.66	16011
AK	ALEUTIANS	BECHEVIN BAY BUOY NO 2	55-05.80	163-28.50	18432.15	47442.82	16011
AK	ALEUTIANS	BECHEVIN BAY BUOY NO 1	55-05.80	163-28.30	18432.26	47441.57	16011
AK	ALEUTIANS	COLD BAY CHANNEL NO 1	55-05.50	162-31.80	18458.15	47087.36	16011
AK	ALEUTIANS	BECHEVIN BAY BUOY NO 3	55-04.80	163-27.70	18429.38	47437.26	16011
AK	ALEUTIANS	BECHEVIN BAY BUOY NO 4	55-04.70	163-27.80	18429.01	47437.82	16011
AK	ALEUTIANS	BECHEVIN BAY BUOY NO 5	55-04.10	163-26.40	18427.82	47428.76	16011
AK	ALEUTIANS	BECHEVIN BAY BUOY NO 6	55-03.90	163-26.50	18427.13	47429.27	16011
AK	ALEUTIANS	CAPE KRENITZIN LIGHT NO 7	55-03.80	163-25.20	18427.49	47421.11	16011
AK	ALEUTIANS	KING COVE HARBOR LIGHT NO 2	55-03.60	162-19.30	18458.17	47008.54	16011
AK	ALEUTIANS	KING COVE HARBOR LIGHT NO 1	55-03.60	162-19.30	18458.17	47008.54	16011
AK	ALEUTIANS	BECHEVIN BAY BUOY NO 8	55-03.00	163-25.50	18424.78	47422.53	16011
AK	ALEUTIANS	BECHEVIN BAY BUOY NO 10	55-02.60	163-25.20	18423.66	47420.44	16011
AK	ALEUTIANS	CHUNAK POINT DAYBEACON 2CP	55-02.50	163-28.00	18421.84	47437.80	16011
AK	ALEUTIANS	MORGAN POINT LIGHT	55-02.50	162-20.10	18454.72	47013.43	16011
AK	ALEUTIANS	ILIASIK ISLANDS LIGHT	55-02.30	161-56.20	18464.30	46863.46	16011
AK	ALEUTIANS	ILIASIK PASSAGE BUOY NO 6	55-02.10	161-55.90	18463.88	46861.59	16011
AK	ALEUTIANS	ILIASIK PASSAGE BUOY NO 5	55-01.80	161-55.20	18463.36	46857.20	16011
AK	ALEUTIANS	BECHEVIN BAY BUOY NO 11	55-01.00	163-25.10	18418.58	47418.91	16011
AK	ALEUTIANS	ST CATHERINE COVE NO 4SC	54-59.90	163-29.30	18412.72	47444.34	16011
AK	ALEUTIANS	STAG POINT LIGHT	54-59.20	162-17.90	18446.33	46999.26	16011

PASSES

STATE/COUNTRY	COUNTY/PROV	NAME	LAT	LON	TD#1	TD#2	CHART NO
AK	ALEUTIANS	UGANIK BAY BUOY NO 22	54-59.10	163-23.10	18413.56	47405.43	16011
AK	ALEUTIANS	ROCKY POINT DAYBEACON 6RP	54-58.30	163-26.40	18409.14	47425.42	16011
AK	ALEUTIANS	FOX ISLAND LIGHT	54-57.40	162-25.90	18437.45	47048.94	16011
AK	ALEUTIANS	UGANIK BAY LIGHT NO 29	54-56.90	163-21.50	18407.35	47394.29	16011
AK	ALEUTIANS	UGANIK BAY BUOY NO 30	54-56.80	163-22.00	18406.75	47397.32	16011
AK	ALEUTIANS	THIN POINT WHISTLE 2TP	54-55.00	162-32.30	18427.32	47088.29	16011
AK	ALEUTIANS	ISANOTSKI STRAIT LIGHT NO 8	54-51.40	163-23.40	18388.31	47402.84	16011
AK	ALEUTIANS	ISANOTSKI STRAIT LIGHT NO 5	54-49.50	163-22.40	18382.65	47395.57	16011
AK	ALEUTIANS	ISANOTSKI STRAIT NO 4	54-49.00	163-21.60	18381.48	47390.36	16011
AK	ALEUTIANS	IKATAN BAY LIGHT NO 3	54-47.00	163-21.80	18374.74	47390.40	16011
AK	ALEUTIANS	IKATAN BAY LIGHT NO 1	54-46.60	163-10.90	18380.11	47323.45	16011
AK	ALEUTIANS	AKUTAN POINT LIGHT NO 2	54-08.70	165-43.60	18088.42	48169.00	16011
AK	ALEUTIANS	AKUN STRAIT LIGHT	54-08.00	165-39.70	18090.54	48146.49	16011
AK	ALEUTIANS	ULAKTA HEAD LIGHT	53-55.50	166-30.40	17953.64	48389.21	16011
AK	ALEUTIANS	ILIULIUK BAY ENTRANCE NO 2	53-54.60	166-29.50	17950.76	48382.62	16011
AK	ALEUTIANS	SPITHEAD LIGHT	53-53.90	166-30.80	17945.06	48387.71	16011
AK	ALEUTIANS	ROCKY POINT SHOAL RP	53-53.50	166-31.20	17942.40	48388.85	16011
AK	ALEUTIANS	ILIULIUK HARB S CHAN NO 13	53-52.60	166-32.90	17934.97	48395.48	16011
AK	ALEUTIANS	ILIULIUK HARB S CHAN NO 10	53-52.60	166-32.70	17935.33	48394.46	16011
AK	ALEUTIANS	ILIULIUK HARB S CHAN NO 11	53-52.60	166-32.70	17935.33	48394.46	16011
AK	ALEUTIANS	UNALASKA CHANNEL NO 5	53-52.60	166-32.00	17936.56	48390.92	16011
AK	ALEUTIANS	BAILEY LEDGE DAYBEACON	53-51.60	166-33.40	17929.15	48395.79	16011
AK	ALEUTIANS	KULUK SHOAL BUOY NO 2	51-52.10	176-36.40	14829.05	49774.35	16012
AK	ALEUTIANS	GANNET ROCKS LIGHT NO 4	51-52.10	176-36.40	14829.05	49774.35	16012
AK	ALEUTIANS	GANNET ROCKS BUOY 4A	51-51.90	176-36.50	14827.70	49774.07	16012
AK	ALEUTIANS	SWEEPER COVE JETTY NO 6	51-51.70	176-37.60	14820.57	49775.01	16012
AK	ALEUTIANS	SWEEPER COVE ENTRANCE NO 5	51-51.50	176-35.30	14833.10	49771.80	16012
AK	ALEUTIANS	FINGER SHOAL BUOY NO 3	51-51.50	176-33.90	14841.20	49770.08	16012
AK	ALEUTIANS	SWEEPER COVE LIGHT NO 7	51-51.30	176-37.60	14819.03	49774.21	16012
AK	BERING SEA	RILEY CHANNEL ENTR LIGHT	66-47.00	161-52.30	17899.71	46567.79	16005
AK	BERING SEA	CAPE ESPENBERG LIGHT	66-34.00	163-36.00	17825.27	46813.03	16005
AK	BERING SEA	CAPE DECEIT LIGHT	66-06.00	162-45.00	17929.26	46707.24	16005
AK	BERING SEA	GRANTLEY HARBOR LIGHT	65-16.70	166-20.80	17783.60	47310.53	16006
AK	BERING SEA	CHEENIK LIGHT NO 6	64-32.50	163-02.70	18100.86	46813.27	16006
AK	BERING SEA	GOLOVNIN BAY LIGHT NO 4	64-31.30	162-55.00	18110.75	46790.79	16006
AK	BERING SEA	NOME RANGE LIGHT	64-30.00	165-24.80	17950.63	47238.23	16006
AK	BERING SEA	NOME HARBOR E JETTY LIGHT	64-29.90	165-24.70	17950.97	47238.10	16006
AK	BERING SEA	GOLOVNIN BAY LIGHT NO 2	64-27.10	162-52.50	18121.90	46786.11	16006
AK	BERING SEA	ROCKY POINT LIGHT	64-24.00	163-09.00	18112.59	46839.18	16006
AK	BERING SEA	SHAKTOOLIK RIVER ENTRANCE	64-22.80	161-14.00	18215.81	46482.04	16006
AK	BERING SEA	UNALAKLEET RIVER S SPIT LIGHT	63-52.10	160-47.00	18297.55	46392.55	16006
AK	BERING SEA	EGG ISLAND LIGHT	63-36.00	161-43.20	18288.24	46584.92	16006
AK	BERING SEA	CAPE STEPHENS LIGHT	63-32.70	162-18.00	18267.03	46707.31	16006
AK	BERING SEA	WHALE ISLAND LIGHT	63-29.50	161-59.70	18288.64	46644.76	16006

PASSES

STATE/COUNTRY	COUNTY/PROV	NAME	LAT	LON	TD#1	TD#2	CHART NO
AK	BERING SEA	POINT ROMANOF LIGHT	63-12.00	162-50.00	18283.69	46835.44	16006
AK	BERING SEA	YUKON RIVER MID ENTRANCE LIGHT	63-04.60	165-37.60	18124.83	47441.26	16006
AK	BERING SEA	YUKON RIVER N ENTRANCE LIGHT	63-02.50	163-23.00	18274.77	46965.35	16006
AK	BERING SEA	KWIGUK PASS ENTRANCE LIGHT	62-47.40	164-51.80	18218.89	47314.33	16006
AK	BERING SEA	YUKON RIVER S ENTRANCE LIGHT	62-35.40	164-59.50	18238.26	47366.42	16006
AK	BERING SEA	MEKORYUK BRKWTR DAYBEACON NO 2	60-23.30	166-10.90	18482.56	48020.67	16006
AK	BERING SEA	KUSKOKWIM BAY BUOY NO 5	59-43.60	162-18.30	18689.92	46876.81	16006
AK	BERING SEA	KUSKOKWIM BAY BELL NO 4	59-35.80	162-16.00	18699.52	46870.25	16006
AK	BERING SEA	KUSKOKWIM BAY BUOY NO 3	59-27.00	162-19.10	18708.31	46895.84	16006
AK	BERING SEA	KUSKOKWIM BAY BUOY NO 2	59-18.90	162-18.50	18716.36	46899.26	16006
AK	BERING SEA	DUCK CREEK LIGHT	58-57.30	157-01.70	18746.81	44978.98	16006
AK	BERING SEA	GRAVEYARD POINT LIGHT	58-52.10	157-00.80	18747.54	44962.71	16006
AK	BERING SEA	THE BEND LIGHT	58-49.80	157-00.30	18747.79	44954.98	16006
AK	BERING SEA	EKUK RANGE LIGHT	58-48.00	158-33.10	18747.15	45520.23	16006
AK	BERING SEA	NAKNEK ENTRANCE NO 1	58-43.40	157-02.80	18748.23	44957.53	16006
AK	BERING SEA	NAKNEK LIGHT	58-42.50	157-04.80	18748.26	44968.05	16006
AK	BERING SEA	NUSHAGAK BAY ENTRANCE NO 2	58-33.70	158-24.20	18748.35	45450.04	16006
ARANGEL/KOROR	MALAKAL	MALAKAL HARBOR NO 6	07-19.30N	134-27.90E	Suggest	GPS	81151
ARANGEL/KOROR	MALAKAL	MALAKAL HARBOR NO 1	07-19.00N	134-27.60E	Suggest	GPS	81151
ARANGEL/KOROR	MALAKAL	MALAKAL PASSAGE NO 17	07-18.80N	134-28.10E	Suggest	GPS	81151
ARANGEL/KOROR	MALAKAL	MALAKAL PASSAGE LIGHT	07-16.70N	134-28.30E	Suggest	GPS	81151
CA	DEL NORTE	ST GEORGE REEF BUOY SG (LNB)	41-50.20	124-23.80	14311.69	43868.41	18600
CA	DEL NORTE	CRESCENT CITY RANGE LIGHT	41-45.00	124-11.30	14376.48	43869.13	18603
CA	DEL NORTE	BATTERY POINT LIGHT	41-44.60	124-12.10	14378.24	43868.31	18600
CA	DEL NORTE	CRESCENT CITY BRKWTR NO 8	41-44.60	124-11.20	14379.92	43868.76	18603
CA	DEL NORTE	CRESCENT CITY RADIOBEACON	41-44.50	124-11.00	14381.11	43868.75	18600
CA	DEL NORTE	CRESCENT CITY NO 7	41-44.30	124-11.30	14382.17	43868.39	18603
CA	DEL NORTE	CRESCENT CITY HARBOR NO 1	41-44.20	124-12.80	14380.17	43867.54	18603
CA	DEL NORTE	CRESCENT CITY ENTRANCE LIGHT	41-44.20	124-11.40	14382.79	43868.24	18600
CA	DEL NORTE	CRESCENT CITY ENTRANCE LIGHT	41-44.20	124-11.40	14382.79	43868.24	18603
CA	DEL NORTE	CRESCENT CITY NO 6	41-44.20	124-11.20	14383.17	43868.34	18603
CA	DEL NORTE	CRESCENT CITY WHISTLE NO 4	41-43.60	124-11.30	14387.86	43867.65	18603
CA	DEL NORTE	CRESCENT CITY WHISTLE NO 2	41-43.00	124-11.70	14391.97	43866.81	18603
CA	DEL NORTE	CRESCENT CITY WHISTLE NO 2	41-43.00	124-11.70	14391.97	43866.81	18600
CA	DEL NORTE	SCRIPPS CURRENT METER N	41-34.90	124-16.80	14447.10	43855.06	18600
CA	DEL NORTE	SCRIPPS CURRENT METER P	41-34.60	124-21.40	14440.44	43852.29	18600
CA	DEL NORTE	SCRIPPS CURRENT METER Q	41-34.20	124-26.90	14432.85	43848.93	18600
CA	DEL NORTE	SCRIPPS CURRENT METER R	41-33.30	124-31.40	14431.13	43845.47	18600
CA	HUMBOLDT	READING ROCKS LIGHT	41-20.50	124-10.60	14573.06	43840.29	18600
CA	HUMBOLDT	TURTLE ROCKS BUOY NO 28	41-08.20	124-11.80	14664.71	43822.08	18600
CA	HUMBOLDT	TRINIDAD HEAD WHISTLE NO 26	41-03.10	124-09.00	14706.53	43815.11	18600
CA	HUMBOLDT	TRINIDAD HEAD LIGHT	41-03.10	124-09.00	14664.71	43822.08	18600
CA	HUMBOLDT	TRINIDAD HARBOR BUOY NO 4	41-03.00	124-08.60	14711.29	43815.96	18620
CA	HUMBOLDT	PILOT ROCK BUOY NO 2	41-02.60	124-09.20	14712.86	43814.98	18620

P A S S E S

STATE/COUNTRY	COUNTY/PROV	NAME	LAT	LON	TD#1	TD#2	CHART NO
CA	HUMBOLDT	SCRIPPS CURRENT METER M	40-50.90	124-28.40	14752.34	43783.94	18620
CA	HUMBOLDT	SAMOA TURNING BASIN BUOY A	40-49.00	124-10.50	14809.63	43791.38	18622
CA	HUMBOLDT	SCRIPPS CURRENT METER L	40-48.60	124-23.90	14779.47	43782.53	18620
CA	HUMBOLDT	HUMBOLDT BAY NO 21	40-48.50	124-10.00	14814.48	43790.79	18622
CA	HUMBOLDT	DOODLEY ISLAND MARINA LIGHT	40-48.40	124-09.90	14815.45	43790.68	18622
CA	HUMBOLDT	HUMBOLDT BAY NO 19	40-48.30	124-10.90	14813.67	43789.88	18622
CA	HUMBOLDT	HUMBOLDT BAY NO 18	40-47.80	124-11.20	14816.51	43788.80	18622
CA	HUMBOLDT	SCRIPPS CURRENT METER K	40-47.50	124-19.60	14797.80	43783.14	18620
CA	HUMBOLDT	HUMBOLDT BAY NO 17	40-46.80	124-11.90	14821.93	43786.57	18622
CA	HUMBOLDT	HUMBOLDT BAY NO 15	40-46.50	124-12.20	14823.32	43785.84	18622
CA	HUMBOLDT	HUMBOLDT BAY ENTRANCE HB	40-46.40	124-16.20	14814.03	43783.21	18622
CA	HUMBOLDT	HUMBOLDT BAY ENTRANCE HB	40-46.40	124-16.20	14814.03	43783.21	18620
CA	HUMBOLDT	HUMBOLDT BAY NO 16	40-46.40	124-12.10	14824.29	43785.72	18622
CA	HUMBOLDT	NOYO RIVER RANGE NO 6	40-46.10	124-14.20	14821.16	43783.89	18626
CA	HUMBOLDT	HUMBOLDT BAY ENTRANCE NO 3	40-46.10	124-14.20	14821.16	43783.89	18622
CA	HUMBOLDT	HUMBOLDT BAY NO 14	40-46.10	124-12.60	14825.17	43784.87	18622
CA	HUMBOLDT	HUMBOLDT BAY ENTRANCE NO 2	40-46.00	124-14.80	14820.37	43783.34	18622
CA	HUMBOLDT	HUMBOLDT BAY NO 13	40-46.00	124-12.90	14825.13	43784.50	18622
CA	HUMBOLDT	HUMBOLDT BAY ENTRANCE NO 4	40-45.90	124-14.50	14821.83	43783.34	18622
CA	HUMBOLDT	HUMBOLDT BAY RANGE LIGHT	40-45.90	124-13.90	14823.34	43783.71	18622
CA	HUMBOLDT	HUMBOLDT BAY LIGHT	40-45.90	124-13.70	14823.84	43783.83	18622
CA	HUMBOLDT	HUMBOLDT BAY LIGHT	40-45.90	124-13.70	14823.84	43783.83	18620
CA	HUMBOLDT	HUMBOLDT BAY NO 12	40-45.90	124-12.80	14826.10	43784.38	18622
CA	HUMBOLDT	HUMBOLDT BAY NO 11	40-45.60	124-13.20	14827.23	43783.59	18622
CA	HUMBOLDT	HUMBOLDT BAY NO 10	40-45.50	124-13.10	14828.19	43783.47	18622
CA	HUMBOLDT	HUMBOLDT BAY ENTRANCE NO 6	40-45.40	124-14.00	14826.64	43782.73	18622
CA	HUMBOLDT	HUMBOLDT BAY ENTRANCE NO 5	40-45.40	124-13.80	14827.14	43782.85	18622
CA	HUMBOLDT	HUMBOLDT BAY NO 7	40-45.40	124-13.50	14827.90	43783.04	18622
CA	HUMBOLDT	HUMBOLDT BAY NO 9	40-45.40	124-13.40	14828.15	43783.10	18622
CA	HUMBOLDT	HUMBOLDT BAY NO 8	40-45.10	124-13.40	14830.28	43782.55	18622
CA	HUMBOLDT	NOAA BUOY EB 46006	40-44.90	124-30.20	14790.07	43772.04	18620
CA	HUMBOLDT	HOOKTON CHANNEL NO 1	40-44.90	124-13.30	14831.96	43782.24	18622
CA	HUMBOLDT	HOOKTON CHANNEL RANGE NO 4	40-44.60	124-13.60	14833.33	43781.51	18622
CA	HUMBOLDT	HOOKTON CHANNEL NO 5	40-44.50	124-13.40	14834.54	43781.45	18622
CA	HUMBOLDT	HOOKTON CHANNEL NO 6	40-44.40	124-13.50	14835.00	43781.20	18622
CA	HUMBOLDT	HOOKTON CHANNEL NO 7	40-44.40	124-13.40	14835.25	43781.26	18622
CA	HUMBOLDT	HOOKTON CHANNEL NO 8	40-44.30	124-13.30	14836.21	43781.14	18622
CA	HUMBOLDT	PACIFIC GAS DIKE LIGHT	40-44.20	124-13.10	14837.43	43781.08	18622
CA	HUMBOLDT	HOOKTON CHANNEL NO 10	40-44.00	124-13.20	14838.59	43780.64	18622
CA	HUMBOLDT	HOOKTON CHANNEL NO 12	40-43.90	124-13.10	14839.55	43780.52	18622
CA	HUMBOLDT	HOOKTON CHANNEL NO 13	40-43.60	124-13.30	14841.17	43779.84	18622
CA	HUMBOLDT	BLUNTS REEF BUOY B (ELB)	40-26.40	124-30.20	14915.38	43735.50	18620
CA	HUMBOLDT	CAPE MENDOCINO LIGHT	40-26.40	124-24.30	14930.76	43739.01	18620
CA	HUMBOLDT	PUNTA GORDA WHISTLE NO 24	40-14.90	124-22.20	15011.45	43715.03	18620

PASSES

STATE/COUNTRY	COUNTY/PROV	NAME	LAT	LON	TD#1	TD#2	CHART NO
CA	HUMBOLDT	SCRIPPS CURRENT METER J	40-10.90	124-21.40	15039.14	43706.26	18620
CA	HUMBOLDT	SHELTER COVE ENTRANCE NO 1	40-00.60	124-03.50	15154.53	43691.84	18620
CA	HUMBOLDT	POINT DELGADA WHISTLE NO 20	40-00.30	124-04.80	15152.61	43690.30	18620
CA	LAKE TAHOE	USCG PIER LIGHT	39-10.80	120-17.10	16283.10	43688.40	18665
CA	LAKE TAHOE	SUGAR PINE POINT LIGHT	39-03.70	120-06.80	16353.80	43651.20	18665
CA	LOS ANGELES	POINT DUME WHISTLE NO 12	33-59.60	118-48.20	28125.32	41227.04	18720
CA	LOS ANGELES	STA CRUZ ISLAND BUOY A	33-58.90	119-39.80	27986.35	41456.48	18729
CA	LOS ANGELES	ANACAPA ISLAND TEST BUOY	33-58.80	119-15.50	28052.24	41350.03	18756
CA	LOS ANGELES	STA CRUZ ISLAND BUOY B	33-58.70	119-39.00	27988.43	41452.28	18729
CA	LOS ANGELES	MARINA DEL REY NO 14	33-58.70	118-26.70	28179.81	41119.65	18744
CA	LOS ANGELES	STA CRUZ METEOROLOGICAL BUOY	33-58.30	119-38.50	27989.58	41448.55	18729
CA	LOS ANGELES	STA CRUZ OCEANOGRAPHIC NO 4	33-58.30	119-06.70	28075.43	41308.26	18729
CA	LOS ANGELES	MARINA DEL REY NO 5	33-58.30	118-26.90	28178.90	41119.22	18744
CA	LOS ANGELES	MARINA DEL REY PIER LIGHT	33-58.20	118-26.80	28179.06	41118.38	18744
CA	LOS ANGELES	MARINA DEL REY N BRKWTR NO 2	33-57.80	118-27.80	28176.14	41121.88	18744
CA	LOS ANGELES	MARINA DEL REY NO 3	33-57.80	118-27.60	28176.64	41120.90	18744
CA	LOS ANGELES	MARINA DEL REY NO 4	33-57.60	118-27.50	28176.70	41119.70	18744
CA	LOS ANGELES	MARINA DEL REY S BRKWTR NO 1	33-57.50	118-27.50	28176.60	41119.35	18744
CA	LOS ANGELES	GULL ISLAND LIGHT	33-56.90	119-49.50	27958.86	41489.08	18728
CA	LOS ANGELES	HYPERION HARBOR BUOY	33-55.30	118-26.30	28177.47	41105.79	18744
CA	LOS ANGELES	EL SEGUNDO NO 10ES	33-55.20	118-26.50	28176.87	41106.42	18744
CA	LOS ANGELES	STA CRUZ METEOROLOGICAL NO 2	33-55.10	119-44.10	27972.73	41459.39	18729
CA	LOS ANGELES	STA CRUZ OCEANOGRAPHIC BUOY	33-55.10	119-43.90	27973.27	41458.56	18729
CA	LOS ANGELES	HYPERION BUOY B	33-55.03	118-26.10	28177.97	41104.81	18744
CA	LOS ANGELES	HYPERION BUOY A	33-55.00	118-26.20	28177.43	41104.26	18744
CA	LOS ANGELES	SCATTERGOOD BUOY NO 8ES	33-55.00	118-26.10	28177.68	41103.77	18744
CA	LOS ANGELES	EL SEGUNDO BUOY A	33-54.80	118-26.80	28175.73	41106.51	18744
CA	LOS ANGELES	EL SEGUNDO DANGER BUOY E	33-54.60	118-25.70	28178.29	41100.44	18744
CA	LOS ANGELES	EL SEGUNDO LIGHT "ES"	33-54.60	118-25.60	28178.54	41099.95	18744
CA	LOS ANGELES	EL SEGUNDO NO 2ES	33-54.50	118-27.50	28173.68	41108.90	18744
CA	LOS ANGELES	EL SEGUNDO NO 6ES	33-54.50	118-26.00	28177.44	41101.57	18744
CA	LOS ANGELES	EL SEGUNDO DANGER BUOY N	33-54.50	118-25.90	28177.69	41101.08	18744
CA	LOS ANGELES	EL SEGUNDO DANGER BUOY S	33-54.50	118-25.80	28177.94	41100.59	18744
CA	LOS ANGELES	EL SEGUNDO NO 4ES	33-54.40	118-25.90	28177.59	41100.74	18744
CA	LOS ANGELES	SOUTH POINT LIGHT	33-53.80	120-07.10	27909.70	41547.84	18728
CA	LOS ANGELES	REDONDO HARBOR LIGHT	33-50.90	118-23.60	28179.92	41077.69	18744
CA	LOS ANGELES	REDONDO BEACH W JETTY NO 3	33-50.50	118-23.70	28179.29	41076.86	18744
CA	LOS ANGELES	REDONDO BEACH E JETTY NO 2	33-50.50	118-23.60	28179.53	41076.37	18744
CA	LOS ANGELES	REDONDO BEACH HARB ENTR	33-50.50	118-23.50	28179.78	41075.88	18744
CA	LOS ANGELES	REDONDO HARBOR ENTR NO 1	33-50.30	118-23.80	28178.85	41076.68	18744
CA	LOS ANGELES	PALOS VERDES POINT NO 10	33-46.40	118-26.60	28168.23	41077.46	18740
CA	LOS ANGELES	LA EAST BASIN CHANN NO 2	33-45.90	118-15.20	28195.59	41020.66	18746
CA	LOS ANGELES	LONG BEACH CHANNEL NO 13	33-45.90	118-13.30	28200.19	41011.38	18746
CA	LOS ANGELES	LONG BEACH BERTH 118	33-45.70	118-13.20	28200.23	41010.27	18746

PASSES

STATE/COUNTRY	COUNTY/PROV	NAME	LAT	LON	TD#1	TD#2	CHART NO
CA	LOS ANGELES	LONG BEACH NAVY LDG ENTR	33-45.70	118-11.90	28203.36	41003.91	18746
CA	LOS ANGELES	SHORELINE MARINA E ENT LIGHT	33-45.60	118-11.50	28204.22	41001.64	18746
CA	LOS ANGELES	DOWNTOWN MARINA JETTY	33-45.60	118-10.80	28205.90	40998.21	18746
CA	LOS ANGELES	DOWNTOWN MARINA MOLE LIGHT	33-45.50	118-11.50	28204.12	41001.34	18746
CA	LOS ANGELES	DOWNTOWN MARINA W ENTR LIGHT	33-45.50	118-11.00	28205.32	40998.89	18746
CA	LOS ANGELES	DOWNTOWN MARINA E ENTR LIGHT	33-45.50	118-11.00	28205.32	40998.89	18746
CA	LOS ANGELES	DOWNTOWN MARINA E BRKWTR	33-45.50	118-10.90	28205.56	40998.40	18746
CA	LOS ANGELES	QUEENSWAY BAY MARINA NO F	33-45.40	118-11.80	28203.30	41002.50	18746
CA	LOS ANGELES	QUEENSWAY BAY MARINA NO E	33-45.40	118-11.70	28203.54	41002.01	18746
CA	LOS ANGELES	QUEENSWAY BAY MARINA NO D	33-45.40	118-11.60	28203.78	41001.52	18746
CA	LOS ANGELES	DOWNTOWN MARINA W BRKWTR	33-45.40	118-10.90	28205.46	40998.10	18746
CA	LOS ANGELES	QUEENSWAY BAY MARINA NO C	33-45.30	118-11.50	28203.92	41000.73	18746
CA	LOS ANGELES	QUEENSWAY BAY MARINA NO A	33-45.30	118-11.40	28204.16	41000.25	18746
CA	LOS ANGELES	QUEENSWAY BAY MARINA NO B	33-45.30	118-11.40	28204.16	41000.25	18746
CA	LOS ANGELES	LA EAST BASIN CHANN NO 1	33-45.20	118-16.00	28192.97	41022.38	18746
CA	LOS ANGELES	ALAMITOS BAY BAFFLE "B"	33-45.20	118-06.70	28215.30	40976.87	18746
CA	LOS ANGELES	ALAMITOS BAY BAFFLE "A"	33-45.10	118-06.70	28215.20	40976.57	18746
CA	LOS ANGELES	STA CATALINA HARBOR LIGHT	33-25.40	118-30.80	28139.74	41033.52	18757
CA	LOS ANGELES	STA CATALINA E END LIGHT	33-18.10	118-19.00	28161.25	40960.18	18757
CA	LOS ANGELES	SAN CLEMENTE ISLAND LIGHT	33-15.50	119-27.90	27995.40	41251.71	18762
CA	MARIN	BODEGA HEAD LIGHT	38-18.00	123-03.20	15861.79	43351.86	18643
CA	MARIN	BODEGA HARBOR APPROACH BA	38-17.20	123-02.30	15867.70	43348.10	18643
CA	MARIN	BODEGA HEAD WHISTLE NO 12	38-16.90	123-04.40	15861.85	43346.82	18640
CA	MARIN	TOMALES POINT LIGHT NO 2	38-15.10	123-00.10	15882.46	43338.30	18643
CA	MARIN	TOMALES BAY OUTSIDE BAR BUOY	38-14.60	122-59.20	15887.19	43335.91	18643
CA	MARIN	NOAA BUOY EB 46013	38-13.90	123-18.10	15828.20	43333.72	18640
CA	MARIN	NAPA RIVER RANGE LIGHT NO 14	38-12.30	122-18.30	16031.47	43320.33	18654
CA	MARIN	PETALUMA RIVER NO 5	38-12.20	122-34.10	15978.71	43321.99	18654
CA	MARIN	PETALUMA RIVER NO 4	38-11.90	122-34.10	15979.71	43320.47	18654
CA	MARIN	SACRAMENTO RIVER NO 2	38-10.60	121-39.80	16167.06	43302.20	18661
CA	MARIN	SACRAMENTO SHIP CHANNEL NO 36A	38-10.30	121-40.20	16166.53	43300.53	18661
CA	MARIN	SACRAMENTO SHIP CHANNEL NO 35	38-09.60	121-41.00	16165.76	43296.61	18661
CA	MARIN	SACRAMENTO SHIP CHANNEL NO 34	38-09.50	121-41.00	16166.04	43296.01	18661
CA	MARIN	RIO VISTA BRIDGE FOG SIGNAL	38-09.50	121-40.90	16166.38	43295.98	18661
CA	MARIN	NAPA RIVER WRECK NO 4WR	38-09.40	122-17.60	16043.01	43304.81	18654
CA	MARIN	SACRAMENTO SHIP CHANNEL NO 32	38-09.30	121-41.10	16166.25	43294.85	18661
CA	MARIN	PACIFIC GAS TOWER LIGHT	38-09.20	122-17.80	16042.97	43303.78	18654
CA	MARIN	SACRAMENTO SHIP CHANNEL NO 28	38-08.90	121-41.20	16167.01	43292.49	18661
CA	MARIN	SACRAMENTO SHIP CHANNEL NO 25	38-08.00	121-41.60	16168.13	43287.26	18661
CA	MARIN	NAPA RIVER NO 2	38-07.80	122-16.60	16051.32	43296.03	18654
CA	MARIN	SACRAMENTO SHIP CHANNEL NO 24	38-07.50	121-41.80	16168.81	43284.34	18661
CA	MARIN	SUISUN SLOUGH ENTRANCE NO 10	38-07.20	122-03.70	16096.27	43289.50	18656
CA	MARIN	SACRAMENTO SHIP CHANNEL NO 22	38-07.00	121-42.20	16168.82	43281.50	18661
CA	MARIN	VALLEJO YACHT CLUB N LIGHT	38-06.30	122-16.00	16057.91	43287.81	18654

PASSES

STATE/COUNTRY	COUNTY/PROV	NAME	LAT	LON	TD#1	TD#2	CHART NO
CA	MARIN	DECKER ISLAND N END LIGHT	38-06.30	121-42.60	16169.38	43277.46	18661
CA	MARIN	SAN JOAQUIN RIVER NO 42	38-06.10	121-36.10	16191.56	43273.68	18661
CA	MARIN	SAN JOAQUIN RIVER NO 33	38-05.90	121-40.10	16178.77	43274.09	18661
CA	MARIN	SACRAMENTO SHIP CHANNEL NO 18	38-05.60	121-44.10	16166.26	43273.85	18661
CA	MARIN	SAN JOAQUIN RIVER NO 32	38-05.60	121-40.30	16178.90	43272.36	18661
CA	MARIN	SAN JOAQUIN RIVER NO 30	38-05.50	121-40.60	16178.17	43271.88	18661
CA	MARIN	SAN JOAQUIN RIVER NO 34	38-05.40	121-39.20	16183.08	43270.70	18661
CA	MARIN	SAN JOAQUIN RIVER NO 37	38-05.40	121-38.10	16186.73	43270.25	18661
CA	MARIN	SAN JOAQUIN RIVER NO 29	38-05.30	121-40.90	16177.69	43270.79	18661
CA	MARIN	SAN JOAQUIN RIVER NO 36	38-05.20	121-38.40	16186.26	43269.16	18661
CA	MARIN	THREE MILE SLOUGH NO 1	38-05.10	121-41.10	16177.56	43269.67	18661
CA	MARIN	SAN JOAQUIN RIVER NO 53	38-04.80	121-34.10	16201.53	43264.84	18661
CA	MARIN	MARE ISLAND STRAIT NO 4	38-04.60	122-14.60	16067.66	43278.21	18654
CA	MARIN	SAN JOAQUIN RIVER NO 54	38-04.60	121-34.00	16202.37	43263.57	18661
CA	MARIN	MARE ISLAND STRAIT NO 3	38-04.50	122-14.80	16067.30	43277.73	18654
CA	MARIN	SAN JOAQUIN RIVER NO 55	38-04.50	121-33.70	16203.61	43262.81	18661
CA	MARIN	PETALUMA RIVER CHANNEL NO 6	38-04.30	122-25.30	16033.20	43279.50	18654
CA	MARIN	MARE ISLAND STRAIT NO 1	38-04.30	122-14.80	16067.89	43276.64	18654
CA	MARIN	SAN PABLO BAY NO 17	38-04.20	122-15.10	16067.20	43276.18	18654
CA	MARIN	MARE ISLAND STRAIT NO 2	38-04.20	122-14.60	16068.85	43276.04	18654
CA	MARIN	SAN JOAQUIN RIVER NO 56	38-04.10	121-33.60	16204.95	43260.30	18661
CA	MARIN	ROE ISLAND RANGE LIGHT	38-04.00	122-02.70	16108.86	43271.22	18656
CA	MARIN	SUISUN BAY CHANNEL NO 14	38-04.00	122-02.40	16109.85	43271.12	18656
CA	MARIN	SUISUN BAY CHANNEL NO 15	38-04.00	122-02.40	16109.85	43271.12	18656
CA	MARIN	SAN JOAQUIN RIVER NO 26	38-04.00	121-40.50	16182.43	43262.78	18661
CA	MARIN	CARQUINEZ BRIDGE PIER NO 2	38-03.90	122-13.50	16073.38	43274.08	18656
CA	MARIN	GLEN COVE MARINA LIGHT	38-03.90	122-12.80	16075.70	43273.87	18656
CA	MARIN	SACRAMENTO SHIP CHANNEL NO 1	38-03.90	121-51.00	16147.93	43266.46	18659
CA	MARIN	SUISUN BAY CHANNEL NO 12	38-03.80	122-03.50	16106.78	43270.76	18656
CA	MARIN	SUISUN BAY CHANNEL NO 16A	38-03.80	122-01.90	16112.08	43269.82	18656
CA	MARIN	SUISUN BAY CHANNEL NO 17	38-03.80	122-01.20	16114.40	43269.58	18656
CA	MARIN	SACRAMENTO SHIP CHANNEL NO 2	38-03.80	121-51.00	16148.20	43265.87	18659
CA	MARIN	SACRAMENTO SHIP CHANNEL NO 11	38-03.80	121-47.50	16159.79	43264.50	18661
CA	MARIN	MIDDLE GROUND OBSTRUCTION B	38-03.70	121-58.60	16123.30	43268.10	18656
CA	MARIN	SACRAMENTO SHIP CHANNEL NO 7	38-03.70	121-48.50	16156.75	43264.30	18659
CA	MARIN	SACRAMENTO SHIP CHANNEL NO 9	38-03.70	121-47.90	16158.74	43264.07	18661
CA	MARIN	SACRAMENTO SHIP CHANNEL NO 12	38-03.70	121-47.60	16159.73	43263.95	18661
CA	MARIN	SAN JOAQUIN RIVER NO 57	38-03.70	121-33.30	16206.94	43257.68	18661
CA	MARIN	CARQUINEZ STRAIT NO 21	38-03.60	122-11.60	16080.55	43271.86	18656
CA	MARIN	SUISUN BAY CHANNEL NO 19	38-03.60	121-60.00	16118.94	43268.03	18656
CA	MARIN	SUISUN BAY CHANNEL NO 21	38-03.60	121-58.90	16122.58	43267.64	18656
CA	MARIN	SUISUN BAY CHANNEL NO 22	38-03.60	121-58.70	16123.25	43267.57	18656
CA	MARIN	MIDDLE GROUND OBSTRUCTION A	38-03.60	121-58.30	16124.57	43267.43	18656
CA	MARIN	SAN JOAQUIN RIVER NO 25	38-03.60	121-40.80	16182.48	43260.49	18661

PASSES

STATE/COUNTRY	COUNTY/PROV	NAME	LAT	LON	TD#1	TD#2	CHART NO
CA	MARIN	SUISUN BAY CHANNEL NO 10	38-03.50	122-04.20	16105.32	43268.91	18656
CA	MARIN	SEAL ISLANDS CHANNEL NO 9	38-03.50	122-02.30	16111.61	43268.26	18656
CA	MARIN	SUISUN BAY PIER 2 W END	38-03.50	122-01.60	16113.92	43268.02	18656
CA	MARIN	SUISUN BAY CHANNEL NO 23	38-03.50	121-57.70	16126.84	43266.64	18656
CA	MARIN	SUISUN BAY LIGHT NO 34	38-03.50	121-52.00	16145.71	43264.50	18656
CA	MARIN	SUISUN BAY LIGHT NO 33	38-03.50	121-52.00	16145.71	43264.50	18656
CA	MARIN	SAN JOAQUIN RIVER NO 58	38-03.50	121-33.30	16207.44	43256.44	18661
CA	MARIN	OLEUM WHARF E LIGHTS	38-03.40	122-15.80	16067.26	43272.04	18654
CA	MARIN	SEAL ISLANDS CHANNEL NO 8	38-03.40	122-02.30	16111.89	43267.69	18656
CA	MARIN	SUISUN BAY RESTRICTED AREA A	38-03.40	121-59.20	16122.15	43266.60	18656
CA	MARIN	SUISUN BAY CHANNEL NO 24	38-03.40	121-57.70	16127.12	43266.06	18656
CA	MARIN	MIDDLE POINT LIGHT	38-03.30	121-59.50	16121.44	43266.14	18656
CA	MARIN	SUISUN BAY CHANNEL NO 24A	38-03.30	121-57.20	16129.05	43265.30	18656
CA	MARIN	SEQUOIA OIL WHARF W LIGHT	38-03.20	122-16.40	16065.87	43271.13	18654
CA	MARIN	CARQUINEZ STRAIT NO 20	38-03.20	122-11.70	16081.38	43269.68	18656
CA	MARIN	SUISUN BAY CHANNEL NO 9	38-03.20	122-04.90	16103.86	43267.46	18656
CA	MARIN	SEAL ISLANDS CHANNEL NO 2	38-03.20	122-04.20	16106.17	43267.22	18656
CA	MARIN	STOCKTON CHANNEL RANGE B	38-03.20	121-30.50	16217.38	43253.20	18661
CA	MARIN	SUISUN BAY CHANNEL NO 26	38-03.10	121-56.90	16130.59	43264.04	18656
CA	MARIN	CARQUINEZ STRAIT NO 22	38-02.90	122-11.00	16084.57	43267.80	18656
CA	MARIN	SUISUN BAY CHANNEL NO 7	38-02.90	122-06.00	16101.08	43266.15	18656
CA	MARIN	AVON WHARF WEST LIGHTS	38-02.90	122-05.60	16102.40	43266.01	18656
CA	MARIN	POINT EDITH RANGE LIGHT	38-02.90	122-05.30	16103.39	43265.91	18656
CA	MARIN	HARRIS YACHT HARBOR NO 1	38-02.90	121-57.30	16129.83	43263.04	18656
CA	MARIN	PETALUMA RIVER ENTRANCE NO 1	38-02.70	122-25.70	16036.76	43271.15	18654
CA	MARIN	NEW YORK SLOUGH NY	38-02.70	121-53.10	16144.25	43260.27	18656
CA	MARIN	STOCKTON CHANNEL RANGE C	38-02.70	121-30.10	16219.91	43249.86	18661
CA	MARIN	CARQUINEZ STRAIT NO 23	38-02.60	122-10.00	16088.73	43265.82	18656
CA	MARIN	BENICIA BRIDGE SEC CHANNEL	38-02.60	122-07.50	16096.98	43264.98	18656
CA	MARIN	BENICIA RR BRIDGE PIER 17	38-02.60	122-07.40	16097.31	43264.95	18656
CA	MARIN	SUISUN BAY CHANNEL NO 6	38-02.60	122-06.60	16099.95	43264.67	18656
CA	MARIN	SUISUN BAY CHANNEL NO 28	38-02.60	121-55.00	16138.25	43260.43	18656
CA	MARIN	SUISUN BAY CHANNEL NO 30	38-02.60	121-53.30	16143.86	43259.76	18656
CA	MARIN	NEW YORK SLOUGH NO 2	38-02.50	121-53.10	16144.79	43259.10	18656
CA	MARIN	SAN JOAQUIN RIVER NO 21	38-02.50	121-42.00	16181.36	43254.38	18661
CA	MARIN	SAN PABLO CHANNEL NO 10	38-02.40	122-21.00	16053.10	43268.19	18654
CA	MARIN	BENICIA WHARF LIGHT	38-02.40	122-08.30	16094.92	43264.14	18656
CA	MARIN	SUISUN BAY CHANNEL NO 5	38-02.40	122-07.10	16098.87	43263.73	18656
CA	MARIN	SUISUN BAY CHANNEL NO 2	38-02.30	122-07.30	16098.50	43263.23	18656
CA	MARIN	SUISUN BAY CHANNEL NO 3	38-02.30	122-07.30	16098.50	43263.23	18656
CA	MARIN	CARQUINEZ BRIDGE PIER SIGNAL	38-02.30	122-07.20	16098.83	43263.20	18656
CA	MARIN	BENICIA RR BRIDGE PIER 13	38-02.30	122-07.20	16098.83	43263.20	18656
CA	MARIN	BENICIA BRIDGE FOG SIGNAL	38-02.30	122-07.20	16098.83	43263.20	18656
CA	MARIN	SUISUN BAY CHANNEL NO 4	38-02.30	122-07.10	16099.16	43263.17	18656

P A S S E S

STATE/COUNTRY	COUNTY/PROV	NAME	LAT	LON	TD#1	TD#2	CHART NO
CA	MARIN	PITTSBURG MARINA NO 1	38-02.20	121-52.80	16146.59	43257.23	18656
CA	MARIN	AMORCO WHARF LIGHTS	38-02.10	122-07.40	16098.74	43262.15	18656
CA	MARIN	CARQUINEZ STRAIT NO 25	38-02.00	122-09.60	16091.78	43262.36	18656
CA	MARIN	SHELL OIL WHARF E END LIGHT	38-02.00	122-07.70	16098.03	43261.70	18656
CA	MARIN	NEW YORK SLOUGH NO 5	38-02.00	121-52.00	16149.76	43255.73	18656
CA	MARIN	SHELL OIL WHARF W END LIGHT	38-01.80	122-08.00	16097.62	43260.69	18656
CA	MARIN	NEW YORK SLOUGH NO 8	38-01.80	121-51.20	16152.93	43254.23	18656
CA	MARIN	POINT BEENAR LIGHT	38-01.80	121-50.20	16156.22	43253.80	18659
CA	MARIN	SAN JOAQUIN RIVER NO 11	38-01.80	121-45.90	16170.36	43251.93	18661
CA	MARIN	SAN PABLO CHANNEL NO 8	38-01.70	122-22.30	16050.92	43264.83	18654
CA	MARIN	MARTINEZ MARINA LIGHT NO 1	38-01.70	122-08.20	16097.24	43260.20	18656
CA	MARIN	NEW YORK SLOUGH NO 11	38-01.70	121-50.60	16155.17	43253.38	18656
CA	MARIN	SAN JOAQUIN RIVER NO 3	38-01.70	121-49.40	16159.12	43252.87	18659
CA	MARIN	SAN JOAQUIN RIVER NO 13	38-01.70	121-45.10	16173.25	43250.97	18661
CA	MARIN	SAN JOAQUIN RIVER NO 10	38-01.70	121-45.10	16173.25	43250.97	18661
CA	MARIN	SAN JOAQUIN RIVER NO 15	38-01.70	121-44.90	16173.90	43250.88	18661
CA	MARIN	NEW YORK SLOUGH NO 10	38-01.60	121-50.70	16155.11	43252.84	18656
CA	MARIN	SAN JOAQUIN RIVER NO 4	38-01.60	121-49.70	16158.40	43252.41	18659
CA	MARIN	SAN JOAQUIN RIVER NO 14	38-01.60	121-45.10	16173.51	43250.38	18661
CA	MARIN	SAN JOAQUIN RIVER NO 16	38-01.60	121-44.90	16174.16	43250.29	18661
CA	MARIN	SAN JOAQUIN RIVER NO 18	38-01.60	121-44.20	16176.46	43249.96	18661
CA	MARIN	STOCKTON CHANNEL NO 16	38-01.50	121-28.10	16229.32	43241.24	18661
CA	MARIN	STOCKTON CHANNEL RANGE D	38-01.50	121-28.00	16229.64	43241.18	18661
CA	MARIN	SAN JOAQUIN RIVER NO 5	38-01.40	121-48.90	16161.55	43250.88	18659
CA	MARIN	STOCKTON CHANNEL RANGE E	38-01.40	121-27.90	16230.20	43240.49	18661
CA	MARIN	SAN JOAQUIN RIVER NO 8	38-01.20	121-48.20	16164.38	43249.38	18659
CA	MARIN	POINT PINOLE LIGHT P	38-01.00	122-22.00	16053.97	43260.98	18654
CA	MARIN	SAN PABLO CHANNEL E	38-00.60	122-24.10	16048.29	43259.51	18654
CA	MARIN	STOCKTON CHANNEL NO 27	37-59.70	121-25.90	16240.65	43228.52	18661
CA	MARIN	STOCKTON CHANNEL NO 28	37-59.60	121-25.90	16240.88	43227.89	18661
CA	MARIN	STOCKTON CHANNEL RANGE J	37-59.20	121-23.50	16249.50	43223.83	18661
CA	MARIN	STOCKTON CHANNEL RANGE H	37-59.10	121-23.30	16250.36	43223.06	18661
CA	MARIN	DRAKES BAY WHISTLE NO 1	37-59.00	122-57.30	15945.80	43260.80	18647
CA	MARIN	SAN RAFAEL CREEK LIGHT	37-58.30	122-29.70	16036.88	43249.13	18649
CA	MARIN	SAN PABLO BAY NO 2	37-58.10	122-25.70	16050.44	43246.69	18654
CA	MARIN	POINT SAN PABLO TERMINAL NO 4	37-57.90	122-25.70	16051.02	43245.62	18654
CA	MARIN	SAN RAFAEL CREEK NO 3	37-57.80	122-28.50	16042.24	43246.07	17649
CA	MARIN	EAST BROTHER ISLAND LIGHT	37-57.80	122-26.00	16050.34	43245.20	18649
CA	MARIN	SF BAY N CHANNEL NO 17	37-57.50	122-27.30	16047.01	43244.05	18649
CA	MARIN	SF BAY N CHANNEL NO 18	37-57.30	122-26.40	16050.50	43242.67	18649
CA	MARIN	POINT ORIENT WHARF S LIGHTS	37-57.30	122-25.60	16053.09	43242.38	18649
CA	MARIN	ROD & GUN CLUB LIGHT	37-57.30	121-20.60	16262.94	43209.59	18661
CA	MARIN	SAN RAFAEL OUTFALL LIGHT	37-56.90	122-27.60	16047.79	43240.97	18649
CA	MARIN	MOLATE POINT WHARF S LIGHT	37-56.70	122-25.60	16054.83	43239.16	18649

PASSES

STATE/COUNTRY	COUNTY/PROV	NAME	LAT	LON	TD#1	TD#2	CHART NO
CA	MARIN	SAN QUENTIN SECURITY ZONE A	37-56.40	122-29.00	16044.72	43238.82	18649
CA	MARIN	SF BAY NORTH CHANNEL NO 15	37-56.20	122-26.70	16052.72	43236.90	18649
CA	MARIN	RUCHMOND E CHANNEL NO 6	37-56.20	122-25.50	16056.59	43236.45	18649
CA	MARIN	CASTRO ROCKS NO 2CR	37-55.90	122-25.20	16058.42	43234.72	18649
CA	MARIN	SF BAY NORTH CHANNEL NO 14	37-55.80	122-26.50	16054.51	43234.69	18649
CA	MARIN	RICHMOND E CHANNEL NO 1	37-55.80	122-25.60	16057.42	43234.34	18649
CA	MARIN	STANDARD OIL INNER FOR SIGNAL	37-55.50	122-24.30	16062.47	43232.22	18649
CA	MARIN	SOUTHAMPTON SHOAL NO 5	37-55.30	122-25.60	16058.85	43231.66	18649
CA	MARIN	STANDARD OIL WHARF FOG SIGNAL	37-55.30	122-24.60	16062.07	43231.26	18649
CA	MARIN	RICHMOND HARBOR CHANNEL NO 2	37-55.10	122-25.00	16061.35	43230.34	18649
CA	MARIN	RICHMOND HARBOR NO 20	37-55.10	122-21.80	16071.65	43229.05	18649
CA	MARIN	POINT POTRERO REACH NO 14	37-55.10	122-21.80	16071.65	43229.05	18649
CA	MARIN	SOUTHAMPTON SHOAL NO 4	37-55.00	122-25.30	16060.67	43229.93	18649
CA	MARIN	SF BAY NORTH CHANNEL C	37-54.80	122-26.90	16056.09	43229.49	18649
CA	MARIN	SF BAY NORTH CHANNEL NO 12	37-54.80	122-26.60	16057.06	43229.37	18649
CA	MARIN	RICHMOND HARBOR CHANNEL NO 5	37-54.50	122-23.90	16066.59	43226.66	18649
CA	MARIN	POINT RICHMOND N PIER LIGHT	37-54.50	122-23.50	16067.87	43226.50	18649
CA	MARIN	POINT RICHMOND S PIER LIGHT	37-54.40	122-23.50	16068.15	43225.95	18649
CA	MARIN	RICHMOND HARBOR NO 7	37-54.40	122-23.10	16069.44	43225.79	18649
CA	MARIN	SF BAY NORTH CHANNEL NO 10	37-54.30	122-26.10	16060.09	43226.48	18649
CA	MARIN	RICHMOND HARBOR JETTY	37-54.20	122-23.50	16068.72	43224.87	18649
CA	MARIN	SF BAY NORTH CHANNEL B	37-54.10	122-26.60	16059.05	43225.61	18649
CA	MARIN	SOUTHAMPTON SHOAL NO 1	37-54.00	122-25.30	16063.50	43224.54	18649
CA	MARIN	SOUTHAMPTON SHOAL NO 2	37-54.00	122-25.10	16064.15	43224.46	18649
CA	MARIN	SF BAY NORTH CHANNEL NO 9	37-53.70	122-26.90	16059.22	43223.59	18649
CA	MARIN	NATL MARINE FISHERIES LIGHT	37-53.50	122-26.70	16060.42	43222.43	18649
CA	MARIN	NATL MARINE FISHERIES LIGHT	37-53.40	122-26.70	16060.71	43221.89	18649
CA	MARIN	SF BAY NORTH CHANNEL NO 8	37-53.10	122-25.00	16066.99	43219.56	18649
CA	MARIN	SOUTHAMPTON SHOAL LIGHT	37-52.90	122-24.00	16070.75	43218.04	18649
CA	MARIN	CORINTHIAN HARBOR NO 5	37-52.80	122-26.30	16063.68	43218.50	18649
CA	MARIN	CORINTHIAN HARBOR NO 1	37-52.30	122-27.30	16061.88	43216.24	18649
CA	MARIN	BELVEDERE COVE NO 1	37-52.30	122-27.20	16062.20	43216.20	18649
CA	MARIN	BERKELEY BRKWTR LIGHT NO 4	37-52.10	122-19.20	16088.31	43211.52	18649
CA	MARIN	BERKELEY BRKWTR LIGHT NO 3	37-52.10	122-19.20	16088.31	43211.52	18649
CA	MARIN	BERKELEY BRKWTR LIGHT NO 2	37-52.00	122-19.20	16088.58	43210.96	18649
CA	MARIN	BERKELEY MARINA NORTH LIGHT	37-52.00	122-19.00	16089.22	43210.87	18649
CA	MARIN	BERKELEY MARINA SOUTH LIGHT	37-52.00	122-19.00	16089.22	43210.87	18649
CA	MARIN	SAUSALITO CHANNEL NO 6	37-51.90	122-29.10	16057.26	43214.87	18649
CA	MARIN	SF BAY NORTH CHANNEL NO 6	37-51.90	122-23.70	16074.49	43212.48	18649
CA	MARIN	CONE ROCK LIGHT	37-51.80	122-28.10	16060.73	43213.90	18649
CA	MARIN	SF BAY NORTH CHANNEL A	37-51.80	122-24.40	16072.53	43212.26	18649
CA	MARIN	CORINTHIAN HARBOR NO 3	37-51.70	122-27.40	16063.24	43213.06	18649
CA	MARIN	RACOON STRAIT NO 4	37-51.70	122-26.70	16065.47	43212.75	18649
CA	MARIN	DUXBURY REEF WHISTLE 1DR	37-51.60	122-41.70	16018.04	43218.51	18647

PASSES

STATE/COUNTRY	COUNTY/PROV	NAME	LAT	LON	TD#1	TD#2	CHART NO
CA	MARIN	BERKELEY MARINA NO 3	37-51.50	122-20.90	16084.52	43209.02	18649
CA	MARIN	RACOON STRAIT NO 2	37-51.20	122-26.60	16067.18	43210.01	18649
CA	MARIN	POINT BLUFF LIGHT	37-51.20	122-25.10	16071.96	43209.32	18649
CA	MARIN	SF BAY NORTH CHANNEL NO 3	37-51.00	122-25.00	16072.83	43208.20	18649
CA	MARIN	SF BAY NORTH CHANNEL NO 4	37-51.00	122-23.70	16076.96	43207.59	18649
CA	MARIN	BERKELEY MARINA NO 2	37-50.90	122-21.60	16083.92	43206.06	18649
CA	MARIN	RACOON STRAIT NO 1	37-50.60	122-27.10	16067.25	43207.00	18649
CA	MARIN	EMERYVILLE MARINA NO 1	37-50.60	122-19.30	16092.05	43203.30	18649
CA	MARIN	EMERYVILLE MARINA NO 3	37-50.60	122-18.90	16093.33	43203.11	18649
CA	MARIN	EMERYVILLE MARINA NO 5	37-50.60	122-18.50	16094.60	43202.91	18649
CA	MARIN	EMERYVILLE MARINA NO 8	37-50.50	122-18.60	16094.55	43202.41	18649
CA	MARIN	EMERYVILLE MARINA NO 7	37-50.50	122-18.60	16094.55	43202.41	18649
CA	MARIN	HARDING ROCK HR	37-50.30	122-26.70	16069.35	43205.20	18649
CA	MARIN	YELLOW BLUFF LIGHT	37-50.20	122-28.30	16064.55	43205.40	18649
CA	MARIN	POINT BONITA WHISTLE NO 2	37-50.00	122-34.00	16047.03	43206.91	18649
CA	MARIN	SF BAY NORTH CHANNEL NO 2	37-50.00	122-23.70	16079.70	43202.15	18649
CA	MARIN	TREASURE ISLAND N END NO 6	37-50.00	122-22.30	16084.14	43201.47	18649
CA	MARIN	HORSESHOE BAY E BRKWTR LIGHT	37-49.90	122-28.50	16064.74	43203.88	18649
CA	MARIN	TREASURE ISLAND N END NO 8	37-49.90	122-21.90	16085.68	43200.73	18649
CA	MARIN	ALCATRAZ BELL	37-49.70	122-25.60	16074.49	43201.43	18649
CA	MARIN	POINT BONITA LIGHT	37-49.60	122-30.00	16060.82	43202.96	18649
CA	MARIN	POINT BONITA NO 3	37-49.60	122-30.00	16060.82	43202.96	18649
CA	MARIN	ALCATRAZ LIGHT	37-49.60	122-25.30	16075.71	43200.75	18649
CA	MARIN	LIME POINT LIGHT	37-49.50	122-28.60	16065.53	43201.77	18649
CA	MARIN	POINT BONITA NO 4	37-49.40	122-33.20	16051.24	43203.37	18649
CA	MARIN	TREASURE ISLAND E CHANNEL NO 4	37-49.30	122-21.10	16089.83	43197.04	18649
CA	MARIN	POINT DIABLO LIGHT	37-49.20	122-29.90	16062.23	43200.77	18649
CA	MARIN	BLOSSOM ROCK BELL BR	37-49.10	122-24.20	16080.55	43197.49	18649
CA	MARIN	OAKLAND OUTER HARBOR NO 7	37-49.00	122-19.20	16096.65	43194.42	18649
CA	MARIN	POINT BONITA LIGHT	37-48.90	122-31.70	27201.99	43200.01	18680
CA	MARIN	OAKLAND OUTER HARBOR NO 5	37-48.90	122-19.50	16095.97	43194.02	18649
CA	MARIN	GOLDEN GATE BRIDGE NO 2	37-48.80	122-28.70	16067.13	43198.05	18649
CA	MARIN	OAKLAND OUTER HARBOR NO 3	37-48.80	122-20.00	16094.65	43193.73	18649
CA	MARIN	FOUR FATHOM BANK BELL	37-48.70	122-32.30	16056.03	43199.23	18649
CA	MARIN	FISHERMAN'S WHARF BRKWTR A	37-48.70	122-25.30	16078.15	43195.86	18649
CA	MARIN	FISHERMAN'S WHARF BRKWTR B	37-48.70	122-25.20	16078.47	43195.81	18649
CA	MARIN	PIER 45 EAST LIGHT	37-48.70	122-25.20	16078.47	43195.81	18649
CA	MARIN	FISHERMAN'S WHARF ENTRANCE NO 2	37-48.70	122-25.10	16078.79	43195.76	18649
CA	MARIN	PIER 39 BRKWTR LIGHT B	37-48.70	122-24.50	16080.68	43195.46	18649
CA	MARIN	PIER 39 BRKWTR LIGHT A	37-48.70	122-24.50	16080.68	43195.46	18649
CA	MARIN	PIER 39 BRKWTR LIGHT C	37-48.70	122-24.40	16081.00	43195.41	18649
CA	MARIN	TREASURE ISLAND E CHANNEL NO 3	37-48.70	122-21.10	16091.44	43193.74	18649
CA	MARIN	BART OBSTRUCTION LIGHTS	37-48.70	122-20.20	16094.28	43193.28	18649
CA	MARIN	AQUATIC PARK ENTRANCE NO 1	37-48.60	122-25.40	16078.11	43195.36	18649

PASSES

STATE/COUNTRY	COUNTY/PROV	NAME	LAT	LON	TD#1	TD#2	CHART NO
CA	MARIN	PIER 39 BRKWTR LIGHT D	37-48.60	122-24.40	16081.27	43194.86	18649
CA	MARIN	PIER 39 BRKWTR LIGHT F	37-48.60	122-24.40	16081.27	43194.86	18649
CA	MARIN	PIER 39 BRKWTR LIGHT E	37-48.60	122-24.40	16081.27	43194.86	18649
CA	MARIN	ANITA ROCK LIGHT	37-48.50	122-27.20	16072.69	43195.71	18649
CA	MARIN	SF SUBMARINE OUTFALL LIGHT	37-48.50	122-26.90	16073.64	43195.56	18649
CA	MARIN	SF WEST YACHT HARBOR NO 2	37-48.50	122-26.30	16075.53	43195.27	18649
CA	MARIN	PIER 39 MARINA LIGHT NO 2	37-48.50	122-24.70	16080.59	43194.47	18649
CA	MARIN	PIER 27-29 WEST LIGHT	37-48.50	122-24.00	16082.80	43194.12	18649
CA	MARIN	YERBA BUENA ISLAND WHARF	37-48.40	122-21.70	16090.34	43192.40	18649
CA	MARIN	OAKLAND OUTER HARBOR NO 1B	37-48.30	122-20.90	16093.13	43191.44	18649
CA	MARIN	OAKLAND 7TH ST TERMINAL NO 2	37-48.30	122-20.50	16094.40	43191.23	18649
CA	MARIN	SAN FRANCISCO N BUOY "N"	37-48.20	122-47.90	27146.77	43203.57	18680
CA	MARIN	OAKLAND HARBOR BAR CHANNEL NO 1	37-48.20	122-21.40	16091.82	43191.15	18649
CA	MARIN	OAKLAND 7TH ST TERMIANL NO 1	37-48.20	122-20.40	16094.98	43190.63	18649
CA	MARIN	PIER D NORTH BUOY	37-48.10	122-22.50	16088.61	43191.17	18649
CA	MARIN	OAKLAND HARBOR BAR CHANNEL NO 2	37-48.10	122-21.10	16093.04	43190.44	18649
CA	MARIN	OAKLAND INNER HARBOR NO 4	37-48.10	122-20.70	16094.30	43190.23	18649
CA	MARIN	OAKLAND MID HARBOR A	37-48.10	122-20.30	16095.56	43190.02	18649
CA	MENDOCINO	SCRIPPS CURRENT METER E	39-38.80	123-49.30	15328.06	43640.61	18620
CA	MENDOCINO	SCRIPPS CURRENT METER F	39-38.50	123-50.50	15326.07	43639.04	18620
CA	MENDOCINO	SCRIPPS CURRENT METER G	39-37.60	123-53.60	15321.65	43634.66	18620
CA	MENDOCINO	SCRIPPS CURRENT METER H	39-37.10	123-59.60	15306.10	43629.91	18620
CA	MENDOCINO	SCRIPPS CURRENT METER B	39-36.80	123-27.00	15410.40	43647.70	18640
CA	MENDOCINO	NOYO WHISTLE BUOY NA	39-25.90	123-49.90	15398.45	43600.95	18620
CA	MENDOCINO	NOYO RIVER ENTRANCE NO 2	39-25.80	123-49.30	15400.88	43600.93	18626
CA	MENDOCINO	ALBION RIVER LIGHT NO 1	39-25.80	123-49.30	15400.88	43600.93	18626
CA	MENDOCINO	NOYO RIVER ENTRANCE NO 3	39-25.80	123-48.90	15402.14	43601.14	18626
CA	MENDOCINO	FORT BRAGG RADIOBEACON	39-25.80	123-48.50	15403.40	43601.34	18620
CA	MENDOCINO	NOYO RIVER ENTRANCE NO 5	39-25.70	123-48.50	15403.94	43601.03	18626
CA	MENDOCINO	POINT CABRILLO LIGHT	39-20.90	123-49.50	15426.60	43585.15	18620
CA	MENDOCINO	MENDOCINO BAY WHISTLE	39-17.80	123-48.70	15444.96	43575.73	18620
CA	MENDOCINO	LITTLE RIVER BUOY	39-15.90	123-48.00	15457.62	43569.43	18620
CA	MENDOCINO	ALBION RIVER BUOY AR	39-13.60	123-47.20	15472.04	43562.08	18620
CA	MENDOCINO	NOAA BUOY EB 46014	39-13.30	123-58.40	15438.28	43556.18	18620
CA	MENDOCINO	POINT ARENA NO 18	38-57.50	123-45.70	15556.34	43506.25	18640
CA	MENDOCINO	POINT ARENA LIGHT	38-57.30	123-44.40	15561.45	43505.97	18640
CA	MENDOCINO	ARENA COVE BUOY A	38-54.60	123-43.50	15577.03	43496.36	18640
CA	MENDOCINO	SAUNDERS REEF BUOY NO 16	38-50.80	123-40.00	15605.87	43483.25	18640
CA	MONTEREY	MOSS LANDING HARB ENTR RB	36-48.40	121-47.20	27521.42	42802.41	18685
CA	MONTEREY	MOSS LANDING HARB ENTR NO 2	36-48.30	121-47.30	27521.09	42801.97	18685
CA	MONTEREY	MOSS LANDING ENTR "MLA"	36-47.90	121-48.00	27518.43	42800.71	18685
CA	MONTEREY	NOAA BUOY 46042	36-45.00	122-24.50	27374.58	42840.34	18680
CA	MONTEREY	MONTEREY BAY DANGER "B"	36-43.40	121-50.90	27511.07	42778.37	18685
CA	MONTEREY	MONTEREY BAY DANGER "A"	36-39.20	121-52.90	27507.62	42756.64	18685

PASSES

STATE/COUNTRY	COUNTY/PROV	NAME	LAT	LON	TD#1	TD#2	CHART NO
CA	MONTEREY	POINT PINOS WHISTLE NO 2	36-38.90	121-56.60	27492.55	42761.32	18680
CA	MONTEREY	POINT PINOS LIGHT	36-38.00	121-56.00	27496.17	42754.95	18680
CA	MONTEREY	MONTEREY BAY NO 4	36-37.50	121-53.70	27506.33	42747.91	18685
CA	MONTEREY	MONTEREY HARB N NO 1	36-36.50	121-53.40	27508.78	42741.41	18685
CA	MONTEREY	MONTEREY HARBOR NO A	36-36.50	121-53.30	27509.20	42741.23	18685
CA	MONTEREY	MONTEREY MAIN CHANNEL NO 2	36-36.40	121-53.40	27508.90	42740.82	18685
CA	MONTEREY	MONTEREY FAIRWAY "A"	36-36.30	121-53.50	27508.61	42740.40	18685
CA	MONTEREY	POINT CYPRESS GONG NO 6	36-35.00	121-59.00	27487.73	42742.52	18680
CA	MONTEREY	POINT SUR LIGHT	36-35.00	121-59.00	27487.73	42742.52	18680
CA	MONTEREY	NOAA BUOY EB 46028	35-45.30	121-52.00	27565.27	42444.01	18700
CA	ORANGE	LONG BEACH MID-CHAN NO B	33-45.00	118-13.00	28200.01	41007.15	18746
CA	ORANGE	LONG BEACH HARBOR MOORING	33-45.00	118-11.10	28204.58	40997.86	18746
CA	ORANGE	ALAMITOS BAY BASIN 1 NO 2	33-45.00	118-06.90	28214.62	40977.25	18746
CA	ORANGE	ALAMITOS BAY BASIN 1 NO 1	33-45.00	118-06.80	28214.86	40976.76	18746
CA	ORANGE	NOAA BUOY EB46025	33-44.80	119-04.10	28072.37	41246.63	18720
CA	ORANGE	LONG BEACH CHANNEL NO 6	33-44.80	118-12.90	28200.05	41006.05	18746
CA	ORANGE	LONG BEACH HARBOR MOORING	33-44.80	118-11.10	28204.38	40997.25	18746
CA	ORANGE	LONG BEACH HARBOR MOORING	33-44.70	118-11.00	28204.52	40996.46	18746
CA	ORANGE	ALAMITOS BAY CHANNEL NO 3	33-44.70	118-07.00	28214.08	40976.85	18746
CA	ORANGE	LONG BCH SE BASIN NO 3	33-44.60	118-11.90	28202.26	41000.56	18746
CA	ORANGE	LONG BEACH HARBOR MOORING	33-44.60	118-10.90	28204.66	40995.68	18746
CA	ORANGE	POINT VINCENT LIGHT	33-44.50	118-24.60	28171.38	41061.76	18740
CA	ORANGE	LONG BEACH HARBOR MOORING	33-44.50	118-10.90	28204.56	40995.37	18746
CA	ORANGE	LONG BEACH MID-CHAN NO A	33-44.40	118-12.60	28200.38	41003.37	18746
CA	ORANGE	LONG BCH SE BASIN ENT NO 1	33-44.40	118-12.30	28201.10	41001.90	18746
CA	ORANGE	LONG BCH HARB MOORING CR 2	33-44.40	118-09.40	28208.05	40987.73	18746
CA	ORANGE	LONG BCH HARB MOORING CR 1	33-44.40	118-09.40	28208.05	40987.73	18746
CA	ORANGE	LONG BCH HARB MOORING CR 3	33-44.40	118-08.80	28209.48	40984.79	18746
CA	ORANGE	LONG BEACH HARBOR PIER "J"	33-44.30	118-11.10	28203.88	40995.74	18746
CA	ORANGE	ALAMITOS BAY W JETTY NO 1	33-44.20	118-07.30	28212.85	40976.84	18746
CA	ORANGE	ALAMITOS BAY E JETTY NO 2	33-44.20	118-07.20	28213.09	40976.35	18746
CA	ORANGE	TERMINAL ISLAND JETTY TI	33-44.10	118-14.80	28194.79	41013.16	18746
CA	ORANGE	LA OUTER HARBOR MOORING D	33-44.10	118-14.40	28195.75	41011.22	18746
CA	ORANGE	ANAHEIM BAY CHANNEL NO 10	33-44.10	118-05.60	28216.79	40968.19	18746
CA	ORANGE	ANAHEIM BAY CHANNEL NO 11	33-44.10	118-05.50	28217.03	40967.70	18746
CA	ORANGE	LA OUTER HARBOR MOORING B	33-44.00	118-14.80	28194.70	41012.86	18746
CA	ORANGE	LA OUTER HARBOR MOORING C	33-44.00	118-14.60	28195.18	41011.89	18746
CA	ORANGE	ANAHEIM BAY CHANNEL NO 13	33-44.00	118-05.40	28217.16	40966.92	18746
CA	ORANGE	LA OUTER HARBOR MOORING A	33-43.90	118-15.00	28194.12	41013.52	18746
CA	ORANGE	ANAHEIM BAY CHANNEL NO 15	33-43.90	118-05.30	28217.30	40966.13	18746
CA	ORANGE	ANAHEIM BAY CHANNEL NO 17	33-43.90	118-05.20	28217.54	40965.64	18746
CA	ORANGE	LA OUTER HARBOR MOORING	33-43.70	118-15.30	28193.20	41014.37	18746
CA	ORANGE	ANAHEIM BAY W JETTY NO 5	33-43.70	118-06.10	28215.20	40969.47	18746
CA	ORANGE	LONG BEACH CHANNEL NO 3	33-43.60	118-11.50	28202.22	40995.59	18746

P A S S E S

STATE/COUNTRY	COUNTY/PROV	NAME	LAT	LON	TD#1	TD#2	CHART NO
CA	ORANGE	ANAHEIM BAY E JETTY NO 6	33-43.60	118-06.00	28215.33	40968.69	18746
CA	ORANGE	LONG BEACH LIGHT	33-43.40	118-11.20	28202.74	40993.52	18746
CA	ORANGE	LONG BEACH CHAN WHISTLE "LB"	33-43.40	118-11.00	28203.22	40992.55	18746
CA	ORANGE	LONG BEACH CHANNEL NO 2	33-43.40	118-10.80	28203.70	40991.57	18746
CA	ORANGE	LONG BEACH BRKWTR E NO 1	33-43.40	118-08.20	28209.90	40978.88	18746
CA	ORANGE	LA MAIN CHANNEL ART NO 6	33-43.30	118-16.00	28191.12	41016.54	18746
CA	ORANGE	LA MAIN CHANNEL ART NO 5	33-43.00	118-16.10	28190.59	41016.11	18746
CA	ORANGE	LA MAIN CHANNEL ART. NO 4	33-43.00	118-15.50	28192.04	41013.21	18746
CA	ORANGE	ANAHEIM BAY ENTR NO 1	33-43.00	118-06.60	28213.30	40969.86	18746
CA	ORANGE	ANAHEIM BAY ENTR NO 2	33-43.00	118-06.50	28213.54	40969.38	18746
CA	ORANGE	LOS ANGELES MARINA LIGHT	33-42.90	118-16.60	28189.29	41018.22	18746
CA	ORANGE	CABRILLO BEACH N RAMP	33-42.80	118-16.90	28188.47	41019.38	18746
CA	ORANGE	SAN PEDRO W CHANNEL NO 3	33-42.80	118-16.60	28189.19	41017.92	18746
CA	ORANGE	SAN PEDRO W CHANNEL NO 2	33-42.80	118-16.40	28189.67	41016.96	18746
CA	ORANGE	SAN PEDRO W CHANNEL NO 1	33-42.80	118-16.40	28189.67	41016.96	18746
CA	ORANGE	LA MAIN CHANNEL ART NO 3	33-42.80	118-15.50	28191.84	41012.60	18746
CA	ORANGE	LA MAIN CHANNEL NO 2	33-42.60	118-14.60	28193.81	41007.64	18746
CA	ORANGE	LOS ANGELES LIGHT	33-42.50	118-15.00	28192.75	41009.27	18746
CA	ORANGE	POINT FERMIN LIGHT	33-42.30	118-17.60	28186.30	41021.22	18740
CA	ORANGE	LOS ANGELES CHANNEL "LA"	33-42.00	118-14.50	28193.47	41005.34	18746
CA	ORANGE	SAN PEDRO BUOY B	33-42.00	118-12.00	28199.45	40993.23	18740
CA	ORANGE	SAN PEDRO BUOY A	33-42.00	118-09.80	28204.69	40982.54	18740
CA	ORANGE	POINT FERMIN NO 6	33-41.90	118-17.50	28186.16	41019.53	18740
CA	ORANGE	SAN PEDRO CHANNEL 8TL	33-40.70	118-24.50	28168.11	41049.38	18740
CA	ORANGE	HUNTINGTON BEACH NO 2HB	33-38.10	118-00.80	28221.97	40927.65	18740
CA	ORANGE	SAN PEDRO CAL BUOY	33-37.80	118-05.10	28211.62	40947.67	18740
CA	ORANGE	SAN PEDRO CHANNEL 7TL	33-37.70	118-27.90	28157.16	41056.26	18740
CA	ORANGE	SAN PEDRO NO 3TL	33-37.70	118-06.50	28208.24	40954.16	18740
CA	ORANGE	HUNTINGTON BCH REEF D	33-37.00	117-58.50	28226.19	40913.48	
CA	ORANGE	RUEBEN E LEE OBSTRUCTION	33-36.90	117-54.20	28235.99	40892.29	18746
CA	ORANGE	LIDO ISLE W LIGHT NO 4	33-36.70	117-55.20	28233.49	40896.63	18746
CA	ORANGE	NEWPORT BAY CHANNEL NO 12	33-36.70	117-54.40	28235.33	40892.73	18746
CA	ORANGE	LIDO ISLE E LIGHT NO 2	33-36.50	117-54.50	28234.89	40892.70	18746
CA	ORANGE	NEWPORT BAY CHANNEL NO 11	33-36.50	117-54.20	28235.58	40891.23	18746
CA	ORANGE	BALBOA ISLAND N CHANNEL NO 2	33-36.50	117-54.00	28236.04	40890.26	18746
CA	ORANGE	NEWPORT BAY CHANNEL NO 10	33-36.20	117-53.80	28236.19	40888.50	18746
CA	ORANGE	NEWPORT BAY CHANNEL NO 6	33-36.00	117-52.80	28238.27	40883.12	18746
CA	ORANGE	NEWPORT BAY E JETTY NO 4	33-35.40	117-52.60	28238.11	40880.59	18746
CA	ORANGE	NEWPORT BAY W JETTY NO 3	33-35.30	117-52.70	28237.77	40880.82	18746
CA	ORANGE	NEWPORT NO 4	33-35.20	117-57.20	28227.36	40902.38	18740
CA	ORANGE	NEWPORT BAY NO 1	33-35.10	117-52.60	28237.80	40879.82	18746
CA	ORANGE	GOBAL MARINE BUOYS (3)	33-30.00	117-51.00	28236.20	40859.35	18746
CA	ORANGE	SHIP ROCK LIGHT	33-27.80	118-29.40	28145.04	41033.95	18757
CA	ORANGE	ISTHMUS COVE N ENTR NO 2	33-27.70	118-30.40	28142.58	41038.25	18757

PASSES

STATE/COUNTRY	COUNTY/PROV	NAME	LAT	LON	TD#1	TD#2	CHART NO
CA	ORANGE	DANA POINT HARBOR NO 8	33-27.40	117-41.60	28254.52	40808.29	18746
CA	ORANGE	DANA POINT JETTY NO 6	33-27.40	117-41.40	28254.96	40807.34	18746
CA	ORANGE	DANA POINT WHISTLE NO 2	33-27.30	117-43.20	28250.87	40815.71	18746
CA	ORANGE	DANA POINT BRKWTR NO 5	33-27.30	117-41.40	28254.85	40807.12	18746
CA	ORANGE	DANA POINT NO 4	33-27.20	117-41.20	28255.19	40805.94	18746
CA	ORANGE	STA CRUZ OCEANOGRAPHIC NO 3	33-27.00	119-49.00	27947.91	41375.40	18729
CA	ORANGE	ISTHMUS COVE N ENTR NO 1	33-26.90	118-29.60	28143.82	41032.29	18757
CA	ORANGE	HARBOR REEF E BUOY	33-26.90	118-29.40	28144.29	41031.38	18757
CA	ORANGE	ISTHMUS COVE E ENTR NO 2	33-26.80	118-29.30	28144.45	41030.64	18757
CA	ORANGE	HARBOR REEF S BUOY	33-26.80	118-29.30	28144.45	41030.64	18757
CA	ORANGE	LONG POINT LIGHT	33-24.40	118-21.90	28159.87	40990.01	18757
CA	ORANGE	STA CRUZ OCEANOGRAPHIC NO 2	33-24.00	119-39.00	27971.85	41324.70	18729
CA	ORANGE	SAN MATEO POINT LIGHT	33-23.20	117-35.70	28263.07	40771.21	18740
CA	ORANGE	BEGG ROCK WHISTLE NO 4	33-22.00	119-41.80	27964.01	41329.42	18755
CA	ORANGE	SAN ONOFRE BUOY A	33-21.70	117-33.80	28265.62	40759.20	18740
CA	ORANGE	AVALON RB	33-20.90	118-19.50	28162.47	40969.70	18757
CA	ORANGE	AVALON BAY NO 2	33-20.90	118-19.40	28162.70	40969.24	18757
CA	ORANGE	SAN ONOFRE NO 2SO	33-20.90	117-34.20	28263.92	40759.47	18740
CA	ORANGE	AVALON BAY NO 1	33-20.70	118-19.30	28162.76	40968.26	18757
CA	ORANGE	CAMP PENDLETON CAL BUOY	33-20.30	117-37.10	28257.04	40771.82	18740
CA	S LUIS OBISPO	PIEDRAS BLANCAS LIGHT	35-39.90	121-17.10	27692.85	42322.54	18700
CA	S LUIS OBISPO	SAN SIMEON NO 1	35-37.70	121-11.30	27714.79	42293.20	18700
CA	S LUIS OBISPO	MOUSE ROCK NO 3MR	35-26.30	120-54.40	27777.85	42175.92	18721
CA	S LUIS OBISPO	CONSTANTINE ROCK NO 1CR	35-26.20	120-56.60	27769.98	42182.40	18721
CA	S LUIS OBISPO	ESTERO SUB TERMINAL BUOY	35-24.90	120-53.40	27781.47	42164.72	18721
CA	S LUIS OBISPO	TORO CREEK SUB TERMINAL BUOY	35-24.40	120-53.10	27782.56	42160.90	18721
CA	S LUIS OBISPO	ESTERO BAY WHISTLE "EB"	35-24.10	120-55.90	27772.60	42168.25	18703
CA	S LUIS OBISPO	MORRO BEACH SUB TERMINAL BUOY	35-24.00	120-52.60	27784.35	42157.00	18703
CA	S LUIS OBISPO	MORRO CREEK OUTFALL "B"	35-23.20	120-52.40	27785.07	42151.82	18703
CA	S LUIS OBISPO	MORRO CREEK SUB TERMINAL BUOY	35-23.00	120-52.90	27783.29	42152.32	18703
CA	S LUIS OBISPO	ESTERO BAY NO 10E	35-23.00	120-52.20	27785.78	42150.03	18703
CA	S LUIS OBISPO	POINT SAN LUIS WHISTLE NO 3	35-22.00	120-51.20	27789.33	42141.10	18703
CA	S LUIS OBISPO	MORRO BAY CHANNEL NO 12	35-22.00	120-51.20	27789.33	42141.10	18703
CA	S LUIS OBISPO	MORRO BAY W BRKWTR LIGHT	35-21.80	120-52.10	27786.14	42142.92	18703
CA	S LUIS OBISPO	MORRO BAY RB	35-21.80	120-52.10	27786.14	42142.92	18700
CA	S LUIS OBISPO	MORRO BAY ENTR NO 1	35-21.70	120-52.40	27785.08	42143.34	18703
CA	S LUIS OBISPO	MORRO BAY CHANNEL NO 14	35-21.70	120-51.20	27789.32	42139.41	18703
CA	S LUIS OBISPO	POINT BUCHON WHISTLE NO 2	35-14.40	120-54.50	27777.95	42109.62	18700
CA	S LUIS OBISPO	SAN LUIS OBISPO NO 5	35-09.70	120-45.00	27810.38	42051.91	18703
CA	S LUIS OBISPO	LANSING ROCK BUOY	35-09.70	120-44.80	27811.06	42051.22	18703
CA	S LUIS OBISPO	SAN LUIS OBISPO LIGHT	35-09.60	120-45.60	27808.33	42053.43	18700
CA	S LUIS OBISPO	SAN LUIS OBISPO NO 2	35-09.40	120-43.80	27814.44	42046.14	18703
CA	S LUIS OBISPO	WESTDAHL ROCK NO 1	35-08.80	120-47.00	27803.53	42053.87	18700
CA	S LUIS OBISPO	SOUZA ROCK GONG	35-07.70	120-44.30	27812.60	42038.61	18700

P A S S E S

STATE/COUNTRY	COUNTY/PROV	NAME	LAT	LON	TD#1	TD#2	CHART NO
CA	SAN DIEGO	CAMP PENDLETON N LIGHT	33-18.60	117-28.90	28272.89	40730.25	18740
CA	SAN DIEGO	CHURCH ROCKS, CATALINA IS	33-17.80	118-19.60	28159.61	40962.13	
CA	SAN DIEGO	SAN NICOLAS N SIDE LIGHT	33-15.50	119-27.90	27995.40	41251.71	18755
CA	SAN DIEGO	CAMP PENDLETON S LIGHT	33-15.40	117-26.10	28275.49	40711.44	18740
CA	SAN DIEGO	SAN NOCOLAS IS SPOT	33-15.00	119-49.50	27942.30	41337.25	
CA	SAN DIEGO	OCEANSIDE'S CLAM BEDS	33-14.30	117-17.30	28292.72	40669.24	
CA	SAN DIEGO	SAN NICOLAS E END LIGHT	33-13.80	119-26.10	27998.96	41239.03	18755
CA	SAN DIEGO	SAN NICOLAS E END NO 3	33-13.40	119-23.80	28004.34	41228.32	18755
CA	SAN DIEGO	SAN NICOLAS S SIDE LIGHT	33-13.00	119-28.10	27993.73	41244.77	18755
CA	SAN DIEGO	DEL MAR BOAT BASIN NO 7	33-12.90	117-24.10	28277.11	40697.92	18774
CA	SAN DIEGO	DEL MAR BOAT BASIN NO 8	33-12.70	117-24.10	28276.90	40697.58	18774
CA	SAN DIEGO	OCEANSIDE NO 9	33-12.50	117-23.70	28277.53	40695.42	18774
CA	SAN DIEGO	OCEANSIDE BRKWTR NO 3	33-12.50	117-24.10	28276.59	40697.07	18774
CA	SAN DIEGO	OCEANSIDE NO 6	33-12.40	117-23.90	28277.01	40696.16	18774
CA	SAN DIEGO	OCEANSIDE S JETTY NO 4	33-12.30	117-23.90	28276.90	40695.99	18774
CA	SAN DIEGO	OCEANSIDE S JETTY NO 4	33-12.30	117-23.90	28276.90	40695.99	18740
CA	SAN DIEGO	CARLSBAD NO 2C	33-08.00	117-21.30	28277.89	40677.21	18740
CA	SAN DIEGO	OCEANSIDE SPOT	33-02.80	117-21.50	28272.24	40670.04	
CA	SAN DIEGO	WILSON COVE N END BUOY A	33-01.60	118-33.70	28114.79	40984.05	18762
CA	SAN DIEGO	WILSON COVE N END LIGHT	33-01.40	118-33.80	28114.42	40983.99	18762
CA	SAN DIEGO	ELEVEN FATHOM SPOT	33-00.50	118-37.60	28105.17	40998.07	
CA	SAN DIEGO	WILSON COVE LIGHT	33-00.20	118-33.10	28115.15	40978.10	18762
CA	SAN DIEGO	TORREY PINES REEF NO 2	32-53.35	117-15.35	28275.36	40630.27	
CA	SAN DIEGO	TORREY PINES REEF NO 1	32-53.12	117-15.50	28274.84	40630.60	
CA	SAN DIEGO	UCSD OCEANOGRAPHIC BUOY A	32-51.90	117-15.80	28273.05	40630.30	18773
CA	SAN DIEGO	POINT LOMA SPOT	32-51.70	119-24.30	27993.01	41167.90	
CA	SAN DIEGO	LA JOLLA KELP BEDS	32-50.00	117-17.50	28267.82	40635.01	
CA	SAN DIEGO	PYRAMID HEAD LIGHT	32-49.20	118-21.10	28133.86	40902.51	18762
CA	SAN DIEGO	PT LOMA BIRD ROCKS	32-48.90	117-16.57	28268.62	40629.72	
CA	SAN DIEGO	CHINA POINT LIGHT	32-48.20	118-25.50	28123.53	40918.85	18762
CA	SAN DIEGO	POINT LOMA SPOT	32-47.90	118-31.50	28110.14	40943.23	
CA	SAN DIEGO	MISSION BAY CHANNEL NO 4	32-45.60	117-14.20	28269.79	40616.70	18773
CA	SAN DIEGO	MISSION BAY NO 1	32-45.50	117-15.80	28266.92	40622.34	18773
CA	SAN DIEGO	MISSION BAY RB	32-45.50	117-15.40	28267.71	40620.70	18773
CA	SAN DIEGO	MISSION BAY S JETTY NO 2	32-45.40	117-15.50	28267.42	40620.99	18773
CA	SAN DIEGO	OCEAN BEACH PIER SIGNAL	32-45.00	117-15.50	28267.04	40620.51	18740
CA	SAN DIEGO	FORTY MILE BANK	32-44.50	118-10.00	28154.34	40846.67	
CA	SAN DIEGO	POINT LOMA SPOT	32-44.50	117-47.80	28201.10	40753.96	
CA	SAN DIEGO	GULF OF SANTA CATALINA	32-44.00	117-20.70	28255.79	40640.68	18740
CA	SAN DIEGO	POINT LOMA SPOT	32-43.60	118-27.50	28115.96	40917.50	
CA	SAN DIEGO	HARBOR ISLAND E BASIN NO 12	32-43.60	117-11.60	28273.40	40602.91	18773
CA	SAN DIEGO	HARBOR ISLAND E BASIN NO 10	32-43.60	117-11.50	28273.59	40602.51	18773
CA	SAN DIEGO	HARBOR ISLAND E BASIN NO 8	32-43.60	117-11.40	28273.79	40602.10	18773
CA	SAN DIEGO	HARBOR ISLAND E BASIN NO 6	32-43.60	117-11.30	28273.98	40601.69	18773

P A S S E S

STATE/COUNTRY	COUNTY/PROV	NAME	LAT	LON	TD#1	TD#2	CHART NO
CA	SAN DIEGO	HARBOR ISLAND E BASIN NO 3	32-43.60	117-11.30	28273.98	40601.69	18773
CA	SAN DIEGO	HARBOR ISLAND E BASIN NO 4	32-43.60	117-11.20	28274.18	40601.29	18773
CA	SAN DIEGO	HARBOR ISLAND LIGHT	32-43.50	117-12.70	28271.14	40607.29	18773
CA	SAN DIEGO	HARBOR ISLAND E BASIN NO 1	32-43.50	117-11.20	28274.08	40601.17	18773
CA	SAN DIEGO	HARBOR ISLAND E BASIN NO 2	32-43.50	117-11.10	28274.28	40600.76	18773
CA	SAN DIEGO	NORTH SAN DIEGO BAY BUOY A	32-43.50	117-10.70	28275.06	40599.14	18773
CA	SAN DIEGO	NORTH SAN DIEGO BAY BUOY C	32-43.50	117-10.50	28275.46	40598.32	18773
CA	SAN DIEGO	NORTH SAN DIEGO BAY BUOY D	32-43.50	117-10.40	28275.65	40597.91	18773
CA	SAN DIEGO	COMMERCIAL BASIN NO 7	32-43.40	117-13.50	28269.47	40610.44	18773
CA	SAN DIEGO	COMMERCIAL BASIN NO 5	32-43.40	117-13.40	28269.67	40610.03	18773
CA	SAN DIEGO	NORTH SAN DIEGO BAY BUOY B	32-43.40	117-10.50	28275.36	40598.21	18773
CA	SAN DIEGO	COMMERCIAL BASIN NO 6	32-43.30	117-13.50	28269.38	40610.32	18773
CA	SAN DIEGO	COMMERCIAL BASIN NO 4	32-43.30	117-13.40	28269.58	40609.91	18773
CA	SAN DIEGO	COMMERCIAL BASIN NO 3	32-43.30	117-13.30	28269.77	40609.51	18773
CA	SAN DIEGO	COMMERICAL BASIN "B"	32-43.30	117-13.20	28269.97	40609.10	18773
CA	SAN DIEGO	SAN DIEGO BAY NO 19	32-43.30	117-11.30	28273.70	40601.35	18773
CA	SAN DIEGO	SAN DIEGO BAY PIER B	32-43.30	117-10.20	28275.85	40596.88	18773
CA	SAN DIEGO	COMMERICAL BASIN NO 2	32-43.20	117-13.30	28269.68	40609.39	18773
CA	SAN DIEGO	COMMERCIAL BASIN NO 1	32-43.20	117-13.00	28270.27	40608.17	18773
CA	SAN DIEGO	POINT LOMA SPOT	32-43.10	118-24.30	28122.56	40903.26	
CA	SAN DIEGO	SAN DIEGO BAY NO 21	32-43.10	117-11.60	28272.92	40602.35	18773
CA	SAN DIEGO	SAN DIEGO BAY NO 19	32-42.90	117-13.10	28269.79	40608.23	18773
CA	SAN DIEGO	SAN DIEGO BAY NO 18	32-42.80	117-12.90	28270.09	40607.30	18773
CA	SAN DIEGO	NORTH ISLAND LIGHT "N"	32-42.80	117-12.50	28270.87	40605.68	18773
CA	SAN DIEGO	SAN DIEGO QUARANTINE BUOY C	32-42.70	117-14.10	28267.64	40612.07	18773
CA	SAN DIEGO	SAN DIEGO QUARANTINE BUOY B	32-42.70	117-14.10	28267.64	40612.07	18773
CA	SAN DIEGO	SAN DIEGO QUARANTINE BUOY A	32-42.70	117-14.00	28267.83	40611.67	18773
CA	SAN DIEGO	SHELTER ISLAND YACHT NO 6	32-42.60	117-14.00	28267.74	40611.56	18773
CA	SAN DIEGO	PT LOMA KELP BEDS	32-42.50	118-16.30	28139.37	40868.99	
CA	SAN DIEGO	SHELTER ISLAND YACHT NO 5	32-42.50	117-14.10	28267.45	40611.85	18773
CA	SAN DIEGO	SAN DIEGO BAY NO 22	32-42.50	117-10.70	28274.11	40598.03	18773
CA	SAN DIEGO	SEAPORT VILLAGE BUOY A	32-42.50	117-10.20	28275.09	40596.00	18773
CA	SAN DIEGO	SAN DIEGO BAY NO 16A	32-42.40	117-13.50	28268.53	40609.29	18773
CA	SAN DIEGO	SAN DIEGO BAY NO 17	32-42.30	117-13.70	28268.05	40609.99	18773
CA	SAN DIEGO	NORTH ISLAND LIGHT NO 2	32-42.20	117-13.40	28268.54	40608.66	18773
CA	SAN DIEGO	SAN DIEGO BAY NO 23	32-42.20	117-10.10	28275.00	40595.27	18773
CA	SAN DIEGO	SAIL AMERICA BUOY	32-42.10	117-29.40	28236.64	40674.03	18740
CA	SAN DIEGO	TENTH AVE PIER N LIGHT	32-42.00	117-09.60	28275.79	40593.02	18773
CA	SAN DIEGO	TENTH AVE PIER S LIGHT	32-41.80	117-09.20	28276.38	40591.20	18773
CA	SAN DIEGO	SAN DIEGO BAY NO 15	32-41.70	117-13.90	28267.09	40610.12	18773
CA	SAN DIEGO	SAN DIEGO BAY NO 14	32-41.60	117-13.80	28267.19	40609.60	18773
CA	SAN DIEGO	SAN DIEGO & CORONADO BRIDGE	32-41.40	117-09.10	28276.19	40590.36	18773
CA	SAN DIEGO	BALLAST POINT LIGHT B	32-41.20	117-13.90	28266.62	40609.55	18773
CA	SAN DIEGO	GLORIETTA BAY NO 2	32-41.20	117-09.30	28275.61	40590.95	18773

PASSES

STATE/COUNTRY	COUNTY/PROV	NAME	LAT	LON	TD#1	TD#2	CHART NO
CA	SAN DIEGO	GLORIETTA BAY NO 1	32-41.20	117-09.10	28276.00	40590.15	18773
CA	SAN DIEGO	SAN DIEGO BAY SUB ZONE A	32-41.00	117-14.00	28266.24	40609.73	18773
CA	SAN DIEGO	SAN DIEGO BAY NO 12	32-41.00	117-13.70	28266.83	40608.52	18773
CA	SAN DIEGO	GLORIETTA BAY NO 3	32-41.00	117-09.40	28275.23	40591.15	18773
CA	SAN DIEGO	SAN DIEGO BAY NO 11	32-40.90	117-13.80	28266.54	40608.81	18773
CA	SAN DIEGO	GLORIETTA BAY NO 15	32-40.90	117-10.40	28273.19	40595.07	18773
CA	SAN DIEGO	GLORIETTA BAY NO 14	32-40.90	117-10.30	28273.38	40594.66	18773
CA	SAN DIEGO	SAN DIEGO BAY RESTRICTED D	32-40.90	117-09.40	28275.13	40591.04	18773
CA	SAN DIEGO	NAVY AMPHIBIOUS BASE LIGHT	32-40.90	117-09.40	28275.13	40591.04	18773
CA	SAN DIEGO	SAN DIEGO BAY MOORING NO 48	32-40.90	117-08.50	28276.88	40587.41	18773
CA	SAN DIEGO	SAN DIEGO BAY RESTRICTED C	32-40.80	117-09.70	28274.46	40592.14	18773
CA	SAN DIEGO	GLORIETTA BAY NO 8	32-40.70	117-10.10	28273.58	40593.64	18773
CA	SAN DIEGO	SAN DIEGO BAY RESTRICTED E	32-40.70	117-09.10	28275.53	40589.62	18773
CA	SAN DIEGO	SAN DIEGO BAY RESTRUCTED B	32-40.60	117-09.90	28273.88	40592.73	18773
CA	SAN DIEGO	SAN DIEGO BAY RESTRICTED A	32-40.50	117-10.00	28273.59	40593.03	18773
CA	SAN DIEGO	SAN DIEGO BAY NO 9	32-40.40	117-13.80	28266.07	40608.25	18773
CA	SAN DIEGO	SAN DIEGO BAY NO 10	32-40.40	117-13.60	28266.47	40607.44	18773
CA	SAN DIEGO	SAN DIEGO BAY RESTRICTED F	32-40.30	117-08.60	28276.12	40587.18	18773
CA	SAN DIEGO	SAN DIEGO BAY RESTRICTED I	32-40.20	117-08.80	28275.64	40587.88	18773
CA	SAN DIEGO	ZUNIGA JETTY LIGHT Z	32-40.00	117-13.30	28266.68	40605.79	18773
CA	SAN DIEGO	SAN DIEGO BAY RESTRICTED G	32-40.00	117-09.00	28275.06	40588.48	18773
CA	SAN DIEGO	POINT LOMA LIGHT	32-39.90	117-14.50	28264.24	40610.52	18740
CA	SAN DIEGO	SOUTH SAN DIEGO BAY MOORING	32-39.80	117-07.60	28277.59	40582.66	18773
CA	SAN DIEGO	SAN DIEGO BAY RESTRICTED J	32-39.60	117-08.90	28274.88	40587.66	18773
CA	SAN DIEGO	SAN DIEGO BAY NO 34	32-39.40	117-07.60	28277.21	40582.25	18773
CA	SAN DIEGO	FORTY THREE FATHOM SPOT	32-39.30	117-58.30	28175.03	40788.87	
CA	SAN DIEGO	SAN DIEGO BAY RESTRICTED H	32-39.30	117-08.80	28274.79	40586.94	18773
CA	SAN DIEGO	SAN DIEGO BAY NO 36	32-39.30	117-07.40	28277.50	40581.35	18773
CA	SAN DIEGO	SAN DIEGO BAY NO 5	32-39.10	117-13.60	28265.26	40605.99	18765
CA	SAN DIEGO	SAN DIEGO BAY NO 6	32-39.10	117-13.40	28265.65	40605.19	18773
CA	SAN DIEGO	TWENTY FOUR FATHOM SPOT	32-39.00	119-34.10	27965.55	41172.53	
CA	SAN DIEGO	SAN DIEGO BAY NO 38	32-39.00	117-07.30	28277.41	40580.64	18773
CA	SAN DIEGO	SAN DIEGO BAY NO 40	32-38.70	117-07.40	28276.94	40580.73	18773
CA	SAN DIEGO	SAN DIEGO BAY NO 41	32-38.70	117-07.30	28277.13	40580.33	18773
CA	SAN DIEGO	CHULA VISTA CHANNEL NO 2	32-38.60	117-04.40	28282.63	40568.70	18773
CA	SAN DIEGO	CHULA VISTA CHANNEL NO 4	32-38.50	117-07.40	28276.75	40580.53	18773
CA	SAN DIEGO	CHULA VISTA CHANNEL NO 3	32-38.50	117-07.30	28276.94	40580.13	18773
CA	SAN DIEGO	CORONADO CAYS CHANNEL NO 2	32-38.30	117-08.00	28275.40	40582.72	18773
CA	SAN DIEGO	CORONADO CAYS CHANNEL NO 1	32-38.30	117-07.90	28275.59	40582.32	18773
CA	SAN DIEGO	CHULA VISTA CHANNEL NO 6	32-38.30	117-07.30	28276.75	40579.93	18773
CA	SAN DIEGO	CHULA VISTA CHANNEL NO 5	32-38.30	117-07.20	28276.95	40579.54	18773
CA	SAN DIEGO	CHULA VISTA CHANNEL NO 7	32-38.20	117-07.10	28277.04	40579.03	18773
CA	SAN DIEGO	CHULA VISTA CHANNEL NO 9	32-38.20	117-07.00	28277.24	40578.63	18773
CA	SAN DIEGO	CHULA VISTA CHANNEL NO 11	32-38.20	117-06.80	28277.63	40577.84	18773

PASSES

STATE/COUNTRY	COUNTY/PROV	NAME	LAT	LON	TD#1	TD#2	CHART NO
CA	SAN DIEGO	CHULA VISTA CHANNEL NO 8	32-38.10	117-07.20	28276.76	40579.33	18773
CA	SAN DIEGO	CHULA VISTA CHANNEL NO 10	32-38.10	117-07.00	28277.14	40578.53	18773
CA	SAN DIEGO	CHULA VISTA CHANNEL NO 12	32-38.10	117-06.80	28277.53	40577.74	18773
CA	SAN DIEGO	CORONADO CAYS CHANNEL NO 8	32-38.00	117-08.00	28275.12	40582.41	18773
CA	SAN DIEGO	CORONADO CAYS CHANNEL NO 7	32-38.00	117-07.90	28275.31	40582.02	18773
CA	SAN DIEGO	CHULA VISTA CHANNEL NO 14	32-38.00	117-06.80	28277.44	40577.64	18773
CA	SAN DIEGO	CHULA VISTA CHANNEL NO 13	32-38.00	117-06.70	28277.63	40577.24	18773
CA	SAN DIEGO	CORONADO CAYS CHANNEL NO 10	32-37.90	117-07.90	28275.21	40581.91	18773
CA	SAN DIEGO	CORONADO CAYS CHANNEL NO 11	32-37.90	117-07.80	28275.41	40581.51	18773
CA	SAN DIEGO	CORONADO CAYS CHANNEL NO 13	32-37.80	117-07.70	28275.51	40581.02	18773
CA	SAN DIEGO	CHULA VISTA CHANNEL NO 16	32-37.80	117-06.70	28277.44	40577.04	18773
CA	SAN DIEGO	CHULA VISTA CHANNEL NO 15	32-37.80	117-06.60	28277.63	40576.64	18773
CA	SAN DIEGO	CORONADO CAY CHANNEL NO 16	32-37.70	117-07.70	28275.41	40580.92	18773
CA	SAN DIEGO	CORONADO CAY CHANNEL NO 15	32-37.70	117-07.70	28275.41	40580.92	18773
CA	SAN DIEGO	CORONADO CAY PIER "C"	32-37.70	117-07.70	28275.41	40580.92	18773
CA	SAN DIEGO	CHULA VISTA CHANNEL NO 17	32-37.70	117-06.50	28277.73	40576.14	18773
CA	SAN DIEGO	CHULA VISTA CHANNEL NO 18	32-37.60	117-06.60	28277.45	40576.45	18773
CA	SAN DIEGO	CHULA VISTA N BASIN LIGHT	32-37.60	117-06.20	28278.21	40574.86	18773
CA	SAN DIEGO	CHULA VISTA CHANNEL NO 21	32-37.50	117-06.50	28277.54	40575.95	18773
CA	SAN DIEGO	CHULA VISTA CHANNEL NO 20	32-37.50	117-06.40	28277.73	40575.55	18773
CA	SAN DIEGO	CHULA VISTA CHANNEL NO 19	32-37.50	117-06.40	28277.73	40575.55	18773
CA	SAN DIEGO	SAN DIEGO BAY WHISTLE "SD"	32-37.30	117-14.70	28261.45	40608.42	18765
CA	SAN DIEGO	CHULA VISTA CHANNEL NO 22	32-37.30	117-06.30	28277.74	40574.96	18773
CA	SAN DIEGO	POINT LOMA SPOT	32-33.50	119-29.70	27973.34	41141.80	
CA	SAN MATEO	PIER D SOUTH BUOY	37-48.00	122-22.40	16089.20	43190.57	18649
CA	SAN MATEO	OAKLAND INNER HARBOR NO 5	37-48.00	122-19.80	16097.41	43189.21	18649
CA	SAN MATEO	OAKLAND INNER HARBOR NO 6	37-47.90	122-19.90	16097.35	43188.71	18649
CA	SAN MATEO	PIER B NORTH BUOY	37-47.80	122-22.80	16088.47	43189.68	18649
CA	SAN MATEO	NOONDAY ROCK WHISTLE NR	37-47.70	123-10.70	27091.38	43210.13	18680
CA	SAN MATEO	PIER 14 DAYBEACON	37-47.70	122-23.30	16087.16	43189.39	18649
CA	SAN MATEO	MILE ROCKS LIGHT	37-47.60	122-30.60	27210.18	43192.53	18680
CA	SAN MATEO	MILE ROCKS LIGHT	37-47.60	122-30.60	16064.42	43192.53	18649
CA	SAN MATEO	PIER 18 DAYBEACON	37-47.60	122-23.20	16087.74	43188.79	18649
CA	SAN MATEO	PIER 20 DAYBEACON	37-47.50	122-23.20	16088.00	43188.24	18649
CA	SAN MATEO	PIER 22 DAYBEACON	37-47.50	122-23.20	16088.00	43188.24	18649
CA	SAN MATEO	OAKLAND INNER HARBOR NO 8	37-47.50	122-18.10	16104.08	43185.53	18649
CA	SAN MATEO	BROOKLYN BASIN S NO 1	37-47.10	122-15.30	16113.94	43181.75	18649
CA	SAN MATEO	SF MAIN SHIP CHANNEL NO 7	37-46.90	122-35.30	16051.55	43191.09	18649
CA	SAN MATEO	RINCON POINT MARINA NO 2	37-46.90	122-23.00	16090.23	43184.85	18649
CA	SAN MATEO	RINCON POINT MARINA NO 1	37-46.90	122-23.00	16090.23	43184.85	18649
CA	SAN MATEO	RINCON POINT MARINA BRKWTR B	37-46.80	122-23.00	16090.49	43184.30	18649
CA	SAN MATEO	RINCON POINT MARINA BRKWTR A	37-46.80	122-23.00	16090.49	43184.30	18649
CA	SAN MATEO	USCG ISLAND PIER N LIGHT	37-46.80	122-15.00	16115.66	43179.90	18649
CA	SAN MATEO	RINCON POINT MARINA S ENTR NO 1	37-46.70	122-23.00	16090.76	43183.75	18649

PASSES

STATE/COUNTRY	COUNTY/PROV	NAME	LAT	LON	TD#1	TD#2	CHART NO
CA	SAN MATEO	RINCON POINT MARINA S ENTR NO 2	37-46.70	122-23.00	16090.76	43183.75	18649
CA	SAN MATEO	USCG ISLAND PIER S LIGHT	37-46.70	122-14.60	16117.17	43179.11	18649
CA	SAN MATEO	SF MAIN SHIP CHANNEL NO 5	37-46.60	122-36.30	16049.24	43189.99	18649
CA	SAN MATEO	ALAMEDA NAS ENTRANCE NO 1	37-46.60	122-20.40	16099.19	43181.80	18649
CA	SAN MATEO	SF MAIN SHIP CHANNEL NO 8	37-46.50	122-35.20	16052.96	43188.92	18649
CA	SAN MATEO	MISSION ROCK NE LIGHT	37-46.50	122-22.80	16091.92	43182.55	18649
CA	SAN MATEO	ALAMEDA NAS ENTRANCE NO 2	37-46.50	122-20.40	16099.46	43181.24	18649
CA	SAN MATEO	SF MAIN SHIP CHANNEL NO 3	37-46.40	122-37.10	16047.28	43189.32	18649
CA	SAN MATEO	MISSION ROCK SE LIGHT	37-46.30	122-22.80	16092.44	43181.45	18649
CA	SAN MATEO	SF MAIN SHIP CHANNEL NO 1	37-46.20	122-37.90	16045.32	43188.65	18649
CA	SAN MATEO	SF MAIN SHIP CHANNEL NO 6	37-46.20	122-36.10	16050.97	43187.77	18649
CA	SAN MATEO	SANTA FE FERRY SLIP FOG SIGNAL	37-46.20	122-23.00	16092.08	43181.01	18649
CA	SAN MATEO	SF BAY S CHANNEL NO 1	37-46.10	122-21.80	16096.11	43179.80	18649
CA	SAN MATEO	ALAMEDA NAS S ENTRANCE NO 3	37-46.10	122-18.60	16106.15	43178.02	18649
CA	SAN MATEO	ALAMEDA NAS S ENTRANCE NO 4	37-46.10	122-18.50	16106.47	43177.97	18649
CA	SAN MATEO	SF MAIN SHIP CHANNEL NO 4	37-46.00	122-36.90	16049.01	43187.11	18649
CA	SAN MATEO	ALAMEDA NAS S ENTRANCE NO 2	37-46.00	122-18.40	16107.04	43177.36	18649
CA	SAN MATEO	RICHMOND HARBOR CHANNEL NO 3	37-45.90	122-24.50	16088.16	43180.18	18649
CA	SAN MATEO	SF MAIN SHIP CHANNEL NO 2	37-45.80	122-37.70	16047.05	43186.45	18649
CA	SAN MATEO	BALLENA BAY LIGHT NO 1	37-45.80	122-16.90	16112.26	43175.39	18649
CA	SAN MATEO	PIER 94/96 CHANNEL NO 2	37-45.50	122-22.00	16097.05	43176.61	18649
CA	SAN MATEO	SAN FRANCISCO BUOY SF (LNB)	37-45.00	122-41.50	27176.72	43184.11	18680
CA	SAN MATEO	BALLENA BAY ANCH 9 BUOY A	37-44.80	122-19.40	16107.00	43171.26	18649
CA	SAN MATEO	PIER 94 N END LIGHT	37-44.70	122-22.30	16098.19	43172.37	18649
CA	SAN MATEO	LASH TERMINAL NO 1	37-44.70	122-22.20	16098.50	43172.31	18649
CA	SAN MATEO	PIER 94/96 CHANNEL NO 4	37-44.30	122-21.60	16101.41	43169.76	18649
CA	SAN MATEO	HUNTERS POINT LIGHT	37-43.80	122-21.40	16103.32	43166.88	18649
CA	SAN MATEO	FARALLON OCEANOGRAPHIC BUOY A	37-42.40	122-35.00	27207.53	43167.00	18645
CA	SAN MATEO	BALLENA BAY DIRECTIONAL LIGHT	37-41.80	122-11.40	16139.39	43149.39	18649
CA	SAN MATEO	SAN BRUNO CHANNEL NO 2	37-41.70	122-20.40	16111.80	43154.60	18651
CA	SAN MATEO	SAN BRUNO SHOAL NO 1	37-41.70	122-20.30	16112.08	43154.56	18651
CA	SAN MATEO	SAN FRANCISCO W BUOY "W"	37-41.50	122-47.60	27166.50	43169.00	18680
CA	SAN MATEO	SAN LEANDRO MARINA NO 12	37-41.50	122-11.70	16139.19	43147.88	18649
CA	SAN MATEO	BRISBANE MARINA NO 8	37-40.30	122-22.70	16108.17	43148.30	18651
CA	SAN MATEO	BRISBANE MARINA NO 1	37-40.30	122-22.10	16110.03	43147.92	18651
CA	SAN MATEO	OYSTER COVE MARINA NO 1	37-40.20	122-22.70	16108.42	43147.75	18651
CA	SAN MATEO	BRISBANE MARINA NO 6	37-40.20	122-22.60	16108.73	43147.68	18651
CA	SAN MATEO	SAN BRUNO CHANNEL NO 3	37-40.20	122-19.50	16118.30	43145.69	18651
CA	SAN MATEO	SAN BRUNO CHANNEL NO 4	37-40.10	122-19.60	16118.23	43145.20	18651
CA	SAN MATEO	OYSTER COVE MARINA LIGHT NO 8	37-39.90	122-22.40	16110.10	43145.89	18651
CA	SAN MATEO	OYSTER COVE MARINA LIGHT NO 1	37-39.90	122-22.10	16111.03	43145.70	18651
CA	SAN MATEO	SAN FRANCISCO S BUOY "S "	37-39.20	122-39.70	27199.14	43152.64	18680
CA	SAN MATEO	SAN BRUNO CHANNEL NO 6	37-38.60	122-18.90	16124.07	43136.34	18651
CA	SAN MATEO	SAN BRUNO CHANNEL NO 5	37-38.60	122-18.70	16124.68	43136.20	18651

PASSES

STATE/COUNTRY	COUNTY/PROV	NAME	LAT	LON	TD#1	TD#2	CHART NO
CA	SAN MATEO	SF AIRPORT DAYBEACON NO 1	37-37.90	122-22.70	16114.13	43135.00	18651
CA	SAN MATEO	COYOTE POINT YACHT HARBOR NO 1	37-35.60	122-18.70	16131.91	43119.35	18651
CA	SAN MATEO	SF BAY SOUTH CHANNEL NO 10	37-35.00	122-15.10	16144.25	43113.29	18651
CA	SAN MATEO	SF BAY SOUTH CHANNEL NO 11	37-35.00	122-14.90	16144.86	43113.14	18651
CA	SAN MATEO	SF BAY S CHANNEL TOWER LIGHT	37-34.90	122-15.00	16144.79	43112.64	18651
CA	SAN MATEO	FARALLON ISLAND WAVE BUOY	37-34.00	122-53.10	27169.99	43133.42	18645
CA	SAN MATEO	REDWOOD CREEK NO 2	37-33.20	122-11.80	16158.36	43100.43	18651
CA	SAN MATEO	REDWOOD CREEK NO 5	37-32.40	122-11.50	16161.06	43095.59	18651
CA	SAN MATEO	POINT MONTARA LIGHT	37-32.20	122-31.10	27249.70	43109.46	18680
CA	SAN MATEO	REDWOOD CREEK NO 18	37-30.80	122-12.70	16161.05	43087.38	18651
CA	SAN MATEO	SF BAY SOUTH CHANNEL NO 14	37-30.80	122-08.00	16175.07	43083.39	18651
CA	SAN MATEO	DUMBARTON HWY BRIDGE	37-30.40	122-07.00	16178.92	43080.19	18651
CA	SAN MATEO	PILLAR POINT INNER LIGHT NO 2	37-30.00	122-29.00	27263.52	43095.86	18682
CA	SAN MATEO	PILLAR POINT INNER LIGHT A	37-30.00	122-28.90	27263.91	43095.79	18682
CA	SAN MATEO	PILLAR POINT INNER LIGHT NO 1	37-30.00	122-28.70	27264.71	43095.63	18682
CA	SAN MATEO	DUMBARTON RR BRIDGE	37-29.90	122-06.50	16181.49	43076.83	18651
CA	SAN MATEO	PILLAR POINT HARB ENTR LIGHT	37-29.70	122-29.00	27264.26	43094.21	18682
CA	SAN MATEO	MAYFIELD SLOUGH NO 2	37-29.50	122-06.90	16181.16	43074.84	18651
CA	SAN MATEO	PILLAR POINT HARB ENTR NO 1	37-29.20	122-30.30	27260.37	43092.46	18682
CA	SAN MATEO	PILLAR POINT HARB ENTR NO 3	37-28.90	122-28.90	27266.63	43089.73	18682
CA	SAN MATEO	PILLAR POINT HARB ENTR NO 2	37-28.40	122-29.00	27267.46	43087.06	18682
CA	SAN MATEO	PILLAR POINT HARBOR "PP"	37-28.30	122-31.20	27259.10	43088.22	18680
CA	SAN MATEO	MAYFIELD SLOUGH NO 8	37-28.10	122-05.80	16187.39	43065.66	18651
CA	SAN MATEO	SOUTHEAST REEF NO 1S	37-27.90	122-28.10	27272.27	43083.59	18682
CA	SAN MATEO	NOAA BUOY EB 46012	37-23.70	122-39.70	27239.22	43069.97	18680
CA	SAN MATEO	PIGEON POINT LIGHT	37-10.90	122-23.60	27328.59	42984.58	18680
CA	SAN MATEO	ANO NUEVO ISLAND NO 8	37-05.80	122-20.40	27351.65	42952.19	18680
CA	SONOMA	SCRIPPS CURRENT METER A	38-38.40	123-24.70	15710.37	43438.35	18640
CA	SONOMA	SCRIPPS CURRENT METER C	38-33.60	123-30.80	15710.58	43417.59	18640
CA	SONOMA	SCRIPPS CURRENT METER D	38-29.80	123-38.60	15701.07	43400.98	18640
CA	SONOMA	FORT ROSS NO 14	38-28.70	123-12.90	15789.03	43399.27	18640
CA	SONOMA	SACRAMENTO RIVER RANGE D	38-28.60	121-35.10	16129.37	43407.18	18662
CA	SONOMA	SPUD POINT BRKWTR LIGHT	38-19.90	123-03.30	15854.47	43360.58	18643
CA	SONOMA	SPUD POINT MARINA NO 1	38-19.90	123-03.10	15855.13	43360.58	18643
CA	SONOMA	BODEGA HARBOR CHANNEL NO 36	38-19.90	123-03.10	15855.13	43360.58	18643
CA	SONOMA	BODEGA CHANNEL RANGE D	38-19.90	123-03.10	15855.13	43360.58	18643
CA	SONOMA	BODEGA CHANNEL NO 38	38-19.90	123-02.90	15855.79	43360.58	18643
CA	SONOMA	BODEGA CHANNEL NO 40	38-19.90	123-02.90	15855.79	43360.58	18643
CA	SONOMA	BODEGA CHANNEL NO 34	38-19.80	123-03.10	15855.50	43360.12	18643
CA	SONOMA	BODEGA CHANNEL NO 33	38-19.80	123-03.10	15855.50	43360.12	18643
CA	SONOMA	BODEGA CHANNEL NO 42	38-19.80	123-02.80	15856.49	43360.13	18643
CA	SONOMA	BODEGA CHANNEL NO 31	38-19.60	123-03.10	15856.24	43359.21	18643
CA	SONOMA	BODEGA CHANNEL NO 46	38-19.60	123-02.60	15857.89	43359.21	18643
CA	SONOMA	BODEGA CHANNEL NO 48	38-19.60	123-02.50	15858.22	43359.21	18643

PASSES

STATE/COUNTRY	COUNTY/PROV	NAME	LAT	LON	TD#1	TD#2	CHART NO
CA	SONOMA	BODEGA CHANNEL NO 29	38-19.50	123-03.10	15856.61	43358.75	18643
CA	SONOMA	BODEGA CHANNEL NO 50	38-19.50	123-02.50	15858.59	43358.75	18643
CA	SONOMA	BODEGA CHANNEL NO 26	38-19.40	123-03.10	15856.98	43358.29	18643
CA	SONOMA	BODEGA CHANNEL DAYBEACON	38-19.40	123-02.40	15859.29	43358.29	18643
CA	SONOMA	BODEGA CHANNEL NO 52	38-19.40	123-02.40	15859.29	43358.29	18643
CA	SONOMA	BODEGA CHANNEL NO 23	38-19.30	123-03.10	15857.35	43357.83	18643
CA	SONOMA	BODEGA CHANNEL NO 13	38-18.80	123-03.20	15858.85	43355.54	18646
CA	SONOMA	BODEGA CHANNEL NO 15	38-18.80	123-03.10	15859.19	43355.54	18646
CA	SONOMA	BODEGA HEAD RADIOBEACON	38-18.70	123-03.90	15856.92	43355.08	18640
CA	SONOMA	BODEGA CHANNEL NO 7	38-18.50	123-03.30	15859.63	43354.16	18646
CA	SONOMA	BODEGA HARBOR RANGE B NO 5	38-18.40	123-03.40	15859.66	43353.70	18643
CA	SONOMA	BODEGA HARBOR NO 4	38-18.40	123-03.30	15859.99	43353.70	18643
CA	SONOMA	BODEGA HARBOR RANGE NO 3	38-18.30	123-03.40	15860.03	43353.24	18643
CA	SONOMA	BODEGA HARBOR ENTRANCE LIGHT	38-18.30	123-02.90	15861.67	43353.23	18643
CA	STA BARBARA	NOAA BUOY 46011 (ODAS)	34-52.70	120-52.40	27785.58	41987.46	18700
CA	STA BARBARA	POINT ARGUELLO LIGHT	34-34.60	120-38.80	27827.22	41849.52	18720
CA	STA BARBARA	KINNETIC LABS BUOY	34-30.20	120-42.80	27814.78	41842.98	18721
CA	STA BARBARA	POINT ARGUELLO WAVE BUOY	34-29.70	120-43.60	27812.36	41843.49	18720
CA	STA BARBARA	PLATFORM HARVEST MOORING	34-28.30	120-40.50	27821.52	41825.72	18721
CA	STA BARBARA	GAVIOTA PIPELINE BUOY A	34-28.10	120-12.30	27905.93	41718.09	18721
CA	STA BARBARA	GAVIOTA TANKER A MOORING	34-27.80	120-12.30	27905.83	41716.68	18721
CA	STA BARBARA	GAVIOTA TANKER G MOORING	34-27.70	120-12.60	27904.89	41717.39	18721
CA	STA BARBARA	GAVIOTA TANKER B MOORING	34-27.70	120-12.20	27906.09	41715.82	18721
CA	STA BARBARA	GAVIOTA TANKER C MOORING	34-27.70	120-12.00	27906.69	41715.03	18721
CA	STA BARBARA	GAVIOTA TANKER D MOORING	34-27.60	120-12.00	27906.66	41714.55	18721
CA	STA BARBARA	GAVIOTA TANKER F MOORING	34-27.50	120-12.30	27905.73	41715.27	18721
CA	STA BARBARA	GAVIOTA TANKER E MOORING	34-27.50	120-12.10	27906.33	41714.48	18721
CA	STA BARBARA	POINT CONCEPTION LIGHT	34-26.90	120-28.20	27858.02	41773.73	18720
CA	STA BARBARA	GAVIOTA WELLHEAD BUOY B	34-26.60	120-16.30	27893.48	41726.73	18721
CA	STA BARBARA	STA BARBARA BRKWTR EXT LIGHT	34-24.50	119-41.20	27996.71	41573.01	18725
CA	STA BARBARA	STA BARBARA RB	34-24.50	119-41.10	27997.00	41572.57	18725
CA	STA BARBARA	STA BARBARA NO 4	34-24.50	119-41.00	27997.29	41572.15	18725
CA	STA BARBARA	STA BARBARA NO 12	34-24.40	119-41.40	27996.06	41573.41	18725
CA	STA BARBARA	SALM BUOY	34-24.30	120-06.00	27923.34	41675.25	18721
CA	STA BARBARA	STA BARBARA BRKWTR LIGHT	34-24.30	119-41.20	27996.59	41572.09	18725
CA	STA BARBARA	STA BARBARA LIGHT	34-23.80	119-43.30	27990.13	41578.80	18720
CA	STA BARBARA	RINCON ISLAND LIGHT	34-20.80	119-26.70	28036.46	41492.61	18725
CA	STA BARBARA	STA BARBARA ISLAND LIGHT	33-29.30	119-01.80	28067.47	41184.30	18756
CA	STA CATALINA	STA CATALINA W END LIGHT	33-28.70	118-36.30	28129.28	41068.15	18757
CA	STA CRUZ	STA CRUZ W BRKWTR LIGHT	36-57.60	122-00.10	27451.54	42878.13	18680
CA	STA CRUZ	STA CRUZ MUNI WHARF	36-57.50	122-00.90	27448.18	42878.68	18685
CA	STA CRUZ	STA CRUZ LIGHT	36-57.10	122-01.60	27445.73	42877.31	18680
CA	STA CRUZ	STA CRUZ WHISTLE "SC"	36-56.30	122-00.50	27451.76	42870.96	18685
CA	STA CRUZ	POINT SANTA CRUZ WAVE BUOY	36-53.40	122-04.30	27439.88	42859.35	18680

PASSES

STATE/COUNTRY	COUNTY/PROV	NAME	LAT	LON	TD#1	TD#2	CHART NO
CA	VENTURA	VENTURA GETTY NO 2VG	34-15.80	119-18.00	28057.60	41431.40	18725
CA	VENTURA	NOAA BUOY 46023	34-15.00	120-40.00	27821.94	41763.09	18720
CA	VENTURA	VENTURA UNION NO 2VU	34-14.90	119-17.10	28059.46	41423.42	18725
CA	VENTURA	VENTURA MARINA S JETTY NO 6	34-14.80	119-16.20	28061.91	41418.89	18725
CA	VENTURA	MANDALAY BEACH NO 2MB	34-12.00	119-16.40	28059.25	41407.86	18725
CA	VENTURA	CHANNEL ISLANDS N JETTY NO 5	34-09.60	119-13.40	28065.77	41384.14	18725
CA	VENTURA	CHANNEL ISLANDS S JETTY NO 4	34-09.50	119-13.40	28065.69	41383.72	18725
CA	VENTURA	PORT HUENEME CHANNEL NO 6	34-09.50	119-13.40	28065.69	41383.72	18725
CA	VENTURA	CHANNEL ISLANDS N JETTY NO 3	34-09.40	119-13.70	28064.79	41384.67	18725
CA	VENTURA	CHANNEL ISLANDS S JETTY NO 2	34-09.40	119-13.60	28065.07	41384.21	18725
CA	VENTURA	CHANNEL ISLANDS S BRKWTR NO 1	34-09.30	119-13.70	28064.71	41384.26	18725
CA	VENTURA	PORT HUENEME CHANNEL NO 5	34-08.70	119-12.70	28067.02	41377.21	18744
CA	VENTURA	PORT HUENEME LIGHT	34-08.70	119-12.50	28067.57	41376.30	18744
CA	VENTURA	PORT HUENEME E JETTY NO 3	34-08.60	119-12.80	28066.67	41377.25	18744
CA	VENTURA	PORT HUENEME E JETTY NO 4	34-08.60	119-12.70	28066.94	41376.80	18744
CA	VENTURA	PORT HUENEME WHISTLE NO 2	34-08.30	119-12.90	28066.17	41376.47	18744
CA	VENTURA	PLATFORM GAIL RACON	34-07.50	119-24.00	28034.97	41423.12	18720
CA	VENTURA	ORMOND BEACH NO 2OB	34-07.40	119-10.50	28072.06	41361.80	18744
CA	VENTURA	US NAVY OCEANOGRAPHIC BUOY	34-06.30	119-09.50	28073.95	41352.73	18744
CA	VENTURA	STA CRUZ OCEANOGRAPHIC NO 5	34-05.30	119-06.80	28080.52	41336.28	18729
CA	VENTURA	MARINA DEL REY E CABLE AREA	34-01.40	118-32.20	28168.45	41156.45	18744
CA	VENTURA	POINT BENNETT WHISTLE NO 6	34-01.30	120-27.80	27854.65	41658.63	18727
CA	VENTURA	ANACAPA ISLAND LIGHT	34-00.90	119-21.50	28037.45	41385.10	18720
CA	VENTURA	STA MONICA BRKWTR N END	34-00.60	118-30.30	28172.53	41144.19	18744
CA	VENTURA	STA MONICA FOG SIGNAL	34-00.50	118-29.80	28173.71	41141.37	18744
CA	VENTURA	STA MONICA BRKWTR S END	34-00.30	118-30.00	28173.00	41141.63	18744
CA	VENTURA	STA MONICA ENTR NO 1	34-00.20	118-30.20	28172.39	41142.25	18744
CANADA	B COLUMBIA	HOLLIDAY ISLAND LIGHT	54-37.40	130-45.50	11554.93	30626.72	18400
CANADA	B COLUMBIA	JACINTO POINT LIGHT	54-34.80	131-04.50	11499.30	30610.31	18400
CANADA	B COLUMBIA	GREEN ISLAND LIGHT	54-34.10	130-42.40	11596.46	30623.21	18400
CANADA	B COLUMBIA	WHITESAND ISLAND LIGHT	54-30.80	130-44.80	11613.43	30616.05	18400
CANADA	B COLUMBIA	TREE BLUFF BUOY D86	54-25.80	130-30.80	11718.45	30616.58	18400
CANADA	B COLUMBIA	SLIPPERY ROCK LIGHT	54-24.00	130-29.70	11738.32	30614.15	18400
CANADA	B COLUMBIA	RYAN POINT REEF LIGHT	54-21.60	130-29.90	11756.95	30609.75	18400
CANADA	B COLUMBIA	LUCY ISLAND LIGHT	54-17.70	130-36.40	11759.13	30598.29	18400
CANADA	B COLUMBIA	LANGARA POINT LIGHT	54-15.40	133-03.50	11395.90	30505.58	17008
CANADA	B COLUMBIA	IPHIGENIA POINT LIGHT	54-11.40	133-00.50	11425.04	30499.40	17008
CANADA	B COLUMBIA	FREDERICK ISLAND LIGHT	53-56.30	133-11.80	11506.40	30463.04	17008
CANADA	B COLUMBIA	HIPPA ISLAND LIGHT	53-32.70	133-00.60	11677.18	30417.58	17008
CANADA	B COLUMBIA	MARBLE ISLAND LIGHT	53-12.10	132-40.00	11857.37	30379.44	17008
CANADA	B COLUMBIA	TASU SOUND LIGHT	52-45.00	132-05.70	12130.32	30326.43	17008
CANADA	B COLUMBIA	DAVISON POINT LIGHT	52-44.50	132-06.70	12130.48	30324.54	17008
CANADA	B COLUMBIA	FLATROCK ISLAND LIGHT	52-06.50	131-10.00	12566.50	30238.92	17008
CANADA	B COLUMBIA	CAPE ST JAMES LIGHT	51-56.20	131-00.90	12662.69	30208.85	17008

PASSES

STATE/COUNTRY	COUNTY/PROV	NAME	LAT	LON	TD#1	TD#2	CHART NO
CANADA	B COLUMBIA	NOAA BUOY 46004 (ODAS)	50-56.30	135-51.90	12155.59	29957.93	530
CANADA	B COLUMBIA	NOAA BUOY 46003	50-51.10	155-54.90	11341.39	30055.35	531
CANADA	B COLUMBIA	CAPE SCOTT LIGHT	50-46.90	128-25.50	13710.67	29982.53	17005
CANADA	B COLUMBIA	OUATSINO ISLAND LIGHT	50-26.50	128-01.90	13898.11	29877.45	17005
CANADA	B COLUMBIA	LOOKOUT ISLAND LIGHT	49-59.90	127-26.80	14141.95	29718.14	17005
CANADA	B COLUMBIA	VENDOVI COVE LIGHT	49-36.90	122-36.60	11117.49	28249.00	18421
CANADA	B COLUMBIA	NOOTKA LIGHT	49-35.60	126-36.80	14422.49	29536.18	17005
CANADA	B COLUMBIA	ESTEVAN POINT LIGHT	49-23.00	126-32.50	14458.59	29444.88	17005
CANADA	B COLUMBIA	POPHAM ISLAND LIGHT	49-21.80	123-29.40	15201.64	29186.61	18400
CANADA	B COLUMBIA	CAPE ROGER CURTIS LIGHT	49-20.40	123-25.90	15212.00	29165.41	18400
CANADA	B COLUMBIA	POINT COWAN LIGHT	49-20.10	123-21.60	15225.80	29153.46	18400
CANADA	B COLUMBIA	POINT ATKINSON LIGHT	49-19.80	123-15.80	15244.16	29138.10	18400
CANADA	B COLUMBIA	POINT GREY BUOY Q62	49-17.40	123-15.90	15241.39	29113.79	18400
CANADA	B COLUMBIA	VANCOUVER APPROACH BUOY QA	49-16.60	123-19.20	15230.10	29112.84	18400
CANADA	B COLUMBIA	WESTERLY JETTY LIGHT	49-15.50	123-16.70	15236.95	29096.21	18400
CANADA	B COLUMBIA	ENTRANCE ISLAND LIGHT	49-12.60	123-48.40	15129.28	29134.32	18400
CANADA	B COLUMBIA	GALLOWS POINT LIGHT	49-10.20	123-55.00	15104.61	29124.69	18400
CANADA	B COLUMBIA	THRASHER ROCK LIGHT	49-09.00	123-38.40	15160.54	29078.87	18400
CANADA	B COLUMBIA	TUGBOAT ISLAND LIGHT	49-08.90	123-41.00	15151.76	29083.44	18400
CANADA	B COLUMBIA	JOAN POINT LIGHT	49-08.10	123-49.10	15123.65	29092.79	18400
CANADA	B COLUMBIA	GABRIOLA REEFS BUOY UM	49-07.70	123-39.30	15156.50	29068.22	18400
CANADA	B COLUMBIA	LENNARD ISLAND LIGHT	49-06.60	125-55.30	14634.34	29286.97	17005
CANADA	B COLUMBIA	SAND HEAD LIGHT	49-06.40	123-18.10	15223.61	29007.76	18400
CANADA	B COLUMBIA	SAND HEADS BUOY S1	49-06.20	123-18.50	15222.17	29006.71	18400
CANADA	B COLUMBIA	ROBERTS BANK LIGHT	49-05.20	123-18.60	15220.90	28996.98	18400
CANADA	B COLUMBIA	ROBERTS BANK BUOY TA	49-04.40	123-22.80	15207.04	28998.91	18400
CANADA	B COLUMBIA	DANGER REEF LIGHT	49-03.30	123-42.80	15141.41	29033.64	18400
CANADA	B COLUMBIA	CANOE PASS BUOY T14	49-02.30	123-15.30	15228.23	28960.24	18400
CANADA	B COLUMBIA	PORLIER PASS RANGE LIGHT	49-00.80	123-35.10	15164.69	28992.39	18400
CANADA	B COLUMBIA	PREEDY HARBOR LIGHT	48-58.10	123-41.00	15143.36	28980.24	18400
CANADA	B COLUMBIA	SOUTHEY POINT LIGHT	48-56.70	123-35.70	15159.41	28954.61	18400
CANADA	B COLUMBIA	GRAPPLER ROCK LIGHT	48-56.40	123-36.10	15157.89	28952.70	18400
CANADA	B COLUMBIA	AMPHITRITE POINT LIGHT	48-55.30	125-32.40	14733.35	29169.24	17005
CANADA	B COLUMBIA	FRANCIS ISLAND LIGHT	48-55.30	125-31.30	14737.72	29167.52	17005
CANADA	B COLUMBIA	VICTORIA SHOAL BUOY U43	48-55.20	123-30.90	15173.43	28928.83	18400
CANADA	B COLUMBIA	GOVERNOR ROCK U45	48-54.80	123-29.80	15176.55	28922.33	18400
CANADA	B COLUMBIA	CHROW ISLAND LIGHT	48-54.60	125-28.20	14750.22	29157.24	17005
CANADA	B COLUMBIA	ACTIVE PASS LIGHT	48-52.40	123-17.40	15212.44	28868.18	18400
CANADA	B COLUMBIA	PHILLIMORE POINT LIGHT	48-52.30	123-23.40	15194.18	28882.48	18400
CANADA	B COLUMBIA	GALLANO LIGHT	48-51.70	123-20.90	15201.25	28870.37	18400
CANADA	B COLUMBIA	MARY ANNE POINT LIGHT	48-51.70	123-18.70	15207.89	28864.74	18400
CANADA	B COLUMBIA	BEN MOHR ROCK BUOY UK	48-51.60	123-23.40	15193.56	28875.76	18400
CANADA	B COLUMBIA	PEILE POINT LIGHT	48-51.00	123-24.20	15190.58	28872.03	18400
CANADA	B COLUMBIA	GANGES HARBOR LIGHT	48-50.20	123-27.20	15180.69	28872.00	18400

PASSES

STATE/COUNTRY	COUNTY/PROV	NAME	LAT	LON	TD#1	TD#2	CHART NO
CANADA	B COLUMBIA	PORTLOCK POINT LIGHT	48-49.70	123-21.00	15199.14	28851.38	18400
CANADA	B COLUMBIA	CONCONI REEF LIGHT	48-49.40	123-17.40	15209.65	28839.15	18400
CANADA	B COLUMBIA	BORDELAIS ISLETS LIGHT	48-49.10	125-13.80	14807.38	29090.22	17005
CANADA	B COLUMBIA	CAPE BEALE LIGHT	48-47.20	125-12.90	14811.01	29073.70	17005
CANADA	B COLUMBIA	SEABIRD ROCKS LIGHT	48-45.00	125-09.20	14825.19	29049.66	17005
CANADA	B COLUMBIA	PACHENA POINT LIGHT	48-43.40	125-05.80	14837.99	29030.68	17005
CANADA	B COLUMBIA	CLO-OOSE WHISTLE YJ	48-38.80	124-49.80	14896.40	28962.24	17005
CANADA	B COLUMBIA	CARMANAH LIGHT	48-36.70	124-45.00	14913.22	28935.21	17005
CAROLINE ISLANDS	KUSAIE ISLAND	OKAT HARBOR DANGER MARKER	05-21.10N	162-57.50E	Suggest	GPS	81488
CAROLINE ISLANDS	KUSAIE ISLAND	OKAT HARBOR LIGHT NO 4	05-21.10N	162-57.10E	Suggest	GPS	81488
CAROLINE ISLANDS	KUSAIE ISLAND	OKAT HARBOR RANGE MARKER	05-21.00N	162-57.40E	Suggest	GPS	81488
CAROLINE ISLANDS	KUSAIE ISLAND	OKAT HARBOR LIGHT NO 3	05-21.00N	162-57.20E	Suggest	GPS	81488
CAROLINE ISLANDS	KUSAIE ISLAND	LELE HARBOR RANGE MARKER	05-19.80N	163-01.40E	Suggest	GPS	81488
CAROLINE ISLANDS	PONAPE ISLAND	JOKAJ PASSAGE LIGHT NO 2	06-59.90N	158-10.80E	Suggest	GPS	81435
CAROLINE ISLANDS	PONAPE ISLAND	JOKAJ PASSAGE NO 6	06-59.80N	158-11.50E	Suggest	GPS	81435
CAROLINE ISLANDS	PONAPE ISLAND	JOKAJ PASSAGE NO 4	06-59.80N	158-11.20E	Suggest	GPS	81435
CAROLINE ISLANDS	PONAPE ISLAND	JOKAJ PASSAGE NO 3	06-59.80N	158-10.70E	Suggest	GPS	81435
CAROLINE ISLANDS	PONAPE ISLAND	JOKAJ PASSAGE NO 5	06-59.60N	158-11.10E	Suggest	GPS	81435
CAROLINE ISLANDS	PONAPE ISLAND	JOKAJ PASSAGE NO 8	06-59.50N	158-11.70E	Suggest	GPS	81435
CAROLINE ISLANDS	PONAPE ISLAND	JOKAJ PASSAGE NO 7	06-59.50N	158-11.50E	Suggest	GPS	81435
CAROLINE ISLANDS	PONAPE ISLAND	JOKAJ PASSAGE NO 9	06-59.30N	158-11.70E	Suggest	GPS	81435
CAROLINE ISLANDS	PONAPE ISLAND	JOKAJ PASSAGE NO 10	06-59.10N	158-11.90E	Suggest	GPS	81435
CAROLINE ISLANDS	PONAPE ISLAND	JOKAJ PASSAGE NO 11	06-59.10N	158-11.80E	Suggest	GPS	81435
CAROLINE ISLANDS	PONAPE ISLAND	JOKAJ PASSAGE RANGE MARKER	06-59.10N	158-11.20E	Suggest	GPS	81435
CAROLINE ISLANDS	PONAPE ISLAND	JOKAJ PASSAGE NO 13	06-58.80N	158-11.90E	Suggest	GPS	81435
CAROLINE ISLANDS	TRUK ISLAND	NORTHEAST PASS NO 2	07-30.20N	151-57.80E	Suggest	GPS	81327
CAROLINE ISLANDS	TRUK ISLAND	NORTHEAST PASS LIGHT	07-30.10N	151-58.70E	Suggest	GPS	81327
CAROLINE ISLANDS	TRUK ISLAND	NORTHEAST PASS NO 4	07-29.90N	151-55.80E	Suggest	GPS	81327
CAROLINE ISLANDS	TRUK ISLAND	NORTHEAST PASS NO 6	07-29.60N	151-54.20E	Suggest	GPS	81327
CAROLINE ISLANDS	TRUK ISLAND	NORTHEAST PASS NO 8	07-29.60N	151-52.50E	Suggest	GPS	81327
CAROLINE ISLANDS	TRUK ISLAND	NORTHEAST PASS NO 10	07-29.20N	151-51.70E	Suggest	GPS	81327
CAROLINE ISLANDS	YAP ISLAND	YAP ISLAND LIGHT	09-31.70N	138-06.90E	Suggest	GPS	81187
CAROLINE ISLANDS	YAP ISLAND	TOMIL HARBOR NO 17	09-31.10N	138-07.60E	Suggest	GPS	81187
CAROLINE ISLANDS	YAP ISLAND	TOMIL HARBOR JUNCTION T	09-31.00N	138-07.60E	Suggest	GPS	81187
CAROLINE ISLANDS	YAP ISLAND	TOMIL HARBOR JUNCTION W	09-30.60N	138-07.70E	Suggest	GPS	81187
CAROLINE ISLANDS	YAP ISLAND	WORWOQ INLET DAYBEACON NO 2	09-30.60N	138-07.40E	Suggest	GPS	81187
CAROLINE ISLANDS	YAP ISLAND	TOMIL HARBOR NO 6	09-29.60N	138-07.80E	Suggest	GPS	81187
CAROLINE ISLANDS	YAP ISLAND	TOMIL HARBOR NO 4	09-29.50N	138-07.80E	Suggest	GPS	81187
CAROLINE ISLANDS	YAP ISLAND	TOMIL HARBOR NO 2	09-29.40N	138-07.90E	Suggest	GPS	81187
CAROLINE ISLANDS	YAP ISLAND	TOMIL HARBOR NO 1	09-29.40N	138-07.90E	Suggest	GPS	81187
HAWAII	HAWAII	KAUHOLA POINT LIGHT	20-15.00	155-46.50	11003.58	37426.67	19320
HAWAII	HAWAII	MAHUKONA LIGHT	20-11.00	155-54.30	11038.90	37446.41	19320
HAWAII	HAWAII	KUKUIHAELE LIGHT	20-07.90	155-33.50	11022.36	37449.29	19320
HAWAII	HAWAII	KAWAIHAE LIGHT	20-02.70	155-50.10	11078.18	37477.97	19320

PASSES

STATE/COUNTRY	COUNTY/PROV	NAME	LAT	LON	TD#1	TD#2	CHART NO
HAWAII	HAWAII	KAWAIHAE ENTRANCE BUOY NO 2	20-02.60	155-50.60	11081.14	37478.61	19320
HAWAII	HAWAII	KAWAIHAE SMALL BOAT NO 1	20-02.50	155-50.10	11079.64	37478.77	19320
HAWAII	HAWAII	KAWAIHAE S BRKWTR NO 6	20-02.40	155-50.20	11080.80	37479.23	19320
HAWAII	HAWAII	KAWAIHAE HARBOR CHAN NO 8	20-02.30	155-50.20	11081.53	37479.63	19320
HAWAII	HAWAII	KAWAIHAE CHANNEL RANGE	20-02.30	155-49.80	11079.79	37479.43	19320
HAWAII	HAWAII	LAUPAHOEHOE POINT LIGHT	19-59.80	155-14.60	11045.20	37472.20	19320
HAWAII	HAWAII	LAUPAHOEHOE HARBOR NO 2	19-59.70	155-14.60	11045.55	37472.59	19320
HAWAII	HAWAII	KEAHOLE POINT LIGHT	19-58.60	155-50.10	11108.07	37494.41	19320
HAWAII	HAWAII	PEPEEKEO POINT LIGHT	19-51.00	155-05.10	11074.11	37501.52	19320
HAWAII	HAWAII	PAUKAA POINT LIGHT	19-45.90	155-05.50	11095.81	37521.28	19320
HAWAII	HAWAII	HILO HARBOR BRKWTR LIGHT	19-44.80	155-04.70	11100.00	37525.06	19320
HAWAII	HAWAII	HILO HARBOR ENTRANCE NO 1	19-44.70	155-05.00	11100.71	37525.61	19320
HAWAII	HAWAII	HILO HARBOR BUOY NO 7	19-44.20	155-03.80	11101.88	37526.88	19320
HAWAII	HAWAII	HILO HARBOR BUOY NO 9	19-44.20	155-03.60	11101.70	37526.77	19320
HAWAII	HAWAII	HILO HARBOR RANGE LIGHT	19-44.10	155-03.40	11101.97	37527.05	19320
HAWAII	HAWAII	COCONUT POINT LIGHT	19-43.80	155-05.30	11105.04	37529.20	19320
HAWAII	HAWAII	WAIAKEA LIGHT	19-43.70	155-04.40	11104.66	37529.10	19320
HAWAII	HAWAII	WAILOA BASIN CHANNEL NO 2	19-43.60	155-04.60	11105.29	37529.59	19320
HAWAII	HAWAII	HONOKOHAU ENTR CHANNEL NO 3	19-40.40	156-01.80	11312.98	37573.13	19320
HAWAII	HAWAII	HONOKOHAU ENTR CHANN LIGHT	19-40.40	156-01.70	11312.27	37573.07	19320
HAWAII	HAWAII	HONOKOHAU HARBOR BUOY NO 1	19-40.30	156-02.00	11315.11	37573.64	19320
HAWAII	HAWAII	KAILUA LIGHT	19-38.50	156-00.20	11315.48	37579.77	19320
HAWAII	HAWAII	KAILUA BAY ENTRANCE LIGHT	19-38.50	155-60.00	11314.13	37579.66	19320
HAWAII	HAWAII	KEAUHOU BAY LIGHT	19-33.90	155-57.90	11333.44	37596.61	19320
HAWAII	HAWAII	CAPE KUMUKAHI LIGHT	19-31.20	154-48.80	11146.04	37567.70	19320
HAWAII	HAWAII	NAPOOPOO LIGHT	19-28.90	155-56.30	11359.41	37615.29	19320
HAWAII	HAWAII	POHOIKI BAY BRKWTR NO 2	19-27.50	154-50.60	11165.32	37582.49	19320
HAWAII	HAWAII	MILOLII POINT LIGHT	19-11.40	155-54.60	11473.88	37681.98	19320
HAWAII	HAWAII	KA LAE LIGHT	18-54.90	155-41.10	11515.87	37735.46	19320
HAWAII	HAWAII	NOAA DATA BUOY 51004	17-31.90	152-37.10	11495.03	37881.01	504
HAWAII	HONOLULU	HALEIWA HARBOR ENTR NO 2	21-36.40	158-07.00	12514.42	37104.61	19357
HAWAII	HONOLULU	HALEIWA HARBOR LIGHT	21-35.90	158-06.50	12508.83	37107.00	19357
HAWAII	HONOLULU	HALEIWA HARBOR RANGE LIGHT	21-35.90	158-06.40	12507.82	37107.00	19357
HAWAII	HONOLULU	KAENA POINT PASSING LIGHT	21-34.70	158-16.90	12614.37	37113.77	19357
HAWAII	HONOLULU	KAENA POINT LIGHT	21-34.50	158-16.00	12604.95	37114.67	19357
HAWAII	HONOLULU	KANEOHE BAY ENTR CHANNEL K	21-31.30	157-48.40	12319.96	37127.27	19357
HAWAII	HONOLULU	KANEOHE BAY CHANNEL NO 2	21-31.10	157-48.80	12323.75	37128.27	19357
HAWAII	HONOLULU	KANEOHE BAY CHANNEL NO 3	21-30.80	157-49.10	12326.39	37129.74	19357
HAWAII	HONOLULU	KANEOHE ENTR RANGE LIGHT	21-29.90	157-50.10	12335.41	37134.16	19357
HAWAII	HONOLULU	SAMPAN CHANNEL ENTR NO 2	21-28.30	157-46.80	12299.94	37141.34	19357
HAWAII	HONOLULU	PYRAMID ROCK LIGHT	21-27.90	157-46.00	12291.32	37143.14	19357
HAWAII	HONOLULU	KANEOHE BAY CHANNEL NO 2	21-27.30	157-47.10	12301.75	37146.14	19357
HAWAII	HONOLULU	KANEOHE BAY CHANNEL NO 4	21-27.20	157-47.10	12301.62	37146.62	19357
HAWAII	HONOLULU	WAIANAE HARBOR RANGE LIGHT	21-27.10	158-11.90	12557.20	37150.38	19357

PASSES

STATE/COUNTRY	COUNTY/PROV	NAME	LAT	LON	TD#1	TD#2	CHART NO
HAWAII	HONOLULU	HEEIA-KEA SMALL BOAT NO 2	21-27.10	157-48.70	12317.82	37147.32	19357
HAWAII	HONOLULU	SAMPAN CHANNEL BUOY 10	21-27.10	157-47.80	12308.64	37147.19	19357
HAWAII	HONOLULU	WAIANAE HARBOR BRKWTR NO 1	21-27.00	158-12.00	12558.17	37150.88	19357
HAWAII	HONOLULU	HEEIA-KEA SMALL BOAT NO 1	21-27.00	157-48.60	12316.67	37147.78	19357
HAWAII	HONOLULU	SAMPAN CHANNEL RANGE LIGHT	21-26.30	157-48.50	12314.84	37151.09	19357
HAWAII	HONOLULU	MAKANI KAI RANGE LIGHT	21-25.30	157-47.60	12304.46	37155.71	19357
HAWAII	HONOLULU	PEARL HARBOR LIGHT NO 29	21-22.60	157-57.50	12403.89	37170.08	19357
HAWAII	HONOLULU	PEARL HARBOR BUOY NO 26	21-22.60	157-56.90	12397.66	37169.98	19357
HAWAII	HONOLULU	FORACS III BUOY	21-22.40	158-08.80	12521.77	37172.75	19357
HAWAII	HONOLULU	PEARL HARBOR LIGHT NO 25	21-22.10	157-56.80	12396.18	37172.36	19357
HAWAII	HONOLULU	PEARL HARBOR ARTIC'TD NO 8	21-21.40	157-59.60	12424.78	37176.15	19357
HAWAII	HONOLULU	PEARL HARBOR W LOCH RANGE	21-21.10	157-59.00	12418.29	37177.49	19357
HAWAII	HONOLULU	MERRY POINT LIGHT	21-21.10	157-56.60	12393.25	37177.10	19357
HAWAII	HONOLULU	PEARL HARBOR LIGHT NO 13	21-20.50	157-58.30	12410.50	37180.25	19357
HAWAII	HONOLULU	PEARL HARBOR LIGHT NO 11	21-20.40	157-58.50	12412.52	37180.75	19357
HAWAII	HONOLULU	PEARL HARBOR ENTR RANGE	21-20.00	158-07.00	12501.42	37184.05	19357
HAWAII	HONOLULU	KEEHI LAGOON BARGE CHANNEL	21-20.00	157-54.10	12366.26	37181.93	19357
HAWAII	HONOLULU	PEARL HARBOR ENTR RANGE	21-19.90	158-07.00	12501.36	37184.53	19357
HAWAII	HONOLULU	PEARL HARBOR RANGE LIGHT	21-19.80	157-58.40	12411.01	37183.61	19357
HAWAII	HONOLULU	KEEHI LAGOON PIPELING B	21-19.80	157-54.10	12366.08	37182.89	19357
HAWAII	HONOLULU	KEEHI LAGOON PIPELINE C	21-19.80	157-54.10	12366.08	37182.89	19357
HAWAII	HONOLULU	KEEHI LAGOON PIPELINE A	21-19.70	157-53.90	12363.92	37183.33	19357
HAWAII	HONOLULU	PEARL HARBOR CHANNEL NO 7	21-19.60	158-07.50	12506.46	37186.05	19357
HAWAII	HONOLULU	PEARL HARBOR CHANNEL NO 6	21-19.50	158-07.40	12505.35	37186.52	19357
HAWAII	HONOLULU	PEARL HARBOR CHANNEL NO 5	21-19.40	158-07.70	12508.45	37187.05	19357
HAWAII	HONOLULU	PEARL HARBOR SE LOCH NO 2	21-19.40	158-07.70	12508.45	37187.05	19357
HAWAII	HONOLULU	MAKAI CHANNEL BUOY NO 2	21-19.40	157-40.20	12221.63	37182.36	19357
HAWAII	HONOLULU	MAKAI CHANNEL BUOY NO 1	21-19.40	157-40.20	12221.63	37182.36	19357
HAWAII	HONOLULU	PEARL HARBOR CHANNEL NO 4	21-19.30	158-07.60	12507.34	37187.52	19357
HAWAII	HONOLULU	MAKAI CHANNEL NO 7	21-19.30	157-40.30	12222.54	37182.85	19357
HAWAII	HONOLULU	MAKAI CHANNEL RANGE LIGHT	21-19.30	157-40.30	12222.54	37182.85	19357
HAWAII	HONOLULU	MAKAI CHANNEL NO 5	21-19.30	157-40.30	12222.54	37182.85	19357
HAWAII	HONOLULU	MAKAI CHANNEL NO 4	21-19.30	157-40.20	12221.51	37182.83	19357
HAWAII	HONOLULU	KAPALAMA BASIN BUOY NO 2	21-19.20	157-53.00	12354.10	37185.55	19357
HAWAII	HONOLULU	PEARL HARBOR LIGHT NO 5	21-18.90	157-58.00	12406.15	37187.84	19357
HAWAII	HONOLULU	MAKAPUU POINT LIGHT	21-18.80	157-39.10	12209.60	37184.98	19357
HAWAII	HONOLULU	KALIHI CHANNEL RANGE LIGHT	21-18.70	157-53.90	12363.08	37188.08	19357
HAWAII	HONOLULU	HONOLULU CHANNEL NO 10	21-18.70	157-52.10	12344.27	37187.77	19357
HAWAII	HONOLULU	HONOLULU CHANNEL NO 8	21-18.50	157-52.10	12344.10	37188.72	19357
HAWAII	HONOLULU	HONOLULU CHANNEL RANGE	21-18.50	157-52.10	12344.10	37188.72	19357
HAWAII	HONOLULU	HICKAM HARBOR CHANNEL NO 1	21-18.40	157-57.30	12398.43	37190.10	19357
HAWAII	HONOLULU	HICKAM HARBOR CHANNEL NO 2	21-18.20	157-57.10	12396.18	37191.02	19357
HAWAII	HONOLULU	KALIHI CHANNEL BUOY NO 5	21-18.20	157-54.00	12363.70	37190.48	19357
HAWAII	HONOLULU	HONOLULU CHANNEL BUOY NO 7	21-18.20	157-52.30	12345.93	37190.18	19357

PASSES

STATE/COUNTRY	COUNTY/PROV	NAME	LAT	LON	TD#1	TD#2	CHART NO
HAWAII	HONOLULU	BARBERS POINT ANCHORAGE	21-18.10	158-04.40	12472.91	37192.75	19357
HAWAII	HONOLULU	PEARL HARBOR ENTR NO 1	21-18.10	157-57.60	12401.35	37191.58	19357
HAWAII	HONOLULU	BARBERS POINT LIGHT	21-18.00	158-06.50	12495.02	37193.59	19357
HAWAII	HONOLULU	HONOLULU CHANNEL BUOY NO 6	21-17.90	157-52.40	12346.73	37191.62	19357
HAWAII	HONOLULU	HONOLULU HARBOR ENTR LIGHT	21-17.90	157-52.30	12345.68	37191.60	19357
HAWAII	HONOLULU	HONOLULU CHANNEL BUOY NO 4	21-17.80	157-52.40	12346.65	37192.09	19357
HAWAII	HONOLULU	KEWALO BASIN RANGE LIGHT	21-17.80	157-51.60	12338.27	37191.95	19357
HAWAII	HONOLULU	KALIHI CHANNEL ENTR NO 1	21-17.60	157-54.10	12364.27	37193.34	19357
HAWAII	HONOLULU	KEWALO BASIN BUOY NO 1	21-17.50	157-51.90	12341.17	37193.43	19357
HAWAII	HONOLULU	ALA WAI CHANNEL RANGE LIGHT	21-17.50	157-50.80	12329.66	37193.23	19357
HAWAII	HONOLULU	HONOLULU HARBOR ENTR H	21-17.00	157-53.00	12352.26	37196.00	19357
HAWAII	HONOLULU	KUAPA ENTR CHANNEL NO 2	21-16.90	157-42.90	12246.78	37194.60	19357
HAWAII	HONOLULU	ALA WAI BOAT HARBOR NO 1	21-16.80	157-51.00	12331.15	37196.58	19357
HAWAII	HONOLULU	ALA WAI BOAT HARBOR NO 2	21-16.80	157-50.90	12330.10	37196.56	19357
HAWAII	HONOLULU	KAISER BOAT CHANNEL NO 1	21-16.80	157-50.60	12326.96	37196.50	19357
HAWAII	HONOLULU	MAUNALUA BAY LIGHT NO 1	21-16.50	157-43.10	12248.44	37196.52	19357
HAWAII	HONOLULU	DIAMOND HEAD LIGHT	21-15.50	157-48.70	12305.96	37202.29	19357
HAWAII	HONOLULU	DIAMOND HEAD REEF NO 2	21-15.00	157-49.10	12309.73	37204.73	19357
HAWAII	HONOLULU	NOAA DATA BUOY 51002	17-11.40	157-49.80	13139.37	38222.46	540
HAWAII	KAUAI	NOAA DATA BUOY EB 51001	23-26.00	162-18.00	14953.56	36375.07	540
HAWAII	KAUAI	KILAUEA POINT LIGHT	22-14.10	159-24.30	13282.59	36996.73	19380
HAWAII	KAUAI	NUALOLO BEACH RANGE MARKER	22-09.70	159-42.20	13498.29	36928.57	19380
HAWAII	KAUAI	KAHALA POINT LIGHT	22-09.00	159-17.90	13252.88	36936.61	19380
HAWAII	KAUAI	MILOLII BEACH RANGE MARKER	22-08.90	159-43.60	13512.57	36932.66	19380
HAWAII	KAUAI	WAIKAEA CHANNEL DIR LIGHT	22-04.50	159-19.00	13263.00	36960.36	19380
HAWAII	KAUAI	NOHILI POINT LIGHT	22-03.90	159-47.10	13549.17	36959.32	19380
HAWAII	KAUAI	LEHUA ROCK LIGHT	22-01.30	160-06.10	13745.16	36970.23	19380
HAWAII	KAUAI	KOKOLE LIGHT	21-58.90	159-45.50	13534.09	36986.82	19380
HAWAII	KAUAI	KUKII RANGE LIGHT	21-57.60	159-21.30	13285.66	36996.70	19380
HAWAII	KAUAI	KUKII POINT LIGHT	21-57.60	159-21.00	13282.59	36996.73	19380
HAWAII	KAUAI	NAWILIWILI HARBOR LIGHT	21-57.50	159-20.30	13275.41	36997.33	19380
HAWAII	KAUAI	NAWILIWILI HARBOR BRKWTR	21-57.40	159-21.10	13283.60	36997.79	19380
HAWAII	KAUAI	NAWILIWILI ENTR BUOY NO 1	21-57.40	159-21.10	13283.60	36997.79	19380
HAWAII	KAUAI	NININI POINT BUOY NO 2	21-57.30	159-20.40	13276.43	36998.38	19380
HAWAII	KAUAI	NAWILIWILI ARTICULATED NO 9	21-57.20	159-21.60	13288.72	36998.80	19380
HAWAII	KAUAI	NAWILIWILI BOAT HARBOR NO 2	21-57.20	159-21.60	13288.72	36998.80	19380
HAWAII	KAUAI	NAWILIWILI BOAT HARBOR NO 1	21-57.20	159-21.60	13288.72	36998.80	19380
HAWAII	KAUAI	HANAPEPE BAY BRKWTR LIGHT	21-54.00	159-35.60	13433.19	37014.50	19380
HAWAII	KAUAI	HANAPEPE BAY LIGHT NO 1	21-53.90	159-35.80	13435.28	37015.01	19380
HAWAII	KAUAI	HANAPEPE BAY BUOY NO 2	21-53.90	159-35.60	13433.21	37015.03	19380
HAWAII	KAUAI	HANAPEPE LIGHT	21-53.80	159-36.40	13441.52	37015.49	19380
HAWAII	KAUAI	KALANIPUAO ROCK BUOY NO 2	21-52.80	159-31.50	13391.02	37021.30	19380
HAWAII	KAUAI	MAKAHUENA POINT LIGHT	21-52.30	159-26.80	13342.47	37024.36	19380
HAWAII	KAUAI	NOAA DATA BUOY 51003	19-11.00	160-49.20	14542.52	37889.20	540

PASSES

STATE/COUNTRY	COUNTY/PROV	NAME	LAT	LON	TD#1	TD#2	CHART NO
HAWAII	MAUI	MOLOKAI LIGHT	21-12.80	156-58.30	11789.79	37204.19	19340
HAWAII	MAUI	LAAU POINT LIGHT	21-06.20	157-18.50	11980.93	37238.86	19340
HAWAII	MAUI	KAUNAKAKAI ENTRANCE LIGHT	21-05.50	157-01.70	11808.14	37237.84	19340
HAWAII	MAUI	KAUNAKAKAI BUOY NO 2	21-04.80	157-02.10	11810.86	37241.08	19340
HAWAII	MAUI	KAAMOLA POINT LIGHT	21-03.20	156-51.10	11697.90	37245.35	19340
HAWAII	MAUI	KAMALO BAY REEF BUOY NO 2	21-02.10	156-52.70	11711.36	37250.67	19340
HAWAII	MAUI	NAKALELE POINT LIGHT	21-01.90	156-35.60	11546.04	37246.88	19340
HAWAII	MAUI	HAWEA POINT LIGHT	21-00.40	156-40.20	11585.28	37254.74	19340
HAWAII	MAUI	PAUWELA POINT LIGHT	20-56.90	156-19.50	11386.25	37263.96	19340
HAWAII	MAUI	POHAKULOA POINT LIGHT	20-55.90	156-59.50	11769.15	37280.16	19340
HAWAII	MAUI	WAIHEE REEF BUOY NO 2	20-55.90	156-28.70	11464.54	37271.04	19340
HAWAII	MAUI	KAHULUI ENTR W BRKWTR LIGHT	20-54.20	156-28.60	11458.52	37278.37	19340
HAWAII	MAUI	KAHULUI ENTR E BRKWTR LIGHT	20-54.20	156-28.50	11457.60	37278.34	19340
HAWAII	MAUI	KAHULUI HARBOR RANGE LIGHT	20-53.60	156-28.50	11455.83	37280.93	19340
HAWAII	MAUI	LAHAINA BOAT BASIN LIGHT	20-52.50	156-40.90	11573.12	37289.55	19320
HAWAII	MAUI	LAHAINA LIGHT	20-52.50	156-40.90	11573.12	37289.55	19340
HAWAII	MAUI	LAHAINA ENTRANCE BUOY L	20-52.30	156-41.20	11575.68	37290.52	19340
HAWAII	MAUI	MAALAEA BASIN RANGE LIGHT	20-47.70	156-30.80	11461.79	37307.16	19340
HAWAII	MAUI	MAALAEA BASIN CHANNEL NO 1	20-47.60	156-30.80	11461.54	37307.60	19340
HAWAII	MAUI	KAUMALAPAU ENTRANCE NO 1	20-47.30	156-59.70	11760.05	37318.38	19340
HAWAII	MAUI	KAUMALAPAU LIGHT	20-47.20	156-59.70	11759.94	37318.82	19340
HAWAII	MAUI	McGREGOR POINT LIGHT	20-46.80	156-31.60	11467.50	37311.32	19340
HAWAII	MAUI	HANA BAY RANGE DAYBEACON	20-45.60	155-59.20	11183.91	37305.47	19340
HAWAII	MAUI	KAUIKI HEAD LIGHT	20-45.60	155-58.90	11181.92	37305.37	19340
HAWAII	MAUI	MANELE SMALL BOAT HARB NO 4	20-44.80	156-53.40	11689.96	37327.31	19340
HAWAII	MAUI	MANELE SMALL BOAT HARB NO 6	20-44.80	156-53.40	11689.96	37327.31	19340
HAWAII	MAUI	MANELE SMALL BOAT HARB NO 2	20-44.80	156-53.30	11688.89	37327.28	19340
HAWAII	MAUI	MANELE SMALL BOAT HARB NO 3	20-44.70	156-53.40	11689.85	37327.75	19340
HAWAII	MAUI	MANELE SMALL BOAT HARB NO 1	20-44.70	156-53.40	11689.85	37327.75	19340
HAWAII	MAUI	MANELE BAY BRKWTR LIGHT	20-44.70	156-53.40	11689.85	37327.75	19340
HAWAII	MAUI	MANELE SMALL BOAT HARB NO 8	20-44.70	156-53.40	11689.85	37327.75	19340
HAWAII	MAUI	MANELE BAY BUOY NO 2	20-44.50	156-53.00	11685.34	37328.49	19340
HAWAII	MAUI	PALAOA POINT LIGHT	20-44.10	156-58.00	11738.65	37331.94	19340
HAWAII	MAUI	MOLOKINI ISLAND LIGHT	20-38.00	156-30.00	11432.70	37348.57	19340
HAWAII	MAUI	HANAMANIOA LIGHT	20-35.20	156-24.90	11374.49	37358.63	19340
HAWAII	MAUI	KAHOOLAWE SW POINT LIGHT	20-30.30	156-40.20	11534.35	37385.41	19340
HAWAII	MAUI	NOAA LIGHTED BUOY 51005	20-21.00	156-04.30	11132.23	37409.87	504
MARIANAS	GUAM ISLAND	RITIDIAN POINT LIGHT	13-38.90N	144-51.60E	Suggest	GPS	81048
MARIANAS	GUAM ISLAND	AGANA SMALL BOAT BASIN NO 2	13-28.90N	144-45.10E	Suggest	GPS	81048
MARIANAS	GUAM ISLAND	AGANA SMALL BOAT BASIN NO 1	13-28.90N	144-44.90E	Suggest	GPS	81048
MARIANAS	GUAM ISLAND	AGANA SMALL BOAT BASIN	13-28.60N	144-45.00E	Suggest	GPS	81048
MARIANAS	GUAM ISLAND	APRA OUTER HARBOR PIER DOG	13-27.70N	144-37.50E	Suggest	GPS	81048
MARIANAS	GUAM ISLAND	CABRAS ISLAND CHANNEL NO 4	13-27.50N	144-39.50E	Suggest	GPS	81048
MARIANAS	GUAM ISLAND	CABRAS ISLAND CHANN NO 2	13-27.50N	144-39.20E	Suggest	GPS	81048

PASSES

STATE/COUNTRY	COUNTY/PROV	NAME	LAT	LON	TD#1	TD#2	CHART NO
MARIANAS	GUAM ISLAND	GLASS BRKWTR LIGHT	13-27.40N	144-37.50E	Suggest	GPS	81048
MARIANAS	GUAM ISLAND	APRA ENTRANCE RANGE LIGHT	13-27.30N	144-39.80E	Suggest	GPS	81048
MARIANAS	GUAM ISLAND	CABRAS ISLAND CHANNEL NO 5	13-27.30N	144-39.70E	Suggest	GPS	81048
MARIANAS	GUAM ISLAND	CABRAS ISLAND CHANNEL A	13-27.30N	144-39.30E	Suggest	GPS	81048
MARIANAS	GUAM ISLAND	APRA OUTER HARBOR NO 3	13-27.20N	144-39.10E	Suggest	GPS	81048
MARIANAS	GUAM ISLAND	APRA ENTRANCE BUOY NO 1	13-27.00N	144-37.30E	Suggest	GPS	81048
MARIANAS	GUAM ISLAND	APRA HARBOR W SHOAL WS	13-26.90N	144-39.10E	Suggest	GPS	81048
MARIANAS	GUAM ISLAND	OROTE POINT LIGHT	13-26.70N	144-37.00E	Suggest	GPS	81048
MARIANAS	GUAM ISLAND	APRA INNER HARBOR RANGE	13-26.50N	144-39.90E	Suggest	GPS	81048
MARIANAS	GUAM ISLAND	APRA OUTER HARBOR LIGHT	13-26.50N	144-39.20E	Suggest	GPS	81048
MARIANAS	GUAM ISLAND	APRA INNER HARBOR RANGE	13-25.00N	144-39.90E	Suggest	GPS	81048
MARIANAS	GUAM ISLAND	MAMAON CHANNEL NO 1	13-16.10N	144-39.30E	Suggest	GPS	81048
MARIANAS	GUAM ISLAND	MERIZO CHANNEL NO 4	13-14.80N	144-41.10E	Suggest	GPS	81048
MARIANAS	GUAM ISLAND	MERIZO CHANNEL NO 3	13-14.60N	144-41.30E	Suggest	GPS	81048
MARIANAS	GUAM ISLAND	MERIZO CHANNEL NO 2	13-14.50N	144-41.30E	Suggest	GPS	81048
MARIANAS	ROTA ISLAND	ROTA WEST HARBOR RANGE	14-08.10N	145-07.90E	Suggest	GPS	81063
MARIANAS	SAIPAN	MANAGAHA ISLAND LIGHT	15-14.40N	145-42.60E	Suggest	GPS	81076
MARIANAS	SAIPAN	TANAPAG CHANNEL NO 8	15-14.00N	145-43.30E	Suggest	GPS	81076
MARIANAS	SAIPAN	TANAPAG HARBOR RANGE LIGHT	15-13.70N	145-44.30E	Suggest	GPS	81076
MARIANAS	SAIPAN	TANAPAG CHANNEL NO 10	15-13.70N	145-44.00E	Suggest	GPS	81076
MARIANAS	SAIPAN	TANAPAG CHANNEL NO 6	15-13.70N	145-42.90E	Suggest	GPS	81076
MARIANAS	SAIPAN	TANAPAG CHANNEL NO 4	15-13.70N	145-42.50E	Suggest	GPS	81076
MARIANAS	SAIPAN	TANAPAG HARBOR NO 2	15-13.70N	145-42.00E	Suggest	GPS	81076
MARIANAS	SAIPAN	TANAPAG CHANNEL NO 7	15-13.60N	145-42.90E	Suggest	GPS	81076
MARIANAS	SAIPAN	TANAPAG CHANNEL NO 5	15-13.60N	145-42.50E	Suggest	GPS	81076
MARIANAS	SAIPAN	TANAPAG CHANNEL NO 3	15-13.60N	145-42.10E	Suggest	GPS	81076
MARIANAS	SAIPAN	OKINO REEF BUOY NO 1	15-12.60N	145-41.60E	Suggest	GPS	81076
MARIANAS	SAIPAN	TANAPAG HARBOR T	15-12.10N	145-40.30E	Suggest	GPS	81076
MARIANAS	TINIAN	TINIAN HARBOR CHANNEL NO 5	14-57.90N	145-37.50E	Suggest	GPS	81071
MARIANAS	TINIAN	TINIAN HARBOR CHANNEL NO 6	14-57.80N	145-37.50E	Suggest	GPS	81071
MARIANAS	TINIAN	TINIAN HARBOR CHANNEL NO 4	14-57.60N	145-37.60E	Suggest	GPS	81071
MARIANAS	TINIAN	TINIAN HARBOR CHANNEL NO 3	14-57.50N	145-37.70E	Suggest	GPS	81071
MARIANAS	TINIAN	TINIAN HARBOR CHANNEL NO 2	14-57.50N	145-37.40E	Suggest	GPS	81071
MARIANAS	TINIAN	TINIAN HARBOR CHANNEL NO 1	14-57.30N	145-37.50E	Suggest	GPS	81071
MARSHALL ISLANDS	KWAJALEIN ATOLL	ROI-NAMUR CHANNEL NO 3	09-23.00N	167-28.10E	Suggest	GPS	81715
MARSHALL ISLANDS	KWAJALEIN ATOLL	ROI-NAMUR CHANNEL DAYBEACON	09-22.40N	167-28.30E	Suggest	GPS	81715
MARSHALL ISLANDS	KWAJALEIN ATOLL	ROI-NAMUR CHANNEL NO 2	09-20.50N	167-27.80E	Suggest	GPS	81715
MARSHALL ISLANDS	KWAJALEIN ATOLL	KWAJALEIN-ROI CHANNEL NO 9	09-18.70N	167-28.60E	Suggest	GPS	81715
MARSHALL ISLANDS	KWAJALEIN ATOLL	KWAJALEIN-ROI CHANNEL NO 7	09-14.30N	167-30.50E	Suggest	GPS	81715
MARSHALL ISLANDS	KWAJALEIN ATOLL	KWAJALEIN-ROI CHANNEL NO 5	09-06.40N	167-34.50E	Suggest	GPS	81715
MARSHALL ISLANDS	KWAJALEIN ATOLL	MECK ISLAND NO 2	09-00.00N	167-42.60E	Suggest	GPS	81715
MARSHALL ISLANDS	KWAJALEIN ATOLL	KWAJALEIN-ROI CHANNEL NO 4	08-59.60N	167-36.80E	Suggest	GPS	81715
MARSHALL ISLANDS	KWAJALEIN ATOLL	MECK ISLAND RANGE MARKER	08-59.60N	167-28.60E	Suggest	GPS	81715
MARSHALL ISLANDS	KWAJALEIN ATOLL	KWAJALEIN-ROI CHANNEL NO 2	08-53.10N	167-38.70E	Suggest	GPS	81715

PASSES

STATE/COUNTRY	COUNTY/PROV	NAME	LAT	LON	TD#1	TD#2	CHART NO
MARSHALL ISLANDS	KWAJALEIN ATOLL	KWAJALEIN BIGEJ CHANN NO 1	08-52.60N	167-45.90E	Suggest	GPS	81715
MARSHALL ISLANDS	KWAJALEIN ATOLL	KWAJALEIN LAGOON BUOY V	08-52.40N	167-43.80E	Suggest	GPS	81715
MARSHALL ISLANDS	KWAJALEIN ATOLL	KWAJALEIN BIGEJ CHANN NO 2	08-52.10N	167-45.50E	Suggest	GPS	81715
MARSHALL ISLANDS	KWAJALEIN ATOLL	KWAJALEIN GEA PASS NO 6	08-49.50N	167-36.90E	Suggest	GPS	81715
MARSHALL ISLANDS	KWAJALEIN ATOLL	KWAJALEIN GEA PASS NO 2	08-49.20N	167-35.80E	Suggest	GPS	81715
MARSHALL ISLANDS	KWAJALEIN ATOLL	KWAJALEIN GEA PASS NO 3	08-49.10N	167-36.20E	Suggest	GPS	81715
MARSHALL ISLANDS	KWAJALEIN ATOLL	KWAJALEIN LAGOON BUOY S	08-48.40N	167-42.10E	Suggest	GPS	81715
MARSHALL ISLANDS	KWAJALEIN ATOLL	KWAJALEIN LAGOON BUOY Y	08-47.70N	167-42.10E	Suggest	GPS	81715
MARSHALL ISLANDS	KWAJALEIN ATOLL	KWAJALEIN HARBOR NO 1	08-47.50N	167-39.70E	Suggest	GPS	81715
MARSHALL ISLANDS	KWAJALEIN ATOLL	KWAJALEIN LAGOON LIGHT R	08-47.00N	167-42.50E	Suggest	GPS	81715
MARSHALL ISLANDS	KWAJALEIN ATOLL	KWAJALEIN S PASS NO 2	08-47.00N	167-38.60E	Suggest	GPS	81715
MARSHALL ISLANDS	KWAJALEIN ATOLL	KWAJALEIN EBEYE REEF ER2	08-45.50N	167-43.90E	Suggest	GPS	81715
MARSHALL ISLANDS	KWAJALEIN ATOLL	KWAJALEIN HARBOR BUOY B	08-45.40N	167-42.70E	Suggest	GPS	81715
MARSHALL ISLANDS	KWAJALEIN ATOLL	KWAJALEIN HARBOR BUOY NO 3	08-45.00N	167-42.50E	Suggest	GPS	81715
MARSHALL ISLANDS	KWAJALEIN ATOLL	KWAJALEIN HARBOR BUOY NO 5	08-44.50N	167-43.00E	Suggest	GPS	81715
MARSHALL ISLANDS	KWAJALEIN ATOLL	KWAJALEIN HARBOR BUOY NO 7	08-44.30N	167-43.30E	Suggest	GPS	81715
MARSHALL ISLANDS	KWAJALEIN ATOLL	KWAJALEIN HARBOR BUOY NO 10	08-44.20N	167-43.50E	Suggest	GPS	81715
MARSHALL ISLANDS	KWAJALEIN ATOLL	KWAJALEIN HARBOR BUOY NO 9	08-44.10N	167-43.50E	Suggest	GPS	81715
MARSHALL ISLANDS	MAJURO ATOLL	MAJURO CHANNEL BUOY NO 2	07-10.20N	171-10.50E	Suggest	GPS	81782
MARSHALL ISLANDS	MAJURO ATOLL	MAJURO CHANNEL BUOY NO 1	07-10.10N	171-10.30E	Suggest	GPS	81782
MARSHALL ISLANDS	MAJURO ATOLL	MAJURO ATOLL LIGHT	07-09.70N	171-09.90E	Suggest	GPS	81782
MARSHALL ISLANDS	MAJURO ATOLL	MAJURO CHANNEL BUOY NO 6	07-08.70N	171-11.30E	Suggest	GPS	81782
MARSHALL ISLANDS	MAJURO ATOLL	MAJURO CHANNEL BUOY NO 11	07-06.40N	171-17.50E	Suggest	GPS	81782
MARSHALL ISLANDS	MAJURO ATOLL	MAJURO CHANNEL BUOY NO 9	07-06.00N	171-15.90E	Suggest	GPS	81782
OR	CLATSOP	CAPE DISAPPOINTMENT	46-15.10	124-06.20	12082.59	28030.30	18521
OR	CLATSOP	COLUMBIA RIVER BUOY "CR"	46-11.10	124-10.90	12119.34	28019.57	18520
OR	COOS	HAYNES INLET CHANNEL NO 1	43-26.20	124-13.60	13501.17	27805.58	18587
OR	COOS	NORTH SLOUGH CHANNEL NO 1	43-26.00	124-14.10	13502.71	27804.17	18587
OR	COOS	COOS BAY CHANNEL NO 29	43-25.70	124-16.60	13504.15	27798.44	18587
OR	COOS	COOS BAY BRIDGE FOG SIGNAL	43-25.60	124-14.10	13506.26	27803.45	18587
OR	COOS	COOS BAY CHANNEL NO 28	43-25.60	124-13.70	13506.46	27804.28	18587
OR	COOS	COOS BAY CHANNEL NO 24	43-25.40	124-15.20	13507.50	27800.80	18587
OR	COOS	JARVIS DIKE 6.8 LIGHT 19	43-25.00	124-16.50	13510.40	27797.38	18587
OR	COOS	COOS BAY CHANNEL NO 35	43-24.60	124-13.00	13515.70	27803.94	18587
OR	COOS	COOS BAY CHANNEL NO 36	43-24.50	124-13.10	13516.54	27803.55	18587
OR	COOS	SMITH RIVER LIGHT NO 2	43-24.40	124-05.10	13521.54	27820.33	18584
OR	COOS	NORTH BAY WHARF LIGHT B	43-24.10	124-16.90	13518.16	27794.91	18587
OR	COOS	NORTH BAY WHARF LIGHT A	43-24.00	124-16.90	13519.05	27794.72	18587
OR	COOS	COOS BAY FISH PEN LIGHT A	43-23.90	124-17.00	13519.88	27794.33	18587
OR	COOS	COOS BAY FISH PEN LIGHT D	43-23.90	124-17.00	13519.88	27794.33	18587
OR	COOS	COOS BAY CHANNEL NO 15	43-23.90	124-16.90	13519.93	27794.54	18587
OR	COOS	COOS BAY FISH PEN LIGHT B	43-23.80	124-17.10	13520.72	27793.94	18587
OR	COOS	COOS BAY FISH PEN LIGHT C	43-23.80	124-16.90	13520.82	27794.36	18587
OR	COOS	COOS BAY CHANNEL NO 37	43-23.00	124-13.00	13529.94	27801.03	18587

PASSES

STATE/COUNTRY	COUNTY/PROV	NAME	LAT	LON	TD#1	TD#2	CHART NO
OR	COOS	COOS BAY CHANNEL NO 11	43-22.70	124-17.90	13530.01	27790.27	18587
OR	COOS	COOS RIVER ENTRANCE NO 1	43-22.60	124-10.90	13534.63	27804.72	18587
OR	COOS	COOS BAY DREDGE BUOY F	43-22.50	124-21.60	13529.83	27782.29	18587
OR	COOS	COOS BAY WHISTLE "K"	43-22.20	124-23.00	13531.72	27778.87	18580
OR	COOS	COOS BAY WHISTLE "K"	43-22.20	124-23.00	13531.72	27778.87	18587
OR	COOS	COOS BAY CHANNEL NO 10A	43-22.20	124-18.40	13534.16	27788.31	18587
OR	COOS	COOS RIVER CHANNEL NO 8	43-22.10	124-10.60	13539.25	27804.45	18587
OR	COOS	COOS BAY ENTRANCE NO 1	43-21.90	124-21.70	13535.04	27780.97	18587
OR	COOS	ISTHMUS SLOUGH LIGHT NO 43	43-21.90	124-12.50	13540.00	27800.07	18587
OR	COOS	COOS RIVER CHANNEL NO 10	43-21.80	124-10.40	13542.04	27804.32	18587
OR	COOS	COOS BAY N JETTY NO 3	43-21.70	124-21.20	13537.06	27781.62	18587
OR	COOS	COOS BAY DREDGE BUOY E	43-21.60	124-22.10	13537.45	27779.59	18587
OR	COOS	COOS RIVER CHANNEL NO 12	43-21.60	124-09.60	13544.27	27805.65	18587
OR	COOS	COOS BAY N JETTY LIGHT 3A	43-21.50	124-20.60	13539.14	27782.48	18587
OR	COOS	COOS BAY CHANNEL NO 7	43-21.50	124-19.20	13539.90	27785.36	18587
OR	COOS	COOS BAY ENTRANCE NO 2	43-21.40	124-20.90	13539.86	27781.68	18587
OR	COOS	BALTIMORE ROCK NO 2BR	43-21.30	124-22.90	13539.65	27777.40	18580
OR	COOS	COOS BAY CHANNEL NO 5	43-21.30	124-20.00	13541.23	27783.34	18587
OR	COOS	COOS BAY CHANNEL NO 5A	43-21.30	124-19.50	13541.50	27784.37	18587
OR	COOS	SOUTH SLOUGH NO 2	43-21.30	124-19.10	13541.72	27785.20	18587
OR	COOS	SOUTH SLOUGH LIGHT NO 1	43-21.30	124-19.00	13541.77	27785.40	18587
OR	COOS	SOUTH SLOUGH NO 4	43-21.20	124-19.10	13542.59	27785.01	18587
OR	COOS	SOUTH SLOUGH NO 5	43-21.10	124-19.00	13543.53	27785.03	18587
OR	COOS	COOS BAY LEADING LIGHT	43-21.00	124-20.10	13543.81	27782.58	18587
OR	COOS	SOUTH SLOUGH NO 6	43-21.00	124-19.10	13544.36	27784.64	18587
OR	COOS	SOUTH SLOUGH NO 8	43-20.90	124-19.10	13545.24	27784.45	18587
OR	COOS	SMALL BOAT WARNING SIGN	43-20.70	124-19.20	13546.94	27783.88	18587
OR	COOS	CAPE ARAGO LIGHT	43-20.50	124-22.50	13546.88	27776.72	18580
OR	COOS	COQUILLE RIVER ENTR NO 2	43-08.20	124-27.90	13650.49	27741.93	18580
OR	COOS	COQUILLE RIVER NO 15	43-07.40	124-24.50	13659.89	27747.29	18588
OR	COOS	COQUILLE RIVER NO 14	43-07.30	124-24.60	13660.69	27746.89	18588
OR	CORRY	NOAA BUOY 46002	42-27.00	130-16.90	13674.63	27291.77	530
OR	CURRY	CAPE BLANCO LIGHT	42-50.20	124-33.80	13799.74	27692.54	18600
OR	CURRY	ORFORD REEF WHISTLE 2OR	42-45.10	124-39.20	13837.42	27670.56	18600
OR	CURRY	PORT ORFORD JETTY NO 3	42-44.30	124-29.80	13853.84	27687.76	18600
OR	CURRY	PORT ORFORD ENTR NO 1	42-43.30	124-30.60	13861.49	27683.89	18600
OR	CURRY	ROGUE RIVER WHISTLE "R"	42-23.60	124-28.50	14029.94	27642.44	18600
OR	CURRY	CHETCO RIVER FRONT RANGE	42-02.90	124-16.00	14220.97	27616.73	18602
OR	CURRY	CHETCO RIVER NO 11	42-02.80	124-16.10	14221.64	27616.25	18602
OR	CURRY	CHETCO RIVER RADIOBEACON	42-02.80	124-16.00	14221.80	27616.47	18602
OR	CURRY	CHETCO RIVER ENTR "RB"	42-02.80	124-16.00	14221.80	27616.47	18600
OR	CURRY	CHETCO RIVER NO 5	42-02.60	124-16.30	14222.97	27615.28	18602
OR	CURRY	CHETCO RIVER NO 2	42-02.10	124-16.50	14226.79	27613.51	18602
OR	CURRY	CHETCO RIVER WHISTLE "CR"	42-01.70	124-17.00	14229.29	27611.34	18600

PASSES

STATE/COUNTRY	COUNTY/PROV	NAME	LAT	LON	TD#1	TD#2	CHART NO
OR	CURRY	CHETCO RIVER WHISTLE "CR"	42-01.70	124-17.00	14229.29	27611.34	18602
OR	DOUGLAS	UMPQUA RIVER NO 21	43-44.90	124-07.80	13335.96	27849.66	18584
OR	DOUGLAS	UMPQUA RIVER NO 23	43-44.90	124-07.80	13335.96	27849.66	18584
OR	DOUGLAS	GARDINER PAPER MILL DOCK	43-44.50	124-07.20	13339.69	27850.24	18584
OR	DOUGLAS	UMPQUA RIVER NO 15	43-43.40	124-09.70	13348.99	27843.29	18584
OR	DOUGLAS	UMPQUA RIVER NO 28	43-43.10	124-07.10	13352.30	27848.16	18584
OR	DOUGLAS	SCHOLFIELD CREEK CHANNEL NO 2	43-42.60	124-06.30	13357.00	27849.00	18584
OR	DOUGLAS	SALMON HARBOR ENTR NO 1	43-41.20	124-10.80	13368.40	27837.39	18584
OR	DOUGLAS	WINCHESTER BAY HARBOR NO 1	43-41.10	124-11.00	13369.24	27836.81	18584
OR	DOUGLAS	SLAMON HARBOR ENTR NO 2	43-41.10	124-10.80	13369.29	27837.22	18584
OR	DOUGLAS	UMPQUA RIVER NO 8	43-41.00	124-11.10	13370.11	27836.44	18584
OR	DOUGLAS	SMALL BOAT WARNING SIGN	43-40.90	124-11.00	13371.03	27836.47	18584
OR	DOUGLAS	UMPQUA RIVER NO 6	43-40.20	124-11.90	13377.03	27833.45	18584
OR	DOUGLAS	UMPQUA RIVER ENTRANCE NO 1	43-40.10	124-13.80	13377.39	27829.39	18584
OR	DOUGLAS	UMPQUA RIVER S JETTY 2A	43-40.00	124-13.10	13378.48	27830.66	18584
OR	DOUGLAS	UMPQUA RIVER WHISTLE "U	43-39.90	124-14.30	13379.03	27828.04	18584
OR	DOUGLAS	UMPQUA RIVER WHISTLE "U"	43-39.90	124-14.30	13379.03	27828.04	18580
OR	DOUGLAS	UMPQUA RIVER ENTRANCE NO 2	43-39.90	124-13.40	13379.29	27829.87	18584
OR	DOUGLAS	UMPQUA RIVER LIGHT	43-39.80	124-11.90	13380.61	27832.78	18584
OR	DOUGLAS	UMPQUA RIVER LIGHT	43-39.80	124-11.90	13380.61	27832.78	18580
OR	LANE	HECETA HEAD LIGHT	44-08.30	124-07.60	13126.26	27886.19	18580
OR	LANE	SIUSLAW RIVER NO 8	44-01.50	124-07.80	13187.06	27875.70	18583
OR	LANE	SIUSLAW RIVER WHISTLE "S"	44-01.20	124-09.40	13189.78	27872.05	18580
OR	LANE	SIUSLAW RIVER N JETTY NO 1	44-01.10	124-09.30	13190.67	27872.10	18583
OR	LANE	SIUSLAW RIVER N JETTY NO 3	44-01.10	124-08.70	13190.66	27873.29	18583
OR	LANE	SIUSLAW RIVER NO 5	44-01.00	124-07.90	13191.53	27874.74	18583
OR	LANE	SIUSLAW RIVER NO 7	44-00.90	124-07.70	13192.42	27874.99	18583
OR	LANE	SIUSLAW CHANNEL NO 9	44-00.50	124-07.70	13196.01	27874.38	18583
OR	LANE	SIUSLAW CHANNEL NO 11	44-00.30	124-07.50	13197.80	27874.48	18583
OR	LANE	SIUSLAW CHANNEL NO 12	44-00.10	124-07.40	13199.58	27874.38	18583
OR	LANE	SIUSLAW CHANNEL NO 14	43-59.40	124-07.20	13205.86	27873.72	18583
OR	LANE	SIUSLAW RIVER DIKE NO 16	43-58.90	124-07.50	13210.34	27872.36	18583
OR	LANE	SIUSLAW LIGHT NO 18	43-58.80	124-07.50	13211.24	27872.20	18583
OR	LANE	SIUSLAW RIVER DIKE NO 18A	43-58.80	124-07.50	13211.24	27872.20	18583
OR	LANE	SIUSLAW RIVER DIKE NO 20	43-58.70	124-07.60	13212.13	27871.85	18583
OR	LANE	SIUSLAW RIVER DIKE NO 22	43-58.40	124-07.40	13214.82	27871.79	18583
OR	LANE	SIUSLAW CHANNEL NO 25	43-58.10	124-07.00	13217.52	27872.14	18583
OR	LANE	SIUSLAW CHANNEL NO 23	43-58.10	124-04.80	13217.57	27876.59	18583
OR	LANE	SIUSLAW CHANNEL NO 29	43-58.10	124-04.80	13217.57	27876.59	18583
OR	LANE	SIUSLAW CHANNEL NO 26	43-57.90	124-06.20	13219.33	27873.45	18583
OR	LANE	SIUSLAW CHANNEL NO 28	43-57.90	124-05.90	13219.34	27874.05	18583
OR	LINCOLN	CAPE LOOKOUT WHISTLE NO 2CL	45-20.30	124-01.30	12497.06	27986.95	18520
OR	LINCOLN	CAPE KIWANDA RB	45-12.90	123-58.20	12555.46	27984.61	18520
OR	LINCOLN	CAPE KIWANDA WHISTLE NO 2	45-12.80	123-59.30	12557.50	27982.56	18520

PASSES

STATE/COUNTRY	COUNTY/PROV	NAME	LAT	LON	TD#1	TD#2	CHART NO
OR	LINCOLN	SMALL BOAT WARNING SIGN	44-48.60	124-03.60	12768.77	27947.34	18561
OR	LINCOLN	DEPOE BAY WHISTLE "DB"	44-48.50	124-05.30	12770.87	27944.08	18520
OR	LINCOLN	DEPOE BAY WHISTLE "DB"	44-48.50	124-05.30	12770.87	27944.08	18561
OR	LINCOLN	DEPOE BAY ENTRANCE NO 2	44-48.50	124-04.30	12770.15	27945.92	18561
OR	LINCOLN	NOAA BUOY 46040	44-46.30	124-17.40	12798.25	27919.29	18520
OR	LINCOLN	YAQUINA HEAD LIGHT	44-40.60	124-04.70	12839.26	27935.47	18580
OR	LINCOLN	YAQUINA BAY CHANNEL NO 9	44-37.70	124-02.90	12863.66	27935.21	18561
OR	LINCOLN	SMALL BOAT WARNING SIGN	44-37.50	124-03.30	12865.64	27934.21	18561
OR	LINCOLN	YAQUINA BAY CHANNEL NO 11	44-37.50	124-02.30	12865.08	27936.10	18561
OR	LINCOLN	SOUTHBEACH MARINA NO 2	44-37.40	124-03.20	12866.47	27934.27	18561
OR	LINCOLN	YAQUINA BAY CHANNEL NO 7	44-37.10	124-03.80	12869.44	27932.76	18561
OR	LINCOLN	BOAT BASIN WEST LIGHT	44-36.90	124-01.20	12869.76	27937.43	18561
OR	LINCOLN	YAQUINA BAY LIGHT NO 14	44-36.90	124-01.20	12869.76	27937.43	18561
OR	LINCOLN	YAQUINA BAY S JETTY NO 4	44-36.50	124-04.70	12875.21	27930.30	18561
OR	LINCOLN	YAQUINA RIVER NO 17	44-36.40	124-00.50	12873.80	27938.13	18561
OR	LINCOLN	YAQUINA BAY ENTRANCE NO 1	44-36.20	124-05.90	12878.50	27927.65	18561
OR	LINCOLN	YAQUINA BAY WHISTLE "Y"	44-35.90	124-06.70	12881.56	27925.76	18561
OR	LINCOLN	YAQUINA BAY WHISTLE "Y"	44-35.90	124-06.70	12881.56	27925.76	18580
OR	LINCOLN	YAQUINA RIVER NO 19	44-35.70	124-00.70	12880.10	27936.86	18561
OR	LINCOLN	YAQUINA RIVER BEND MOORING	44-35.30	124-01.10	12883.86	27935.59	18561
OR	LINCOLN	YAQUINA RIVER NO 42	44-35.20	123-56.60	12882.36	27944.08	18561
OR	LINCOLN	YAQUINA RIVER NO 22	44-35.10	124-01.40	12885.79	27934.77	18561
OR	LINCOLN	CLEFT OF THE ROCK LIGHT	44-17.50	124-06.50	13044.04	27901.49	18580
OR	TILLAMOOK	NEHALEM RIVER WHISTLE "NR"	45-39.30	123-57.50	12337.38	28012.32	18556
OR	TILLAMOOK	NEHALEM RIVER WHISTLE "NR"	45-39.30	123-57.50	12337.38	28012.32	18520
OR	TILLAMOOK	TILLAMOOK BAY WHISTLE "T"	45-34.30	123-59.50	12380.31	28004.14	18520
OR	TILLAMOOK	TILLAMOOK BAY ENTR NO 1	45-34.30	123-58.60	12379.06	28005.66	18558
OR	TILLAMOOK	GARIBALDI CHANNEL NO 6	45-34.00	123-56.80	12378.99	28008.44	18558
OR	TILLAMOOK	GARIBALDI CHANNEL NO 10	45-33.50	123-56.00	12381.94	28009.32	18558
OR	TILLAMOOK	GARIBALDI CHANNEL NO 11	45-33.30	123-55.60	12383.02	28009.81	18558
OR	TILLAMOOK	GARIBALDI CHANNEL NO 13	45-33.30	123-55.40	12382.74	28010.15	18558
OR	TILLAMOOK	SMALL BOAT WARNING SIGN	45-33.30	123-55.00	12382.19	28010.83	18558
OR	TILLAMOOK	GARIBALDI CHANNEL NO 12	45-33.20	123-55.70	12383.97	28009.54	18558
OR	TILLAMOOK	GARIBALDI CHANNEL NO 19	45-33.20	123-54.80	12382.73	28011.08	18558
OR	TILLAMOOK	CAPE MEARES LIGHT	45-29.20	123-58.60	12420.46	28000.66	18520
OR/WA	COLUMBIA RIVER	BAYVIEW LIGHT	46-16.50	123-29.20	12001.11	28089.86	18523
OR/WA	COLUMBIA RIVER	ROCKLAND LIGHT NO 27	46-16.30	123-30.20	12004.60	28088.10	18523
OR/WA	COLUMBIA RIVER	THREE TREE POINT NO 23	46-16.10	123-31.20	12008.08	28086.35	18523
OR/WA	COLUMBIA RIVER	DESDEMONA SANDS CHANNEL LIGHT	46-16.00	124-02.20	12068.84	28037.26	18521
OR/WA	COLUMBIA RIVER	SAND ISLAND RANGE LIGHT	46-16.00	123-59.50	12063.78	28041.47	18521
OR/WA	COLUMBIA RIVER	SKAMOKAWA CREEK NO 33	46-15.90	123-27.90	12002.92	28091.52	18523
OR/WA	COLUMBIA RIVER	COLUMBIA R NORTH JETTY 9	46-15.60	124-05.10	12077.05	28032.43	18521
OR/WA	COLUMBIA RIVER	ELLIOT POINT NO 13	46-15.60	123-36.90	12023.09	28076.84	18523
OR/WA	COLUMBIA RIVER	JIM CROW POINT NO 19	46-15.60	123-33.80	12016.95	28081.81	18523

PASSES

STATE/COUNTRY	COUNTY/PROV	NAME	LAT	LON	TD#1	TD#2	CHART NO
OR/WA	COLUMBIA RIVER	JIM CROW NO 22	46-15.60	123-32.20	12013.76	28084.38	18523
OR/WA	COLUMBIA RIVER	PILLAR ROCK RANGE LIGHT	46-15.60	123-30.80	12010.96	28086.63	18523
OR/WA	COLUMBIA RIVER	PILLAR ROCK CHANNEL NO 17	46-15.50	123-35.20	12020.46	28079.49	18523
OR/WA	COLUMBIA RIVER	JIM CROW POINT NO 19A	46-15.50	123-33.50	12017.09	28082.22	18523
OR/WA	COLUMBIA RIVER	HARRINGTON PT RANGE LIGHT	46-15.40	123-40.50	12031.63	28070.95	18521
OR/WA	COLUMBIA RIVER	MILLER SANDS DIKE NO 5	46-15.40	123-40.00	12030.65	28071.74	18523
OR/WA	COLUMBIA RIVER	MILLER SANDS CHANNEL NO 12	46-15.40	123-38.20	12027.11	28074.62	18523
OR/WA	COLUMBIA RIVER	PILLAR ROCK RANGE NO 18	46-15.40	123-33.80	12018.42	28081.66	18523
OR/WA	COLUMBIA RIVER	PILLAR ROCK DIKE NO 14A	46-15.20	123-35.40	12023.06	28078.95	18523
OR/WA	COLUMBIA RIVER	PILLAR ROCK RANGE LIGHT	46-15.20	123-32.50	12017.31	28083.60	18523
OR/WA	COLUMBIA RIVER	PEACOCK SPIT NO 7	46-15.10	124-06.20	12082.59	28030.30	18521
OR/WA	COLUMBIA RIVER	CLATSOP SPIT WHISTLE NO 14	46-14.90	124-00.60	12073.62	28038.84	18521
OR/WA	COLUMBIA RIVER	MILLER SANDS CHANNEL NO 2	46-14.90	123-40.70	12035.66	28070.25	18523
OR/WA	COLUMBIA RIVER	MILLER SANDS RANGE LIGHT	46-14.90	123-40.70	12035.66	28070.25	18523
OR/WA	COLUMBIA RIVER	COLUMBIA RIVER DREDGE B	46-14.60	124-10.60	12094.15	28023.07	18521
OR/WA	COLUMBIA RIVER	HARRINGTON PT CHANNEL NO 54	46-14.60	123-41.80	12039.99	28068.26	18521
OR/WA	COLUMBIA RIVER	COLUMBIA RIVER ENTR NO 1	46-14.40	124-09.50	12093.55	28024.60	18521
OR/WA	COLUMBIA RIVER	COLUMBIA R ENTR DREDGE D	46-14.40	123-56.80	12070.07	28044.38	18521
OR/WA	COLUMBIA RIVER	COLUMBIA R CHANNEL NO 20	46-14.20	123-59.50	12076.54	28039.98	18521
OR/WA	COLUMBIA RIVER	COLUMBIA R SOUTH JETTY 2SJ	46-14.10	124-05.70	12088.71	28030.23	18521
OR/WA	COLUMBIA RIVER	SKAMOKAWA CREEK RANGE LIGHT	46-14.10	123-25.40	12011.31	28094.27	18523
OR/WA	COLUMBIA RIVER	HARRINGTON PT CHANNEL LIGHT	46-14.00	123-42.80	12046.31	28066.21	18521
OR/WA	COLUMBIA RIVER	HUNTING ISLAND LIGHT NO 39	46-13.70	123-25.30	12014.11	28094.15	18523
OR/WA	COLUMBIA RIVER	PUGET SOUND RANGE LIGHT	46-13.70	123-25.20	12013.91	28094.31	18523
OR/WA	COLUMBIA RIVER	COLUMBIA R CHANNEL NO 22	46-13.50	123-58.30	12079.30	28041.28	18521
OR/WA	COLUMBIA RIVER	COLUMBIA RIVER ENTRANCE LIGHT	46-13.50	123-57.20	12077.26	28043.01	18521
OR/WA	COLUMBIA RIVER	COLUMBIA RIVER DREDGE A	46-12.80	124-05.90	12098.28	28028.81	18521
OR/WA	COLUMBIA RIVER	COLUMBIA R CHANNEL NO 25	46-12.80	123-56.70	12081.35	28043.22	18521
OR/WA	COLUMBIA RIVER	ELOCHOMAN DAYBEACON NO 2	46-12.50	123-23.20	12018.96	28096.71	18523
OR/WA	COLUMBIA RIVER	FORT STEVENS WHARF NO 26	46-12.40	123-57.00	12084.78	28042.42	18521
OR/WA	COLUMBIA RIVER	CATHLAMET DAYBEACON NO 2	46-12.40	123-24.60	12022.51	28094.36	18523
OR/WA	COLUMBIA RIVER	ELOCHOMAN BUOY NO 1	46-12.30	123-23.30	12020.68	28096.41	18523
OR/WA	COLUMBIA RIVER	TANSY POINT ROCK BUOY	46-11.90	123-47.60	12070.81	28056.90	18521
OR/WA	COLUMBIA RIVER	TANSY POINT BRKWTR E ENTR	46-11.80	123-47.90	12072.11	28056.35	18521
OR/WA	COLUMBIA RIVER	TANSY POINT BRKWTR W ENTR	46-11.70	123-48.30	12073.59	28055.63	18521
OR/WA	COLUMBIA RIVER	TANSY POINT BRKWTR W LIGHT	46-11.70	123-48.30	12073.59	28055.63	18521
OR/WA	COLUMBIA RIVER	DESDEMONA LOWER SANDS NO 31	46-11.60	123-53.00	12083.13	28048.08	18521
OR/WA	COLUMBIA RIVER	HUNTS MILL POINT NO 44	46-11.60	123-25.90	12031.13	28091.66	18523
OR/WA	COLUMBIA RIVER	TANSY POINT RANGE LIGHT	46-11.50	123-50.10	12078.44	28052.60	18521
OR/WA	COLUMBIA RIVER	ASTORIA WEST BASIN N LIGHT	46-11.40	123-51.30	12081.41	28050.62	18521
OR/WA	COLUMBIA RIVER	ASTORIA WEST BASIN S LIGHT	46-11.40	123-51.20	12081.22	28050.77	18521
OR/WA	COLUMBIA RIVER	TANSY POINT RANGE LIGHT	46-11.30	123-55.10	12089.20	28044.51	18521
OR/WA	COLUMBIA RIVER	BUNKER HILL LIGHT NO 85	46-11.30	123-08.30	11998.12	28120.40	18524
OR/WA	COLUMBIA RIVER	STELLA RANGE LIGHT	46-11.30	123-07.40	11996.29	28121.89	18524

PASSES

STATE/COUNTRY	COUNTY/PROV	NAME	LAT	LON	TD#1	TD#2	CHART NO
OR/WA	COLUMBIA RIVER	OAK POINT LIGHT NO 81	46-11.10	123-10.80	12004.76	28116.12	18523
OR/WA	COLUMBIA RIVER	PUGET SOUNT NO 47	46-10.90	123-25.50	12035.65	28091.81	18523
OR/WA	COLUMBIA RIVER	BEAVER PIER W END LIGHT	46-10.80	123-11.10	12007.70	28115.42	18523
OR/WA	COLUMBIA RIVER	CRIMS ISLAND DIKE NO 2	46-10.70	123-07.40	12000.98	28121.49	18524
OR/WA	COLUMBIA RIVER	EUREKA DIKE LIGHT NO 80	46-10.10	123-12.90	12016.77	28111.97	18523
OR/WA	COLUMBIA RIVER	FISHER ISLAND CHANNEL NO 5	46-09.80	123-04.30	12001.75	28126.07	18524
OR/WA	COLUMBIA RIVER	WAUNA LOWER LIGHT	46-09.70	123-24.50	12042.83	28092.58	18523
OR/WA	COLUMBIA RIVER	CROWN ZELLERBACH INTAKE	46-09.20	123-23.80	12045.29	28093.36	18523
OR/WA	COLUMBIA RIVER	WATERFORD LIGHT NO 69	46-09.20	123-15.90	12029.74	28106.39	18523
OR/WA	COLUMBIA RIVER	FISHER ISLAND CHANNEL NO 10	46-09.20	123-03.40	12004.67	28127.18	18524
OR/WA	COLUMBIA RIVER	DRISCOLL RANGE LIGHT	46-09.10	123-23.60	12045.66	28093.62	18523
OR/WA	COLUMBIA RIVER	PANCAKE POINT DIKE NO 59	46-08.90	123-22.30	12044.66	28095.61	18523
OR/WA	COLUMBIA RIVER	CATHLAMET DIKE NO 67	46-08.90	123-17.80	12035.83	28103.04	18523
OR/WA	COLUMBIA RIVER	EUREKA CHANNEL NO 70	46-08.90	123-15.60	12031.48	28106.68	18523
OR/WA	COLUMBIA RIVER	WALLACE ISLAND DAYBEACON NO 1	46-08.90	123-13.80	12027.91	28109.66	18523
OR/WA	COLUMBIA RIVER	WAUNA RANGE LIGHT	46-08.60	123-22.90	12048.14	28094.41	18523
OR/WA	COLUMBIA RIVER	WESTPORT RANGE LIGHT	46-08.50	123-21.20	12045.59	28097.14	18523
OR/WA	COLUMBIA RIVER	LONGVIEW CHANNEL NO 17	46-08.20	123-00.60	12006.97	28131.23	18524
OR/WA	COLUMBIA RIVER	MOUNT COFFIN LIGHT NO 1	46-07.70	122-59.20	12008.15	28133.27	18524
OR/WA	COLUMBIA RIVER	SLAUGHTERS CHANNEL NO 23	46-07.50	122-59.40	12010.16	28132.80	18524
OR/WA	COLUMBIA RIVER	LONGVIEW RANGE LIGHT	46-07.40	122-58.60	12009.35	28134.09	18524
OR/WA	COLUMBIA RIVER	LONGVIEW LONG POND LIGHT	46-07.20	122-58.70	12011.16	28133.79	18524
OR/WA	COLUMBIA RIVER	DIBBLEE DIKE NO 22	46-07.10	122-59.10	12012.78	28133.06	18524
OR/WA	COLUMBIA RIVER	SLAUGHTERS DIKE LIGHT NO 26	46-06.60	122-58.50	12015.61	28133.75	18524
OR/WA	COLUMBIA RIVER	LONGVIEW BRIDGE FOG SIGNAL	46-06.30	122-57.80	12016.63	28134.75	18524
OR/WA	COLUMBIA RIVER	COTTONWOOD ISLAND DIKE NO 29A	46-05.50	122-54.90	12017.33	28139.16	18524
OR/WA	COLUMBIA RIVER	SHAVER TRANSP MOORING BARGE B	46-05.40	122-55.80	12019.95	28137.57	18524
OR/WA	COLUMBIA RIVER	SHAVER TRANSP MOORING BARGE A	46-05.40	122-55.80	12019.95	28137.57	18524
OR/WA	COLUMBIA RIVER	COTTONWOOD ISLAND RANGE LIGHT	46-05.00	122-53.80	12019.23	28140.71	18524
OR/WA	COLUMBIA RIVER	COTTONWOOD ISLAND RANGE LIGHT	46-04.10	122-52.90	12024.84	28141.69	18524
OR/WA	COLUMBIA RIVER	COFFIN ROCK LIGHT	46-02.10	122-52.80	12041.21	28140.62	18524
OR/WA	COLUMBIA RIVER	KALAMA RANGE LIGHT	46-00.60	122-50.90	12050.03	28142.95	18524
OR/WA	COLUMBIA RIVER	AHLE POINT LIGHT NO 49	45-59.90	122-50.60	12055.33	28143.03	18524
OR/WA	COLUMBIA RIVER	HUNTER BAR LIGHT NO 1	45-59.50	122-51.10	12059.67	28141.92	18524
OR/WA	COLUMBIA RIVER	KALAMA RANGE LIGHT	45-58.70	122-50.30	12064.88	28142.80	18524
OR/WA	COLUMBIA RIVER	BYBEE BUOY NO 60	45-58.20	122-49.30	12067.21	28144.23	18524
OR/WA	COLUMBIA RIVER	MARTIN ISLAND RANGE LIGHT	45-57.50	122-48.50	12071.65	28145.18	18524
OR/WA	COLUMBIA RIVER	MARTIN ISLAND DIKE NO 63	45-57.20	122-48.30	12073.83	28145.35	18524
OR/WA	COLUMBIA RIVER	MARTIN ISLAND RANGE LIGHT	45-56.30	122-48.10	12081.16	28145.13	18524
OR/WA	COLUMBIA RIVER	SHELL CHEMICAL DOCK LIGHTS	45-54.80	122-48.80	12095.34	28142.97	18524
OR/WA	COLUMBIA RIVER	MARTIN ISLAND CHANNEL NO 75	45-54.50	122-48.30	12096.99	28143.66	18524
OR/WA	COLUMBIA RIVER	ST HELENS JUNCTION LIGHT	45-52.90	122-47.80	12109.91	28143.54	18524
OR/WA	COLUMBIA RIVER	ST HELENS JETTY NO 79	45-52.20	122-47.00	12114.54	28144.50	18524
OR/WA	COLUMBIA RIVER	ST HELENS RANGE LIGHT	45-51.90	122-46.90	12116.97	28144.49	18524

PASSES

STATE/COUNTRY	COUNTY/PROV	NAME	LAT	LON	TD#1	TD#2	CHART NO
OR/WA	COLUMBIA RIVER	ST HELENS DIKE NO 80	45-51.80	122-47.30	12118.57	28143.72	18524
OR/WA	COLUMBIA RIVER	WARRIOR ROCK RANGE LIGHT	45-51.30	122-46.70	12121.85	28144.47	18524
OR/WA	COLUMBIA RIVER	WARRIOR ROCK LIGHT	45-50.90	122-47.20	12126.24	28143.33	18524
OR/WA	COLUMBIA RIVER	WARRIOR ROCK REEF NO 4	45-50.40	122-47.30	12130.79	28142.84	18524
OR/WA	COLUMBIA RIVER	DUCK CLUB LIGHT NO 8	45-49.00	122-47.80	12143.95	28141.06	18524
OR/WA	COLUMBIA RIVER	HENRICI RANGE LIGHT	45-48.70	122-47.80	12146.58	28140.87	18524
OR/WA	COLUMBIA RIVER	KNAPP POINT LIGHT NO 19	45-44.70	122-45.20	12177.58	28142.95	18524
OR/WA	COLUMBIA RIVER	LAKE UMATILLA NO 4	45-44.20	120-38.70	11995.17	28376.30	18535
OR/WA	COLUMBIA RIVER	HOOD RIVER RANGE LIGHT	45-43.50	121-29.60	12065.23	28281.49	18531
OR/WA	COLUMBIA RIVER	WILLOW DIKE NO 26	45-43.40	122-45.90	12190.39	28140.85	18524
OR/WA	COLUMBIA RIVER	LAKE UMATILLA LIGHT NO 1	45-43.40	120-41.30	12006.73	28371.46	18535
OR/WA	COLUMBIA RIVER	LAKE UMATILLA NO 2	45-43.40	120-41.20	12006.64	28371.65	18535
OR/WA	COLUMBIA RIVER	HOOD RIVER NO 35A	45-43.20	121-29.60	12068.38	28281.41	18531
OR/WA	COLUMBIA RIVER	HOOD RIVER NO 37	45-43.10	121-29.50	12069.28	28281.56	18531
OR/WA	COLUMBIA RIVER	HOOD RIVER BRKWTR LIGHT	45-42.90	121-30.40	12072.71	28279.83	18531
OR/WA	COLUMBIA RIVER	HOOD R MARINA W LIGHT	45-42.80	121-29.80	12072.87	28280.92	18531
OR/WA	COLUMBIA RIVER	HOOD R MARINA E LIGHT	45-42.80	121-29.80	12072.87	28280.92	18531
OR/WA	COLUMBIA RIVER	COOK POINT RANGE NO 27	45-42.50	121-39.60	12090.73	28262.51	18531
OR/WA	COLUMBIA RIVER	BONNEVILLE POOL NO 47	45-42.40	121-22.70	12066.86	28294.10	18531
OR/WA	COLUMBIA RIVER	LITTLE WHITE SALMON RANGE 30	45-42.30	121-36.70	12088.39	28267.87	18531
OR/WA	COLUMBIA RIVER	BONNEVILLE POOL NO 39	45-42.30	121-27.80	12075.21	28284.52	18531
OR/WA	COLUMBIA RIVER	BINGEN BOAT BASIN NO 3	45-42.20	121-27.20	12075.40	28285.62	18531
OR/WA	COLUMBIA RIVER	WIND MOUNTAIN RANGE NO 17	45-42.10	121-50.70	12112.05	28241.64	18531
OR/WA	COLUMBIA RIVER	MEMALOOSE ISLAND S NO 2	45-42.00	121-20.50	12068.07	28298.12	18531
OR/WA	COLUMBIA RIVER	BONNEVILLE POOL NO 41	45-41.90	121-25.30	12075.86	28289.10	18531
OR/WA	COLUMBIA RIVER	BONNEVILLE POOL NO 45A	45-41.90	121-23.20	12072.90	28293.03	18531
OR/WA	COLUMBIA RIVER	BINGEN RANGE LIGHT NO 40	45-41.70	121-26.60	12079.83	28286.61	18531
OR/WA	COLUMBIA RIVER	BONNEVILLE POOL NO 54	45-41.70	121-18.30	12068.28	28302.17	18531
OR/WA	COLUMBIA RIVER	WIND MOUNTAIN RANGE NO 26	45-41.60	121-42.10	12103.80	28257.53	18531
OR/WA	COLUMBIA RIVER	CASCADE RAPIDS RANGE NO 15	45-41.30	121-53.10	12123.86	28236.84	18531
OR/WA	COLUMBIA RIVER	BONNEVILLE POOL NO 56	45-41.10	121-17.10	12073.16	28304.29	18531
OR/WA	COLUMBIA RIVER	MORGAN RANGE LIGHT	45-41.00	122-46.60	12213.11	28138.01	18524
OR/WA	COLUMBIA RIVER	WILLOW RANGE LIGHT	45-41.00	122-46.60	12213.11	28138.01	18524
OR/WA	COLUMBIA RIVER	BONNEVILLE POOL NO 14	45-40.90	121-53.20	12128.03	28236.49	18531
OR/WA	COLUMBIA RIVER	STEVENSON RANGE LIGHT	45-40.70	121-53.90	12131.12	28235.10	18531
OR/WA	COLUMBIA RIVER	BONNEVILLE POOL NO 12	45-40.20	121-53.80	12135.98	28235.09	18531
OR/WA	COLUMBIA RIVER	CASCADE RAPIDS RANGE NO 8	45-39.60	121-53.90	12142.17	28234.65	18531
OR/WA	COLUMBIA RIVER	VANCOUVER RANGE LIGHT	45-39.50	122-45.90	12225.54	28138.29	18524
OR/WA	COLUMBIA RIVER	KELLEY POINT JUNCTION LIGHT	45-39.20	122-45.70	12227.94	28138.46	18524
OR/WA	COLUMBIA RIVER	BONNEVILLE DAM MOORING C	45-38.90	122-55.40	12246.02	28120.64	18531
OR/WA	COLUMBIA RIVER	VANCOUVER CHANNEL NO 47	45-38.90	122-44.70	12229.08	28140.09	18524
OR/WA	COLUMBIA RIVER	BONNEVILLE DAM MOORING B	45-38.80	121-55.50	12152.65	28231.31	18531
OR/WA	COLUMBIA RIVER	BONNEVILLE POOL NO 3	45-38.50	121-56.00	12156.42	28230.25	18531
OR/WA	COLUMBIA RIVER	BONNEVILLE POOL NO 4	45-38.50	121-55.80	12156.12	28230.63	18531

PASSES

STATE/COUNTRY	COUNTY/PROV	NAME	LAT	LON	TD#1	TD#2	CHART NO
OR/WA	COLUMBIA RIVER	VANCOUVER RANGE LIGHT	45-38.40	122-42.70	12230.47	28143.41	18524
OR/WA	COLUMBIA RIVER	BONNEVILLE POOL NO 2	45-38.40	121-56.00	12157.43	28230.21	18531
OR/WA	COLUMBIA RIVER	TANNER CREEK DAYBEACON NO 94	45-38.00	121-57.60	12163.86	28227.03	18531
OR/WA	COLUMBIA RIVER	WARRENDALE RANGE LIGHT	45-36.90	122-00.50	12179.23	28221.08	18531
OR/WA	COLUMBIA RIVER	MULTNOMAH FALLS RANGE LIGHT	45-36.80	122-02.00	12182.48	28218.21	18531
OR/WA	COLUMBIA RIVER	WARRENDALE RANGE LIGHT	45-36.80	122-02.00	12182.48	28218.21	18531
OR/WA	COLUMBIA RIVER	BONNEVILLE POOL NO 69	45-36.60	121-08.70	12112.11	28319.26	18531
OR/WA	COLUMBIA RIVER	NORTH PORTLAND DAYBEACON 1	45-36.40	122-40.20	12244.94	28146.71	18531
OR/WA	COLUMBIA RIVER	VANCOUVER CHANNEL NO 14	45-36.40	122-37.50	12240.77	28151.69	18531
OR/WA	COLUMBIA RIVER	SKAMANIA LIGHT NO 58	45-36.40	122-03.30	12188.41	28215.57	18531
OR/WA	COLUMBIA RIVER	NORTH PORTLAND DIKE LIGHT	45-36.20	122-38.00	12243.39	28150.64	18531
OR/WA	COLUMBIA RIVER	NORTH PORTLAND E RANGE LIGHT	45-36.10	122-38.40	12244.94	28149.84	18531
OR/WA	COLUMBIA RIVER	PORTLAND AIRPORT DIKE NO 16	45-36.10	122-35.90	12241.09	28154.46	18531
OR/WA	COLUMBIA RIVER	THE DALLES BOAT BASIN NO 2	45-36.10	121-10.40	12119.60	28315.93	18531
OR/WA	COLUMBIA RIVER	LIESER POINT CHANNEL NO 18	45-36.00	122-34.20	12239.41	28157.55	18531
OR/WA	COLUMBIA RIVER	AIRPORT BAR RANGE LIGHT	45-36.00	122-33.30	12238.02	28159.22	18531
OR/WA	COLUMBIA RIVER	GOVT ISLAND S CHANNEL NO 1	45-35.90	122-34.70	12241.11	28156.56	18531
OR/WA	COLUMBIA RIVER	GOVT ISLAND S CHANNEL NO 2	45-35.80	122-34.70	12242.05	28156.50	18531
OR/WA	COLUMBIA RIVER	INTERSTATE 205 BRIDGE NO 19	45-35.80	122-33.00	12239.44	28159.65	18531
OR/WA	COLUMBIA RIVER	INTERSTATE 205 BRIDGE NO 21	45-35.80	122-32.80	12239.13	28160.03	18531
OR/WA	COLUMBIA RIVER	GOVT ISLAND S CHANNEL NO 3	45-35.50	122-34.20	12244.09	28157.24	18531
OR/WA	COLUMBIA RIVER	GOVT ISLAND S CHANNEL NO 5	45-35.20	122-33.70	12246.13	28157.98	18531
OR/WA	COLUMBIA RIVER	GOVT ISLAND RANGE LIGHT	45-35.20	122-31.80	12243.24	28161.52	18531
OR/WA	COLUMBIA RIVER	FASHION REEF NO 75	45-35.10	122-08.40	12208.90	28205.33	18531
OR/WA	COLUMBIA RIVER	FASHION REEF RANGE LIGHT	45-35.10	122-07.60	12207.71	28206.84	18531
OR/WA	COLUMBIA RIVER	GOVT ISLAND S CHANNEL NO 7	45-34.90	122-33.10	12248.04	28158.92	18531
OR/WA	COLUMBIA RIVER	GOVT ISLAND RANGE LIGHT	45-34.90	122-29.90	12243.19	28164.87	18531
OR/WA	COLUMBIA RIVER	HASSALO ROCK NO 1	45-34.90	122-27.90	12240.16	28168.61	18531
OR/WA	COLUMBIA RIVER	PRINDLE DIKE NO 73	45-34.90	122-09.40	12212.36	28203.34	18531
OR/WA	COLUMBIA RIVER	FASHION REEF NO 74	45-34.90	122-08.60	12211.17	28204.85	18531
OR/WA	COLUMBIA RIVER	FASHION REEF NO 76	45-34.90	122-07.90	12210.13	28206.17	18531
OR/WA	COLUMBIA RIVER	MULTNOMAH FALLS NO 83	45-34.90	122-06.40	12207.91	28209.01	18531
OR/WA	COLUMBIA RIVER	MULTNOMAH FALLS DIKE NO 82	45-34.90	122-06.30	12207.76	28209.20	18531
OR/WA	COLUMBIA RIVER	HASSALO ROCK DAYBEACON NO 2	45-34.80	122-27.90	12241.10	28168.55	18531
OR/WA	COLUMBIA RIVER	MULTNOMAH FALLS BAR RANGE	45-34.80	122-06.40	12208.90	28208.96	18531
OR/WA	COLUMBIA RIVER	CAPE HORN DIKE NO 71	45-34.70	122-10.50	12215.95	28201.16	18531
OR/WA	COLUMBIA RIVER	GOVT ISLAND S CHANNEL NO 9	45-34.60	122-32.70	12250.25	28159.47	18531
OR/WA	COLUMBIA RIVER	FISHER QUARRY CHANNEL RANGE	45-34.60	122-28.00	12243.15	28168.24	18531
OR/WA	COLUMBIA RIVER	CAMA RANGE LIGHT	45-34.50	122-26.10	12241.24	28171.74	18531
OR/WA	COLUMBIA RIVER	LADY ISLAND RANGE LIGHT	45-34.40	122-23.90	12238.89	28175.80	18531
OR/WA	COLUMBIA RIVER	GOVT ISLAND S CHANNEL NO 11	45-34.30	122-32.20	12252.33	28160.22	18531
OR/WA	COLUMBIA RIVER	WASHOUGAL NO 48	45-34.30	122-21.80	12236.70	28179.68	18531
OR/WA	COLUMBIA RIVER	GOVT ISLAND RANGE LIGHT	45-34.20	122-27.70	12246.50	28168.57	18531
OR/WA	COLUMBIA RIVER	WASHOUGAL NO 50	45-34.10	122-21.30	12237.88	28180.51	18531

PASSES

STATE/COUNTRY	COUNTY/PROV	NAME	LAT	LON	TD#1	TD#2	CHART NO
OR/WA	COLUMBIA RIVER	CAPE HORN RANGE LIGHT NO 68A	45-34.10	122-11.50	12223.33	28198.97	18531
OR/WA	COLUMBIA RIVER	GOVT ISLAND S CHANNEL NO 13	45-34.00	122-31.20	12253.65	28161.91	18531
OR/WA	COLUMBIA RIVER	GOVT ISLAND S CHANNEL NO 14	45-34.00	122-30.40	12252.45	28163.40	18531
OR/WA	COLUMBIA RIVER	WASHOUGAL RANGE LIGHT	45-34.00	122-20.50	12237.65	28181.96	18531
OR/WA	COLUMBIA RIVER	McGUIRE ISLAND MID DIKE NO 34	45-33.90	122-27.10	12248.46	28169.51	18531
OR/WA	COLUMBIA RIVER	GOVT ISLAND RANGE LIGHT	45-33.90	122-26.80	12248.01	28170.07	18531
OR/WA	COLUMBIA RIVER	GOVT ISLAND RANGE NO 35	45-33.90	122-26.40	12247.42	28170.82	18531
OR/WA	COLUMBIA RIVER	IONE REEF NO 1	45-33.90	122-24.80	12245.03	28173.82	18531
OR/WA	COLUMBIA RIVER	GOVT ISLAND S CHANNEL NO 15	45-33.80	122-29.30	12252.70	28165.33	18531
OR/WA	COLUMBIA RIVER	LADY ISLAND RANGE LIGHT	45-33.80	122-26.80	12248.97	28170.02	18531
OR/WA	COLUMBIA RIVER	GOVT ISLAND S CHANNEL NO 17	45-33.70	122-28.50	12252.45	28166.77	18531
OR/WA	COLUMBIA RIVER	GOVT ISLAND S CHANNEL NO 21	45-33.70	122-26.80	12249.92	28169.96	18531
OR/WA	COLUMBIA RIVER	GOVT ISLAND S CHANNEL NO 19	45-33.60	122-27.70	12252.21	28168.21	18531
OR/WA	COLUMBIA RIVER	McGUIRE ROCK DAYBEACON NO 20	45-33.60	122-27.30	12251.62	28168.96	18531
OR/WA	COLUMBIA RIVER	GARY ISLAND DIKE NO 52	45-33.60	122-20.70	12241.81	28181.35	18531
OR/WA	COLUMBIA RIVER	GARY ISLAND DIKE NO 54	45-33.40	122-20.60	12243.59	28181.43	18531
OR/WA	COLUMBIA RIVER	WASHOUGAL RANGE LIGHT	45-33.10	122-20.30	12246.05	28181.83	18531
OR/WA	COLUMBIA RIVER	REED ISLAND RANGE LIGHT	45-33.10	122-20.30	12246.05	28181.83	18531
OR/WA	COLUMBIA RIVER	SAND ISLAND LIGHT NO 66	45-33.10	122-14.10	12236.95	28193.54	18531
OR/WA	COLUMBIA RIVER	TUNNEL POINT LIGHT NO 64	45-32.60	122-16.50	12245.34	28188.73	18531
OR/WA	COLUMBIA RIVER	CORBETT DIKE DAYBEACON NO 60	45-32.50	122-18.80	12249.67	28184.33	18531
PACIFIC OCEAN	JOHNSTON ATOLL	JOHNSTON HARBOR NO 18	16-44.70	169-31.40	Suggest	GPS	83637
PACIFIC OCEAN	JOHNSTON ATOLL	JOHNSTON ATOLL RANGE LIGHT	16-44.70	169-31.10	Suggest	GPS	83637
PACIFIC OCEAN	JOHNSTON ATOLL	JOHNSTON ATOLL RANGE	16-44.70	169-31.10	Suggest	GPS	83637
PACIFIC OCEAN	JOHNSTON ATOLL	JOHNSTON HARBOR NO 20	16-44.60	169-31.70	Suggest	GPS	83637
PACIFIC OCEAN	JOHNSTON ATOLL	JOHNSTON ATOLL NO 16	16-44.60	169-31.10	Suggest	GPS	83637
PACIFIC OCEAN	JOHNSTON ATOLL	JOHNSTON HARBOR NO 22	16-44.40	169-32.10	Suggest	GPS	83637
PACIFIC OCEAN	JOHNSTON ATOLL	JOHNSTON ATOLL NO 13	16-44.40	169-31.20	Suggest	GPS	83637
PACIFIC OCEAN	JOHNSTON ATOLL	JOHNSTON ATOLL NO 14	16-44.40	169-31.10	Suggest	GPS	83637
PACIFIC OCEAN	JOHNSTON ATOLL	JOHNSTON HARBOR NO 24	16-44.20	169-32.20	Suggest	GPS	83637
PACIFIC OCEAN	JOHNSTON ATOLL	JOHNSTON ATOLL NO 11	16-44.20	169-31.20	Suggest	GPS	83637
PACIFIC OCEAN	JOHNSTON ATOLL	JOHNSTON ATOLL NO 12	16-44.20	169-31.10	Suggest	GPS	83637
PACIFIC OCEAN	JOHNSTON ATOLL	JOHNSTON HARBOR NO 25	16-44.10	169-32.60	Suggest	GPS	83637
PACIFIC OCEAN	JOHNSTON ATOLL	JOHNSTON HARBOR NO 23	16-44.10	169-32.10	Suggest	GPS	83637
PACIFIC OCEAN	JOHNSTON ATOLL	JOHNSTON HARBOR NO 26	16-44.00	169-32.60	Suggest	GPS	83637
PACIFIC OCEAN	JOHNSTON ATOLL	JOHNSTON ATOLL NO 9	16-44.00	169-31.20	Suggest	GPS	83637
PACIFIC OCEAN	JOHNSTON ATOLL	JOHNSTON ATOLL NO 10	16-44.00	169-31.10	Suggest	GPS	83637
PACIFIC OCEAN	JOHNSTON ATOLL	JOHNSTON HARBOR NO 28	16-43.90	169-33.00	Suggest	GPS	83637
PACIFIC OCEAN	JOHNSTON ATOLL	JOHNSTON HARBOR NO 27	16-43.80	169-33.00	Suggest	GPS	83637
PACIFIC OCEAN	JOHNSTON ATOLL	JOHNSTON ATOLL NO 7	16-43.80	169-31.20	Suggest	GPS	83637
PACIFIC OCEAN	JOHNSTON ATOLL	JOHNSTON HARBOR NO 29	16-43.70	169-33.00	Suggest	GPS	83637
PACIFIC OCEAN	JOHNSTON ATOLL	JOHNSTON HARBOR NO 30	16-43.60	169-33.10	Suggest	GPS	83637
PACIFIC OCEAN	JOHNSTON ATOLL	JOHNSTON HARBOR NO 31	16-43.60	169-33.00	Suggest	GPS	83637
PACIFIC OCEAN	JOHNSTON ATOLL	JOHNSTON ATOLL NO 6	16-43.60	169-31.10	Suggest	GPS	83637

PASSES

STATE/COUNTRY	COUNTY/PROV	NAME	LAT	LON	TD#1	TD#2	CHART NO
PACIFIC OCEAN	JOHNSTON ATOLL	JOHNSTON HARBOR NO 32	16-43.30	169-32.90	Suggest	GPS	83637
PACIFIC OCEAN	JOHNSTON ATOLL	JOHNSTON ATOLL CHANNEL NO 2	16-42.80	169-31.10	Suggest	GPS	83637
PACIFIC OCEAN	MIDWAY	MIDWAY CHANNEL RANGE LIGHT	28-13.70	177-21.30	Suggest	GPS	19022
PACIFIC OCEAN	MIDWAY	EASTERN ISLAND RANGE MARKER	28-13.70	177-21.30	Suggest	GPS	19022
PACIFIC OCEAN	MIDWAY	MIDWAY CHANNEL ENTR NO 1	28-11.40	177-21.40	Suggest	GPS	19022
PHILIPPINES	LUZON ISLAND	SUBIC BAY NW CHANNEL NO 4	14-51.10N	120-13.30E	Suggest	GPS	91286
PHILIPPINES	LUZON ISLAND	SUBIC BAY NW CHANNEL NO 5	14-51.10N	120-12.90E	Suggest	GPS	91286
PHILIPPINES	LUZON ISLAND	SUBIC BAY NW CHANNEL NO 2	14-49.90N	120-13.90E	Suggest	GPS	91286
PHILIPPINES	LUZON ISLAND	KALAKLAN POINT LIGHT	14-49.50N	120-16.00E	Suggest	GPS	91286
PHILIPPINES	LUZON ISLAND	PORT OLONGAPO LIGHT A	14-48.80N	120-15.10E	Suggest	GPS	91286
PHILIPPINES	LUZON ISLAND	PORT OLONGAPO BUOY S	14-48.70N	120-14.50E	Suggest	GPS	91286
PHILIPPINES	LUZON ISLAND	CUBI SHOAL LIGHT NO 8	14-48.60N	120-15.50E	Suggest	GPS	91286
PHILIPPINES	LUZON ISLAND	AGUSUHIN POINT BUOY NO 7	14-48.60N	120-12.80E	Suggest	GPS	91286
PHILIPPINES	LUZON ISLAND	NAGCABAN POINT BUOY NO 2	14-48.10N	120-17.10E	Suggest	GPS	91286
PHILIPPINES	LUZON ISLAND	SIXTEEN FOOT SHOAL NO 6	14-47.90N	120-14.50E	Suggest	GPS	91286
PHILIPPINES	LUZON ISLAND	GRAND ISLAND SHOAL NO 4	14-46.70N	120-13.10E	Suggest	GPS	91286
PHILIPPINES	LUZON ISLAND	MACMANY POINT NO 3	14-46.60N	120-12.20E	Suggest	GPS	91286
PHILIPPINES	LUZON ISLAND	ILANIN BAY LIGHT NO 1	14-46.20N	120-15.00E	Suggest	GPS	91286
PHILIPPINES	LUZON ISLAND	ILANIN BAY LIGHT NO 3	14-46.10N	120-15.30E	Suggest	GPS	91286
PHILIPPINES	LUZON ISLAND	ILANIN BAY DIR LIGHT	14-46.00N	120-15.20E	Suggest	GPS	91286
PHILIPPINES	LUZON ISLAND	TWENTY-FOUR FOOT SHOAL NO 2	14-45.20N	120-13.40E	Suggest	GPS	91286
SAMOA ISLANDS	AUNUU ISLAND	AUNUU ISLAND BRKWTR NO 1	14-17.30	170-33.60	Suggest	GPS	83484
SAMOA ISLANDS	AUNUU ISLAND	AUNUU ISLAND LIGHT	14-17.00	170-32.90	Suggest	GPS	83484
SAMOA ISLANDS	OFU HARBOR	OFU HARBOR DAYBEACON NO 3	14-10.20	169-40.80	Suggest	GPS	83484
SAMOA ISLANDS	OFU HARBOR	OFU HARBOR LIGHT NO 1	14-10.20	169-40.80	Suggest	GPS	83484
SAMOA ISLANDS	OFU HARBOR	OFU HARBOR DAYBEACON NO 2	14-10.10	169-40.80	Suggest	GPS	83484
SAMOA ISLANDS	PAGO PAGO	WHALE ROCK BUOY NO 2	14-17.30	170-40.10	Suggest	GPS	83484
SAMOA ISLANDS	PAGO PAGO	PAGO PAGO HARBOR NO 5	14-16.70	170-40.20	Suggest	GPS	83484
SAMOA ISLANDS	PAGO PAGO	PAGO PAGO HARBOR NO 6	14-16.60	170-41.40	Suggest	GPS	83484
SAMOA ISLANDS	PAGO PAGO	PAGO PAGO HARBOR RANGE	14-16.30	170-40.40	Suggest	GPS	83484
SAMOA ISLANDS	TA'U HARBOR	TA'U HARBOR RANGE MARKER	14-14.50	169-30.60	Suggest	GPS	83484
TOAGEL MLUNGUI	PALAU ISLANDS	WEST PASSAGE NO 36	07-28.00N	134-28.20E	Suggest	GPS	81148
TOAGEL MLUNGUI	PALAU ISLANDS	WEST PASSAGE NO 38	07-27.30N	134-27.80E	Suggest	GPS	81148
TOAGEL MLUNGUI	PALAU ISLANDS	WEST PASSAGE NO 40	07-26.80N	134-27.20E	Suggest	GPS	81148
TOAGEL MLUNGUI	PALAU ISLANDS	WEST PASSAGE NO 42	07-25.80N	134-26.40E	Suggest	GPS	81148
SAMOA ISLANDS	TUTUILA ISLAND	STEPS POINT LIGHT	14-22.50	170-45.40	Suggest	GPS	83484
SAMOA ISLANDS	TUTUILA ISLAND	TAEMA BANK LIGHT NO 1	14-19.60	170-40.40	Suggest	GPS	83484
SAMOA ISLANDS	TUTUILA ISLAND	BREAKERS POINT LIGHT	14-17.60	170-39.80	Suggest	GPS	83484
Canada	B Columbia	CARMANAH LIGHT	48-36.70	124-45.00	11462.64	28078.27	18460
Canada	B Columbia	PORT SAN JUAN WHISTLE YK	48-32.10	124-29.00	11446.14	28094.24	18460
Canada	B Columbia	SAN JUAN POINT LIGHT	48-31.90	124-27.40	11443.64	28096.01	18460
WA	CLALLAM	STRAIT OF S JUAN DE FUCA J	48-29.20	124-43.60	11483.78	28075.42	18460
WA	CLALLAM	STRAIT OF S JUAN DE FUCA J	48-29.20	124-43.60	11483.78	28075.42	18480
Canada	B Columbia	FISGARD LIGHT	48-25.80	123-26.80	11338.82	28166.19	18465

PASSES

STATE/COUNTRY	COUNTY/PROV	NAME	LAT	LON	TD#1	TD#2	CHART NO
WA	CLALLAM	DUNTZE ROCK WHISTLE 2D	48-24.90	124-44.90	11500.53	28071.28	18460
WA	CLALLAM	DUNTZE ROCK WHISTLE 2D	48-24.90	124-44.90	11500.53	28071.28	18480
Canada	B Columbia	SCROGGS ROCKS LIGHT	48-24.40	123-26.30	11341.84	28166.19	18465
WA	CLALLAM	CAPE FLATTERY LIGHT	48-23.50	124-44.10	11503.68	28071.36	18460
WA	CLALLAM	CAPE FLATTERY LIGHT	48-23.50	124-44.10	11503.68	28071.36	18480
WA	CLALLAM	WAADAH ISLAND LIGHT	48-23.20	124-35.90	11488.57	28080.89	18460
WA	CLALLAM	ALBERT HEAD LIGHT	48-23.20	123-28.60	11350.24	28162.80	18465
Canada	B Columbia	SHERINGHAM POINT LIGHT	48-22.70	123-55.20	11407.63	28129.74	18465
WA	CLALLAM	DTOKOAH POINT NO 1	48-22.60	124-35.10	11489.01	28081.48	18460
WA	CLALLAM	NEAH BAY INNER NO 2	48-22.50	124-35.90	11490.93	28080.47	18460
WA	CLALLAM	SWINOMISH S CHANNEL NO 11A	48-22.00	122-31.90	11231.96	28233.74	18421
Canada	B Columbia	WHIFFIN SPIT LIGHT	48-21.50	123-42.60	11385.03	28144.66	18465
WA	CLALLAM	HEIN BANK LIGHTED BUOY	48-21.10	123-02.70	11300.82	28194.37	18465
Canada	B Columbia	WILLIAM HEAD LIGHT	48-20.60	123-31.60	11364.47	28157.89	18465
Canada	B Columbia	RACE ROCKS LIGHT	48-17.90	123-31.80	11373.29	28156.39	18465
WA	CLALLAM	ROSARIO STRAIT BUOY R	48-16.50	123-06.50	11322.44	28187.73	18465
WA	CLALLAM	CLALLAM REEF NO 1	48-16.10	124-15.40	11471.33	28101.46	18460
Canada	B Columbia	RACE ROCKS E BUOY VG	48-16.10	123-27.70	11370.10	28160.72	18465
WA	CLALLAM	SLIP POINT LIGHT	48-15.90	124-14.90	11470.99	28101.96	18460
WA	CLALLAM	CALIBRATION LIGHTED BELL	48-14.20	123-21.70	11363.00	28167.45	18465
WA	CLALLAM	STRAIT OF JUAN DE FUCA PA	48-12.40	123-27.60	11381.80	28159.14	18465
WA	CLALLAM	PUGET SOUND BUOY S	48-12.40	123-06.50	11334.92	28186.06	18465
WA	CLALLAM	NEW DUNGENESS SAND SPIT NO 2	48-11.50	123-05.60	11335.71	28186.85	18465
WA	CLALLAM	UMATILLA REEF WHISTLE 2UR	48-11.20	124-49.20	11557.25	28057.52	18480
WA	CLALLAM	NEW DUNGENESS LIGHT	48-10.90	123-06.50	11339.62	28185.45	18465
Canada	B Columbia	CRESCENT BAY NO 2	48-10.20	123-43.40	11423.81	28138.07	18465
WA	CLALLAM	IDEAL CEMENT RANGE DAYBEACON	48-10.00	123-57.50	11454.97	28120.23	18465
WA	CLALLAM	SALMON PEN LIGHT C	48-08.40	123-25.20	11389.79	28160.35	18465
WA	CLALLAM	SALMON PEN LIGHT E	48-08.40	123-25.10	11389.56	28160.48	18465
WA	CLALLAM	SALMON PEN LIGHT D	48-08.40	123-25.10	11389.56	28160.48	18465
WA	CLALLAM	SALMON PEN LIGHT F	48-08.40	123-24.90	11389.12	28160.73	18465
WA	CLALLAM	SALMON PEN LIGHT G	48-08.40	123-24.90	11389.12	28160.73	18465
WA	CLALLAM	SALMON PEN LIGHT A	48-08.40	123-24.90	11389.12	28160.73	18465
WA	CLALLAM	EDIZ HOOK LIGHT	48-08.40	123-24.50	11388.22	28161.25	18465
WA	CLALLAM	EDIZ HOOK NO 2	48-08.40	123-23.90	11386.88	28162.02	18465
WA	CLALLAM	PORT ANGELES BOAT HAVEN NO 3	48-07.80	123-26.80	11395.40	28158.02	18465
WA	CLALLAM	PORT ANGELES BOAT HAVEN LIGHT	48-07.60	123-27.00	11396.53	28157.67	18465
WA	CLALLAM	SEQUIM BAY ENTRANCE NO 2	48-05.10	123-01.60	11347.18	28189.42	18471
WA	CLALLAM	SEQUIM BAY NO 5	48-04.60	123-02.50	11350.92	28188.04	18471
WA	CLALLAM	SEQUIM BAY ENTRANCE NO 4	48-04.60	123-02.50	11350.92	28188.04	18471
WA	CLALLAM	SEQUIM BAY NO 7	48-04.50	123-02.50	11351.25	28188.00	18471
WA	CLALLAM	QUILLAYUTE R BOAT BASIN NO 1	47-54.60	124-38.20	11599.47	28060.10	18480
WA	CLALLAM	QUILLAYUTE R BOAT BASIN NO 2	47-54.60	124-38.20	11599.47	28060.10	18480
WA	CLALLAM	QUILLAYUTE RIVER NO 3	47-54.50	124-38.60	11600.70	28059.54	18480

PASSES

STATE/COUNTRY	COUNTY/PROV	NAME	LAT	LON	TD#1	TD#2	CHART NO
WA	CLALLAM	QUILLAYUTE RIVER DIR LIGHT	47-54.50	124-38.60	11600.70	28059.54	18480
WA	CLALLAM	JAMES ISLAND LIGHT	47-54.30	124-38.80	11601.93	28059.16	18480
WA	CLALLAM	QUILLAYUTE RIVER NO 2	47-53.70	124-38.70	11604.18	28058.88	18480
WA	CLALLAM	QUILLAYUTE RIVER WHISTLE Q	47-53.10	124-40.40	11610.14	28056.36	18480
WA	GEORGIA STRAIT	INTERNATL BOUNDARY RANGE A	49-00.10	123-05.30	11215.54	28205.51	18421
WA	GEORGIA STRAIT	INTERNATL BOUNDARY RANGE A	49-00.10	123-03.90	11213.05	28207.14	18421
WA	GEORGIA STRAIT	INTERNATL BOUNDARY RANGE B	49-00.10	123-03.90	11213.05	28207.14	18421
WA	GEORGIA STRAIT	INTERNATL BOUNDARY RANGE B	49-00.10	123-02.00	11209.67	28209.37	18421
WA	GEORGIA STRAIT	INTERNATL BOUNDARY OBSTR	49-00.10	123-01.10	11208.07	28210.42	18421
WA	GEORGIA STRAIT	INTERNATL BOUNDARY RANGE C	49-00.10	122-45.30	11180.36	28228.97	18421
WA	GEORGIA STRAIT	SEMIAHMOO BAY LIGHT	48-59.60	122-47.00	11184.16	28226.82	18421
WA	GEORGIA STRAIT	SEMIAHMOO BAY NO 2	48-59.40	122-47.40	11185.21	28226.28	18421
WA	GEORGIA STRAIT	THE BASIN BRKWTR LIGHT	48-58.50	123-03.60	11215.54	28206.95	18421
WA	GEORGIA STRAIT	BOUNDARY BAY BASIN LIGHT 1	48-58.40	123-03.80	11216.09	28206.68	18421
WA	GEORGIA STRAIT	BOUNDARY BAY BASIN LIGHT 2	48-58.40	123-03.70	11215.91	28206.79	18421
WA	GEORGIA STRAIT	POINT ROBERTS LIGHT	48-58.30	123-04.90	11218.26	28205.35	18421
WA	GEORGIA STRAIT	INTALCO N & S LIGHTS	48-50.60	122-43.20	11193.43	28228.58	18421
WA	GEORGIA STRAIT	SOCONY MOBIL N & S LIGHTS	48-49.50	122-43.10	11195.30	28228.36	18421
Canada	B Columbia	ROSENFELD ROCK NO U59	48-48.20	123-01.60	11232.47	28205.73	18421
WA	GEORGIA STRAIT	PATOS ISLAND LIGHT	48-47.30	122-58.20	11227.91	28209.50	18421
WA	GEORGIA STRAIT	ALDEN BANK BUOY B	48-47.10	122-48.90	11210.75	28220.62	18421
Canada	B Columbia	SATURNA ISLAND LIGHT	48-47.00	123-02.70	11237.11	28203.99	18421
WA	GEORGIA STRAIT	BOUNDARY PASS SHOAL B	48-45.90	123-00.80	11235.83	28205.88	18421
WA	GEORGIA STRAIT	SUCIA ISLAND DAYBEACON NO 1	48-45.80	122-55.10	11225.15	28212.72	18421
WA	GEORGIA STRAIT	CLEMENTS REEF BUOY	48-45.80	122-52.00	11219.24	28216.46	18421
WA	GEORGIA STRAIT	EWING ISLAND REEF DAYBEACON	48-45.70	122-52.50	11220.40	28215.82	18421
WA	GEORGIA STRAIT	BELLINGTON BRKWTR NO 4	48-45.50	122-30.60	11179.60	28242.29	18421
WA	GEORGIA STRAIT	AQUALICUM CREEK ENTRANCE NO 2	48-45.40	122-30.80	11180.16	28242.01	18421
WA	GEORGIA STRAIT	ROSARIO STRAIT BUOY CA	48-45.30	122-46.40	11209.62	28223.06	18421
WA	GEORGIA STRAIT	POINT MIGLEY BUOY	48-45.30	122-43.40	11203.94	28226.70	18421
WA	GEORGIA STRAIT	BELLINGTON BRKWTR NO 2	48-45.20	122-30.40	11179.78	28242.44	18421
WA	GEORGIA STRAIT	I&J WATERWAY NO 2	48-45.00	122-29.80	11179.03	28243.12	18421
WA	GEORGIA STRAIT	I&J WATERWAY NO 1	48-44.90	122-30.00	11179.59	28242.85	18421
WA	GEORGIA STRAIT	WHATCOM WATERWAY SECTOR LIGHT	48-44.60	122-29.60	11179.39	28243.25	18421
Canada	B Columbia	GOWLLAND POINT LIGHT	48-44.10	123-11.00	11259.51	28192.95	18421
WA	GEORGIA STRAIT	LUMMI POINT NO 5	48-44.10	122-41.10	11201.95	28229.12	18421
WA	GEORGIA STRAIT	SKIPJACK ISLAND LIGHT	48-44.00	123-02.30	11242.85	28203.40	18421
WA	GEORGIA STRAIT	GEORGIA PACIFIC OUTFALL	48-44.00	122-30.90	11182.92	28241.49	18421
WA	GEORGIA STRAIT	LUMMI ISLAND FERRY LANDING	48-43.20	122-40.70	11202.98	28229.32	18421
WA	GEORGIA STRAIT	ORCAS ISLAND N SHORE BUOY	48-42.90	122-53.50	11228.21	28213.67	18421
WA	GEORGIA STRAIT	ORCAS ISLAND N SHORE BUOY	48-42.90	122-53.30	11227.82	28213.91	18421
Canada	B Columbia	POINT FAIRFAX LIGHT	48-42.00	123-17.80	11277.72	28183.95	18421
WA	GEORGIA STRAIT	THE SISTERS LIGHT NO 17	48-41.70	122-45.40	11215.06	28223.13	18421
WA	GEORGIA STRAIT	POINT FRANCIS SHOAL NO 4	48-41.70	122-38.20	11201.19	28231.91	18421

PASSES

STATE/COUNTRY	COUNTY/PROV	NAME	LAT	LON	TD#1	TD#2	CHART NO
WA	GEORGIA STRAIT	LUMMI ISLAND LIGHT NO 3	48-41.50	122-38.60	11202.35	28231.37	18421
WA	GEORGIA STRAIT	TURN POINT LIGHT	48-41.30	123-14.20	11272.31	28188.02	18421
Canada	B Columbia	ARACHNE REEF LIGHT	48-41.10	123-17.60	11279.50	28183.84	18421
WA	GEORGIA STRAIT	ROSARIO STRAIT BUOY C	48-40.50	122-42.80	11212.51	28225.92	18421
WA	GEORGIA STRAIT	INATI BAY REEF BUOY	48-40.50	122-37.10	11201.47	28232.90	18421
WA	GEORGIA STRAIT	ROCKS JUNCTION BUOY	48-40.50	122-35.40	11198.20	28234.98	18421
WA	GEORGIA STRAIT	LUMMI ROCKS NO 16A	48-40.20	122-40.10	11207.89	28229.13	18421
WA	GEORGIA STRAIT	NEW CHANNEL NORI BUOYS	48-39.90	123-09.30	11265.95	28193.41	18421
Canada	B Columbia	TOM POINT LIGHT	48-39.80	123-16.30	11280.08	28184.89	18421
WA	GEORGIA STRAIT	ROSARIO STRAIT NO 16	48-38.50	122-42.70	11216.52	28225.41	18421
WA	GEORGIA STRAIT	SINCLAIR ISLAND NO 4	48-38.30	122-40.00	11211.64	28228.66	18421
WA	GEORGIA STRAIT	SPEIDEN CHANNEL NO 3	48-38.10	123-09.60	11270.86	28192.36	18421
WA	GEORGIA STRAIT	GREEN POINT LIGHT	48-38.00	123-06.30	11264.50	28196.35	18421
WA	GEORGIA STRAIT	VITI ROCKS LIGHT	48-38.00	122-37.30	11206.97	28231.89	18421
WA	GEORGIA STRAIT	HARBOR ROCK DAYBEACON	48-37.80	122-58.60	11249.59	28205.68	18421
WA	GEORGIA STRAIT	VITI ROCKS NO 9	48-37.80	122-37.10	11207.00	28232.08	18421
WA	GEORGIA STRAIT	JONES ISLAND ROCKS	48-37.20	123-02.50	11258.80	28200.69	18421
WA	GEORGIA STRAIT	PEARL ISLAND LIGHT NO 1	48-37.00	123-10.10	11274.54	28191.33	18421
WA	GEORGIA STRAIT	CYPRESS REEF DAYBEACON C	48-36.80	122-43.30	11221.36	28224.13	18421
WA	GEORGIA STRAIT	VENDOVI ISLAND NO 2	48-36.50	122-35.80	11207.15	28233.29	18421
WA	GEORGIA STRAIT	BELLINGTON CHANNEL NO 8	48-36.20	122-37.70	11211.54	28230.85	18421
WA	GEORGIA STRAIT	BIRD ROCKS LIGHT	48-35.90	123-00.80	11258.47	28202.30	18421
WA	GEORGIA STRAIT	LYDIA SHOAL NO 13	48-35.90	122-46.70	11230.13	28219.64	18421
WA	GEORGIA STRAIT	BELLINGTON CHANNEL NO 6	48-35.50	122-39.00	11215.62	28229.02	18421
WA	GEORGIA STRAIT	KELLETT BLUFF LIGHT	48-35.30	123-12.10	11282.79	28188.23	18421
WA	GEORGIA STRAIT	SHIRT TAIL REEF NO 1	48-35.30	123-01.20	11260.72	28201.59	18421
WA	GEORGIA STRAIT	TIDE POINT NO 12	48-35.10	122-44.40	11227.30	28222.22	18421
WA	GEORGIA STRAIT	MOSQUITO PASS NO 2	48-35.00	123-10.20	11279.69	28190.44	18421
WA	GEORGIA STRAIT	BLIND BAY ROCK DAYBEACON	48-35.00	122-55.90	11250.71	28208.00	18421
WA	GEORGIA STRAIT	WILLIAM POINT LIGHT	48-35.00	122-33.50	11205.74	28235.68	18421
WA	GEORGIA STRAIT	TAILFIN FISH PEN LIGHT A	48-34.90	122-41.00	11220.93	28226.36	18421
WA	GEORGIA STRAIT	PADILLA BAY NO 4	48-34.70	122-35.60	11210.56	28232.99	18421
WA	GEORGIA STRAIT	UPRIGHT HEAD FERRY LANDING	48-34.30	122-52.90	11246.28	28211.45	18421
WA	GEORGIA STRAIT	BLAKELY ISLAND SHOAL BS	48-34.20	122-50.70	11242.06	28214.13	18421
Canada	B Columbia	D'ARCY ISLAND LIGHT	48-34.00	123-17.00	11296.07	28181.71	18421
WA	GEORGIA STRAIT	BELLINGTON CHANNEL NO 5	48-34.00	122-40.00	11220.90	28227.31	18421
WA	GEORGIA STRAIT	SCAN AM FISH FARM LIGHTS	48-33.50	122-41.00	11224.03	28225.91	18421
WA	GEORGIA STRAIT	PADILLA BAY NO 5	48-33.50	122-34.40	11210.74	28234.11	18421
WA	GEORGIA STRAIT	SHOAL BAY AQUACULTURE LIGHT	48-33.40	122-52.40	11247.38	28211.76	18421
WA	GEORGIA STRAIT	FLAT POINT LIGHT	48-33.20	122-55.10	11253.36	28208.35	18421
WA	GEORGIA STRAIT	CYPRESS SALMON FARM A & B	48-33.20	122-41.00	11224.70	28225.82	18421
Canada	B Columbia	KELP REEFS LIGHT	48-32.90	123-14.10	11292.99	28184.83	18421
WA	GEORGIA STRAIT	REID ROCK BUOY	48-32.90	122-59.30	11262.67	28203.05	18421
WA	GEORGIA STRAIT	BLACK ROCK LIGHT NO 9	48-32.80	122-45.90	11235.55	28219.61	18421

PASSES

STATE/COUNTRY	COUNTY/PROV	NAME	LAT	LON	TD#1	TD#2	CHART NO
WA	GEORGIA STRAIT	FRIDAY HARBOR N BRKWTR	48-32.40	123-00.90	11267.18	28200.89	18421
WA	GEORGIA STRAIT	MINNESOTA ISLAND NO 2	48-32.20	122-59.20	11264.19	28202.92	18421
WA	GEORGIA STRAIT	BELLINGTON CHANNEL NO 4	48-32.20	122-40.00	11224.92	28226.74	18421
WA	GEORGIA STRAIT	HUCKLEBERRY ISLAND NO 6	48-32.20	122-33.90	11212.55	28234.34	18421
WA	GEORGIA STRAIT	SADDLEBAG ISLAND NO 7	48-32.10	122-33.40	11211.76	28234.93	18421
WA	GEORGIA STRAIT	TURN ROCK LIGHT NO 3	48-32.00	122-57.80	11261.80	28204.58	18421
Canada	B Columbia	LITTLE ZERO ROCK NO V30	48-31.90	123-19.70	11307.12	28177.54	18421
WA	GEORGIA STRAIT	BLAKELY ISLAND LIGHT	48-31.90	122-48.50	11242.96	28216.08	18421
WA	GEORGIA STRAIT	LAWSON ROCK JUNCTION	48-31.90	122-47.20	11240.30	28217.69	18421
WA	GEORGIA STRAIT	YELLOW BLUFF REEF NO 2	48-31.90	122-39.50	11224.58	28227.27	18421
WA	GEORGIA STRAIT	REEF POINT JUNCTION	48-31.70	122-43.50	11233.20	28222.23	18421
WA	GEORGIA STRAIT	FISHERMAN BAY SECTOR LIGHT	48-31.50	122-55.10	11257.47	28207.75	18421
Canada	B Columbia	ZERO ROCK LIGHT	48-31.40	123-17.40	11303.71	28180.16	18421
WA	GEORGIA STRAIT	UNDERTAKERS REEF NO 8	48-31.40	122-49.70	11246.61	28214.41	18421
WA	GEORGIA STRAIT	GUEMES CHANNEL NO 5	48-31.40	122-38.40	11223.47	28228.48	18421
WA	GEORGIA STRAIT	GUEMES CHANNEL NO 3	48-31.30	122-39.30	11225.53	28227.33	18421
WA	GEORGIA STRAIT	GUEMES CHANNEL NO 4	48-31.20	122-39.10	11225.34	28227.55	18421
WA	GEORGIA STRAIT	ANACORTES FERRY BRKWTR LIGHT	48-31.20	122-37.40	11221.88	28229.67	18421
WA	GEORGIA STRAIT	LIME KILN LIGHT	48-31.00	123-09.10	11287.63	28190.23	18421
WA	GEORGIA STRAIT	CAPSANTE WATERWAY NO 1	48-30.70	122-35.90	11219.94	28231.38	18421
WA	GEORGIA STRAIT	ANACORTES CHANNEL NO 3	48-30.70	122-35.50	11219.12	28231.88	18421
WA	GEORGIA STRAIT	SWINOMISH N CHANNEL NO 2	48-30.70	122-33.30	11214.63	28234.64	18421
WA	GEORGIA STRAIT	GUEMES CHANNEL NO 2	48-30.60	122-41.80	11232.26	28223.99	18421
WA	GEORGIA STRAIT	SHANNON POINT LIGHT	48-30.60	122-40.90	11230.41	28225.11	18421
WA	GEORGIA STRAIT	FIDALGO BAY SHOAL NO 2	48-30.60	122-35.00	11218.32	28232.48	18421
WA	GEORGIA STRAIT	TEXACO OIL WHARF LIGHTS	48-30.60	122-34.60	11217.50	28232.98	18421
WA	GEORGIA STRAIT	ANACORTES CHANNEL NO 4	48-30.50	122-35.80	11220.18	28231.45	18421
WA	GEORGIA STRAIT	SHELL OIL WHARF LIGHTS	48-30.50	122-34.10	11216.71	28233.57	18421
WA	GEORGIA STRAIT	SWINOMISH N CHANNEL NO 6	48-30.00	122-32.80	11215.16	28235.05	18421
WA	GEORGIA STRAIT	SWINOMISH N CHANNEL NO 7	48-29.80	122-32.50	11214.99	28235.37	18421
WA	GEORGIA STRAIT	SWINOMISH N CHANNEL NO 12	48-29.20	122-32.20	11215.72	28235.56	18421
WA	GEORGIA STRAIT	CENTER ISLAND REEF DAYBEACON	48-29.10	122-50.10	11253.00	28213.13	18421
WA	GEORGIA STRAIT	CENTER ISLAND NO 6	48-29.10	122-50.10	11253.00	28213.13	18421
WA	GEORGIA STRAIT	BURROWS ISLAND LIGHT	48-28.60	122-42.70	11238.82	28222.21	18421
WA	GEORGIA STRAIT	RAM ISLAND ROCKS NO 4	48-28.40	122-50.20	11254.94	28212.76	18421
WA	GEORGIA STRAIT	SWINOMISH N CHANNEL NO 22	48-28.40	122-31.50	11216.08	28236.20	18421
WA	GEORGIA STRAIT	HUNTER BAY AQUACULTURE BUOYS	48-28.10	122-51.30	11257.98	28211.28	18421
WA	GEORGIA STRAIT	SWINOMISH N CHANNEL NO 30	48-27.70	122-30.90	11216.42	28236.74	18421
WA	GEORGIA STRAIT	DENNIS SHOAL NO 6	48-27.50	122-42.80	11241.67	28221.72	18421
Canada	B Columbia	HARO STRAIT BUOY VD	48-27.10	123-10.80	11301.52	28186.58	18421
WA	GEORGIA STRAIT	CATTLE POINT LIGHT	48-27.10	122-57.70	11273.95	28202.92	18421
WA	GEORGIA STRAIT	KELLETT LEDGE NO 3	48-27.00	122-47.40	11252.54	28215.78	18421
WA	GEORGIA STRAIT	WILLIAMSON ROCKS NO 4	48-26.90	122-42.30	11242.08	28222.15	18421
WA	GEORGIA STRAIT	TWIN ROCKS DAYBEACON	48-26.80	122-54.60	11268.20	28206.69	18421

PASSES

STATE/COUNTRY	COUNTY/PROV	NAME	LAT	LON	TD#1	TD#2	CHART NO
WA	GEORGIA STRAIT	ICEBERG POINT LIGHT NO 2	48-26.80	122-54.60	11268.20	28206.69	18421
WA	GEORGIA STRAIT	SALMON BANK NO 3	48-25.60	122-58.50	11279.56	28201.36	18465
WA	GEORGIA STRAIT	DISCOVERY ISLAND LIGHT	48-25.50	123-13.50	11311.62	28182.58	18421
Canada	B Columbia	DISCOVERY ISLAND LIGHT	48-25.50	123-13.50	11311.62	28182.58	18465
WA	GEORGIA STRAIT	SWINOMISH S CHANNEL NO 21	48-25.50	122-30.10	11219.80	28237.09	18421
WA	GEORGIA STRAIT	SWINOMISH S CHANNEL NO 22	48-25.50	122-29.90	11219.38	28237.34	18421
WA	GEORGIA STRAIT	SWINOMISH S CHANNEL NO 19	48-25.20	122-30.00	11220.29	28237.13	18421
WA	GEORGIA STRAIT	OGDEN POINT BRKWTR LIGHT	48-24.80	123-23.60	11334.97	28169.72	18465
WA	GEORGIA STRAIT	LA CONNER RANGE LIGHT NO 18	48-24.80	122-29.70	11220.59	28237.39	18421
WA	GEORGIA STRAIT	AMERICAN AQUA FISH PEN LIGHTS	48-24.50	122-33.60	11229.53	28232.36	18421
WA	GEORGIA STRAIT	BROTCHIE LEDGE LIGHT	48-24.40	123-23.20	11335.28	28170.04	18465
WA	GEORGIA STRAIT	BEN URE ISLAND LIGHT NO 2	48-24.20	122-37.60	11238.74	28227.20	18421
WA	GEORGIA STRAIT	LAWSON REEF JUNCTION BELL	48-24.10	122-42.90	11250.26	28220.46	18421
WA	GEORGIA STRAIT	TRIAL ISLANDS LIGHT	48-23.70	123-18.20	11326.69	28175.97	18465
WA	GEORGIA STRAIT	SWINIMISH S CHANNEL NO 16	48-23.00	122-30.30	11226.12	28236.08	18421
WA	GEORGIA STRAIT	VICTORIA HARBOR WHISTLE VH	48-22.50	123-23.50	11341.47	28168.84	18465
WA	GEORGIA STRAIT	SWINOMISH S CHANNEL NO 15	48-22.50	122-30.60	11227.96	28235.55	18421
WA	GEORGIA STRAIT	SEAL ROCKS LIGHT NO 12	48-22.40	122-33.70	11234.84	28231.58	18421
WA	GEORGIA STRAIT	SWINOMISH S CHANNEL NO 13	48-22.30	122-30.60	11228.45	28235.49	18421
WA	GEORGIA STRAIT	SWINOMISH S CHANNEL NO 11C	48-22.20	122-31.20	11229.97	28234.70	18421
WA	GEORGIA STRAIT	SWINOMISH S CHANNEL NO 11B	48-22.10	122-31.60	11231.07	28234.16	18421
WA	GRAYS HARBOR	NOAA BUOY 46041	47-24.90	124-31.90	11719.34	28047.77	18500
WA	GRAYS HARBOR	POINT GRENVILLE	47-18.30	124-16.60	11719.74	28063.62	18500
WA	GRAYS HARBOR	GRAYS HARBOR LIGHT NO 3	46-58.70	123-47.60	11762.44	28090.96	18502
WA	GRAYS HARBOR	GRAYS HARBOR LIGHT NO 1	46-58.50	123-48.30	11765.19	28089.81	18502
WA	GRAYS HARBOR	ABERDEEN REACH RANGE L LIGHT	46-58.50	123-48.20	11764.96	28089.96	18502
WA	GRAYS HARBOR	GRAYS HARBOR N CHANNEL RANGE	46-58.20	123-55.70	11783.43	28078.93	18502
WA	GRAYS HARBOR	GRAYS HARBOR N CHANNEL RANGE	46-58.20	123-55.00	11781.88	28079.94	18502
WA	GRAYS HARBOR	GRAYS HARBOR N CHANNEL NO 40	46-58.10	123-55.30	11783.12	28079.43	18502
WA	GRAYS HARBOR	GRAYS HARBOR N CHANNEL NO 44	46-58.00	123-54.10	11781.05	28081.09	18502
WA	GRAYS HARBOR	GRAYS HARBOR N CHANNEL NO 46	46-58.00	123-53.50	11779.72	28081.96	18502
WA	GRAYS HARBOR	GRAYS HARBOR N CHANNEL NO 46A	46-58.00	123-53.30	11779.27	28082.25	18502
WA	GRAYS HARBOR	GRAYS HARBOR N CHANNEL NO 35	46-57.90	123-56.90	11787.81	28076.99	18502
WA	GRAYS HARBOR	COW POINT RANGE J LIGHT	46-57.90	123-49.00	11770.26	28088.40	18502
WA	GRAYS HARBOR	GRAYS HARBOR N CHANNEL RANGE	46-57.80	123-58.50	11791.91	28074.62	18502
WA	GRAYS HARBOR	GRAYS HARBOR N CHANNEL NO 36	46-57.80	123-56.30	11787.07	28077.79	18502
WA	GRAYS HARBOR	GRAYS HARBOR N CHANNEL NO 55	46-57.80	123-49.60	11772.19	28087.46	18502
WA	GRAYS HARBOR	GRAYS HARBOR N CHANNEL NO 34	46-57.70	123-57.90	11791.17	28075.42	18502
WA	GRAYS HARBOR	GRAYS HARBOR N CHANNEL RANGE	46-57.60	123-59.20	11794.60	28073.48	18502
WA	GRAYS HARBOR	GRAYS HARBOR N CHANNEL NO 32	46-57.60	123-58.60	11793.29	28074.34	18502
WA	GRAYS HARBOR	COW POINT TURNING BASIN NO 50	46-57.60	123-50.90	11776.26	28085.44	18502
WA	GRAYS HARBOR	COW POINT RANGE H LIGHT	46-57.60	123-49.40	11772.91	28087.62	18502
WA	GRAYS HARBOR	COW POINT TURNING BASIN NO 48	46-57.50	123-50.90	11776.85	28085.38	18502
WA	GRAYS HARBOR	WEYERHAEUSER OUTFALL LIGHTS	46-57.40	123-50.90	11777.43	28085.31	18502

COASTAL LORAN COORDINATES - 1990
West Coast & Pacific Edition
P A S S E S

STATE/COUNTRY	COUNTY/PROV	NAME	LAT	LON	TD#1	TD#2	CHART NO
WA	GRAYS HARBOR	CHARLEY CREEK DIKE NO 2	46-57.40	123-50.60	11776.76	28085.74	18502
WA	GRAYS HARBOR	COW POINT REACH RANGE LIGHT	46-57.40	123-50.20	11775.87	28086.32	18502
WA	GRAYS HARBOR	ABERDEEN REACH RANGE K LIGHT	46-57.40	123-50.20	11775.87	28086.32	18502
WA	GRAYS HARBOR	CHELALIS RIVER NO 4	46-57.40	123-46.00	11766.44	28092.42	18502
WA	GRAYS HARBOR	DAMON POINT LIGHT	46-57.10	124-06.20	11812.68	28063.10	18502
WA	GRAYS HARBOR	GRAYS HARBOR N CHANNEL NO 29	46-57.10	123-59.50	11798.17	28072.70	18502
WA	GRAYS HARBOR	GRAYS HARBOR N CHANNEL NO 27	46-56.50	124-00.30	11803.41	28071.13	18502
WA	GRAYS HARBOR	GRAYS HARBOR N BAY NO 1	46-55.90	124-06.60	11820.52	28061.66	18502
WA	GRAYS HARBOR	GRAYS HARBOR N CHANNEL NO 25	46-55.90	124-01.10	11808.66	28069.55	18502
WA	GRAYS HARBOR	GRAYS HARBOR BAR RANGE LIGHT	46-55.80	124-09.40	11827.08	28057.59	18502
WA	GRAYS HARBOR	GRAYS HARBOR N CHANNEL RANGE	46-55.50	124-01.60	11812.08	28068.55	18502
WA	GRAYS HARBOR	GRAYS HARBOR CHANNEL NO 13	46-55.40	124-07.40	11825.15	28060.15	18502
WA	GRAYS HARBOR	GRAYS HARBOR S REACH NO 15	46-55.40	124-06.20	11822.58	28061.87	18502
WA	GRAYS HARBOR	GRAYS HARBOR S REACH NO 15A	46-55.30	124-05.40	11821.45	28062.94	18502
WA	GRAYS HARBOR	GRAYS HARBOR S REACH NO 17	46-55.30	124-04.20	11818.87	28064.67	18502
WA	GRAYS HARBOR	GRAYS HARBOR S REACH SC	46-55.30	124-02.70	11815.64	28066.82	18502
WA	GRAYS HARBOR	GRAYS HARBOR RANGE A LIGHT	46-55.20	124-02.90	11816.65	28066.46	18502
WA	GRAYS HARBOR	GRAYS HARBOR S REACH NO 16	46-55.10	124-04.90	11821.55	28063.52	18502
WA	GRAYS HARBOR	GRAYS HARBOR S REACH RANGE	46-55.10	124-03.60	11818.75	28065.38	18502
WA	GRAYS HARBOR	GRAYS HARBOR WHISTLE NO 3	46-55.00	124-14.70	11842.92	28049.45	18502
WA	GRAYS HARBOR	POINT CHEHALIS NO 4	46-54.90	124-06.80	11826.79	28060.65	18502
WA	GRAYS HARBOR	POINT CHEHALIS NO 2	46-54.80	124-07.10	11828.01	28060.14	18502
WA	GRAYS HARBOR	WESTHAVEN COVE NO 7	46-54.80	124-06.30	11826.31	28061.29	18502
WA	GRAYS HARBOR	GRAYS HARBOR GONG NO 5	46-54.70	124-12.50	11840.05	28052.35	18502
WA	GRAYS HARBOR	GRAYS HARBOR ENTRANCE NO 9	46-54.70	124-09.80	11834.34	28056.21	18502
WA	GRAYS HARBOR	GRAYS HARBOR CHANNEL NO 11	46-54.70	124-08.70	11832.01	28057.78	18502
WA	GRAYS HARBOR	GRAYS HARBOR BOAT WARNING	46-54.70	124-06.80	11827.96	28060.50	18502
WA	GRAYS HARBOR	WESTHAVEN COVE BRKWTR NO 8	46-54.60	124-06.40	11827.69	28061.00	18502
WA	GRAYS HARBOR	WESTHAVEN COVE SE NO 1	46-54.40	124-06.10	11828.22	28061.29	18502
WA	GRAYS HARBOR	GRAYS HARBOR WHISTLE NO 6	46-54.30	124-11.10	11839.43	28054.05	18502
WA	GRAYS HARBOR	GRAYS HARBOR WHISTLE NO 4	46-53.70	124-11.70	11844.22	28052.75	18502
WA	GRAYS HARBOR	GRAYS HARBOR LIGHT	46-53.30	124-06.90	11836.42	28059.33	18500
WA	GRAYS HARBOR	GRAYS HARBOR LIGHT	46-53.30	124-06.90	11836.42	28059.33	18502
WA	GRAYS HARBOR	GRAYS HARBOR WHISTLE GH	46-51.90	124-14.30	11860.27	28047.68	18502
WA	GRAYS HARBOR	GRAYS HARBOR WHISTLE GH	46-51.90	124-14.30	11860.27	28047.68	18500
WA	JEFFERSON	DESTRUCTION ISLAND LIGHT	47-40.50	124-29.10	11640.59	28062.24	18500
WA	PACIFIC	WILLAPA LIGHT	46-44.10	124-04.90	11887.91	28055.40	18504
WA	PACIFIC	WILLAPA BAY LIGHT	46-44.10	124-04.90	11887.91	28055.40	18500
WA	PACIFIC	WILLAPA BAY ENTRANCE NO 8	46-43.50	124-05.30	11892.46	28054.37	18504
WA	PACIFIC	WILLAPA BAY ENTRANCE NO 10	46-43.40	124-03.90	11890.17	28056.34	18504
WA	PACIFIC	WILLAPA BAY ENTRANCE NO 6	46-43.30	124-06.10	11895.37	28053.04	18504
WA	PACIFIC	WILLAPA BAY ENTRANCE B	46-42.90	124-07.30	11900.34	28050.98	18504
WA	PACIFIC	WILLAPA RIVER RANGE LIGHT	46-42.60	123-51.20	11868.32	28074.56	18504
WA	PACIFIC	TOKE POINT JETTY NO 3	46-42.50	123-57.90	11883.21	28064.53	18504

(900315clc)   Page 67   Copyright 1990

PASSES

STATE/COUNTRY	COUNTY/PROV	NAME	LAT	LON	TD#1	TD#2	CHART NO
WA	PACIFIC	TOKE POINT BASIN NO 4	46-42.50	123-57.90	11883.21	28064.53	18504
WA	PACIFIC	WILLAPA BAY ENTRANCE A	46-42.30	124-09.10	11907.79	28047.88	18504
WA	PACIFIC	WILLAPA RIVER CHANNEL NO 19	46-42.20	123-53.20	11875.13	28071.29	18504
WA	PACIFIC	CEDAR RIVER FLATS NO 2	46-42.10	123-57.60	11885.10	28064.68	18504
WA	PACIFIC	WILLAPA BAY ENTRANCE NO 13	46-42.00	124-01.00	11892.88	28059.57	18504
WA	PACIFIC	WILLAPA BAY CHANNEL NO 15	46-41.90	124-00.10	11891.62	28060.83	18504
WA	PACIFIC	WILLAPA BAY WHISTLE W	46-41.80	124-10.80	11914.38	28045.00	18500
WA	PACIFIC	WILLAPA BAY WHISTLE W	46-41.80	124-10.80	11914.38	28045.00	18504
WA	PACIFIC	WILLAPA BAY CHANNEL NO 16	46-41.80	123-58.30	11888.47	28063.42	18504
WA	PACIFIC	WILLAPA RIVER NO 1	46-41.80	123-57.60	11887.00	28064.46	18504
WA	PACIFIC	WILLAPA RIVER CHANNEL NO 10	46-41.80	123-54.90	11881.29	28068.47	18504
WA	PACIFIC	WILLAPA RIVER RANGE LIGHT	46-41.60	123-57.30	11887.63	28064.76	18504
WA	PACIFIC	WILLAPA RIVER RANGE C	46-41.40	123-49.10	11871.45	28076.84	18504
WA	PACIFIC	S WILLAPA BAY NO 3	46-41.20	123-59.50	11894.78	28061.19	18504
WA	PACIFIC	WILLAPA RIVER CHANNEL NO 59	46-40.80	123-45.90	11868.40	28081.21	18504
WA	PACIFIC	BAY CENTER CHANNEL NO 11	46-38.80	123-57.00	11904.85	28063.13	18504
WA	PACIFIC	BAY CENTER CHANNEL NO 2	46-38.60	123-59.30	11910.92	28059.54	18504
WA	PACIFIC	LEADBETTER POINT NO 1	46-38.40	124-07.20	11928.45	28047.66	18504
WA	PACIFIC	LEADBETTER POINT NO 1	46-38.40	124-07.20	11928.45	28047.66	18500
WA	PACIFIC	BAY CENTER CHANNEL NO 6	46-38.40	123-58.20	11909.92	28061.04	18504
WA	PACIFIC	PALIX RIVER NO 15	46-37.90	123-56.50	11909.60	28063.20	18504
WA	PACIFIC	S WILLAPA BAY NO 7	46-36.60	123-58.40	11921.95	28059.38	18504
WA	PACIFIC	NEMAH RIVER CHANNEL NO 1	46-34.60	123-56.80	11931.67	28060.27	18504
WA	PACIFIC	NAHCOTTA CHANNEL NO 10	46-34.30	123-58.60	11937.34	28057.34	18504
WA	PACIFIC	LONG ISLAND JUNCTION LIGHT	46-32.30	123-58.60	11950.49	28055.80	18504
WA	PACIFIC	STANLEY CHANNEL DAYBEACON NO 2	46-31.20	123-58.50	11957.57	28055.11	18504
WA	PACIFIC	STANLEY CHANNEL NO 4	46-29.00	123-57.80	11970.85	28054.47	18504
WA	PACIFIC	NAHCOTTA CHANNEL NO 17	46-27.20	124-00.30	11987.95	28049.25	18504
WA	PACIFIC	NORTH HEAD LIGHT	46-18.00	124-04.60	12059.33	28035.21	18500
WA	PACIFIC	CAPE DISAPPOINTMENT LIGHT	46-16.60	124-03.10	12066.30	28036.37	18500
WA	PACIFIC	NOAA BUOY 46005	46-05.00	130-60.00	12594.53	27562.69	530
WA	PUGET SOUND	SWINOMISH S CHANNEL NO 1	48-21.80	122-33.20	11235.24	28232.03	18421
WA	PUGET SOUND	SWINOMISH S CHANNEL NO 4	48-21.70	122-33.10	11235.27	28232.12	18421
WA	PUGET SOUND	SWINOMISH RANGE LIGHT	48-21.60	122-34.00	11237.45	28230.95	18421
WA	PUGET SOUND	SKAGIT BAY NO 10	48-21.10	122-32.90	11236.33	28232.19	18421
WA	PUGET SOUND	ROSARIO STRAIT BUOY RA	48-19.80	122-58.60	11295.57	28199.06	18465
WA	PUGET SOUND	MINOR ISLAND LIGHT	48-19.50	122-49.10	11275.68	28211.02	18465
WA	PUGET SOUND	SKAGIT BAY NO 6	48-19.50	122-30.60	11235.34	28234.63	18421
WA	PUGET SOUND	SMITH ISLAND LIGHT	48-19.10	122-50.60	11280.05	28208.96	18465
WA	PUGET SOUND	SKAGIT BAY NO 4	48-18.20	122-29.00	11235.13	28236.29	18421
WA	PUGET SOUND	STRAWBERRY POINT NO 3	48-18.00	122-30.10	11238.04	28234.81	18421
WA	PUGET SOUND	POINT POLNELL LIGHT	48-16.40	122-33.50	11249.68	28229.94	18441
WA	PUGET SOUND	OAK HARBOR NO 7	48-16.30	122-38.90	11261.92	28222.96	18441
WA	PUGET SOUND	SKAGIT BAY NO 2	48-16.30	122-30.20	11242.64	28234.16	18421

PASSES

STATE/COUNTRY	COUNTY/PROV	NAME	LAT	LON	TD#1	TD#2	CHART NO
WA	PUGET SOUND	PARTRIDGE BANK NO 3	48-15.50	122-50.00	11288.81	28208.43	18465
WA	PUGET SOUND	OAK HARBOR NO 2	48-15.50	122-37.50	11260.97	28224.50	18441
WA	PUGET SOUND	PENN COVE SEA FARM LIGHT	48-14.00	122-43.00	11277.43	28216.90	18441
WA	PUGET SOUND	SNATELUM POINT NO 1	48-13.70	122-37.10	11265.01	28224.42	18441
WA	PUGET SOUND	POINT PARTRIDGE LIGHT	48-13.40	122-46.10	11286.10	28212.69	18465
WA	PUGET SOUND	POINT PARTRIDGE NO 5	48-13.20	122-46.90	11288.48	28211.59	18465
WA	PUGET SOUND	PENN CCOVE MUSSEL RAFT LIGHT	48-13.20	122-42.10	11277.67	28217.79	18441
WA	PUGET SOUND	WEST COAST BLUE MUSSEL LIGHT	48-13.10	122-42.60	11279.08	28217.11	18441
WA	PUGET SOUND	ONAMAC POINT REEF A	48-11.30	122-32.40	11261.07	28229.73	18441
WA	PUGET SOUND	ONAMAC POINT REEF B	48-11.10	122-32.40	11261.63	28229.66	18441
WA	PUGET SOUND	KEYSTONE HARBOR NO 1	48-09.40	122-40.30	11284.59	28218.81	18441
WA	PUGET SOUND	KEYSTONE HARBOR NO 2	48-09.40	122-40.20	11284.36	28218.94	18441
WA	PUGET SOUND	POINT WILSON NO 6	48-09.20	122-45.80	11297.80	28211.58	18471
WA	PUGET SOUND	McCURDY POINT NO 4	48-08.70	122-50.60	11310.34	28205.15	18471
WA	PUGET SOUND	POINT HUDSON LIGHT	48-07.00	122-44.90	11302.44	28211.96	18441
WA	PUGET SOUND	PROTECTION ISLAND SPIT NO 1	48-06.90	122-57.80	11332.55	28195.09	18471
WA	PUGET SOUND	PORT OF PORT TOWNSEND DOLPHIN	48-06.90	122-45.20	11303.44	28211.53	18441
WA	PUGET SOUND	PORT OF PORT TOWNSEND DOLPHIN	48-06.90	122-45.10	11303.21	28211.66	18441
WA	PUGET SOUND	PORT TOWNSEND BRKWTR NO 1	48-06.50	122-46.20	11307.00	28210.08	18441
WA	PUGET SOUND	BLUE WATER SALMON FARM	48-06.20	122-46.50	11308.64	28209.58	18441
WA	PUGET SOUND	HOLMES HARBOR NO 1	48-06.20	122-31.80	11274.38	28228.86	18441
WA	PUGET SOUND	MARROWSTONE POINT LIGHT	48-06.10	122-41.20	11296.61	28216.48	18441
WA	PUGET SOUND	KILLSUT HARBOR NO 2	48-04.80	122-44.50	11308.37	28211.69	18441
WA	PUGET SOUND	TULALIP TRIBES BRKWTR A	48-03.70	122-16.70	11246.19	28248.04	18441
WA	PUGET SOUND	KALA POINT LIGHT NO 2	48-03.50	122-45.90	11315.80	28209.37	18441
WA	PUGET SOUND	TULALIP BAY BUOY NO 2	48-03.30	122-17.60	11249.48	28246.73	18441
WA	PUGET SOUND	CAMANO HEAD ROCKS NO 1	48-03.00	122-21.20	11258.90	28241.87	18441
WA	PUGET SOUND	NEPTUNE SEA FARM LIGHTS	48-02.80	122-31.90	11284.93	28227.62	18441
WA	PUGET SOUND	RACE LAGOON SEAFOODS LIGHTS	48-02.70	122-31.80	11285.00	28227.71	18441
WA	PUGET SOUND	LANGLEY BRKWTR LIGHT A	48-02.30	122-24.10	11267.89	28237.80	18441
WA	PUGET SOUND	LANGLEY BRKWTR LIGHT B	48-02.30	122-24.10	11267.89	28237.80	18441
WA	PUGET SOUND	LANGLEY BRKWTR LIGHT C	48-02.30	122-24.00	11267.66	28237.93	18441
WA	PUGET SOUND	LANGLEY BRKWTR LIGHT D	48-02.30	122-24.00	11267.66	28237.93	18441
WA	PUGET SOUND	SANDY POINT LIGHT NO 1	48-02.10	122-22.50	11264.68	28239.87	18441
WA	PUGET SOUND	PUGET SOUND TRAFFIC BUOY SC	48-01.90	122-38.10	11302.49	28219.10	18441
WA	PUGET SOUND	BUSH POINT LIGHT	48-01.80	122-36.30	11298.52	28221.45	18441
WA	PUGET SOUND	SNOHOMISH RIVER NO 5A	48-01.20	122-12.90	11244.38	28252.39	18441
WA	PUGET SOUND	ANTHONYS LIGHTHOUSE RANGE C	48-01.10	122-13.10	11245.15	28252.10	18441
WA	PUGET SOUND	STEAMBOAT FLATS LIGHT	48-00.90	122-16.20	11253.18	28247.90	18441
WA	PUGET SOUND	ANTHONYS LIGHTHOUSE RANGE B	48-00.90	122-13.40	11246.46	28251.64	18441
WA	PUGET SOUND	ANTHONYS LIGHTHOUSE RANGE A	48-00.60	122-13.50	11247.58	28251.42	18441
WA	PUGET SOUND	GEDNEY ISLAND NO 1	48-00.30	122-17.70	11258.59	28245.72	18441
WA	PUGET SOUND	OAK BAY NO 2	48-00.20	122-41.50	11316.11	28213.99	18441
WA	PUGET SOUND	GEDNEY ISLAND FISHING REEF B	47-59.90	122-18.40	11261.50	28244.67	18441

PASSES

STATE/COUNTRY	COUNTY/PROV	NAME	LAT	LON	TD#1	TD#2	CHART NO
WA	PUGET SOUND	GEDNEY ISLAND FISHING REEF A	47-59.80	122-18.60	11262.28	28244.38	18441
WA	PUGET SOUND	ANTHONYS LIGHTHOUSE	47-59.70	122-13.40	11250.01	28251.30	18441
WA	PUGET SOUND	SNOHOMISH RIVER RANGE LIGHT	47-59.50	122-13.30	11250.37	28251.38	18441
WA	PUGET SOUND	PORT GARDNER NO 1	47-59.40	122-15.10	11255.03	28248.94	18441
WA	PUGET SOUND	PORT GARDNER ANCHORAGE AO	47-58.90	122-14.70	11255.57	28249.33	18441
WA	PUGET SOUND	SNOHOMISH RIVER NO 3	47-58.90	122-13.90	11253.63	28250.41	18441
WA	PUGET SOUND	CLINTON SHOAL BUOY	47-58.60	122-20.90	11271.57	28240.94	18441
WA	PUGET SOUND	DOUBLE BLUFF LIGHT	47-58.10	122-32.70	11301.83	28224.98	18441
WA	PUGET SOUND	PUGET SOUND TRAFFIC BUOY SD	47-57.90	122-34.70	11307.34	28222.24	18441
WA	PUGET SOUND	MATS MATS BAY NO 1	47-57.80	122-40.20	11320.99	28214.86	18441
WA	PUGET SOUND	MATS MATS BAY RANGE LIGHT	47-57.70	122-41.10	11323.50	28213.62	18441
WA	PUGET SOUND	MATS MATS BAY CHANNEL NO 5	47-57.70	122-41.00	11323.26	28213.75	18441
WA	PUGET SOUND	MATS MATS BAY CHANNEL NO 3	47-57.70	122-40.80	11322.78	28214.02	18441
WA	PUGET SOUND	KLAS ROCKS NO 2	47-57.70	122-40.20	11321.33	28214.82	18441
WA	PUGET SOUND	MATS MATS BAY CHANNEL NO 6	47-57.60	122-41.10	11323.84	28213.58	18441
WA	PUGET SOUND	MATS MATS BAY CHANNEL NO 7	47-57.40	122-41.10	11324.52	28213.51	18441
WA	PUGET SOUND	MATS MATS BAY CHANNEL NO 8	47-57.40	122-41.10	11324.52	28213.51	18441
WA	PUGET SOUND	COLVOS ROCKS LIGHT	47-57.10	122-40.10	11323.12	28214.74	18441
WA	PUGET SOUND	WASHINGTON STATE FERRY DOLPHIN	47-57.00	122-18.10	11269.76	28244.21	18441
WA	PUGET SOUND	MUKILTEO LIGHT	47-56.90	122-18.30	11270.57	28243.91	18441
WA	PUGET SOUND	PORT LUDLOW NO 2	47-56.50	122-39.40	11323.47	28215.46	18441
WA	PUGET SOUND	TALA POINT JUNCTION LIGHT	47-55.90	122-39.30	11325.28	28215.38	18441
WA	PUGET SOUND	FOUL WEATHER BLUFF NO 1	47-55.90	122-37.10	11319.91	28218.33	18441
WA	PUGET SOUND	PUGET SOUND TRAFFIC BUOY SE	47-55.40	122-29.50	11302.99	28228.37	18441
WA	PUGET SOUND	PORT LUDLOW NO 4	47-55.30	122-40.80	11331.01	28213.15	18441
WA	PUGET SOUND	SKUNK BAY LIGHT	47-55.20	122-34.10	11314.96	28222.11	18441
WA	PUGET SOUND	POINT NO POINT LIGHT	47-54.70	122-31.50	11310.28	28225.44	18441
WA	PUGET SOUND	SCATCHET HEAD NO 1	47-54.50	122-26.20	11297.87	28232.52	18441
WA	PUGET SOUND	CUTLUS BAY ENTRANCE NO 1	47-54.50	122-24.00	11292.42	28235.49	18441
WA	PUGET SOUND	POSSESSION POINT REEF A	47-53.80	122-23.60	11293.77	28235.81	18441
WA	PUGET SOUND	POSSESSION POINT REEF B	47-53.80	122-23.20	11292.78	28236.35	18441
WA	PUGET SOUND	POSSESSION POINT NO 1	47-53.80	122-23.00	11292.28	28236.62	18441
WA	PUGET SOUND	POINT HANNON NO 2	47-53.30	122-36.50	11327.46	28218.21	18441
WA	PUGET SOUND	ALLSEASONS AQUAFARM BUOYS	47-52.90	122-36.70	11329.36	28217.80	18441
WA	PUGET SOUND	PORT GAMBLE RANGE LIGHT	47-52.80	122-34.60	11324.51	28220.60	18441
WA	PUGET SOUND	BYWATER BAY AQUACULTURE	47-52.30	122-37.60	11333.71	28216.37	18441
WA	PUGET SOUND	BRIDGE WEST CHANNEL SIGNAL	47-52.00	122-38.00	11335.78	28215.72	18441
WA	PUGET SOUND	PORT GAMBLE LIGHT NO 1	47-51.80	122-34.60	11328.05	28220.25	18441
WA	PUGET SOUND	CASE SHOAL DAYBEACON	47-51.50	122-40.40	11343.52	28212.29	18441
WA	PUGET SOUND	SISTERS ROCK NO 4	47-51.50	122-38.40	11338.57	28215.00	18441
WA	PUGET SOUND	CASE SHOAL NO 6	47-50.70	122-40.10	11345.69	28212.41	18441
WA	PUGET SOUND	CASE SHOAL NO 5	47-49.50	122-38.80	11346.86	28213.73	18441
WA	PUGET SOUND	APPLE COVE POINT LIGHT	47-48.90	122-28.80	11323.93	28227.13	18441
WA	PUGET SOUND	EDMONDS UNDERWATER PARK BUOYS	47-48.90	122-23.10	11309.48	28234.92	18441

PASSES

STATE/COUNTRY	COUNTY/PROV	NAME	LAT	LON	TD#1	TD#2	CHART NO
WA	PUGET SOUND	CASE SHOAL NO 8	47-48.80	122-42.80	11359.45	28208.03	18441
WA	PUGET SOUND	EDMONDS FISHING REEF	47-48.70	122-23.30	11310.70	28234.58	18441
WA	PUGET SOUND	EDMONDS BOAT HARBOR NO 1	47-48.60	122-23.40	11311.32	28234.41	18441
WA	PUGET SOUND	EDMONDS STORM SEWER OUTFALL	47-48.40	122-23.70	11312.80	28233.94	18441
WA	PUGET SOUND	EDMONDS S BRKWTR LIGHT	47-48.40	122-23.60	11312.54	28234.08	18441
WA	PUGET SOUND	QUILCENE BAY PISH PEN A	47-47.30	122-51.00	11385.58	28196.30	18441
WA	PUGET SOUND	QUILCENE BAY FISH PEN B	47-47.30	122-51.00	11385.58	28196.30	18441
WA	PUGET SOUND	SANDY POINT LIGHT NO 2	47-47.20	122-42.70	11365.27	28207.56	18421
WA	PUGET SOUND	POINT WELLS RANGE LIGHT	47-47.00	122-23.60	11317.62	28233.62	18441
WA	PUGET SOUND	POINT WELLS FOG SIGNAL	47-46.90	122-23.80	11318.49	28233.31	18441
WA	PUGET SOUND	QUILCENE BAY NO 2	47-46.70	122-51.10	11388.16	28195.93	18441
WA	PUGET SOUND	PUGET SOUND TRAFFIC BUOY SF	47-45.90	122-26.20	11328.34	28229.69	18441
WA	PUGET SOUND	BANGOR EXPLOSIVE ANCHORAGE A	47-45.80	122-43.40	11372.42	28206.07	18441
WA	PUGET SOUND	WHITNEY POINT WARNING LIGHT	47-45.70	122-51.00	11391.84	28195.65	18441
WA	PUGET SOUND	TRIDENT SUBMARINE RANGE LIGHT	47-45.20	122-45.30	11379.54	28203.24	18441
WA	PUGET SOUND	KENMORE CHANNEL NO 2	47-45.20	122-15.70	11303.83	28243.93	18447
WA	PUGET SOUND	KENMORE CHANNEL NO 4	47-45.20	122-15.60	11303.57	28244.07	18447
WA	PUGET SOUND	BOEING CREEK REEF A	47-45.10	122-23.10	11323.36	28233.69	18441
WA	PUGET SOUND	BOEING CREEK REEF B	47-44.90	122-23.10	11324.11	28233.63	18441
WA	PUGET SOUND	TABOOK POINT NO 18	47-44.80	122-48.50	11389.15	28198.71	18441
WA	PUGET SOUND	BANGOR EXPLOSIVE ANCHORAGE B	47-44.40	122-44.40	11380.43	28204.16	18441
WA	PUGET SOUND	PULALI POINT LIGHT	47-44.20	122-51.00	11397.80	28195.04	18441
WA	PUGET SOUND	SEAL ROCK DAYBEACON	47-42.90	122-52.90	11407.81	28191.91	18441
WA	PUGET SOUND	AGATE PASSAGE NO 4	47-42.50	122-34.10	11361.71	28217.62	18441
WA	PUGET SOUND	POINT MONROE LIGHT	47-42.50	122-30.60	11352.69	28222.45	18441
WA	PUGET SOUND	LIBERTY BAY DAYBEACON NO 2	47-42.40	122-37.60	11371.09	28212.75	18441
WA	PUGET SOUND	AGATE PASS SLAMON PEN LIGHT	47-42.30	122-34.60	11363.79	28216.85	18441
WA	PUGET SOUND	TREASURE ISLAND SHOAL NO 2	47-41.90	122-32.10	11358.93	28220.17	18441
WA	PUGET SOUND	POINT BOLIN REEF NO 6	47-41.80	122-34.50	11365.52	28216.81	18441
WA	PUGET SOUND	MEADOW POINT NO 1	47-41.80	122-24.50	11339.60	28230.66	18441
WA	PUGET SOUND	JUANITA BAY SHOAL DAYBEACON	47-41.80	122-13.00	11309.42	28246.64	18447
WA	PUGET SOUND	HAZEL POINT LIGHT	47-41.60	122-46.10	11395.98	28200.72	18441
WA	PUGET SOUND	HOOD CANAL NO 11	47-41.60	122-44.80	11392.68	28202.51	18441
WA	PUGET SOUND	TSKUTSKO POINT LIGHT	47-41.50	122-49.90	11406.01	28195.45	18441
WA	PUGET SOUND	DOSEWALLIPS FLATS NO 15	47-41.20	122-52.60	11414.04	28191.61	18441
WA	PUGET SOUND	PARK DEPT BOAT RAMP LIGHT	47-41.20	122-24.20	11341.17	28230.88	18441
WA	PUGET SOUND	OAK HEAD LIGHT NO 12	47-40.90	122-48.60	11405.20	28196.99	18441
WA	PUGET SOUND	SHILSHOLE BAY APPROACH	47-40.90	122-25.10	11344.71	28229.53	18441
WA	PUGET SOUND	SHILSHOLE ENTRANCE NO 1	47-40.80	122-24.80	11344.32	28229.91	18447
WA	PUGET SOUND	SHILSHOLE ENTRANCE NO 2	47-40.60	122-24.90	11345.37	28229.70	18447
WA	PUGET SOUND	SHILSHOLE BAY BRKWTR NO 3	47-40.60	122-24.70	11344.85	28229.98	18441
WA	PUGET SOUND	SHILSHOLE INNER NO 8	47-40.30	122-24.40	11345.25	28230.30	18447
WA	PUGET SOUND	LOWER GUIDE WALL LIGHT	47-40.10	122-24.30	11345.79	28230.37	18447
WA	PUGET SOUND	SHILSHOLE APPROACH BELL	47-40.00	122-24.10	11345.66	28230.62	18447

PASSES

STATE/COUNTRY	COUNTY/PROV	NAME	LAT	LON	TD#1	TD#2	CHART NO
WA	PUGET SOUND	SHILSHOLE RANGE LIGHT	47-40.00	122-24.10	11345.66	28230.62	18447
WA	PUGET SOUND	HOOD CANAL NO 11A	47-39.70	122-47.10	11406.37	28198.58	18441
WA	PUGET SOUND	PUGET SOUND TRAFFIC BUOY SG	47-39.70	122-27.80	11356.56	28225.36	18441
WA	PUGET SOUND	WEST POINT LIGHT	47-39.70	122-26.10	11352.11	28227.73	18441
WA	PUGET SOUND	MISERY POINT REEF BUOY A	47-39.60	122-49.60	11413.14	28195.08	18441
WA	PUGET SOUND	MISERY POINT REEF BUOY B	47-39.40	122-49.90	11414.74	28194.58	18441
WA	PUGET SOUND	HOOD CANAL NO 13	47-39.40	122-49.60	11413.98	28195.00	18441
WA	PUGET SOUND	WEBSTER POINT LIGHT NO 33	47-38.90	122-16.50	11329.96	28240.87	18447
WA	PUGET SOUND	LAKE UNION TEST AREA A	47-38.40	122-20.20	11341.79	28235.53	18447
WA	PUGET SOUND	NATL OCEAN SERVICE DOLPHIN	47-38.20	122-19.80	11341.53	28236.03	18447
WA	PUGET SOUND	LAKE UNION SHOAL NO 2	47-37.80	122-20.20	11344.21	28235.33	18447
WA	PUGET SOUND	SMITH COVE NO 1	47-37.70	122-23.00	11352.05	28231.38	18448
WA	PUGET SOUND	ELLIOTT BAY FISH HAVEN A	47-37.50	122-22.40	11351.28	28232.15	18448
WA	PUGET SOUND	ELLIOTT BAY FISH HAVEN B	47-37.50	122-22.30	11351.01	28232.29	18448
WA	PUGET SOUND	EAGLE HARBOR NO 4	47-37.30	122-29.80	11371.64	28221.72	18441
WA	PUGET SOUND	SHIPMATES LIGHT	47-37.30	122-21.80	11350.50	28232.93	18448
WA	PUGET SOUND	WING POINT REEF NO 2	47-36.80	122-29.10	11371.89	28222.53	18441
WA	PUGET SOUND	TYEE SHOAL LIGHT	47-36.60	122-29.20	11372.99	28222.31	18441
WA	PUGET SOUND	N LESCHI BRKWTR LIGHTS	47-36.30	122-16.80	11341.26	28239.63	18447
WA	PUGET SOUND	S LESCHI BRKWTR LIGHTS	47-36.10	122-16.90	11342.35	28239.42	18447
WA	PUGET SOUND	DUWAMISH HEAD LIGHT	47-35.90	122-23.20	11360.03	28230.49	18448
WA	PUGET SOUND	BASS POINT LIGHT	47-35.70	122-39.60	11404.03	28207.42	18441
WA	PUGET SOUND	BLAKELY ROCK LIGHT	47-35.70	122-28.80	11375.72	28222.55	18441
WA	PUGET SOUND	RICH PASSAGE NO 8	47-35.60	122-32.50	11385.90	28217.33	18441
WA	PUGET SOUND	WATERMAN POINT NO 11	47-35.10	122-34.20	11392.51	28214.76	18441
WA	PUGET SOUND	ALASKA RAIL CAR CO NO 2	47-35.10	122-22.20	11360.71	28231.63	18448
WA	PUGET SOUND	ALASKA RAIL CAR CO NO 1	47-35.10	122-22.10	11360.44	28231.77	18448
WA	PUGET SOUND	DECATUR REEF LIGHT NO 2	47-34.90	122-28.50	11378.33	28222.69	18448
WA	PUGET SOUND	ORCHARD ROCKS FISH PEN	47-34.60	122-31.70	11388.08	28218.08	18441
WA	PUGET SOUND	VIKING SALMON PEN LIGHT	47-34.60	122-31.70	11388.08	28218.08	18441
WA	PUGET SOUND	PUGET SOUND TRAFFIC BUOY T	47-34.60	122-27.00	11375.63	28224.70	18448
WA	PUGET SOUND	ALKI POINT LIGHT	47-34.60	122-25.20	11370.84	28227.23	18448
WA	PUGET SOUND	WEST WATERWAY CONTROL LIGHTS	47-34.30	122-21.30	11361.69	28232.63	18448
WA	PUGET SOUND	BAINBRIDGE REEF BUOY NO 4	47-34.20	122-31.10	11388.22	28218.78	18441
WA	PUGET SOUND	POINT HERRON NO 12	47-33.90	122-36.70	11404.27	28210.79	18441
WA	PUGET SOUND	ORCHARD POINT LIGHT	47-33.90	122-31.80	11391.37	28217.69	18441
WA	PUGET SOUND	WEST SEATTLE REEF BUOY	47-33.40	122-24.40	11373.85	28227.95	18448
WA	PUGET SOUND	GEORGETOWN REACH RANGE LIGHT	47-32.60	122-20.10	11365.74	28233.76	18448
WA	PUGET SOUND	BLAKE ISLAND EAST LIGHT	47-32.50	122-28.80	11389.52	28221.41	18448
WA	PUGET SOUND	BLAKE ISLAND REEF BUOY A	47-31.80	122-29.40	11394.21	28220.31	18448
WA	PUGET SOUND	BLAKE ISLAND REEF BUOY B	47-31.70	122-29.40	11394.65	28220.27	18448
WA	PUGET SOUND	FAUNTLEROY COVE FOG SIGNAL	47-31.40	122-23.70	11380.69	28228.25	18448
WA	PUGET SOUND	POINT VASHON LIGHT	47-30.80	122-28.30	11395.71	28221.51	18448
WA	PUGET SOUND	THREE TREE POINT LIGHT	47-27.00	122-22.80	11398.15	28228.00	18448

PASSES

STATE/COUNTRY	COUNTY/PROV	NAME	LAT	LON	TD#1	TD#2	CHART NO
WA	PUGET SOUND	PUGET SOUND TRAFFIC BUOY TA	47-26.90	122-24.20	11402.43	28225.96	18448
WA	PUGET SOUND	POINT HEYER REEF BUOY B	47-25.20	122-25.50	11413.94	28223.49	18448
WA	PUGET SOUND	POINT HEYER REEF BUOY A	47-25.10	122-25.60	11414.69	28223.31	18448
WA	PUGET SOUND	ROBINSON POINT LIGHT	47-23.30	122-22.40	11414.56	28227.28	18448
WA	PUGET SOUND	PUGET SOUND TRAFFIC BUOY TB	47-23.10	122-21.10	11411.95	28229.09	18448
WA	PUGET SOUND	POINT VASHON NO 6	47-22.70	122-32.30	11444.41	28212.76	18448
WA	PUGET SOUND	SALTWATER STATE PARK	47-22.40	122-19.60	11411.21	28231.02	18448
WA	PUGET SOUND	QUARTERMASTER HARB SHOAL NO 2	47-21.00	122-28.60	11442.78	28217.47	18448
WA	PUGET SOUND	PUGET SOUND TRAFFIC BUOY TC	47-19.50	122-27.30	11446.75	28218.79	18448
WA	PUGET SOUND	POINT DEFIANCE LIGHT	47-19.00	122-32.80	11464.24	28210.60	18448
WA	PUGET SOUND	KOPACHUCK STATE PARK BUOY	47-18.60	122-41.40	11489.33	28197.95	18448
WA	PUGET SOUND	BROWNS POINT LIGHT	47-18.40	122-26.60	11450.42	28219.40	18448
WA	PUGET SOUND	HYLEBOS WATERWAY LIGHT NO 1	47-17.20	122-24.70	11451.37	28221.73	18448
WA	PUGET SOUND	HYLEBOS WATERWAY W FOG SIGNAL	47-17.10	122-24.80	11452.16	28221.55	18448
WA	PUGET SOUND	HYLEBOS WATERWAY E FOG SIGNAL	47-17.10	122-24.60	11451.61	28221.85	18448
WA	PUGET SOUND	BLAIR WATERWAY LIGHT	47-16.70	122-24.80	11454.23	28221.40	18448
WA	PUGET SOUND	FOX ISLAND ROCK NO 1	47-16.50	122-38.70	11493.00	28201.00	18448
WA	PUGET SOUND	VON GELDERN COVE LIGHT	47-16.30	122-45.40	11511.84	28191.15	18448
WA	PUGET SOUND	COMMENCEMENT BAY SHOAL A	47-16.30	122-25.90	11459.34	28219.64	18448
WA	PUGET SOUND	SITCUM WATERWAY LIGHT	47-16.30	122-25.10	11457.14	28220.82	18448
WA	PUGET SOUND	PUYALLUP WATERWAY JETTY NO 1	47-16.20	122-25.50	11458.76	28220.19	18448
WA	PUGET SOUND	STATE FISHERIES SALMON PENS	47-16.10	122-38.70	11495.09	28200.83	18448
WA	PUGET SOUND	TACOMA CITY WATERWAY LIGHT	47-15.70	122-26.10	11463.03	28219.13	18448
WA	PUGET SOUND	KOPACHUCK TEST BUOY H	47-14.90	122-39.10	11502.49	28199.75	18448
WA	PUGET SOUND	KOPACHUCK STATE PART BUOY L	47-14.90	122-38.90	11501.96	28200.04	18448
WA	PUGET SOUND	KOPACHUCK TEST BUOY G	47-14.80	122-39.00	11502.76	28199.85	18448
WA	PUGET SOUND	WYCKOFF SHOAL NO 1	47-14.50	122-42.80	11514.47	28194.17	18448
WA	PUGET SOUND	PITT PASSAGE N SHOAL	47-13.60	122-42.70	11519.02	28193.92	18448
WA	PUGET SOUND	GIBSON POINT NO 6	47-13.10	122-36.00	11503.80	28203.55	18448
WA	PUGET SOUND	JOHNSON LIGHT	47-12.30	123-01.80	11575.68	28165.42	18448
WA	PUGET SOUND	TOLIVA SHOAL	47-12.20	122-36.40	11509.75	28202.59	18448
WA	PUGET SOUND	SQUAXIN ISLAND FISH PEN B	47-12.10	122-54.20	11557.26	28176.41	18448
WA	PUGET SOUND	ARCADIA LIGHT	47-11.90	122-56.20	11563.52	28173.39	18448
WA	PUGET SOUND	PEALE PASSAGE FISH PEN A	47-11.70	122-54.20	11559.44	28176.22	18448
WA	PUGET SOUND	EAGLE ISLAND REEF NO 9	47-11.40	122-41.90	11528.82	28194.14	18448
WA	PUGET SOUND	TOTTEN INLET DAYBEACON NO 1	47-11.30	122-56.50	11567.56	28172.67	18448
WA	PUGET SOUND	EAGLE ISLAND SECTOR LIGHT	47-11.30	122-41.70	11528.84	28194.40	18448
WA	PUGET SOUND	CARLYON BEACH LIGHT	47-10.90	122-56.20	11568.98	28172.91	18448
WA	PUGET SOUND	JOHNSON POINT NO 5	47-10.60	122-48.80	11551.42	28183.63	18448
WA	PUGET SOUND	BRAYTON PASSAGE NO 2	47-10.60	122-44.50	11540.11	28189.96	18448
WA	PUGET SOUND	HUNTER POINT LIGHT	47-10.50	122-55.10	11568.34	28174.34	18448
WA	PUGET SOUND	ITSAMI LEDGE REEF BUOY A	47-10.50	122-50.50	11556.41	28181.09	18448
WA	PUGET SOUND	ITSAMI LEDGE NO 7	47-10.40	122-50.10	11555.92	28181.63	18448
WA	PUGET SOUND	DEVILS HEAD LIGHT NO 4	47-09.90	122-45.80	11547.41	28187.73	18448

PASSES

STATE/COUNTRY	COUNTY/PROV	NAME	LAT	LON	TD#1	TD#2	CHART NO
WA	PUGET SOUND	DOFFLEMYER POINT LIGHT	47-08.50	122-54.40	11577.64	28174.41	18448
WA	PUGET SOUND	KAMILCHE SEA FARM A	47-07.50	123-01.20	11600.68	28163.90	18448
WA	PUGET SOUND	TOLMIE BEACH STATE PARK BUOY	47-07.50	122-46.20	11561.92	28186.06	18448
WA	PUGET SOUND	NISQUALLY FLATS NO 3	47-06.70	122-41.90	11555.11	28192.09	18448
WA	PUGET SOUND	BUDD INLET LIGHT NO 2	47-05.50	122-55.80	11598.25	28170.88	18448
WA	PUGET SOUND	WEST OPLYMPIA SHOAL NO 1	47-05.50	122-55.40	11597.22	28171.48	18448
WA	PUGET SOUND	OLYMPIA SHOAL LIGHT	47-05.50	122-55.10	11596.45	28171.92	18448
WA	PUGET SOUND	OLYMPIA ENTRANCE NO 2A	47-05.10	122-55.70	11600.29	28170.84	18448
WA	PUGET SOUND	OLYMPIA ENTRANCE NO 3	47-05.10	122-55.50	11599.78	28171.13	18448
WA	PUGET SOUND	OLYMPIA CHANNEL NO 4	47-04.40	122-55.70	11604.33	28170.49	18448
WA	PUGET SOUND	OLYMPIA INNER RANGE LIGHT	47-04.10	122-54.40	11602.72	28172.28	18448
WA	PUGET SOUND	EAST BAY JUNCTION DAYBEACON	47-03.90	122-54.40	11603.89	28172.18	18448
WA	PUGET SOUND	OLYMPIA RANGE LIGHT	47-03.90	122-54.30	11603.63	28172.33	18448
WA	PUGET SOUND	EAST BAY LIGHT NO 1	47-03.70	122-53.90	11603.76	28172.83	18448

CHAPTER 7

HEAVENLY HAVENS

The controlling coordinates in this chapter and those that follow — the coordinates to use when you input waypoints — are the TDs, not the latitudes and longitudes. Each pair of TDs in Chapters 7 through 13 was measured on site with the ASF function disabled, and if you track them down the same way (ASF function off) you should find pretty near the exact spot whose coordinates we recorded. The "local alignment" process described near the end of Chapter 3 isn't necessary when you're working with raw TDs in this fashion. You can, conceivably, jump aboard your freshly chartered or just-arrived boat in the marina, punch in the TDs for an anchorage 10 miles down the bay, and expect the loran to guide you to it with good precision.

Many loran receiver models, when operated in Lat/Lon mode, will automatically sift through and override available secondaries based on such variables as crossing angles and SNRs (see Chapter 3) to get the best fix. With these lorans, you may choose to navigate to the approximate waypoint in the Lat/Lon mode, then switch to TDs for the final zeroing in.

When giving the coordinates for havens, we offer no guarantees of privacy, solitude, quiet, or fine neighbors. When you find one or more of these, consider yourself in hog heaven and then hope for a good bottom.

Coordinates for these havens are included to provide a convenient listing of some of the places we have stayed and enjoyed. While the list is only rudimentary, it may serve a useful purpose to those who want to know what makes for a good "gunkhole."

Coordinates in this chapter are listed by state (or province or island group), county, description, latitude, longitude, time delay one, and time delay two. Review an updated chart of the area along with a local tide table whenever it is necessary to know for sure the high/low mean or actual water depth at any of these havens.

FOOD, FUN, FRIENDSHIP

People at most places will tolerate just about any legal activity around a boat and appreciate that a vacation is a time for fun. We have learned over the years that the nicest people can be found around boats, and there is no better time than evenings to spread good will and happiness around.

Share your catch with another boater and you're sure to meet some of the nicest people in the world. We often arrange to offer the meat for dinner if our new-found friends will bring the salad. (We have found that it is easier to procure fresh fish than fresh vegetables for salads.)

We share our bounty and catches with people we meet freely and encourage them to join in our fun. Look for the boat Sancho, with Captain Rod and First Mate Susie. Offer us a handshake and we will have fun from then on.

HAVENS

STATE/COUNTRY	COUNTY/PROV	NAME	LAT	LON	TD#1	TD#2	CHART NO
AK		ELFIN COVE ENTRANCE LIGHT NO 2	58-11.70	136-21.00	14747.46	28869.78	17300
AK		KNUDSON COVE BRKWTR	55-28.40	131-47.70	14503.70	26186.80	17420
AK		KNUDSON COVE DAYBEACON	55-28.40	131-47.70	14503.70	26186.80	17420
AK		LETNIKOF COVE LIGHT NO 2	59-10.40	135-23.90	15142.39	29234.64	17300
AK		NORWAY POINT MOORING BUOYS	58-18.50	134-26.40	14955.73	28495.46	17300
AK		POINT BAKER ANCHORAGE	56-21.60	133-37.00	14523.44	27148.33	17360
AK		PORT VALDEZ MOORING BUOY BM	61-05.30	146-24.60	14529.93	32231.65	16700
AK		REFUGE COVE DAYBEACON NO 3	55-24.10	131-44.90	14493.56	26149.35	17420
AK		REFUGE COVE ENTRANCE NO 2	55-24.00	131-44.90	14493.23	26148.90	17420
AK		SHELTER COVE BRKWTR NO 2	55-28.40	133-08.50	14373.83	26610.43	17400
AK		SWARD COAL DOLPHIN LIGHT	60-06.90	149-25.60	13280.51	31968.85	16680
AK		VIEW COVE ENTRANCE LIGHT	55-03.20	132-57.80	14305.61	26446.02	17400
AK	ALEUTIANS	KING COVE HARBOR LIGHT NO 2	55-03.60	162-19.30	18458.17	47008.54	16011
AK	ALEUTIANS	MASSACRE BAY MOORING BUOY	52-50.50	173-13.50	16205.30	49599.50	16012
AK	ALEUTIANS	ST CATHERINE COVE NO 4SC	54-59.90	163-29.30	18412.72	47444.34	16011
AK	ALEUTIANS	SWEEPER COVE ENTRANCE NO 5	51-51.50	176-35.30	14833.10	49771.80	16012
AK	ALEUTIANS	SWEEPER COVE JETTY NO 6	51-51.70	176-37.60	14820.57	49775.01	16012
AK	BERING SEA	CROWLEY MOORING BUOY	59-01.90	158-27.00	18744.26	45498.94	16006
AK	BERING SEA	CROWLEY MOORING LIGHTED BUOY	58-43.00	157-03.70	18748.25	44962.27	16006
CA	HUMBOLDT	SAMOA TURNING BASIN BUOY A	40-49.00	124-10.50	14809.63	43791.38	18622
CA	HUMBOLDT	SHELTER COVE ENTRANCE NO 1	40-00.60	124-03.50	15154.53	43691.84	18620
CA	LOS ANGELES	AVALON BAY, CATALINA IS	33-20.83	118-19.42	28162.59	40969.15	
CA	LOS ANGELES	BELMONT PIER ART REEF	33-45.30	118-08.80	28210.39	40987.49	
CA	LOS ANGELES	BELMONT PIER FOG SIGNAL	33-45.30	118-08.90	28210.15	40987.98	18746
CA	LOS ANGELES	HERMOSA BEACH PIER	33-51.70	118-24.30	28178.96	41083.77	18744
CA	LOS ANGELES	HYPERION HARBOR BUOY	33-55.30	118-26.30	28177.47	41105.79	18744
CA	LOS ANGELES	LONG BEACH PIER A	33-45.20	118-12.00	28202.62	41002.87	18746
CA	LOS ANGELES	LONG BEACH PIER D LIGHT A	33-45.90	118-13.10	28200.67	41010.40	18746
CA	LOS ANGELES	LONG BEACH PIER D LIGHT B	33-45.90	118-13.20	28200.43	41010.89	18746
CA	LOS ANGELES	MANHATTAN BEACH PIER REEF	33-53.00	118-24.80	28178.98	41090.59	
CA	LOS ANGELES	MARINA DEL REY PIER LIGHT	33-58.20	118-26.80	28179.06	41118.38	18744
CA	LOS ANGELES	REDONDO BEACH HARB ENTR	33-50.50	118-23.50	28179.78	41075.88	18744
CA	LOS ANGELES	REDONDO HARBOR ENTR NO 1	33-50.30	118-23.80	28178.85	41076.68	18744
CA	LOS ANGELES	REDONDO HARBOR LIGHT	33-50.90	118-23.60	28179.92	41077.69	18744
CA	LOS ANGELES	STA CATALINA HARBOR LIGHT	33-25.40	118-30.80	28139.74	41033.52	18757
CA	LOS ANGELES	VENICE FISHING PIER	33-58.60	118-28.20	28175.91	41126.68	18744
CA	LOS ANGELES	VENICE PIER REEF	33-59.10	118-28.60	28175.39	41130.43	
CA	MARIN	BELVEDERE COVE NO 1	37-52.30	122-27.20	16062.20	43216.20	18649
CA	MARIN	GLEN COVE MARINA LIGHT	38-03.90	122-12.80	16075.70	43273.87	18656
CA	MENDOCINO	ARENA COVE BUOY A	38-54.60	123-43.50	15577.03	43496.36	18640
CA	MONTEREY	MONTEREY HARB N NO 1	36-36.50	121-53.40	27508.78	42741.41	18685
CA	MONTEREY	MONTEREY HARBOR NO A	36-36.50	121-53.30	27509.20	42741.23	18685
CA	MONTEREY	MOSS LANDING ANCHORAGE	36-48.90	121-48.00	27517.24	42806.81	18685
CA	MONTEREY	MOSS LANDING HARB ENTR NO 2	36-48.30	121-47.30	27521.09	42801.97	18685

HAVENS

STATE/COUNTRY	COUNTY/PROV	NAME	LAT	LON	TD#1	TD#2	CHART NO
CA	MONTEREY	MOSS LANDING HARB ENTR RB	36-48.40	121-47.20	27521.42	42802.41	18685
CA	ORANGE	CABRILLO PIER ART REEF	33-42.70	118-16.80	28188.61	41018.58	
CA	ORANGE	DANA POINT HARBOR NO 8	33-27.40	117-41.60	28254.52	40808.29	18746
CA	ORANGE	FISH HARBOR CHANNEL NO 2	33-43.50	118-15.60	28192.28	41015.21	18746
CA	ORANGE	HARBOR REEF S BUOY	33-26.80	118-29.30	28144.45	41030.64	18757
CA	ORANGE	LA OUTER HARBOR MOORING	33-43.70	118-15.30	28193.20	41014.37	18746
CA	ORANGE	LA OUTER HARBOR MOORING A	33-43.90	118-15.00	28194.12	41013.52	18746
CA	ORANGE	LA OUTER HARBOR MOORING B	33-44.00	118-14.80	28194.70	41012.86	18746
CA	ORANGE	LA OUTER HARBOR MOORING C	33-44.00	118-14.60	28195.18	41011.89	18746
CA	ORANGE	LA OUTER HARBOR MOORING D	33-44.10	118-14.40	28195.75	41011.22	18746
CA	ORANGE	LONG BCH FIREBOAT PIER	33-44.90	118-12.90	28200.15	41006.36	18746
CA	ORANGE	LONG BCH HARB MOORING CR 1	33-44.40	118-09.40	28208.05	40987.73	18746
CA	ORANGE	LONG BCH HARB MOORING CR 2	33-44.40	118-09.40	28208.05	40987.73	18746
CA	ORANGE	LONG BCH HARB MOORING CR 3	33-44.40	118-08.80	28209.48	40984.79	18746
CA	ORANGE	LONG BEACH HARBOR MOORING	33-45.00	118-11.10	28204.58	40997.86	18746
CA	ORANGE	LONG BEACH HARBOR MOORING	33-44.80	118-11.10	28204.38	40997.25	18746
CA	ORANGE	LONG BEACH HARBOR MOORING	33-44.70	118-11.00	28204.52	40996.46	18746
CA	ORANGE	LONG BEACH HARBOR MOORING	33-44.60	118-10.90	28204.66	40995.68	18746
CA	ORANGE	LONG BEACH HARBOR MOORING	33-44.50	118-10.90	28204.56	40995.37	18746
CA	ORANGE	LONG BEACH HARBOR PIER "J"	33-44.30	118-11.10	28203.88	40995.74	18746
CA	ORANGE	LONG BEACH PIER F LIGHT F	33-44.40	118-12.40	28200.86	41002.39	18746
CA	ORANGE	LONG BEACH PIER J LIGHT 4	33-43.30	118-12.20	28200.25	40998.09	18746
CA	ORANGE	NEWPORT BAY ANCHORAGE "A"	33-36.00	117-54.30	28234.83	40890.41	18746
CA	ORANGE	NEWPORT BAY ANCHORAGE "B"	33-36.50	117-54.30	28235.35	40891.72	18746
CA	ORANGE	NEWPORT BAY ANCHORAGE "C"	33-36.60	117-54.40	28235.22	40892.47	18746
CA	ORANGE	NEWPORT BAY ANCHORAGE "D"	33-36.50	117-54.50	28234.89	40892.70	18746
CA	SAN DIEGO	CORONADO CAY PIER "C"	32-37.70	117-07.70	28275.41	40580.92	18773
CA	SAN DIEGO	HARBOR ISLAND E BASIN NO 1	32-43.50	117-11.20	28274.08	40601.17	18773
CA	SAN DIEGO	HARBOR ISLAND E BASIN NO 10	32-43.60	117-11.50	28273.59	40602.51	18773
CA	SAN DIEGO	HARBOR ISLAND E BASIN NO 12	32-43.60	117-11.60	28273.40	40602.91	18773
CA	SAN DIEGO	HARBOR ISLAND E BASIN NO 2	32-43.50	117-11.10	28274.28	40600.76	18773
CA	SAN DIEGO	HARBOR ISLAND E BASIN NO 3	32-43.50	117-11.30	28273.98	40601.69	18773
CA	SAN DIEGO	HARBOR ISLAND E BASIN NO 4	32-43.60	117-11.20	28274.18	40601.29	18773
CA	SAN DIEGO	HARBOR ISLAND E BASIN NO 6	32-43.60	117-11.30	28273.98	40601.69	18773
CA	SAN DIEGO	HARBOR ISLAND E BASIN NO 8	32-43.60	117-11.40	28273.79	40602.10	18773
CA	SAN DIEGO	HARBOR ISLAND LIGHT	32-43.50	117-12.70	28271.14	40607.29	18773
CA	SAN DIEGO	NAVY ANCHORAGE S END LIGHT	32-58.50	118-31.90	28116.64	40968.94	18762
CA	SAN DIEGO	OCEAN BEACH PIER SIGNAL	32-45.00	117-15.50	28267.04	40620.51	18740
CA	SAN DIEGO	PYRAMID COVE ANCHORAGE	32-50.00	118-22.90	28130.51	40911.77	18762
CA	SAN DIEGO	SAN DIEGO BAY PIER B	32-43.30	117-10.20	28275.85	40596.88	18773
CA	SAN DIEGO	SOUTH SAN DIEGO BAY MOORING	32-39.80	117-07.60	28277.59	40582.66	18773
CA	SAN DIEGO	SWEETWATER ANCHORAGE A	32-39.20	117-07.70	28276.83	40582.44	18773
CA	SAN DIEGO	TENTH AVE PIER N LIGHT	32-42.00	117-09.60	28275.79	40593.02	18773
CA	SAN DIEGO	TENTH AVE PIER S LIGHT	32-41.80	117-09.20	28276.38	40591.20	18773

HAVENS

STATE/COUNTRY	COUNTY/PROV	NAME	LAT	LON	TD#1	TD#2	CHART NO
CA	SAN MATEO	BALLENA BAY ANCH 9 BUOY A	37-44.80	122-19.40	16107.00	43171.26	18649
CA	SAN MATEO	OYSTER COVE MARINA LIGHT NO 1	37-39.90	122-22.10	16111.03	43145.70	18651
CA	SAN MATEO	OYSTER COVE MARINA LIGHT NO 8	37-39.90	122-22.40	16110.10	43145.89	18651
CA	SAN MATEO	OYSTER COVE MARINA NO 1	37-40.20	122-22.70	16108.42	43147.75	18651
CA	SAN MATEO	PILLAR POINT HARB ENTR LIGHT	37-29.70	122-29.00	27264.26	43094.21	18682
CA	SAN MATEO	PILLAR POINT HARB ENTR NO 1	37-29.20	122-30.30	27260.37	43092.46	18682
CA	SAN MATEO	PILLAR POINT HARB ENTR NO 2	37-28.40	122-29.00	27267.46	43087.06	18682
CA	SAN MATEO	PILLAR POINT HARB ENTR NO 3	37-28.90	122-28.90	27266.63	43089.73	18682
CA	SAN MATEO	PILLAR POINT HARBOR "PP"	37-28.30	122-31.20	27259.10	43088.22	18680
CA	STA BARBARA	COJO ANCHORAGE BUOY	34-26.50	120-23.60	27871.66	41754.42	18721
CA	STA BARBARA	GAVIOTA TANKER A MOORING	34-27.80	120-12.30	27905.83	41716.68	18721
CA	STA BARBARA	GAVIOTA TANKER B MOORING	34-27.70	120-12.20	27906.09	41715.82	18721
CA	STA BARBARA	GAVIOTA TANKER C MOORING	34-27.70	120-12.00	27906.69	41715.03	18721
CA	STA BARBARA	GAVIOTA TANKER D MOORING	34-27.60	120-12.00	27906.66	41714.55	18721
CA	STA BARBARA	GAVIOTA TANKER E MOORING	34-27.50	120-12.10	27906.33	41714.48	18721
CA	STA BARBARA	GAVIOTA TANKER F MOORING	34-27.50	120-12.30	27905.73	41715.27	18721
CA	STA BARBARA	GAVIOTA TANKER G MOORING	34-27.70	120-12.60	27904.89	41717.39	18721
CA	STA BARBARA	PLATFORM HARVEST MOORING	34-28.30	120-40.50	27821.52	41825.72	18721
HAWAII	HAWAII	KAWAIHAE SMALL BOAT NO 1	20-02.50	155-50.10	11079.64	37478.77	19320
HAWAII	HAWAII	PUAKO SMALL BOAT HARBOR	19-58.60	155-50.10	11108.07	37494.41	19320
HAWAII	HONOLULU	ALA WAI BOAT HARBOR NO 2	21-16.80	157-50.90	12330.10	37196.56	19357
HAWAII	HONOLULU	BARBERS POINT ANCHORAGE	21-18.10	158-04.40	12472.91	37192.75	19357
HAWAII	HONOLULU	BARBERS POINT ANCHORAGE A	21-16.70	158-04.20	12470.00	37199.43	19357
HAWAII	HONOLULU	BARBERS POINT ANCHORAGE B	21-16.70	158-04.70	12475.29	37199.52	19357
HAWAII	HONOLULU	BARBERS POINT ANCHORAGE C	21-17.00	158-04.70	12475.45	37198.08	19357
HAWAII	HONOLULU	BARBERS POINT ANCHORAGE D	21-17.00	158-04.20	12470.17	37197.99	19357
HAWAII	HONOLULU	HEEIA-KEA SMALL BOAT NO 1	21-27.00	157-48.60	12316.67	37147.78	19357
HAWAII	MAUI	MANELE SMALL BOAT HARB NO 1	20-44.70	156-53.40	11689.85	37327.75	19340
HAWAII	MAUI	MANELE SMALL BOAT HARB NO 2	20-44.80	156-53.30	11688.89	37327.28	19340
HAWAII	MAUI	MANELE SMALL BOAT HARB NO 3	20-44.70	156-53.40	11689.85	37327.75	19340
HAWAII	MAUI	MANELE SMALL BOAT HARB NO 6	20-44.80	156-53.40	11689.96	37327.31	19340
HAWAII	MAUI	MANELE SMALL BOAT HARB NO 8	20-44.70	156-53.40	11689.85	37327.75	19340
MARIANAS	GUAM ISLAND	AGANA SMALL BOAT BASIN	13-28.60N	144-45.00E	Suggest	GPS	81048
WA	CLALLAM	MOORING BASIN W LIGHT	48-07.60	123-27.10	11396.75	28157.54	18465
WA	CLALLAM	PORT ANGELES BOAT HAVEN LIGHT	48-07.60	123-27.00	11396.53	28157.67	18465
WA	CLALLAM	PORT ANGELES BOAT HAVEN NO 3	48-07.80	123-26.80	11395.40	28158.02	18465
WA	CLALLAM	QUILLAYUTE R BOAT BASIN NO 1	47-54.60	124-38.20	11599.47	28060.10	18480
WA	CLALLAM	QUILLAYUTE R BOAT BASIN NO 2	47-54.60	124-38.20	11599.47	28060.10	18480
WA	GRAYS HARBOR	GRAYS HARBOR BOAT WARNING	46-54.70	124-06.80	11827.96	28060.50	18502
WA	PACIFIC	NAHCOTTA MOORING BASIN NO 1	46-30.00	124-01.40	11971.39	28049.79	18504
WA	PUGET SOUND	COE NORTH MOORING BUOY	47-41.10	122-24.50	11342.35	28230.43	18441
WA	PUGET SOUND	COE SOUTH MOORING BUOY	47-40.30	122-25.30	11347.61	28229.04	18441
WA	PUGET SOUND	EDMONDS BOAT HARBOR NO 1	47-48.60	122-23.40	11311.32	28234.41	18441
WA	PUGET SOUND	PARK DEPT BOAT RAMP LIGHT	47-41.20	122-24.20	11341.17	28230.88	18441
WA	PUGET SOUND	STEAMBOAT FLATS LIGHT	48-00.90	122-16.20	11253.18	28247.90	18441

CHAPTER 8

PLENTIFUL PORTS

To us, a port is a place where a boater can get major services for his boat, with restaurants, shopping malls, and grocery stores nearby. Obviously, diesel, gasoline, and mechanical services must likewise be available.

Here are listings of places that we have been to and places that have been sent to us for publication. Of course, this list is not exhaustive, and should you have a place you would like to see published for others to enjoy, or for your own convenience, turn your ASF off and send us your time delay and latitude/longitude readings, along with the name of the port, marina, or gas dock. There is no charge for publishing this information, and we do not presume or assume anything about the convenience of any facility contained herein.

Coordinates for the ports' sea buoys are included for convenience, along with state, county, description, latitude, longitude, time delay one, and time delay two coordinates.

Please review the first two paragraphs of Chapter 7 for tips on using these coordinates.

HELPFUL HINT
Lots of polish on the deck makes for a pretty boat, teaches everyone the value of yoga, and provides quick lessons in aerobic exercise.

WIT & WISDOM

Captain Jack Bolack of Gulfwind Marine regularly delivers boats from the greater Tampa Bay area to Mobile, Alabama. On one of our more memorable trips together, we came face to face with fate and luck, but allowed a basic lack of faith in the tales of years gone by to cloud our eyes to the opportunity of a lifetime.

As Captain Jack and I headed west from Steinhatchee, Florida, early one morning, we found ourselves contentedly discussing the previous evening's dinner and the size of the fine steak we devoured. Just about the time our conversation settled to a couple of yeps, we came upon a small squall line that actually followed our course as far as we could see.

About three or four miles ahead, we could see small whitecaps and rain obscuring the horizon. Wet gear in place, we ran up on the rain about the same time the sun peeked over the horizon, casting its rays into the rain and thereby painting a beautiful rainbow within our grasp. As we drove under the rainbow, we could actually see its ends touching the water.

Immediately, I took the loran numbers down and pleaded for an opportunity to stop to dive for our pots of gold, but Captain Jack kept on going, muttering something about bilge water, authors, dreamers, and fairy tales.

I have the loran listings of the rainbow's end if anyone is still in the pursuit of a dream and a legend of love and luck. On a nice day, you might even find Sancho there, searching for the impossible dream.

PORTS

STATE/COUNTRY	COUNTY/PROV	NAME	LAT	LON	TD#1	TD#2	CHART
AK		ALASKA RAILROAD DOCK E LIGHT	60-07.10	149-25.50	13282.87	31970.07	16680
AK		ALASKA RAILROAD DOCK W LIGHT	60-07.10	149-25.60	13282.50	31970.16	16680
AK		BAR HARBOR ENTRANCE NO 2	55-21.00	131-41.00	14489.22	26117.09	17420
AK		BAR HARBOR ENTRANCE NO 3	55-21.00	131-41.00	14489.22	26117.09	17420
AK		BAR HARBOR N ENTRANCE NO 2N	55-21.10	131-41.30	14489.10	26118.95	17420
AK		BAR HARBOR S ENTRANCE NO 2S	55-20.90	131-40.60	14489.51	26114.73	17420
AK		BAR HARBOR S ENTRANCE NO 3S	55-20.90	131-40.60	14489.51	26114.73	17420
AK		CHATHAM STRAIT SEAFOOD PIER	56-48.80	132-57.70	14691.83	27244.00	17360
AK		CLOVER PASSAGE ENTRANCE LIGHT	55-28.70	131-48.70	14503.18	26193.90	17420
AK		COLLIER PIER LIGHTS	60-40.40	151-23.40	13227.36	32251.14	16660
AK		CONTAINER TERMINAL PIER 3	57-46.90	152-26.00	11225.72	31350.84	16580
AK		CORDOVA BOAT HARBOR LIGHT NO 2	60-32.80	145-46.00	14360.51	31918.68	16700
AK		DELONG PIER LIGHTS	60-46.80	148-39.80	13841.09	32198.83	16700
AK		DOG BAY N ENTRANCE LIGHT NO 1	57-47.00	152-24.40	11229.56	31349.21	16580
AK		DOG BAY N ENTRANCE LIGHT NO 2	57-47.00	152-24.40	11229.56	31349.21	16580
AK		DOG BAY S ENTR DAYBEACON NO 3	57-46.70	152-24.80	11225.51	31348.18	16580
AK		DOG BAY S ENTRANCE LIGHT NO 4	57-46.70	152-24.80	11225.51	31348.18	16580
AK		DRIFT RIVER TERMINAL LIGHTS	60-33.20	152-08.10	13033.29	32233.24	16660
AK		DRY SPRUCE BAY ENTRANCE LIGHT	57-57.40	153-06.10	11309.74	31456.55	16580
AK		EAST BARGE SLIP LIGHT	60-46.70	148-40.20	13838.63	32198.42	16700
AK		EDNA BAY ENTRANCE LIGHT	55-56.40	133-36.90	14427.33	26940.70	17400
AK		ELLAMAR ENTRANCE BUOY NO 2	60-53.70	146-43.20	14348.09	32156.63	16700
AK		ENTRANCE ISLAND LIGHT NO 24	57-17.50	135-36.20	14558.12	28176.34	17320
AK		ENTRANCE POINT LIGHT NO 12	61-03.80	146-39.60	14458.91	32232.88	16700
AK		ENTRY POINT LIGHT NO 1	57-02.00	135-14.90	14525.44	27944.39	17320
AK		FUNTER BAY ENTRANCE LIGHT NO 1	58-14.60	134-54.90	14896.91	28561.88	17300
AK		GAMBIER BAY ENTRANCE NO 2	57-27.90	133-55.10	14769.17	27861.91	17360
AK		HAWK INLET ENTRANCE NO 1	58-05.50	134-46.70	14864.88	28439.00	17300
AK		HOMER FUEL DOCK N LIGHT	59-36.30	151-24.90	12569.51	31886.87	16640
AK		HYDER HARBOR ENTRANCE NO 1	55-54.30	130-00.50	14741.82	26313.93	17420
AK		JAPONSKI HARBOR ENTR NO 6	57-02.90	135-20.70	14519.20	27977.76	17320
AK		JAPONSKI HARBOR ENTRANCE NO 5	57-02.80	135-20.70	14518.75	27976.87	17320
AK		KAKE ENTRANCE LIGHT NO 2	56-59.10	134-01.30	14636.14	27601.75	17360
AK		KASILOF ENTRANCE CHANNEL NO 1	60-23.40	151-23.50	13057.82	32155.59	16660
AK		KENAI ENTRANCE CHANNEL NO 1KE	60-31.30	151-20.50	13145.65	32198.58	16660
AK		KENNEDY ENTRANCE BUOY KE	59-06.40	151-26.50	12249.21	31716.28	16640
AK		KETCHIKAN PORT DOCK NO 1	55-20.50	131-38.90	14490.78	26104.93	17420
AK		KETCHIKAN PORT DOCK NO 2	55-20.50	131-38.90	14490.78	26104.93	17420
AK		KILLISNOO HARBOR ENTRANCE NO 2	57-27.70	134-34.50	14707.92	28015.30	17320
AK		KLAWOCK HARBOR ENTRANCE NO 2	55-33.50	133-06.20	14395.67	26628.24	17400
AK		KLAWOCK LOGGING DOCK LIGHT	55-33.20	133-06.50	14394.10	26627.97	17400
AK		KLAWOCK TOW CHANNEL ENTR 2TC	55-29.90	133-11.50	14374.04	26634.39	17400
AK		KNUDSON COVE BRKWTR	55-28.40	131-47.70	14503.70	26186.80	17420
AK		KODIAK CITY DOCK PIER 2 LIGHTS	54-47.10	152-25.40	11128.75	30485.88	16580

PORTS

STATE/COUNTRY	COUNTY/PROV	NAME	LAT	LON	TD#1	TD#2	CHART NO
AK		KODIAK HARBOR ENTRANCE NO 16	57-47.10	152-24.40	11230.68	31349.74	16580
AK		KODIAK N ENTR CHANNEL NO 8	57-48.80	152-19.40	11259.58	31351.95	16580
AK		KODIAK PIER DOCK LIGHTS	57-47.20	152-24.00	11232.51	31349.72	16580
AK		LARSEN BAY ENTRANCE ROCK NO 1	57-32.70	153-58.50	11164.05	31398.84	16580
AK		LITUYA BAY ENTR RANGE LIGHT	58-37.60	137-39.40	14752.99	29427.00	16760
AK		MARGINAL WHARF LIGHT	60-46.70	148-40.40	13837.89	32198.55	16700
AK		MARINE HIGHWAY TERMINAL	56-48.50	132-58.50	14689.45	27243.99	17360
AK		MARINE HIGHWAY WHARF LIGHTS	55-21.30	131-41.80	14488.99	26122.17	17420
AK		METLAKATLA PIER LIGHTS	55-07.80	131-34.10	14456.55	26070.59	17420
AK		NICHOLS BAY ENTRANCE DAYBEACON	54-42.10	132-05.30	14324.75	26179.94	17400
AK		NINILCHIK CHANNEL ENTRANCE LIGHT	60-03.30	151-39.60	12808.05	32052.37	16640
AK		NORTH FORELAND DOCK LIGHTS	61-02.60	151-09.70	13483.67	32368.80	16660
AK		PELICAN ENTRANCE LIGHT	57-57.30	136-13.60	14685.81	28702.52	17300
AK		PETERSBURG FISHERIES DOCK	56-48.90	132-57.50	14692.52	27244.27	17360
AK		PHILLIPS LNG DOCK LIGHTS	60-40.70	151-23.70	13229.44	32252.96	16660
AK		PORT CHATHAM ENTRANCE LIGHT	59-12.60	151-46.40	12258.39	31771.83	16640
AK		PORT GRAHAM ENTRANCE LIGHT	59-22.40	151-53.00	12345.07	31833.18	16640
AK		PORT GRAHAM ENTRANCE SHOAL NO 1	59-22.80	151-54.10	12346.44	31836.42	16640
AK		PORT VALDEZ BERTH 1 E LIGHT	61-05.30	146-21.80	14540.46	32229.12	16700
AK		PORT VALDEZ BERTH 1 LIGHT	61-05.40	146-22.10	14540.29	32230.20	16700
AK		PORT VALDEZ BERTH 1 W LIGHT	61-05.40	146-22.30	14539.54	32230.38	16700
AK		PORT VALDEZ BERTH 3 E LIGHT	61-05.40	146-22.80	14537.66	32230.83	16700
AK		PORT VALDEZ BERTH 3 LIGHT	61-05.40	146-23.00	14536.91	32231.01	16700
AK		PORT VALDEZ BERTH 3 W LIGHT	61-05.30	146-23.10	14535.57	32230.30	16700
AK		PORT VALDEZ BERTH 4 E LIGHT	61-05.30	146-23.50	14534.07	32230.66	16700
AK		PORT VALDEZ BERTH 4 LIGHT	61-05.30	146-23.70	14533.31	32230.84	16700
AK		PORT VALDEZ BERTH 4 W LIGHT	61-05.30	146-23.90	14532.56	32231.02	16700
AK		PORT VALDEZ BERTH 5 LIGHT	61-05.40	146-24.20	14532.40	32232.10	16700
AK		PORT VALDEZ BERTH 5 W LIGHT	61-05.40	146-24.50	14531.27	32232.37	16700
AK		PORT VALDEZ ENTR ISLAND NO 14	61-05.10	146-36.70	14482.38	32240.66	16700
AK		RAILROAD PIER BUOY NO 2	60-06.90	149-25.30	13281.60	31968.58	16680
AK		RATZ HARBOR ENTRANCE LIGHT	55-53.30	132-35.80	14515.67	26618.04	17420
AK		REID LANDING DOCK LIGHT	56-47.00	132-58.70	14683.21	27229.44	17360
AK		SELDOVIA BAY ENTRANCE LIGHT	59-27.20	151-43.20	12422.09	31851.26	16640
AK		SETTLERS COVE BRKWTR LIGHT 2	57-52.40	152-51.70	11262.46	31412.98	16580
AK		SETTLERS COVE DAYBEACON NO 1	57-52.20	152-51.40	11260.52	31411.57	16580
AK		SEWARD COAL DOCK BUOY	60-06.80	149-25.70	13279.15	31968.29	16680
AK		SEWARD COAL MOORING BUOY	60-06.80	149-25.70	13279.15	31968.29	16680
AK		ST PAUL HARBOR ENTRANCE LIGHT	57-44.40	152-25.70	11198.32	31337.35	16580
AK		STANDARD OIL PIER LIGHTS	58-17.90	134-24.80	14955.05	28483.46	17300
AK		STANDARD OIL PIER LIGHTS	56-48.60	132-58.20	14690.29	27243.87	17360
AK		STANDARD OIL PIER LIGHTS	55-20.10	131-37.60	14491.45	26097.34	17420
AK		SURGE BAY ENTR LIGHT	57-58.60	136-33.50	14657.50	28795.64	16016
AK		SWANSON HARBOR ENTRANCE NO 2	58-11.60	135-04.60	14868.04	28568.71	17300

PORTS

STATE/COUNTRY	COUNTY/PROV	NAME	LAT	LON	TD#1	TD#2	CHART NO
AK		TAMGAS HARBOR ENTRANCE LIGHT	55-01.30	131-30.80	14440.71	26061.77	17420
AK		TENAKEE ENTRANCE NO 1	57-46.40	134-56.00	14760.14	28284.79	17300
AK		THOMAS BASIN ENTRANCE NO 2	55-20.30	131-38.50	14490.73	26102.36	17420
AK		THOMAS BASIN ENTRANCE NO 3	55-20.30	131-38.50	14490.73	26102.36	17420
AK		THOMAS BAY ENTRANCE NO 1	56-59.30	132-58.20	14733.02	27354.27	17360
AK		THOMAS BAY ENTRANCE NO 2	56-59.10	132-57.80	14732.80	27350.72	17360
AK		THORNE BAY ENTRANCE NO 2	55-40.80	132-27.40	14484.51	26477.35	17420
AK		TOKEEN HARBOR ENTRANCE LIGHT	55-56.20	133-19.80	14455.21	26855.14	17400
AK		U S ARMY DOCK LIGHTS	59-16.80	135-27.00	15172.75	29310.74	17300
AK		UNION OIL PIER LIGHTS	57-47.10	152-25.20	11229.29	31350.81	16580
AK		VALDEZ BOAT HARBOR NO 2	61-27.40	146-21.10	14754.92	32405.37	16700
AK		VALDEZ BOAT HARBOR NO 3	61-07.40	146-21.20	14562.93	32245.50	16700
AK		VALDEZ CONTAINER TERMINAL	61-07.30	146-18.40	14572.48	32242.18	16700
AK		WINDHAM BAY ENTRANCE LIGHT	57-33.70	133-32.50	14827.17	27836.89	17360
AK		WRANGELL DOCK LIGHTS	56-28.20	132-23.20	14663.29	26901.42	17360
AK		WRANGELL NARROWS N ENTR WN	56-49.80	132-55.70	14698.75	27246.68	17360
AK		YAKUTAT BAY ENTR BUOY NO 2	59-31.90	139-57.10	14838.74	30458.80	16760
AK		YAKUTAT BAY ENTR NO 2	59-31.90	139-57.10	14838.74	30458.80	16016
AK	ALEUTIANS	BECHEVIN BAY ENTRANCE BB	55-06.20	163-28.60	18433.38	47443.66	16011
AK	ALEUTIANS	EGEGIK ENTRANCE BUOY NO 1	58-15.50	157-42.00	18746.46	45162.67	16006
AK	ALEUTIANS	ILIULIUK BAY ENTRANCE NO 2	53-54.60	166-29.50	17950.76	48382.62	16011
AK	ALEUTIANS	PIRATE COVE DAYBEACON	55-21.80	160-21.60	18542.46	46258.11	16011
AK	ALEUTIANS	POPOF STRAIT ENTR LIGHT NO 1	55-21.40	160-30.30	18539.33	46313.78	16011
AK	ALEUTIANS	PORT MOLLER ENTRANCE NO 2	55-60.00	160-39.10	18615.11	46350.54	16011
AK	ALEUTIANS	PORT MOLLER ENTRANCE NO 3	55-59.40	160-36.70	18614.35	46335.06	16011
AK	ALEUTIANS	SAND POINT DOCK LIGHT	55-19.90	160-30.10	18536.10	46313.36	16011
AK	ALEUTIANS	UGANIK AERO DOCK LIGHTS	55-12.50	162-41.50	18474.03	47150.00	16011
AK	ALEUTIANS	UGASHIK RIVER ENTRANCE UR	57-37.50	157-52.30	18732.68	45205.11	16006
AK	ALEUTIANS	KWIGUK PASS ENTRANCE LIGHT	62-47.40	164-51.80	18218.89	47314.33	16006
AK	ALEUTIANS	NAKNEK ENTRANCE NO 1	58-43.40	157-02.80	18748.23	44957.53	16006
AK	BERING SEA	NOME HARBOR E JETTY LIGHT	64-29.90	165-24.70	17950.97	47238.10	16006
AK	BERING SEA	NOME TERMINAL BRIDGE E LIGHT	64-30.00	165-26.00	17949.16	47241.69	16006
AK	BERING SEA	NOME TERMINAL BRIDGE W LIGHT	64-30.00	165-26.10	17949.04	47241.98	16006
AK	BERING SEA	NOME TERMINAL LIGHT	64-29.60	165-26.20	17949.76	47242.93	16006
AK	BERING SEA	NUSHAGAK BAY ENTRANCE NO 2	58-33.70	158-24.20	18748.35	45450.04	16006
AK	BERING SEA	RILEY CHANNEL ENTR LIGHT	66-47.00	161-52.30	17899.71	46567.79	16005
AK	BERING SEA	SHAKTOOLIK RIVER ENTRANCE	64-22.80	161-14.00	18215.81	46482.04	16006
AK	BERING SEA	YUKON RIVER MID ENTRANCE LIGHT	63-04.60	165-37.60	18124.83	47441.26	16006
AK	BERING SEA	YUKON RIVER N ENTRANCE LIGHT	63-02.50	163-23.00	18274.77	46965.35	16006
AK	BERING SEA	YUKON RIVER S ENTRANCE LIGHT	62-35.40	164-59.50	18238.26	47366.42	16006
CA	HUMBOLDT	DOODLEY ISLAND MARINA LIGHT	40-48.40	124-09.90	14815.45	43790.68	18622
CA	LOS ANGELES	DOWNTOWN MARINA E BRKWTR	33-45.50	118-10.90	28205.56	40998.40	18746
CA	LOS ANGELES	DOWNTOWN MARINA E ENTR LIGHT	33-45.50	118-11.00	28205.32	40998.89	18746
CA	LOS ANGELES	DOWNTOWN MARINA JETTY	33-45.60	118-10.80	28205.90	40998.21	18746

PORTS

STATE/COUNTRY	COUNTY/PROV	NAME	LAT	LON	TD#1	TD#2	CHART NO
CA	LOS ANGELES	DOWNTOWN MARINA MOLE LIGHT	33-45.50	118-11.50	28204.12	41001.34	18746
CA	LOS ANGELES	DOWNTOWN MARINA W BRKWTR	33-45.40	118-10.90	28205.46	40998.10	18746
CA	LOS ANGELES	DOWNTOWN MARINA W ENTR LITE	33-45.50	118-11.00	28205.32	40998.89	18746
CA	LOS ANGELES	MARINA DEL REY N BRKWTR NO 2	33-57.80	118-27.80	28176.14	41121.88	18744
CA	LOS ANGELES	MARINA DEL REY NO 14	33-58.70	118-26.70	28179.81	41119.65	18744
CA	LOS ANGELES	MARINA DEL REY NO 3	33-57.80	118-27.60	28176.64	41120.90	18744
CA	LOS ANGELES	MARINA DEL REY NO 4	33-57.60	118-27.50	28176.70	41119.70	18744
CA	LOS ANGELES	MARINA DEL REY NO 5	33-58.30	118-26.90	28178.90	41119.22	18744
CA	LOS ANGELES	MARINA DEL REY PIER LIGHT	33-58.20	118-26.80	28179.06	41118.38	18744
CA	LOS ANGELES	MARINA DEL REY S BRKWTR NO 1	33-57.50	118-27.50	28176.60	41119.35	18744
CA	LOS ANGELES	QUEENSWAY BAY MARINA NO A	33-45.30	118-11.40	28204.16	41000.25	18746
CA	LOS ANGELES	QUEENSWAY BAY MARINA NO B	33-45.30	118-11.40	28204.16	41000.25	18746
CA	LOS ANGELES	QUEENSWAY BAY MARINA NO C	33-45.30	118-11.50	28203.92	41000.73	18746
CA	LOS ANGELES	QUEENSWAY BAY MARINA NO D	33-45.40	118-11.60	28203.78	41001.52	18746
CA	LOS ANGELES	QUEENSWAY BAY MARINA NO E	33-45.40	118-11.70	28203.54	41002.01	18746
CA	LOS ANGELES	QUEENSWAY BAY MARINA NO F	33-45.40	118-11.80	28203.30	41002.50	18746
CA	LOS ANGELES	SHORELINE MARINA E ENT LITE	33-45.60	118-11.50	28204.22	41001.64	18746
CA	MARIN	AMORCO WHARF LIGHTS	38-02.10	122-07.40	16098.74	43262.15	18656
CA	MARIN	AVON WHARF WEST LIGHTS	38-02.90	122-05.60	16102.40	43266.01	18656
CA	MARIN	BENICIA RR BRIDGE PIER 13	38-02.30	122-07.20	16098.83	43263.20	18656
CA	MARIN	BENICIA RR BRIDGE PIER 17	38-02.60	122-07.40	16097.31	43264.95	18656
CA	MARIN	BENICIA WHARF LIGHT	38-02.40	122-08.30	16094.92	43264.14	18656
CA	MARIN	BERKELEY MARINA NO 2	37-50.90	122-21.60	16083.92	43206.06	18649
CA	MARIN	BERKELEY MARINA NO 3	37-51.50	122-20.90	16084.52	43209.02	18649
CA	MARIN	BERKELEY MARINA NORTH LIGHT	37-52.00	122-19.00	16089.22	43210.87	18649
CA	MARIN	BERKELEY MARINA SOUTH LIGHT	37-52.00	122-19.00	16089.22	43210.87	18649
CA	MARIN	CARQUINEZ BRIDGE PIER NO 2	38-03.90	122-13.50	16073.38	43274.08	18656
CA	MARIN	CARQUINEZ BRIDGE PIER SIGNAL	38-02.30	122-07.20	16098.83	43263.20	18656
CA	MARIN	EMERYVILLE MARINA NO 1	37-50.60	122-19.30	16092.05	43203.30	18649
CA	MARIN	EMERYVILLE MARINA NO 3	37-50.60	122-18.90	16093.33	43203.11	18649
CA	MARIN	EMERYVILLE MARINA NO 5	37-50.60	122-18.50	16094.60	43202.91	18649
CA	MARIN	EMERYVILLE MARINA NO 7	37-50.50	122-18.60	16094.55	43202.41	18649
CA	MARIN	EMERYVILLE MARINA NO 8	37-50.50	122-18.60	16094.55	43202.41	18649
CA	MARIN	FISHERMANS WHARF BRKWTR A	37-48.70	122-25.30	16078.15	43195.86	18649
CA	MARIN	FISHERMANS WHARF BRKWTR B	37-48.70	122-25.20	16078.47	43195.81	18649
CA	MARIN	FISHERMANS WHARF ENTRANCE NO 2	37-48.70	122-25.10	16078.79	43195.76	18649
CA	MARIN	GLEN COVE MARINA LIGHT	38-03.90	122-12.80	16075.70	43273.87	18656
CA	MARIN	HARRIS YACHT HARBOR NO 1	38-02.90	121-57.30	16129.83	43263.04	18656
CA	MARIN	MARTINEZ MARINA LIGHT NO 1	38-01.70	122-08.20	16097.24	43260.20	18656
CA	MARIN	MOLATE POINT WHARF S LIGHT	37-56.70	122-25.60	16054.83	43239.16	18649
CA	MARIN	OAKLAND 7TH ST TERMIANL NO 1	37-48.20	122-20.40	16094.98	43190.63	18649
CA	MARIN	OAKLAND 7TH ST TERMINAL NO 2	37-48.30	122-20.50	16094.40	43191.23	18649
CA	MARIN	OLEUM WHARF E LIGHTS	38-03.40	122-15.80	16067.26	43272.04	18654
CA	MARIN	PIER 27-29 WEST LIGHT	37-48.50	122-24.00	16082.80	43194.12	18649

P O R T S

STATE/COUNTRY	COUNTY/PROV	NAME	LAT	LON	TD#1	TD#2	CHART N
CA	MARIN	PIER 39 BRKWTR LIGHT A	37-48.70	122-24.50	16080.68	43195.46	18649
CA	MARIN	PIER 39 BRKWTR LIGHT B	37-48.70	122-24.50	16080.68	43195.46	18649
CA	MARIN	PIER 39 BRKWTR LIGHT C	37-48.70	122-24.40	16081.00	43195.41	18649
CA	MARIN	PIER 39 BRKWTR LIGHT D	37-48.60	122-24.40	16081.27	43194.86	18649
CA	MARIN	PIER 39 BRKWTR LIGHT E	37-48.60	122-24.40	16081.27	43194.86	18649
CA	MARIN	PIER 39 BRKWTR LIGHT F	37-48.60	122-24.40	16081.27	43194.86	18649
CA	MARIN	PIER 39 MARINA LIGHT NO 2	37-48.50	122-24.70	16080.59	43194.47	18649
CA	MARIN	PIER 45 EAST LIGHT	37-48.70	122-25.20	16078.47	43195.81	18649
CA	MARIN	PIER D NORTH BUOY	37-48.10	122-22.50	16088.61	43191.17	18649
CA	MARIN	PITTSBURG MARINA NO 1	38-02.20	121-52.80	16146.59	43257.23	18656
CA	MARIN	POINT ORIENT WHARF S LIGHTS	37-57.30	122-25.60	16053.09	43242.38	18649
CA	MARIN	POINT RICHMOND N PIER LIGHT	37-54.50	122-23.50	16067.87	43226.50	18649
CA	MARIN	POINT RICHMOND S PIER LIGHT	37-54.40	122-23.50	16068.15	43225.95	18649
CA	MARIN	ROD & GUN CLUB LIGHT	37-57.30	121-20.60	16262.94	43209.59	18661
CA	MARIN	SEQUOIA OIL WHARF W LIGHT	38-03.20	122-16.40	16065.87	43271.13	18654
CA	MARIN	SF WEST YACHT HARBOR NO 2	37-48.50	122-26.30	16075.53	43195.27	18649
CA	MARIN	SHELL OIL WHARF E END LIGHT	38-02.00	122-07.70	16098.03	43261.70	18656
CA	MARIN	SHELL OIL WHARF W END LIGHT	38-01.80	122-08.00	16097.62	43260.69	18656
CA	MARIN	STANDARD OIL WHARF FOG SIGNAL	37-55.30	122-24.60	16062.07	43231.26	18649
CA	MARIN	SUISUN BAY PIER 2 W END	38-03.50	122-01.60	16113.92	43268.02	18656
CA	MARIN	VALLEJO YACHT CLUB N LIGHT	38-06.30	122-16.00	16057.91	43287.81	18654
CA	MARIN	YERBA BUENA ISLAND WHARF	37-48.40	122-21.70	16090.34	43192.40	18649
CA	ORANGE	LOS ANGELES MARINA LIGHT	33-42.90	118-16.60	28189.29	41018.22	18746
CA	S LUIS OBISPO	MORRO CREEK SUB TERMINAL BUOY	35-23.00	120-52.90	27783.29	42152.32	18703
CA	S LUIS OBISPO	TORO CREEK SUB TERMINAL BUOY	35-24.40	120-53.10	27782.56	42160.90	18721
CA	SAN DIEGO	SHELTER ISLAND YACHT NO 5	32-42.50	117-14.10	28267.45	40611.85	18773
CA	SAN DIEGO	SHELTER ISLAND YACHT NO 6	32-42.60	117-14.00	28267.74	40611.56	18773
CA	SAN MATEO	ALAMEDA NAS S ENTRANCE NO 2	37-46.00	122-18.40	16107.04	43177.36	18649
CA	SAN MATEO	ALAMEDA NAS S ENTRANCE NO 3	37-46.10	122-18.60	16106.15	43178.02	18649
CA	SAN MATEO	ALAMEDA NAS S ENTRANCE NO 4	37-46.10	122-18.50	16106.47	43177.97	18649
CA	SAN MATEO	BRISBANE MARINA NO 1	37-40.30	122-22.10	16110.03	43147.92	18651
CA	SAN MATEO	BRISBANE MARINA NO 6	37-40.20	122-22.60	16108.73	43147.68	18651
CA	SAN MATEO	BRISBANE MARINA NO 8	37-40.30	122-22.70	16108.17	43148.30	18651
CA	SAN MATEO	COYOTE POINT YACHT HARBOR NO 1	37-35.60	122-18.70	16131.91	43119.35	18651
CA	SAN MATEO	DUMBARTON HWY BRIDGE	37-30.40	122-07.00	16178.92	43080.19	18651
CA	SAN MATEO	LASH TERMINAL NO 1	37-44.70	122-22.20	16098.50	43172.31	18649
CA	SAN MATEO	OYSTER COVE MARINA LIGHT NO 1	37-39.90	122-22.10	16111.03	43145.70	18651
CA	SAN MATEO	OYSTER COVE MARINA LIGHT NO 8	37-39.90	122-22.40	16110.10	43145.89	18651
CA	SAN MATEO	OYSTER COVE MARINA NO 1	37-40.20	122-22.70	16108.42	43147.75	18651
CA	SAN MATEO	PIER 14 DAYBEACON	37-47.70	122-23.30	16087.16	43189.39	18649
CA	SAN MATEO	PIER 18 DAYBEACON	37-47.60	122-23.20	16087.74	43188.79	18649
CA	SAN MATEO	PIER 20 DAYBEACON	37-47.50	122-23.20	16088.00	43188.24	18649
CA	SAN MATEO	PIER 22 DAYBEACON	37-47.50	122-23.20	16088.00	43188.24	18649
CA	SAN MATEO	PIER 94 N END LIGHT	37-44.70	122-22.30	16098.19	43172.37	18649

P O R T S

STATE/COUNTRY	COUNTY/PROV	NAME	LAT	LON	TD#1	TD#2	CHART NO
CA	SAN MATEO	PIER 94/96 CHANNEL NO 2	37-45.50	122-22.00	16097.05	43176.61	18649
CA	SAN MATEO	PIER 94/96 CHANNEL NO 4	37-44.30	122-21.60	16101.41	43169.76	18649
CA	SAN MATEO	PIER B NORTH BUOY	37-47.80	122-22.80	16088.47	43189.68	18649
CA	SAN MATEO	PIER D SOUTH BUOY	37-48.00	122-22.40	16089.20	43190.57	18649
CA	SAN MATEO	RINCON POINT MARINA BRKWTR A	37-46.80	122-23.00	16090.49	43184.30	18649
CA	SAN MATEO	RINCON POINT MARINA BRKWTR B	37-46.80	122-23.00	16090.49	43184.30	18649
CA	SAN MATEO	RINCON POINT MARINA NO 1	37-46.90	122-23.00	16090.23	43184.85	18649
CA	SAN MATEO	RINCON POINT MARINA NO 2	37-46.90	122-23.00	16090.23	43184.85	18649
CA	SAN MATEO	RINCON POINT MARINA S ENTR NO 1	37-46.70	122-23.00	16090.76	43183.75	18649
CA	SAN MATEO	RINCON POINT MARINA S ENTR NO 2	37-46.70	122-23.00	16090.76	43183.75	18649
CA	SAN MATEO	SAN LEANDRO MARINA NO 12	37-41.50	122-11.70	16139.19	43147.88	18649
CA	SAN MATEO	SANTA FE FERRY SLIP FOG SIGNAL	37-46.20	122-23.00	16092.08	43181.01	18649
CA	SAN MATEO	SF AIRPORT DAYBEACON NO 1	37-37.90	122-22.70	16114.13	43135.00	18651
CA	SAN MATEO	USCG ISLAND PIER N LIGHT	37-46.80	122-15.00	16115.66	43179.90	18649
CA	SAN MATEO	USCG ISLAND PIER S LIGHT	37-46.70	122-14.60	16117.17	43179.11	18649
CA	SONOMA	SPUD POINT MARINA NO 1	38-19.90	123-03.10	15855.13	43360.58	18643
CA	VENTURA	MARINA DEL REY E CABLE AREA	34-01.40	118-32.20	28168.45	41156.45	18744
CA	VENTURA	VENTURA MARINA S JETTY NO 6	34-14.80	119-16.20	28061.91	41418.89	18725
CANADA	B COLUMBIA	ACTIVE PASS LIGHT	48-52.40	123-17.40	15212.44	28868.18	18400
CANADA	B COLUMBIA	ENTRANCE ISLAND LIGHT	49-12.60	123-48.40	15129.28	29134.32	18400
CANADA	B COLUMBIA	GANGES HARBOR LIGHT	48-50.20	123-27.20	15180.69	28872.00	18400
CANADA	B COLUMBIA	PREEDY HARBOR LIGHT	48-58.10	123-41.00	15143.36	28980.24	18400
HAWAII	HAWAII	HILO HARBOR BRKWTR LIGHT	19-44.80	155-04.70	11100.00	37525.06	19320
HAWAII	HAWAII	HILO HARBOR ENTRANCE NO 1	19-44.70	155-05.00	11100.71	37525.61	19320
HAWAII	HAWAII	HONOKOHAU ENTR CHANN LIGHT	19-40.40	156-01.70	11312.27	37573.07	19320
HAWAII	HAWAII	HONOKOHAU ENTR CHANNEL NO 3	19-40.40	156-01.80	11312.98	37573.13	19320
HAWAII	HAWAII	HONOKOHAU HARBOR BUOY NO 1	19-40.30	156-02.00	11315.11	37573.64	19320
HAWAII	HAWAII	KAILUA BAY ENTRANCE LIGHT	19-38.50	155-60.00	11314.13	37579.66	19320
HAWAII	HONOLULU	ALA WAI BOAT HARBOR NO 1	21-16.80	157-51.00	12331.15	37196.58	19357
HAWAII	HONOLULU	BARBERS PT TANK TERMINAL B	21-16.40	158-05.50	12483.60	37201.10	19357
HAWAII	HONOLULU	HALEIWA HARBOR ENTR NO 2	21-36.40	158-07.00	12514.42	37104.61	19357
HAWAII	HONOLULU	HEEIA-KEA SMALL BOAT NO 2	21-27.10	157-48.70	12317.82	37147.32	19357
HAWAII	HONOLULU	HONOLULU HARBOR ENTR H	21-17.00	157-53.00	12352.26	37196.00	19357
HAWAII	HONOLULU	HONOLULU HARBOR ENTR LIGHT	21-17.90	157-52.30	12345.68	37191.60	19357
HAWAII	HONOLULU	KAISER BOAT CHANNEL NO 1	21-16.80	157-50.60	12326.96	37196.50	19357
HAWAII	HONOLULU	KANEOHE BAY ENTR CHANNEL K	21-31.30	157-48.40	12319.96	37127.27	19357
HAWAII	HONOLULU	KANEOHE ENTR RANGE LIGHT	21-29.90	157-50.10	12335.41	37134.16	19357
HAWAII	HONOLULU	KAPALAMA BASIN BUOY NO 2	21-19.20	157-53.00	12354.10	37185.55	19357
HAWAII	HONOLULU	KEEHI LAGOON BARGE CHANNEL	21-20.00	157-54.10	12366.26	37181.93	19357
HAWAII	HONOLULU	PEARL HARBOR ENTR NO 1	21-18.10	157-57.60	12401.35	37191.58	19357
HAWAII	HONOLULU	PEARL HARBOR ENTR RANGE	21-19.90	158-07.00	12501.36	37184.53	19357
HAWAII	HONOLULU	SAMPAN CHANNEL ENTR NO 2	21-28.30	157-46.80	12299.94	37141.34	19357
HAWAII	HONOLULU	WAIANAE HARBOR BRKWTR NO 1	21-27.00	158-12.00	12558.17	37150.88	19357
HAWAII	KAUAI	NAWILIWILI BOAT HARBOR NO 1	21-57.20	159-21.60	13288.72	36998.80	19380

PORTS

STATE/COUNTRY	COUNTY/PROV	NAME	LAT	LON	TD#1	TD#2	CHART NO
HAWAII	KAUAI	NAWILIWILI BOAT HARBOR NO 2	21-57.20	159-21.60	13288.72	36998.80	19380
HAWAII	KAUAI	NAWILIWILI ENTR BUOY NO 1	21-57.40	159-21.10	13283.60	36997.79	19380
HAWAII	MAUI	KAHULUI ENTR E BRKWTR LIGHT	20-54.20	156-28.50	11457.60	37278.34	19340
HAWAII	MAUI	KAUMALAPAU ENTRANCE NO 1	20-47.30	156-59.70	11760.05	37318.38	19340
HAWAII	MAUI	KAUNAKAKAI ENTRANCE LIGHT	21-05.50	157-01.70	11808.14	37237.84	19340
HAWAII	MAUI	KAUNAKAKAI PIER LIGHT NO 6	21-05.00	157-01.90	11809.22	37240.13	19340
HAWAII	MAUI	LAHAINA BOAT BASIN LIGHT	20-52.50	156-40.90	11573.12	37289.55	19320
HAWAII	MAUI	LAHAINA ENTRANCE BUOY L	20-52.30	156-41.20	11575.68	37290.52	19340
HAWAII	MAUI	MANELE BAY BRKWTR LIGHT	20-44.70	156-53.40	11689.85	37327.75	19340
HAWAII	MAUI	MANELE SMALL BOAT HARB NO 4	20-44.80	156-53.40	11689.96	37327.31	19340
OR	COOS	COOS BAY BRIDGE FOG SIGNAL	43-25.60	124-14.10	13506.26	27803.45	18587
OR	COOS	COOS BAY ENTRANCE NO 1	43-21.90	124-21.70	13535.04	27780.97	18587
OR	COOS	COOS BAY ENTRANCE NO 2	43-21.40	124-20.90	13539.86	27781.68	18587
OR	COOS	COOS RIVER ENTRANCE NO 1	43-22.60	124-10.90	13534.63	27804.72	18587
OR	COOS	COQUILLE RIVER ENTR NO 2	43-08.20	124-27.90	13650.49	27741.93	18580
OR	COOS	NORTH BAY WHARF LIGHT A	43-24.00	124-16.90	13519.05	27794.72	18587
OR	COOS	NORTH BAY WHARF LIGHT B	43-24.10	124-16.90	13518.16	27794.91	18587
OR	CURRY	CHETCO RIVER ENTR "RB"	42-02.80	124-16.00	14221.80	27616.47	18600
OR	DOUGLAS	GARDINER PAPER MILL DOCK	43-44.50	124-07.20	13339.69	27850.24	18584
OR	DOUGLAS	SALMON HARBOR ENTR NO 1	43-41.20	124-10.80	13368.40	27837.39	18584
OR	DOUGLAS	SLAMON HARBOR ENTR NO 2	43-41.10	124-10.80	13369.29	27837.22	18584
OR	DOUGLAS	UMPQUA RIVER ENTRANCE NO 1	43-40.10	124-13.80	13377.39	27829.39	18584
OR	DOUGLAS	UMPQUA RIVER ENTRANCE NO 2	43-39.90	124-13.40	13379.29	27829.87	18584
OR	LINCOLN	DEPOE BAY ENTRANCE NO 2	44-48.50	124-04.30	12770.15	27945.92	18561
OR	LINCOLN	SOUTHBEACH MARINA NO 2	44-37.40	124-03.20	12866.47	27934.27	18561
WA	CLALLAM	JOHN WAYNE MARINA NO 2	48-03.80	123-02.30	11353.13	28187.97	18471
WA	CLALLAM	JOHN WAYNE MARINA NO 3	48-03.80	123-02.30	11353.13	28187.97	18471
WA	CLALLAM	SEQUIM BAY ENTRANCE NO 2	48-05.10	123-01.60	11347.18	28189.42	18471
WA	CLALLAM	SEQUIM BAY ENTRANCE NO 4	48-04.60	123-02.50	11350.92	28188.04	18471
WA	GEORGIA STRAIT	ANACORTES MARINA LIGHT	48-30.10	122-36.00	11221.50	28231.07	18421
WA	GEORGIA STRAIT	AQUALICUM CREEK ENTRANCE NO 2	48-45.40	122-30.80	11180.16	28242.01	18421
WA	GEORGIA STRAIT	FERRY TERMINAL A	48-30.50	122-40.50	11229.82	28225.58	18421
WA	GEORGIA STRAIT	FRIDAY HARBOR MARINA NO 1	48-32.30	123-00.80	11267.23	28200.98	18421
WA	GEORGIA STRAIT	FRIDAY HARBOR MARINA NO 2	48-32.30	123-00.80	11267.23	28200.98	18421
WA	GEORGIA STRAIT	FRIDAY HARBOR PIER LIGHTS	48-32.70	123-00.60	11265.83	28201.37	18421
WA	GEORGIA STRAIT	LA CONNER MARINA LIGHT	48-24.00	122-29.70	11222.47	28237.15	18421
WA	GEORGIA STRAIT	SKYLINE ISLAND MARINA NO 1	48-29.40	122-40.60	11232.58	28225.10	18421
WA	GEORGIA STRAIT	SKYLINE ISLAND MARINA NO 2	48-29.30	122-40.60	11232.81	28225.07	18421
WA	GRAYS HARBOR	ABERDEEN TERMINAL PIER NO 1	46-57.90	123-51.30	11775.40	28085.07	18502
WA	GRAYS HARBOR	ABERDEEN TERMINAL PIER NO 2	46-57.80	123-51.20	11775.76	28085.14	18502
WA	GRAYS HARBOR	GRAYS HARBOR ENTRANCE NO 9	46-54.70	124-09.80	11834.34	28056.21	18502
WA	GRAYS HARBOR	ITT RAYONIER PIER LIGHTS	46-58.20	123-54.70	11781.21	28080.37	18502
WA	PACIFIC	WILLAPA BAY ENTRANCE A	46-42.30	124-09.10	11907.79	28047.88	18504
WA	PACIFIC	WILLAPA BAY ENTRANCE B	46-42.90	124-07.30	11900.34	28050.98	18504

PORTS

STATE/COUNTRY	COUNTY/PROV	NAME	LAT	LON	TD#1	TD#2	CHART NO
WA	PACIFIC	WILLAPA BAY ENTRANCE NO 10	46-43.40	124-03.90	11890.17	28056.34	18504
WA	PACIFIC	WILLAPA BAY ENTRANCE NO 13	46-42.00	124-01.00	11892.88	28059.57	18504
WA	PACIFIC	WILLAPA BAY ENTRANCE NO 6	46-43.30	124-06.10	11895.37	28053.04	18504
WA	PACIFIC	WILLAPA BAY ENTRANCE NO 8	46-43.50	124-05.30	11892.46	28054.37	18504
WA	PUGET SOUND	BECKS PIER LIGHT	47-36.60	122-12.60	11328.74	28245.63	18447
WA	PUGET SOUND	BLAIR TERMINAL LIGHT A	47-15.50	122-22.80	11454.98	28223.90	18448
WA	PUGET SOUND	BLAIR TERMINAL LIGHT B	47-15.60	122-23.10	11455.29	28223.49	18448
WA	PUGET SOUND	COLMAN FERRY TERMINAL LIGHTS	47-36.20	122-20.40	11351.31	28234.53	18448
WA	PUGET SOUND	CUTLUS BAY ENTRANCE NO 1	47-54.50	122-24.00	11292.42	28235.49	18441
WA	PUGET SOUND	DES MOINES MARINA BRKWTR LIGHT	47-23.80	122-19.80	11405.00	28231.21	18448
WA	PUGET SOUND	DES MOINES MARINA NO 1	47-24.10	122-20.00	11404.12	28231.03	18448
WA	PUGET SOUND	DES MOINES MARINA NO 1A	47-24.10	122-19.90	11403.85	28231.17	18448
WA	PUGET SOUND	DES MOINES MARINA NO 4	47-24.10	122-19.90	11403.85	28231.17	18448
WA	PUGET SOUND	DES MOINES MARINA NO 5	47-24.10	122-19.80	11403.57	28231.31	18448
WA	PUGET SOUND	DES MOINSE MARINA NO 3	47-24.10	122-19.80	11403.57	28231.31	18448
WA	PUGET SOUND	EAST WATERWAY PIER LIGHT	47-35.40	122-20.70	11355.44	28233.84	18448
WA	PUGET SOUND	HAT ISLAND MARINA BRKWTR NO 1	48-01.30	122-19.20	11259.19	28244.02	18441
WA	PUGET SOUND	HAT ISLAND MARINA BRKWTR NO 2	48-01.20	122-19.20	11259.49	28243.99	18441
WA	PUGET SOUND	INDIANOLA PIER LIGHT	47-44.70	122-31.50	11346.47	28221.99	18441
WA	PUGET SOUND	MEYDENBAUER BAY YACHT CLUB	47-36.50	122-12.50	11328.88	28245.74	18447
WA	PUGET SOUND	MEYDENBAUER YACHT CLUB PIER	46-55.00	122-41.40	11623.96	28187.56	18441
WA	PUGET SOUND	OAK HARBOR MARINA NO 1	48-17.10	122-38.00	11257.77	28224.38	18441
WA	PUGET SOUND	OLYMPIA ENTRANCE NO 2A	47-05.10	122-55.70	11600.29	28170.84	18448
WA	PUGET SOUND	OLYMPIA ENTRANCE NO 3	47-05.10	122-55.50	11599.78	28171.13	18448
WA	PUGET SOUND	PIERCE BARGE TERMINAL LIGHT	47-15.20	122-22.80	11456.56	28223.79	18448
WA	PUGET SOUND	POINT HUDSON MARINA LIGHT	48-06.90	122-44.90	11302.75	28211.92	18441
WA	PUGET SOUND	PORT LUDLOW MARINA BUOY	47-55.30	122-41.00	11331.50	28212.88	18441
WA	PUGET SOUND	PORT OF TACOMA PIER 23 LIGHT A	47-17.00	122-24.70	11452.40	28221.66	18448
WA	PUGET SOUND	PORT OF TACOMA PIER 23 LIGHT B	47-17.00	122-24.50	11451.85	28221.95	18448
WA	PUGET SOUND	PORT OF TACOMA PIER 25 LIGHT	47-17.10	122-24.60	11451.61	28221.85	18448
WA	PUGET SOUND	PORT OF TACOMA PIER NO 1	47-16.60	122-24.80	11454.75	28221.37	18448
WA	PUGET SOUND	POULSBO YACHT CLUB BRKWTR	47-43.60	122-38.50	11368.63	28211.96	18441
WA	PUGET SOUND	ROLLING HILLS PIER LIGHT	48-14.20	122-42.50	11275.74	28217.61	18441
WA	PUGET SOUND	SEABECK MARINA LIGHT A	47-38.70	122-49.70	11417.18	28194.57	18441
WA	PUGET SOUND	SHILSHOLE ENTRANCE NO 1	47-40.80	122-24.80	11344.32	28229.91	18447
WA	PUGET SOUND	SHILSHOLE ENTRANCE NO 2	47-40.60	122-24.90	11345.37	28229.70	18447
WA	PUGET SOUND	TYEE MARINA ENTRANCE LIGHT	47-17.70	122-25.10	11449.89	28221.33	18448

CHAPTER 9

REACHING ROCKS

Coordinates for rocks are included to provide boaters with a comprehensive listing of the rocky bottom structures that are available to them. This is not to be taken as an exhaustive list of all the rocks in a given area; rather, it should provide you with fine examples of substantial habitats that offer excellent fishing opportunities.

Fishing the rocky areas is probably best accomplished by either trolling or drifting. Susie's favorite method is drifting while dangling fresh bait on a three-foot monofilament leader, using a chunk of lead just large enough to keep the line about two feet from the bottom.

When trolling, we like to use leaded jigs sweetened with a piece of cut bait. We also use surgical tubing (blue fish rigs), Chartreuse Bombers, spoons, and — before the day is out — the tackle box.

Susie has found the secret to catching fish: keep the bait in the water and concentrate on what you are doing. I tend to fall asleep.

There's something you should know about anchoring in rocky areas: to date we have turned three "Danforth" anchors inside out, and we once broke our teak anchor pulpit completely off trying to get free to go home. While drifting may seem impractical, it sure is a lot cheaper than anchoring.

As usual, coordinates in this chapter are listed by state (or province or island group), county, depth, description, latitude, longitude, time delay one, and time delay two. Depths listed as "00," have yet to be confirmed, and if you plan to dive at any of the coordinates, be sure to use the depth-finding equipment on your boat or charter boat to determine water depth prior to making the actual dive. Also, the time delay (TD) numbers are the authority in this case and should be used in lieu of the latitude and longitude listings, as described in the introduction to Chapter 7.

We strongly endorse having up-to-date charts of the area aboard, which should be consulted along with tide tables to determine the proper course of action prior to venturing into unfamiliar waters.

DAFFYNITION
COVE: (1) A quiet indentation within the landmass where sailors and powerboat drivers attempt to anchor their boats for the night so that they can use the phrase "trust me." (2) A place where boats gather to tell lies about their adventures. (3) A haven. (4) A wonderful place to camp on the boat while playing soft music, cooking dinner, relaxing, and making plans for the next day's journey while your neighbor shows off his bigger boat.

HELPFUL HINT
We know that fish must eat something. We have tried every pretty-looking lure, fresh-cut bait, and live bait we could muster and have had only marginal luck with all of them. This year we are going to follow Madison Avenue's approach to baiting; we are going to troll with naked lures.

ROCKS

STATE/COUNTRY	COUNTY/PROV	NAME	DEPTH	LAT	LON	TD#1	TD#2
AK		PORT VALDEZ ROCK BUOY	00	61-05.40	146-24.60	14530.89	32232.46
AK		MIDDLE ROCK LIGHT NO 13	00	61-04.90	146-39.00	14471.75	32241.03
AK		ROCKY POINT LIGHT NO 10	00	60-57.10	146-46.00	14370.24	32185.91
AK		NORTH ISLAND ROCK LIGHT NO 10	00	60-37.70	145-42.60	14419.77	31955.39
AK		CHANNEL ISLAND ROCK NO 7	00	60-36.50	145-48.70	14385.99	31953.61
AK		HANKS ISLAND ROCK BOUY NO 5	00	60-36.00	145-59.40	14341.81	31963.73
AK		PENNSYLVANIA ROCK BUOY NO 2	00	60-26.80	147-24.00	13933.72	31990.58
AK		SCHOONER ROCK LIGHT NO 1	00	60-18.40	146-54.30	13966.84	31892.10
AK		SEAL ROCKS SHOAL NO 1	00	60-10.00	146-44.80	13923.36	31814.09
AK		SEAL ROCKS SHOAL NO 1	00	60-10.00	146-44.80	13923.36	31814.09
AK		SEAL ROCKS LIGHT	00	60-09.80	146-50.20	13900.75	31819.77
AK		SEAL ROCKS LIGHT	00	60-09.80	146-50.20	13900.75	31819.77
AK		NINILCHIK ROCK SILL N MARKER	00	60-03.30	151-39.70	12807.77	32052.44
AK		PILOT ROCK LIGHT	00	59-44.60	149-28.10	13049.30	31825.49
AK		COHEN ISLAND ROCK LIGHT	00	59-33.00	151-27.90	12526.20	31870.54
AK		SEAL ROCKS LIGHT	00	59-31.30	149-37.70	12881.18	31749.61
AK		INDIAN ROCK LIGHT	00	59-16.40	135-23.90	15174.35	29295.40
AK		PERL ROCK LIGHT	00	59-05.40	151-41.50	12195.00	31726.23
AK		ELDRED ROCK LIGHT	00	58-58.30	135-13.20	15092.25	29072.79
AK		LATAX ROCKS LIGHT	00	58-41.40	152-28.90	11820.63	31644.02
AK		LATAX ROCKS LIGHT	00	58-41.40	152-28.90	11820.63	31644.02
AK		POUNDSTONE ROCK BUOY PR	00	58-31.70	134-55.90	14979.79	28738.82
AK		POINT STEPHENS ROCK NO 2	00	58-25.40	134-46.10	14962.13	28638.43
AK		FAUST ROCK BUOY	00	58-25.10	134-55.60	14947.46	28670.70
AK		ANCON ROCK BUOY NO 2	00	58-22.40	135-55.80	14844.42	28874.28
AK		GIBBY ROCK LIGHT NO 2	00	58-19.60	134-41.20	14940.66	28561.21
AK		GEORGE ROCK LIGHT	00	58-18.90	134-41.90	14936.29	28556.67
AK		ROCK DUMP BUOY NO 2A	00	58-17.20	134-23.70	14953.21	28472.26
AK		ROCKY ISLAND LIGHT NO 13	00	58-10.70	135-03.00	14866.01	28553.56
AK		ALTHORP ROCK LIGHT NO 3	00	58-10.10	136-21.40	14738.41	28856.02
AK		PINTA ROCK BUOY NO 2	00	58-10.00	135-27.10	14826.02	28639.97
AK		DRY SPRUCE ISLAND ROCK NO 7	00	57-57.90	153-04.10	11314.84	31456.65
AK		ILKOGNAK ROCK LIGHT NO 1	00	57-54.90	152-46.90	11290.55	31419.78
AK		HANIN ROCK LIGHT	00	57-50.10	152-18.70	11275.64	31357.87
AK		STAR ROCK BUOY	00	57-49.80	136-28.00	14622.22	28690.89
AK		CYANE ROCK BUOY NO 15	00	57-47.50	152-23.10	11237.53	31350.09
AK		HUMPBACK ROCK WHISTLE NO 1	00	57-42.80	152-14.10	11205.79	31313.05
AK		HUMPBACK ROCK WHISTLE NO 1	00	57-42.80	152-14.10	11205.79	31313.05
AK		BLACK BAY ROCKS DAYBEACON NO 4	00	57-42.40	136-09.20	14618.77	28544.47
AK		SNIPE ROCK DAYBEACON NO 1	00	57-38.30	136-10.60	14596.04	28512.28
AK		LARSEN BAY ENTRANCE ROCK NO 1	00	57-32.70	153-58.50	11164.05	31398.84
AK		KENASNOW ROCK NO 2	00	57-30.00	134-36.20	14715.61	28044.66
AK		LONE ROCK DAYBEACON NO 4	00	57-27.90	134-33.40	14710.56	28012.83
AK		ROSE ISLAND ROCK LIGHT NO 19	00	57-27.30	135-32.30	14610.63	28250.07

ROCKS

STATE/COUNTRY	COUNTY/PROV	NAME	DEPTH	LAT	LON	TD#1	TD#2
AK		McCLELLAN ROCK LIGHT	00	57-27.20	135-01.50	14662.12	28120.80
AK		WEST FRANCIS ROCK BUOY NO 6	00	57-24.30	135-38.30	14586.11	28247.55
AK		BRAD ROCK BUOY NO 3	00	57-22.40	135-41.30	14571.92	28242.81
AK		ROUND ROCK LIGHT	00	57-15.60	133-56.10	14714.40	27742.24
AK		BIRD ROCK LIGHT NO 2	00	57-12.50	133-35.30	14732.65	27629.74
AK		OLD SITKA ROCKS LIGHT NO 2	00	57-06.90	135-24.60	14530.23	28030.53
AK		EAST PINTA ROCKS NO 1	00	57-05.60	133-58.40	14668.17	27652.79
AK		WEST PINTA ROCKS LIGHT	00	57-05.20	134-00.60	14663.02	27657.89
AK		CHANNEL ROCK BUOY NO 7	00	57-03.80	135-21.80	14521.27	27990.59
AK		CHANNEL ROCK LIGHT NO 8	00	57-03.60	135-22.10	14519.84	27990.12
AK		USHER ROCK SHOAL NO 5	00	57-03.10	135-23.70	14514.76	27992.65
AK		MAKHNATI ROCK WHISTLE NO 2	00	57-02.20	135-23.70	14510.73	27984.65
AK		ROCKWELL LIGHT	00	57-02.20	135-19.90	14517.49	27968.03
AK		ROCKY PATCH BUOY RP	00	57-01.70	135-18.30	14518.10	27956.57
AK		TSARITSA ROCK BUOY NO 7	00	57-01.30	135-19.40	14514.37	27957.83
AK		SIMPSON ROCK BUOY NO 5	00	57-01.20	135-20.60	14511.79	27962.20
AK		KULICHKOF ROCK BUOY NO 2	00	56-60.00	135-26.90	14495.17	27979.24
AK		ELOVOI ROCK DAYBEACON NO 1	00	56-49.30	135-22.60	14455.73	27867.19
AK		MIDWAY ROCK LIGHT MR	00	56-31.80	132-57.80	14625.12	27073.18
AK		FOREMOST ROCK DAYBEACON	00	56-30.10	133-00.30	14614.71	27066.80
AK		VICHNEFSKI ROCK LIGHT	00	56-26.30	133-00.80	14599.30	27032.01
AK		HELM ROCK BUOY NO 8	00	56-22.20	133-38.40	14523.49	27160.01
AK		WEST ROCK LIGHT	00	56-21.20	133-38.10	14520.08	27149.83
AK		CALDER ROCKS WHISTLE NO 6	00	56-15.50	133-43.30	14489.32	27124.67
AK		VILLAGE ISLANDS ROCK NO 15	00	56-13.20	132-18.90	14613.95	26730.47
AK		VILLAGE ROCK DAYBEACON NO 12	00	56-12.90	132-17.50	14614.94	26721.90
AK		MIDCHANNEL ROCK DAYBEACON	00	56-12.20	132-16.20	14614.33	26709.68
AK		TRAP ROCK BUOY NO 3	00	56-11.30	132-13.30	14615.37	26689.16
AK		FOUND ISLAND ROCK NO 2	00	56-11.10	132-12.70	14615.54	26684.78
AK		FOUND ISLAND ROCK DAYBEACON	00	56-06.80	132-04.30	14612.46	26608.22
AK		LEMON POINT ROCK LIGHT	00	56-04.40	134-06.60	14406.75	27146.47
AK		LINCOLN ROCK WEST LIGHT	00	56-03.40	132-41.80	14542.93	26734.34
AK		HUB ROCK DAYBEACON NO 3	00	55-56.50	133-17.70	14459.80	26847.19
AK		BROWNSON ISLAND ROCKS BI	00	55-56.00	132-06.70	14570.23	26509.62
AK		AIKENS ROCK DAYBEACON NO 3	00	55-54.10	133-15.60	14454.41	26818.30
AK		VILLAGE ROCK DAYBEACON VR	00	55-53.50	133-15.30	14452.69	26812.23
AK		PEEP ROCK LIGHT	00	55-49.20	133-19.80	14429.44	26802.58
AK		HIGHWATER ROCK DAYBEACON NO 1	00	55-33.60	133-06.20	14396.02	26628.85
AK		ST IGNACE ROCK LIGHT	00	55-25.70	133-23.60	14338.63	26673.49
AK		SOLA ROCK DAYBEACON SR	00	55-25.60	133-28.80	14329.30	26699.63
AK		OHIO ROCK BUOY	00	55-23.80	131-46.20	14490.56	26154.89
AK		IDAHO ROCK BUOY NO 4	00	55-20.90	131-41.00	14488.89	26116.78
AK		CALIFORNIA ROCK BUOY NO 3	00	55-18.90	131-36.10	14489.78	26087.27
AK		POTTER ROCK BUOY	00	55-18.10	131-34.50	14489.59	26078.31

ROCKS

STATE/COUNTRY	COUNTY/PROV	NAME	DEPTH	LAT	LON	TD#1	TD#2
AK		CUTTER ROCKS DAYBEACON CR	00	55-17.40	131-31.40	14492.01	26063.50
AK		WALDEN ROCK LIGHT WR	00	55-16.30	131-36.60	14480.45	26085.27
AK		MASTIC ROCK DAYBEACON	00	55-15.50	131-23.90	14497.18	26034.17
AK		BAILEY ROCK DAYBEACON BR	00	55-15.40	131-35.90	14478.56	26081.06
AK		HOG ROCKS LIGHT	00	55-10.70	131-16.90	14492.19	26019.31
AK		KELP ROCKS NO 1	00	55-09.50	131-37.80	14456.36	26084.77
AK		LIVELY ROCK BUOY NO 9	00	55-09.50	131-35.10	14460.53	26074.38
AK		MOIRA ROCK LIGHT	00	55-05.00	131-59.80	14407.13	26173.77
AK		INDIAN ROCK NO 6	00	55-01.80	131-20.70	14457.86	26035.01
AK		MELLEN ROCK LIGHT	00	55-01.60	132-39.90	14330.49	26354.26
AK		BLACK ROCK LIGHT	00	55-01.40	131-03.50	14482.67	26008.44
AK		WALLACE ROCK BUOY NO 2	00	54-51.10	132-26.90	14317.84	26273.68
AK		GUIDE ROCKS DAYBEACON NO 4	00	54-49.60	132-21.40	14322.13	26248.20
AK		BOAT ROCK LIGHT	00	54-46.80	130-47.90	14460.63	26005.76
AK		LORD ROCK LIGHT	00	54-43.60	130-49.10	14449.04	26008.01
AK	ALEUTIANS	ROCKY POINT DAYBEACON 6RP	00	54-58.30	163-26.40	18409.14	47425.42
AK	ALEUTIANS	GANNET ROCKS LIGHT NO 4	00	51-52.10	176-36.40	14829.05	49774.35
AK	ALEUTIANS	GANNET ROCKS BUOY 4A	00	51-51.90	176-36.50	14827.70	49774.07
CA	HUMBOLDT	READING ROCKS LIGHT	00	41-20.50	124-10.60	14573.06	43840.29
CA	HUMBOLDT	TURTLE ROCKS BUOY NO 28	00	41-08.20	124-11.80	14664.71	43822.08
CA	HUMBOLDT	PILOT ROCK BUOY NO 2	00	41-02.60	124-09.20	14712.86	43814.98
CA	MARIN	CASTRO ROCKS NO 2CR	00	37-55.90	122-25.20	16058.42	43234.72
CA	MARIN	CONE ROCK LIGHT	00	37-51.80	122-28.10	16060.73	43213.90
CA	MARIN	HARDING ROCK HR	00	37-50.30	122-26.70	16069.35	43205.20
CA	MARIN	BLOSSOM ROCK BELL BR	00	37-49.10	122-24.20	16080.55	43197.49
CA	MARIN	ANITA ROCK LIGHT	00	37-48.50	122-27.20	16072.69	43195.71
CA	ORANGE	SHIP ROCK LIGHT	00	33-27.80	118-29.40	28145.04	41033.95
CA	ORANGE	BEGG ROCK WHISTLE NO 4	00	33-22.00	119-41.80	27964.01	41329.42
CA	ORANGE	BEGG ROCKS	00	33-21.76	119-41.60	27964.41	41327.81
CA	S LUIS OBISPO	MOUSE ROCK NO 3MR	00	35-26.30	120-54.40	27777.85	42175.92
CA	S LUIS OBISPO	CONSTANTINE ROCK NO 1CR	00	35-26.20	120-56.60	27769.98	42182.40
CA	S LUIS OBISPO	CHURCH ROCKS @ MORRO BAY	00	35-20.50	120-59.90	27758.80	42160.86
CA	S LUIS OBISPO	PECHO ROCKS	90	35-10.70	120-48.90	27797.14	42070.67
CA	S LUIS OBISPO	LANSING ROCK BUOY	00	35-09.70	120-44.80	27811.06	42051.22
CA	S LUIS OBISPO	WESTDAHL ROCK NO 1	00	35-08.80	120-47.00	27803.53	42053.87
CA	S LUIS OBISPO	SOUZA ROCK GONG	00	35-07.70	120-44.30	27812.60	42038.61
CA	SAN DIEGO	CHURCH ROCKS, CATALINA IS	00	33-17.80	118-19.60	28159.61	40962.13
CA	SAN DIEGO	OCEANSIDE'S CLAM BEDS	50	33-14.30	117-17.30	28292.72	40669.24
CA	SAN DIEGO	PT LOMA BIRD ROCKS	15	32-48.90	117-16.57	28268.62	40629.72
CA	SAN DIEGO	ROCKPILE FISHING	60	32-25.60	117-08.00	28263.76	40570.52
CA	SAN MATEO	NOONDAY ROCK WHISTLE NR	00	37-47.70	123-10.70	27091.38	43210.13
CA	SAN MATEO	MILE ROCKS LIGHT	00	37-47.60	122-30.60	16064.42	43192.53
CA	SAN MATEO	MILE ROCKS LIGHT	00	37-47.60	122-30.60	27210.18	43192.53
CA	SAN MATEO	MISSION ROCK NE LIGHT	00	37-46.50	122-22.80	16091.92	43182.55

ROCKS

STATE/COUNTRY	COUNTY/PROV	NAME	DEPTH	LAT	LON	TD#1	TD#2
CA	SAN MATEO	MISSION ROCK SE LIGHT	00	37-46.30	122-22.80	16092.44	43181.45
CA	VENTURA	BASS ROCK	78	34-06.40	119-11.60	28068.30	41362.75
CA	VENTURA	LAS FLORES ROCKS	33	34-01.80	118-37.80	28154.39	41185.29
CA	VENTURA	MALIBU ROCKPILE FISHING	60	34-01.50	118-39.70	28149.19	41193.38
CA	VENTURA	SCATTERED ROCKS	50	34-01.50	118-34.22	28163.36	41166.71
CANADA	B COLUMBIA	SLIPPERY ROCK LIGHT	00	54-24.00	130-29.70	11738.32	30614.15
CANADA	B COLUMBIA	THRASHER ROCK LIGHT	00	49-09.00	123-38.40	15160.54	29078.87
CANADA	B COLUMBIA	GRAPPLER ROCK LIGHT	00	48-56.40	123-36.10	15157.89	28952.70
CANADA	B COLUMBIA	GOVERNOR ROCK U45	00	48-54.80	123-29.80	15176.55	28922.33
CANADA	B COLUMBIA	BEN MOHR ROCK BUOY UK	00	48-51.60	123-23.40	15193.56	28875.76
CANADA	B COLUMBIA	SEABIRD ROCKS LIGHT	00	48-45.00	125-09.20	14825.19	29049.66
HAWAII	HONOLULU	PYRAMID ROCK LIGHT	00	21-27.90	157-46.00	12291.32	37143.14
HAWAII	KAUAI	LEHUA ROCK LIGHT	00	22-01.30	160-06.10	13745.16	36970.23
HAWAII	KAUAI	KALANIPUAO ROCK BUOY NO 2	00	21-52.80	159-31.50	13391.02	37021.30
OR	COOS	BALTIMORE ROCK NO 2BR	00	43-21.30	124-22.90	13539.65	27777.40
OR	LINCOLN	CLEFT OF THE ROCK LIGHT	00	44-17.50	124-06.50	13044.04	27901.49
WA	CLALLAM	DUNTZE ROCK WHISTLE 2D	00	48-24.90	124-44.90	11500.53	28071.28
WA	CLALLAM	DUNTZE ROCK WHISTLE 2D	00	48-24.90	124-44.90	11500.53	28071.28
WA	CLALLAM	SCROGGS ROCKS LIGHT	00	48-24.40	123-26.30	11341.84	28166.19
Canada	B Columbia	RACE ROCKS LIGHT	00	48-17.90	123-31.80	11373.29	28156.39
Canada	B Columbia	RACE ROCKS E BUOY VG	00	48-16.10	123-27.70	11370.10	28160.72
Canada	B Columbia	ROSENFELD ROCK NO U59	00	48-48.20	123-01.60	11232.47	28205.73
WA	GEORGIA STRAIT	ROCKS JUNCTION BUOY	00	48-40.50	122-35.40	11198.20	28234.98
WA	GEORGIA STRAIT	LUMMI ROCKS NO 16A	00	48-40.20	122-40.10	11207.89	28229.13
WA	GEORGIA STRAIT	VITI ROCKS LIGHT	00	48-38.00	122-37.30	11206.97	28231.89
WA	GEORGIA STRAIT	HARBOR ROCK DAYBEACON	00	48-37.80	122-58.60	11249.59	28205.68
WA	GEORGIA STRAIT	VITI ROCKS NO 9	00	48-37.80	122-37.10	11207.00	28232.08
WA	GEORGIA STRAIT	JONES ISLAND ROCKS	00	48-37.20	123-02.50	11258.80	28200.69
WA	GEORGIA STRAIT	BIRD ROCKS LIGHT	00	48-35.90	123-00.80	11258.47	28202.30
WA	GEORGIA STRAIT	BLIND BAY ROCK DAYBEACON	00	48-35.00	122-55.90	11250.71	28208.00
WA	GEORGIA STRAIT	REID ROCK BUOY	00	48-32.90	122-59.30	11262.67	28203.05
WA	GEORGIA STRAIT	BLACK ROCK LIGHT NO 9	00	48-32.80	122-45.90	11235.55	28219.61
WA	GEORGIA STRAIT	TURN ROCK LIGHT NO 3	00	48-32.00	122-57.80	11261.80	28204.58
Canada	B Columbia	LITTLE ZERO ROCK NO V30	00	48-31.90	123-19.70	11307.12	28177.54
WA	GEORGIA STRAIT	LAWSON ROCK JUNCTION	00	48-31.90	122-47.20	11240.30	28217.69
Canada	B Columbia	ZERO ROCK LIGHT	00	48-31.40	123-17.40	11303.71	28180.16
WA	GEORGIA STRAIT	RAM ISLAND ROCKS NO 4	00	48-28.40	122-50.20	11254.94	28212.76
WA	GEORGIA STRAIT	WILLIAMSON ROCKS NO 4	00	48-26.90	122-42.30	11242.08	28222.15
WA	GEORGIA STRAIT	TWIN ROCKS DAYBEACON	00	48-26.80	122-54.60	11268.20	28206.69
WA	GEORGIA STRAIT	SEAL ROCKS LIGHT NO 12	00	48-22.40	122-33.70	11234.84	28231.58
WA	PUGET SOUND	CAMANO HEAD ROCKS NO 1	00	48-03.00	122-21.20	11258.90	28241.87
WA	PUGET SOUND	KLAS ROCKS NO 2	00	47-57.70	122-40.20	11321.33	28214.82
WA	PUGET SOUND	COLVOS ROCKS LIGHT	00	47-57.10	122-40.10	11323.12	28214.74
WA	PUGET SOUND	SISTERS ROCK NO 4	00	47-51.50	122-38.40	11338.57	28215.00

ROCKS

STATE/COUNTRY	COUNTY/PROV	NAME	DEPTH	LAT	LON	TD#1	TD#2
WA	PUGET SOUND	SEAL ROCK DAYBEACON	00	47-42.90	122-52.90	11407.81	28191.91
WA	PUGET SOUND	BLAKELY ROCK LIGHT	00	47-35.70	122-28.80	11375.72	28222.55
WA	PUGET SOUND	ORCHARD ROCKS FISH PEN	00	47-34.60	122-31.70	11388.08	28218.08
WA	PUGET SOUND	FOX ISLAND ROCK NO 1	00	47-16.50	122-38.70	11493.00	28201.00

CHAPTER 10

LOVELY LEDGES

When at anchor, we have found it is not easy to keep the stern of the boat right above a ledge, what with the tides, winds, and current all trying to keep us away from the fish. We have found that a marker placed on the ledge will at least let us know how far we have drifted away from our ideal fishing location.

When we are going to troll a ledge, we place markers about every hundred yards or so apart. Then we troll a zigzagging course, trying not to catch our markers. Unfortunately, this technique doesn't work worth a hoot when there's lots of traffic!

We have also found that other fishermen will pull up to our markers and anchor there, just *knowing* that there must be fish by a marker. To alleviate this situation, we start trolling at about 3:30 in the evening and finish well after dark; this improves our chance to creel fish without interference.

Fishing at night is great fun, especially when we catch a real lunker that doesn't want to go home with us. We can't see what we are about to catch until just before we boat it. We heartily recommend that you give night-fishing a try.

Coordinates in this chapter are listed by state (or province or island group), county, description, latitude, longitude, time delay one, and time delay two. When diving near ledges, as elsewhere, use the depth-finding equipment on your boat or charter boat to determine actual water depth. Also, use the time delay (TD) numbers in lieu of the latitude/longitude listings near ledges (see the introduction to Chapter 7).

WIT & WISDOM

If free-board is the amount of boat above the water line, then expensive-board is when the free-board finds itself below the water line.

DAFFYNITION

LORAN: Acronym for LOng RAnge Navigation. The coastal waters of the United States are covered with several Group Repetition Intervals (GRIs): GRI 7960 (Gulf of Alaska Chain), GRI 5990 (Canadian West Coast Chain), GRI 9940 (US West Coast Chain), GRI 9960 (Northeast US Chain), GRI 8970 (Great Lakes Chain), and GRI 7980 (Southeast US Chain). While the credentials of the loran are impressive, the machine cannot think for itself and should not be used as a substitute for good common sense.

LEDGES

STATE/COUNTRY	COUNTY/PROV	NAME	DEPTH	LAT	LON	TD#1	TD#2
AK		KNIK ARM SHOAL BUOY NO 7	00	61-12.20	150-05.20	13782.00	32401.73
AK		KNOWLES HEAD SHOAL BUOY NO 4	00	60-40.50	146-44.00	14217.95	32053.40
AK		LONE ISLAND SHOAL NO 2	00	60-38.30	147-47.20	13956.35	32098.32
AK		MIDDLE GROUND SHOAL BUOY NO 2	00	60-32.50	146-22.00	14224.08	31963.91
AK		APPLEGATE SHOALS LIGHT	00	60-21.30	147-23.50	13882.68	31948.64
AK		SEAL ROCKS SHOAL NO 1	00	60-10.00	146-44.80	13923.36	31814.09
AK		SEAL ROCKS SHOAL NO 1	00	60-10.00	146-44.80	13923.36	31814.09
AK		NINILCHIK ROCK SILL N MARKER	00	60-03.30	151-39.70	12807.77	32052.44
AK		ARCHIMANSRITOF SHOALS BUOY NO 3	00	59-35.50	151-26.10	12557.64	31883.32
AK		PORT GRAHAM ENTRANCE SHOAL NO 1	00	59-22.80	151-54.10	12346.44	31836.42
AK		SUGARLOAF ISLAND SHOAL NO 2	00	58-17.40	136-53.20	14722.19	29052.67
AK		HORSE SHOAL LIGHT NO 1	00	58-15.30	134-42.10	14918.60	28520.80
AK		HAWK INLET EAST SHOAL NO 2	00	58-06.20	134-46.30	14868.81	28444.53
AK		ENTRANCE POINT SHOAL NO 5	00	57-54.80	152-31.50	11305.00	31399.50
AK		WOMENS BAY MIDDLE SHOAL NO 19	00	57-43.80	152-31.00	11184.52	31341.37
AK		HIGHWATER ISLAND SHOAL NO 23	00	57-16.90	135-36.00	14555.70	28170.02
AK		KASIANA ISLAND SHOAL NO 1	00	57-05.40	135-24.30	14524.01	28015.79
AK		USHER ROCK SHOAL NO 5	00	57-03.10	135-23.70	14514.76	27992.65
AK		YASHA ISLAND SHOAL NO 2	00	56-58.90	134-34.50	14581.17	27740.77
AK		FIVE FATHOM SHOAL BUOY	00	56-21.70	133-13.90	14561.07	27045.36
AK		BUTTON ISLAND SHOAL NO 5	00	56-12.10	132-14.80	14616.05	26703.18
AK		AMELIUS ISLAND SHOAL A	00	56-10.20	133-49.60	14458.27	27110.44
AK		EDNA BAY SHOAL BUOYS	00	55-57.80	133-37.30	14431.90	26953.26
AK		SALMON RIVER SHOAL NO 3	00	55-54.50	130-00.20	14742.86	26315.88
AK		POINT SWIFT SHOAL NO 2	00	55-46.30	133-18.80	14420.53	26776.81
AK		KLAWOCK LEDGE DAYBEACON NO 3	00	55-33.40	133-06.10	14395.48	26627.11
AK		KLAWOCK INLET SHOAL NO 8	00	55-32.60	133-07.00	14391.14	26626.95
AK		CRAIG SHOAL NO 7	00	55-29.20	133-08.70	14376.30	26615.96
AK		SALTERY POINT SHOAL NO 6	00	55-28.90	133-08.70	14375.25	26614.26
AK		BALANDRA SHOAL NO 3	00	55-28.60	133-13.70	14365.74	26638.40
AK		BALLENA ISLAND SHOAL NO 2	00	55-28.30	133-13.10	14365.70	26633.62
AK		SHOE ISLAND SHOAL BUOY NO 2	00	54-57.40	132-45.40	14307.39	26369.99
AK	ALEUTIANS	BLUFF POINT SHOAL NO 1	00	55-11.50	161-52.30	18490.30	46838.40
AK	ALEUTIANS	ROCKY POINT SHOAL RP	00	53-53.50	166-31.20	17942.40	48388.85
AK	ALEUTIANS	BAILEY LEDGE DAYBEACON	00	53-51.60	166-33.40	17929.15	48395.79
AK	ALEUTIANS	KULUK SHOAL BUOY NO 2	00	51-52.10	176-36.40	14829.05	49774.35
AK	ALEUTIANS	FINGER SHOAL BUOY NO 3	00	51-51.50	176-33.90	14841.20	49770.08
CA	MARIN	YELLOW BLUFF LIGHT	00	37-50.20	122-28.30	16064.55	43205.40
CANADA	B COLUMBIA	ROBERTS BANK LIGHT	00	49-05.20	123-18.60	15220.90	28996.98
CANADA	B COLUMBIA	ROBERTS BANK BUOY TA	00	49-04.40	123-22.80	15207.04	28998.91
CANADA	B COLUMBIA	VICTORIA SHOAL BUOY U43	00	48-55.20	123-30.90	15173.43	28928.83
MARIANAS	GUAM ISLAND	APRA HARBOR W SHOAL WS	00	13-26.90N	144-39.10E	Suggest	GPS
PHILIPPINES	LUZON ISLAND	CUBI SHOAL LIGHT NO 8	00	14-48.60N	120-15.50E	Suggest	GPS
PHILIPPINES	LUZON ISLAND	SIXTEEN FOOT SHOAL NO 6	16	14-47.90N	120-14.50E	Suggest	GPS

LEDGES

STATE/COUNTRY	COUNTY/PROV	NAME	DEPTH	LAT	LON	TD#1	TD#2
PHILIPPINES	LUZON ISLAND	GRAND ISLAND SHOAL NO 4	00	14-46.70N	120-13.10E	Suggest	GPS
PHILIPPINES	LUZON ISLAND	TWENTY-FOUR FOOT SHOAL NO 2	24	14-45.20N	120-13.40E	Suggest	GPS
WA	GEORGIA STRAIT	BOUNDARY PASS SHOAL B	00	48-45.90	123-00.80	11235.83	28205.88
WA	GEORGIA STRAIT	POINT FRANCIS SHOAL NO 4	00	48-41.70	122-38.20	11201.19	28231.91
WA	GEORGIA STRAIT	LYDIA SHOAL NO 13	00	48-35.90	122-46.70	11230.13	28219.6
WA	GEORGIA STRAIT	BLAKELY ISLAND SHOAL BS	00	48-34.20	122-50.70	11242.06	28214.13
WA	GEORGIA STRAIT	SHOAL BAY AQUACULTURE LIGHT	00	48-33.40	122-52.40	11247.38	28211.76
WA	GEORGIA STRAIT	FIDALGO BAY SHOAL NO 2	00	48-30.60	122-35.00	11218.32	28232.48
WA	GEORGIA STRAIT	DENNIS SHOAL NO 6	00	48-27.50	122-42.80	11241.67	28221.72
WA	PUGET SOUND	CLINTON SHOAL BUOY	00	47-58.60	122-20.90	11271.57	28240.94
WA	PUGET SOUND	CASE SHOAL DAYBEACON	00	47-51.50	122-40.40	11343.52	28212.2
WA	PUGET SOUND	CASE SHOAL NO 6	00	47-50.70	122-40.10	11345.69	28212.41
WA	PUGET SOUND	CASE SHOAL NO 5	00	47-49.50	122-38.80	11346.86	28213.7
WA	PUGET SOUND	CASE SHOAL NO 8	00	47-48.80	122-42.80	11359.45	28208.03
WA	PUGET SOUND	TREASURE ISLAND SHOAL NO 2	00	47-41.90	122-32.10	11358.93	28220.17
WA	PUGET SOUND	JUANITA BAY SHOAL DAYBEACON	00	47-41.80	122-13.00	11309.42	28246.64
WA	PUGET SOUND	LAKE UNION SHOAL NO 2	00	47-37.80	122-20.20	11344.21	28235.33
WA	PUGET SOUND	TYEE SHOAL LIGHT	00	47-36.60	122-29.20	11372.99	28222.31
WA	PUGET SOUND	QUARTERMASTER HARB SHOAL NO 2	00	47-21.00	122-28.60	11442.78	28217.47
WA	PUGET SOUND	COMMENCEMENT BAY SHOAL A	00	47-16.30	122-25.90	11459.34	28219.64
WA	PUGET SOUND	WYCKOFF SHOAL NO 1	00	47-14.50	122-42.80	11514.47	28194.17
WA	PUGET SOUND	PITT PASSAGE N SHOAL	00	47-13.60	122-42.70	11519.02	28193.9
WA	PUGET SOUND	TOLIVA SHOAL	00	47-12.20	122-36.40	11509.75	28202.59
WA	PUGET SOUND	WEST OPLYMPIA SHOAL NO 1	00	47-05.50	122-55.40	11597.22	28171.48
WA	PUGET SOUND	OLYMPIA SHOAL LIGHT	00	47-05.50	122-55.10	11596.45	28171.92

CHAPTER 11

REEFS

The thought of vessels split open by reefs and sent down to Davy Jones' Locker makes our skin crawl with excitement and conjures up visions of hauling in countless treasures. While this sort of treasure-hunting is certainly a possibility, the real treasure of a reef lies in its beauty and in the beauty of the living creatures that call it home.

But don't be lulled into carelessness by the beauty of a reef. Right under the surface lurk rocks that can cause great harm and loss without a whimper of a warning. The anticipation and excitement that comes with the desire for discovery is very strong, but if it isn't tempered with caution, this emotion may give birth to a trip fraught with hazards that might threaten equipment, if not lives.

If you plan to venture to open-water diving and fishing spots, we urge you to consult with those who have made the trip and take heed of any warnings. Most places are safe and can be great fun to visit, but there are those that require special precautions.

We strongly endorse having up-to-date charts of the area aboard, along with tide tables. Both should be consulted to determine the proper course of action prior to venturing into unfamiliar waters. Listings are as usual (please refer to the first two paragraphs of Chapter 7), and again we urge divers to determine water depth prior to venturing beneath the surface.

Diving most of these structures is easy, but some of the dives are deep and should be attempted only by the experienced. Those who are not as experienced as others need not feel bad about missing out, as they can gain the necessary experience over time. In the meantime, there are lots of pretties listed in this publication that can be found in dives less than 30 feet deep. And that's where we find all of the color anyway!

Reef diving and fishing require special skills. If you're new to this type of diving and fishing, it would be wise to seek out local knowledge before attempting something that could become dangerous very quickly.

Then good luck and happy hunting!

HELPFUL HINT

Fish for savory things near ledges, wrecks, reefs, rocks, and most structures. It is best to drift about a ledge, bounce over rocks, and set a hook at reefs and wrecks.

REEFS

STATE/COUNTRY	COUNTY/PROV	NAME	DEPTH	LAT	LON	TD#1	TD#2
AK		BLIGH REEF BUOY NO 6	00	60-50.50	146-54.30	14275.24	32142.08
AK		WESSELS REEF WHISTLE NO 1	00	59-47.80	146-06.00	13865.38	31578.05
AK		VANDERBILT REEF LIGHT	00	58-35.50	135-01.00	14991.81	28796.31
AK		COHEN REEF DAYBEACON CR	00	58-25.90	134-48.10	14961.83	28650.92
AK		FAVORITE REEF LIGHT NO 2	00	58-22.80	134-51.60	14941.74	28632.44
AK		HANUS REEF LIGHT	00	58-07.90	134-59.80	14857.11	28513.23
AK		SKIPWITH REEFS BUOY NO 2	00	58-00.70	152-39.20	11359.66	31440.22
AK		WILLIAMS REEF WHISTLE NO 1	00	57-50.30	152-09.30	11301.79	31346.23
AK		WILLIAMS REEF WHISTLE NO 1	00	57-50.30	152-09.30	11301.79	31346.23
AK		TENAKEE REEF LIGHT	00	57-46.20	135-13.50	14731.44	28352.77
AK		MINNIE REEF DAYBEACON NO 5	00	57-43.20	136-10.20	14620.95	28556.06
AK		COZIAN REEF BUOY NO 3	00	57-34.10	135-25.50	14654.25	28285.60
AK		WYVILLE REEF BUOY NO 22	00	57-16.30	135-35.40	14553.99	28162.00
AK		NEVA POINT REEF LIGHT NO 12	00	57-14.10	135-33.00	14548.11	28131.75
AK		AKHOIK REEF BUOY NO 1	00	56-54.80	154-07.70	11040.93	31231.60
AK		POINT HIGHFIELD REEF	00	56-28.90	132-23.60	14665.33	26910.20
AK		McARTHUR REEF BUOY	00	56-23.70	133-10.60	14573.99	27049.44
AK		NESBITT REEF LIGHT	00	56-13.20	132-51.70	14563.77	26868.54
AK		KEY REEF LIGHT	00	56-09.60	132-49.80	14553.30	26826.84
AK		DESCONOCIDA REEF BUOY NO 10	00	55-41.30	133-31.40	14381.04	26806.54
AK		CURACAO REEF BUOY NO 8	00	55-39.30	133-28.20	14379.25	26777.29
AK		LARZATITA ISLAND REEF LIGHT	00	55-35.10	133-19.60	14378.79	26706.93
AK		HERMANOS ISLANDS REEF NO 8	00	55-33.80	133-17.70	14377.38	26689.26
AK		PIEDRAS ISLAND REEF NO 9	00	55-33.70	133-17.80	14376.85	26689.17
AK		KLAWOCK REEF BUOY NO 1	00	55-30.60	133-11.10	14377.19	26636.35
AK		KLAWOCK REEF BUOY NO 3	00	55-30.50	133-10.40	14378.02	26632.17
AK		KLAWOCK REEF BUOY NO 2	00	55-30.40	133-11.10	14376.48	26635.20
AK		PARIDA ISLAND SOUTH REEF NO 5	00	55-30.10	133-13.30	14371.71	26644.82
AK		FERN REEF BUOY NO 3A	00	55-29.10	133-15.80	14363.94	26652.03
AK		FISH EGG REEF BUOY NO 3	00	55-28.50	133-09.50	14372.49	26616.15
AK		POND REEF NO 16	00	55-26.30	131-48.80	14494.94	26180.83
AK		ROSA REEF NO 15	00	55-24.80	131-48.10	14490.99	26169.56
AK		PENINSULA POINT REEF NO 2	00	55-23.10	131-44.30	14491.15	26141.89
AK		LEWIS REEF LIGHT NO 11	00	55-22.50	131-44.20	14489.30	26138.97
AK		PENNOCK ISLAND REEF PR	00	55-20.30	131-40.00	14488.44	26109.90
AK		SPIRE ISLAND REEF LIGHT SI	00	55-16.10	131-29.90	14490.03	26056.28
AK		REEF ISLAND LIGHT	00	55-04.80	130-12.10	14568.26	26030.01
AK		HID REEF WHISTLE NO 2	00	55-04.20	131-40.40	14435.12	26093.24
AK		AJAX REEF LIGHT NO 3	00	55-00.10	131-27.60	14441.83	26053.38
AK		CENTER ISLAND REEF NO 3	00	54-48.20	132-22.90	14315.15	26252.96
AK		TONGASS REEF DAYBEACON	00	54-47.20	130-44.60	14466.80	26004.10
AK	ALEUTIANS	CROW REEF BUOY NO CR	00	55-45.60	160-43.40	18586.94	46385.59
CA	DEL NORTE	ST GEORGE REEF BUOY SG (LNB)	00	41-50.20	124-23.80	14311.69	43868.41
CA	HUMBOLDT	BLUNTS REEF BUOY B (ELB)	00	40-26.40	124-30.20	14915.38	43735.50

REEFS

STATE/COUNTRY	COUNTY/PROV	NAME	DEPTH	LAT	LON	TD#1	TD#2
CA	LOS ANGELES	OCEAN PARK REEF	60	33-59.20	118-30.20	28171.42	41138.65
CA	LOS ANGELES	VENICE PIER REEF	20	33-59.10	118-28.60	28175.39	41130.43
CA	LOS ANGELES	VENICE ART REEF	60	33-58.70	118-29.60	28172.46	41133.91
CA	LOS ANGELES	MARINA DEL RAY ART REEF	60	33-57.50	118-29.05	28172.68	41126.95
CA	LOS ANGELES	MANHATTAN BEACH PIER REEF	20	33-53.00	118-24.80	28178.98	41090.59
CA	LOS ANGELES	HERMOSA BEACH ART REEF	20	33-51.70	118-24.30	28178.96	41083.77
CA	LOS ANGELES	HERMOSA BEACH ART REEF	20	33-51.18	118-24.36	28178.31	41082.33
CA	LOS ANGELES	KINGS HARBOR ART REEF	80	33-50.30	118-24.60	28176.87	41080.57
CA	LOS ANGELES	REDONDO BEACH ART REEF	110	33-50.20	118-24.35	28177.39	41079.03
CA	LOS ANGELES	TORRANCE BCH ART REEF	60	33-48.80	118-24.30	28176.17	41074.18
CA	LOS ANGELES	VOLCANIC REEF	300	33-47.60	118-29.80	28161.43	41096.75
CA	LOS ANGELES	BELMONT PIER ART REEF	15	33-45.30	118-08.80	28210.39	40987.49
CA	MARIN	SOUTHAMPTON SHOAL NO 5	00	37-55.30	122-25.60	16058.85	43231.66
CA	MARIN	SOUTHAMPTON SHOAL NO 4	00	37-55.00	122-25.30	16060.67	43229.93
CA	MARIN	SOUTHAMPTON SHOAL NO 1	00	37-54.00	122-25.30	16063.50	43224.54
CA	MARIN	SOUTHAMPTON SHOAL NO 2	00	37-54.00	122-25.10	16064.15	43224.46
CA	MARIN	SOUTHAMPTON SHOAL LIGHT	00	37-52.90	122-24.00	16070.75	43218.04
CA	MARIN	DUXBURY REEF WHISTLE 1DR	00	37-51.60	122-41.70	16018.04	43218.51
CA	MENDOCINO	SAUNDERS REEF BUOY NO 16	00	38-50.80	123-40.00	15605.87	43483.25
CA	ORANGE	SEVENTEEN FATHOM REEF	102	33-43.60	119-09.70	28057.12	41267.41
CA	ORANGE	CABRILLO PIER ART REEF	20	33-42.70	118-16.80	28188.61	41018.58
CA	ORANGE	HUNTINGTON BCH REEF A	50	33-40.00	118-03.00	28218.75	40943.65
CA	ORANGE	BOLSA CHICA 4 ART REEF	85	33-39.32	118-06.40	28210.08	40958.26
CA	ORANGE	BOLSA CHICA 6 ART REEF	83	33-39.28	118-06.09	28210.77	40956.64
CA	ORANGE	HUNTINGTON BCH REEF B	66	33-37.27	117-59.48	28224.19	40918.97
CA	ORANGE	HUNTINGTON BCH REEF D	45	33-37.00	117-58.50	28226.19	40913.48
CA	ORANGE	NEWPORT BEACH ART REEF	120	33-36.07	117-57.54	28227.46	40906.33
CA	ORANGE	HIDDEN SEVEN FATHOM REEF	45	33-29.50	119-04.40	28061.16	41196.35
CA	ORANGE	HUNTINGTON BCH REEF C	66	33-27.12	117-59.18	28214.81	40891.17
CA	ORANGE	HARBOR REEF E BUOY	00	33-26.90	118-29.40	28144.29	41031.38
CA	ORANGE	HARBOR REEF S BUOY	00	33-26.80	118-29.30	28144.45	41030.64
CA	SAN DIEGO	C PENDELTON ART REEF	40	33-19.30	117-31.42	28268.24	40743.32
CA	SAN DIEGO	PENDLETON ART REEF	40	33-18.92	117-33.20	28264.03	40750.88
CA	SAN DIEGO	THREE MILE REEF	66	33-18.60	119-27.60	27997.63	41260.23
CA	SAN DIEGO	BOILER REEF	18	33-16.50	119-36.40	27975.05	41289.60
CA	SAN DIEGO	SEVEN FATHOM REEF	42	33-15.80	119-37.80	27971.32	41293.04
CA	SAN DIEGO	OCEANSIDE ART REEF	60	33-11.00	117-24.00	28275.36	40694.25
CA	SAN DIEGO	NINE FATHOM REEF	54	33-02.60	118-37.50	28106.86	41002.82
CA	SAN DIEGO	TORREY PINES REEF NO 2	60	32-53.35	117-15.35	28275.36	40630.27
CA	SAN DIEGO	TORREY PINES REEF NO 1	55	32-53.12	117-15.50	28274.84	40630.60
CA	SAN DIEGO	POINT LOMA SPOT	342	32-47.90	118-31.50	28110.14	40943.23
CA	SAN MATEO	SAN BRUNO SHOAL NO 1	00	37-41.70	122-20.30	16112.08	43154.56
CA	SAN MATEO	SOUTHEAST REEF NO 1S	00	37-27.90	122-28.10	27272.27	43083.59
CA	STA BARBARA	NAPLES REEF	48	34-25.00	119-57.80	27947.96	41645.18

R E E F S

STATE/COUNTRY	COUNTY/PROV	NAME	DEPTH	LAT	LON	TD#1	TD#2
CA	STA BARBARA	MOHAWK REEF	45	34-24.20	119-45.30	27984.48	41589.18
CA	STA BARBARA	ARROYO BURRO BEACH REEF	60	34-23.80	119-44.90	27985.43	41585.63
CA	STA BARBARA	STA BARBARA CAMBY'S REEF	120	34-22.60	119-42.20	27992.65	41568.59
CA	STA BARBARA	RINCOR ISLAND ART REEF	45	34-20.50	119-26.41	28037.09	41489.97
CA	STA BARBARA	SANTA BARBARA ARCH REEF	18	33-28.90	119-03.50	28063.00	41190.48
CA	VENTURA	RINCOR REEF	100	34-19.40	119-27.00	28034.62	41487.70
CA	VENTURA	PITAS PT ART REEF	24	34-18.08	119-22.06	28047.79	41459.72
CA	VENTURA	VENTURA ART REEF	55	34-14.30	119-19.19	28053.14	41430.32
CA	VENTURA	TWELVE MILE REEF	525	34-14.00	119-42.00	27988.33	41529.31
CA	VENTURA	FOOTPRINT REEF	525	34-14.00	119-42.00	27988.33	41529.31
CA	VENTURA	VENTURA FISHING REEF	60	34-14.00	119-19.00	28053.46	41428.17
CA	VENTURA	CHANNEL IS ART REEF	36	34-09.00	119-16.12	28057.82	41394.01
CA	VENTURA	HOLLYWOOD BEACH ART REEF	60	34-09.00	119-16.10	28057.87	41393.91
CA	VENTURA	HARRISON'S REEF	60	34-02.60	118-58.00	28102.00	41284.73
CA	VENTURA	BEL AIR REEF	26	34-02.22	118-33.00	28167.19	41163.39
CA	VENTURA	BURNT HOUSE REEF	40	34-02.00	118-36.00	28159.24	41177.26
CA	VENTURA	CARBON BCH ART REEF	30	34-01.90	118-39.20	28150.86	41192.46
CA	VENTURA	TEMESCAL FISHING REEF	22	34-01.90	118-31.75	28170.09	41156.07
CA	VENTURA	BIG KELP REEF	120	34-01.80	118-45.30	28134.86	41221.49
CA	VENTURA	CORRAL BEACH REEF	25	34-01.70	118-44.55	28136.73	41217.52
CA	VENTURA	MALIBU REEFS	36	34-01.54	118-39.72	28149.17	41193.63
CA	VENTURA	OBSTRUCTION REEF	50	34-01.50	118-33.40	28165.46	41162.70
CA	VENTURA	SUNSET BEACH REEF	39	34-01.50	118-33.30	28165.72	41162.20
CA	VENTURA	HUNTINGTON BEACH REEFS	54	34-01.00	119-21.50	28037.51	41385.50
CA	VENTURA	ESCONDIDO BEACH ART REEF	60	34-01.00	118-46.00	28132.31	41221.82
CA	VENTURA	SANTA MONICA ART REEF	48	34-00.36	118-31.80	28168.46	41150.68
CANADA	B COLUMBIA	RYAN POINT REEF LIGHT	00	54-21.60	130-29.90	11756.95	30609.75
CANADA	B COLUMBIA	WESTERLY JETTY LIGHT	00	49-15.50	123-16.70	15236.95	29096.21
CANADA	B COLUMBIA	GABRIOLA REEFS BUOY UM	00	49-07.70	123-39.30	15156.50	29068.22
CANADA	B COLUMBIA	DANGER REEF LIGHT	00	49-03.30	123-42.80	15141.41	29033.64
CANADA	B COLUMBIA	CONCONI REEF LIGHT	00	48-49.40	123-17.40	15209.65	28839.15
HAWAII	HONOLULU	DIAMOND HEAD REEF NO 2	00	21-15.00	157-49.10	12309.73	37204.73
HAWAII	MAUI	KAMALO BAY REEF BUOY NO 2	00	21-02.10	156-52.70	11711.36	37250.67
HAWAII	MAUI	WAIHEE REEF BUOY NO 2	00	20-55.90	156-28.70	11464.54	37271.04
MARIANAS	SAIPAN	OKINO REEF BUOY NO 1	00	15-12.60N	145-41.60E	Suggest	GPS
MARSHALL ISLANDS	KWAJALEIN ATOLL	KWAJALEIN EBEYE REEF ER2	00	08-45.50N	167-43.90E	Suggest	GPS
OR	CURRY	ORFORD REEF WHISTLE 2OR	00	42-45.10	124-39.20	13837.42	27670.56
WA	CLALLAM	CLALLAM REEF NO 1	00	48-16.10	124-15.40	11471.33	28101.46
WA	CLALLAM	UMATILLA REEF WHISTLE 2UR	00	48-11.20	124-49.20	11557.25	28057.52
WA	GEORGIA STRAIT	CLEMENTS REEF BUOY	00	48-45.80	122-52.00	11219.24	28216.46
WA	GEORGIA STRAIT	EWING ISLAND REEF DAYBEACON	00	48-45.70	122-52.50	11220.40	28215.82
WA	GEORGIA STRAIT	ARACHNE REEF LIGHT	00	48-41.10	123-17.60	11279.50	28183.84
WA	GEORGIA STRAIT	INATI BAY REEF BUOY	00	48-40.50	122-37.10	11201.47	28232.90
WA	GEORGIA STRAIT	CYPRESS REEF DAYBEACON C	00	48-36.80	122-43.30	11221.36	28224.13

REEFS

STATE/COUNTRY	COUNTY/PROV	NAME	DEPTH	LAT	LON	TD#1	TD#2
WA	GEORGIA STRAIT	SHIRT TAIL REEF NO 1	00	48-35.30	123-01.20	11260.72	28201.59
WA	GEORGIA STRAIT	KELP REEFS LIGHT	00	48-32.90	123-14.10	11292.99	28184.83
WA	GEORGIA STRAIT	YELLOW BLUFF REEF NO 2	00	48-31.90	122-39.50	11224.58	28227.27
WA	GEORGIA STRAIT	REEF POINT JUNCTION	00	48-31.70	122-43.50	11233.20	28222.23
WA	GEORGIA STRAIT	UNDERTAKERS REEF NO 8	00	48-31.40	122-49.70	11246.61	28214.41
WA	GEORGIA STRAIT	CENTER ISLAND REEF DAYBEACON	00	48-29.10	122-50.10	11253.00	28213.13
WA	GEORGIA STRAIT	LAWSON REEF JUNCTION BELL	00	48-24.10	122-42.90	11250.26	28220.46
WA	PUGET SOUND	ONAMAC POINT REEF A	00	48-11.30	122-32.40	11261.07	28229.73
WA	PUGET SOUND	ONAMAC POINT REEF B	00	48-11.10	122-32.40	11261.63	28229.66
WA	PUGET SOUND	GEDNEY ISLAND FISHING REEF B	00	47-59.90	122-18.40	11261.50	28244.67
WA	PUGET SOUND	GEDNEY ISLAND FISHING REEF A	00	47-59.80	122-18.60	11262.28	28244.38
WA	PUGET SOUND	POSSESSION POINT REEF A	00	47-53.80	122-23.60	11293.77	28235.81
WA	PUGET SOUND	POSSESSION POINT REEF B	00	47-53.80	122-23.20	11292.78	28236.35
WA	PUGET SOUND	EDMONDS FISHING REEF	00	47-48.70	122-23.30	11310.70	28234.58
WA	PUGET SOUND	BOEING CREEK REEF A	00	47-45.10	122-23.10	11323.36	28233.69
WA	PUGET SOUND	BOEING CREEK REEF B	00	47-44.90	122-23.10	11324.11	28233.63
WA	PUGET SOUND	POINT BOLIN REEF NO 6	00	47-41.80	122-34.50	11365.52	28216.81
WA	PUGET SOUND	MISERY POINT REEF BUOY A	00	47-39.60	122-49.60	11413.14	28195.08
WA	PUGET SOUND	MISERY POINT REEF BUOY B	00	47-39.40	122-49.90	11414.74	28194.58
WA	PUGET SOUND	WING POINT REEF NO 2	00	47-36.80	122-29.10	11371.89	28222.53
WA	PUGET SOUND	DECATUR REEF LIGHT NO 2	00	47-34.90	122-28.50	11378.33	28222.69
WA	PUGET SOUND	BAINBRIDGE REEF BUOY NO 4	00	47-34.20	122-31.10	11388.22	28218.78
WA	PUGET SOUND	WEST SEATTLE REEF BUOY	00	47-33.40	122-24.40	11373.85	28227.95
WA	PUGET SOUND	BLAKE ISLAND REEF BUOY A	00	47-31.80	122-29.40	11394.21	28220.31
WA	PUGET SOUND	BLAKE ISLAND REEF BUOY B	00	47-31.70	122-29.40	11394.65	28220.27
WA	PUGET SOUND	POINT HEYER REEF BUOY B	00	47-25.20	122-25.50	11413.94	28223.49
WA	PUGET SOUND	POINT HEYER REEF BUOY A	00	47-25.10	122-25.60	11414.69	28223.31
WA	PUGET SOUND	EAGLE ISLAND REEF NO 9	00	47-11.40	122-41.90	11528.82	28194.14
WA	PUGET SOUND	ITSAMI LEDGE REEF BUOY A	00	47-10.50	122-50.50	11556.41	28181.09

CHAPTER 12

WRECKS

Navigating in waters that have caused wrecks in the past can be very hazardous. Most of the wrecks in the Florida Keys and Bahamas, for example, are on the ocean floor because they ventured into shallow water and ran afoul of coral reefs so sharp and hard that they literally cut their way right into the heart of the boats. Just about any kind of boat can be ripped apart, and some of these reefs lie right in the middle of vast expanses of open water. Only a heart-stopping bump will alert you to their presence.

As always, check charts, tide tables, and exercise caution. See the introduction to Chapter 7 for tips on using these coordinates.

WIT & WISDOM

There has never been anything said nearer the truth than the old adage, "It is not important to catch fish; it is important to go fishing."

It would take a lot of words to explain the thrill of getting a hard strike at night without knowing what's on the other end of the line. Or to find a lunker at the end of the fight staring up at you in defiance. Or to watch a 100-pound woman land a 150-pound tarpon. There is nothing quite so heartbreaking as losing a fish that pulled so hard you had to cut the line to save the pole, and there is no laughter so fulfilling as watching a loved one catch a fish smaller than the hook.

Then there's the love you feel when you watch your child catch his first "keeper" fish and then argue for its life by insisting it be put in a glass of water instead of being killed for the supper table. There is no sorrow quite like losing a pet rod and reel or having someone step on a brand-new pole and break the tip off. There is no sound quite like that of line whizzing off the reel, and there is no finer feeling of joy than knowing you have caught what might be a prize.

Fishing is fast, slow, frustrating, rewarding, pensive, and promising all at the same time, but most of all, it's just plain fun.

When Susie and I fish as a team, which is most of the time, we are constantly teasing each other about who might lose the bets on the first, smallest, and biggest fish. We bet things like who cooks dinner, who has to clean and fillet the fish, who does the dishes, and — by far the worst bet I have ever made and lost — who was going to be boss the next day. Susie had great fun with the "Honey, get me . . ." game.

We used to try to fill our freezers with fish during the winter so that we could have fish during the summer until we found out that during the summer, it is by far cheaper to catch fish at a local fish market than to run the boat out to water depths of 70 to 80 feet. Now, we have great fun fishing without having to catch anything. The bets are the same.

WRECKS

STATE/COUNTRY	COUNTY/PROV	NAME	DEPTH	LAT	LON	TD#1	TD#2
AK		WRECK BUOY WR6 (Barge)	00	55-20.70	131-40.30	14489.30	26112.59
CA	LOS ANGELES	VESSEL STAR OF SCOTLAND	42	33-59.80	118-31.20	28169.45	41145.71
CA	MARIN	NAPA RIVER WRECK NO 4WR	00	38-09.40	122-17.60	16043.01	43304.81

CHAPTER 13

FINE FISH'N

Coordinates for fishing are included to provide you with a listing of bottom structures that have proved to be productive fishing grounds. We've also listed areas that produce fish for reasons that seem unfathomable.

Before you head to the marina, be sure to investigate local regulations regarding the taking of some special species of fish, clams, conch, scallops, and other sea creatures. Such restrictions are not uncommon. A state may have one restriction and some counties may have additional restrictions. A quick phone call to the local wildlife people may save you from gaining some expensive experience.

Several states are making an effort to require saltwater fishing licenses, but we have yet to see a marker out at sea telling us when we cross from one state into another. When we're fishing, we remain alert to our location relative to state lines. This can be done by monitoring the latitude or longitude of our present position on the loran. We have yet to find a source to provide the state and county lines in latitude/longitude, but it may be wise to have this information handy when fishing waters near the line.

Coordinates in this chapter are listed by state (or province or island group), county, depth, latitude, longitude, time delay one, and time delay two. Once again, some of the depths contained in this chapter are listed as "00," indicating that the water depths have yet to be confirmed and should be checked using your boat or charter boat's equipment. Use the time delay numbers (TDs) in lieu of the Lat/Lon coordinates, as explained in Chapter 7.

F I S H ' N

STATE/COUNTRY	COUNTY/PROV	NAME	DEPTH	LAT	LON	TD#1	TD#2
AK		KNIK ARM SHOAL BUOY NO 7	00	61-12.20	150-05.20	13782.00	32401.73
AK		PORT VALDEZ ROCK BUOY	00	61-05.40	146-24.60	14530.89	32232.46
AK		MIDDLE ROCK LIGHT NO 13	00	61-04.90	146-39.00	14471.75	32241.03
AK		ROCKY POINT LIGHT NO 10	00	60-57.10	146-46.00	14370.24	32185.91
AK		BLIGH REEF BUOY NO 6	00	60-50.50	146-54.30	14275.24	32142.08
AK		KNOWLES HEAD SHOAL BUOY NO 4	00	60-40.50	146-44.00	14217.95	32053.40
AK		LONE ISLAND SHOAL NO 2	00	60-38.30	147-47.20	13956.35	32098.32
AK		NORTH ISLAND ROCK LIGHT NO 10	00	60-37.70	145-42.60	14419.77	31955.39
AK		CHANNEL ISLAND ROCK NO 7	00	60-36.50	145-48.70	14385.99	31953.61
AK		HANKS ISLAND ROCK BOUY NO 5	00	60-36.00	145-59.40	14341.81	31963.73
AK		MIDDLE GROUND SHOAL BUOY NO 2	00	60-32.50	146-22.00	14224.08	31963.91
AK		PENNSYLVANIA ROCK BUOY NO 2	00	60-26.80	147-24.00	13933.72	31990.58
AK		APPLEGATE SHOALS LIGHT	00	60-21.30	147-23.50	13882.68	31948.64
AK		SCHOONER ROCK LIGHT NO 1	00	60-18.40	146-54.30	13966.84	31892.10
AK		SEAL ROCKS SHOAL NO 1	00	60-10.00	146-44.80	13923.36	31814.09
AK		SEAL ROCKS SHOAL NO 1	00	60-10.00	146-44.80	13923.36	31814.09
AK		SEAL ROCKS LIGHT	00	60-09.80	146-50.20	13900.75	31819.77
AK		SEAL ROCKS LIGHT	00	60-09.80	146-50.20	13900.75	31819.77
AK		NINILCHIK ROCK SILL N MARKER	00	60-03.30	151-39.70	12807.77	32052.44
AK		WESSELS REEF WHISTLE NO 1	00	59-47.80	146-06.00	13865.38	31578.05
AK		PILOT ROCK LIGHT	00	59-44.60	149-28.10	13049.30	31825.49
AK		ARCHIMANSRITOF SHOALS BUOY NO 3	00	59-35.50	151-26.10	12557.64	31883.32
AK		COHEN ISLAND ROCK LIGHT	00	59-33.00	151-27.90	12526.20	31870.54
AK		SEAL ROCKS LIGHT	00	59-31.30	149-37.70	12881.18	31749.61
AK		PORT GRAHAM ENTRANCE SHOAL NO 1	00	59-22.80	151-54.10	12346.44	31836.42
AK		INDIAN ROCK LIGHT	00	59-16.40	135-23.90	15174.35	29295.40
AK		PERL ROCK LIGHT	00	59-05.40	151-41.50	12195.00	31726.23
AK		ELDRED ROCK LIGHT	00	58-58.30	135-13.20	15092.25	29072.79
AK		LATAX ROCKS LIGHT	00	58-41.40	152-28.90	11820.63	31644.02
AK		LATAX ROCKS LIGHT	00	58-41.40	152-28.90	11820.63	31644.02
AK		VANDERBILT REEF LIGHT	00	58-35.50	135-01.00	14991.81	28796.31
AK		POUNDSTONE ROCK BUOY PR	00	58-31.70	134-55.90	14979.79	28738.82
AK		COHEN REEF DAYBEACON CR	00	58-25.90	134-48.10	14961.83	28650.92
AK		POINT STEPHENS ROCK NO 2	00	58-25.40	134-46.10	14962.13	28638.43
AK		FAUST ROCK BUOY	00	58-25.10	134-55.60	14947.46	28670.70
AK		FAVORITE REEF LIGHT NO 2	00	58-22.80	134-51.60	14941.74	28632.44
AK		ANCON ROCK BUOY NO 2	00	58-22.40	135-55.80	14844.42	28874.28
AK		GIBBY ROCK LIGHT NO 2	00	58-19.60	134-41.20	14940.66	28561.21
AK		GEORGE ROCK LIGHT	00	58-18.90	134-41.90	14936.29	28556.67
AK		SUGARLOAF ISLAND SHOAL NO 2	00	58-17.40	136-53.20	14722.19	29052.67
AK		ROCK DUMP BUOY NO 2A	00	58-17.20	134-23.70	14953.21	28472.26
AK		HORSE SHOAL LIGHT NO 1	00	58-15.30	134-42.10	14918.60	28520.80
AK		ROCKY ISLAND LIGHT NO 13	00	58-10.70	135-03.00	14866.01	28553.56
AK		ALTHORP ROCK LIGHT NO 3	00	58-10.10	136-21.40	14738.41	28856.02

F I S H ' N

STATE/COUNTRY	COUNTY/PROV	NAME	DEPTH	LAT	LON	TD#1	TD#2
AK		PINTA ROCK BUOY NO 2	00	58-10.00	135-27.10	14826.02	28639.97
AK		HANUS REEF LIGHT	00	58-07.90	134-59.80	14857.11	28513.23
AK		HAWK INLET EAST SHOAL NO 2	00	58-06.20	134-46.30	14868.81	28444.53
AK		SKIPWITH REEFS BUOY NO 2	00	58-00.70	152-39.20	11359.66	31440.22
AK		DRY SPRUCE ISLAND ROCK NO 7	00	57-57.90	153-04.10	11314.84	31456.65
AK		ILKOGNAK ROCK LIGHT NO 1	00	57-54.90	152-46.90	11290.55	31419.78
AK		ENTRANCE POINT SHOAL NO 5	00	57-54.80	152-31.50	11305.00	31399.50
AK		WILLIAMS REEF WHISTLE NO 1	00	57-50.30	152-09.30	11301.79	31346.23
AK		WILLIAMS REEF WHISTLE NO 1	00	57-50.30	152-09.30	11301.79	31346.23
AK		HANIN ROCK LIGHT	00	57-50.10	152-18.70	11275.64	31357.87
AK		STAR ROCK BUOY	00	57-49.80	136-28.00	14622.22	28690.89
AK		CYANE ROCK BUOY NO 15	00	57-47.50	152-23.10	11237.53	31350.09
AK		TENAKEE REEF LIGHT	00	57-46.20	135-13.50	14731.44	28352.77
AK		WOMENS BAY MIDDLE SHOAL NO 19	00	57-43.80	152-31.00	11184.52	31341.37
AK		MINNIE REEF DAYBEACON NO 5	00	57-43.20	136-10.20	14620.95	28556.06
AK		HUMPBACK ROCK WHISTLE NO 1	00	57-42.80	152-14.10	11205.79	31313.05
AK		HUMPBACK ROCK WHISTLE NO 1	00	57-42.80	152-14.10	11205.79	31313.05
AK		BLACK BAY ROCKS DAYBEACON NO 4	00	57-42.40	136-09.20	14618.77	28544.47
AK		SNIPE ROCK DAYBEACON NO 1	00	57-38.30	136-10.60	14596.04	28512.28
AK		COZIAN REEF BUOY NO 3	00	57-34.10	135-25.50	14654.25	28285.60
AK		LARSEN BAY ENTRANCE ROCK NO 1	00	57-32.70	153-58.50	11164.05	31398.84
AK		KENASNOW ROCK NO 2	00	57-30.00	134-36.20	14715.61	28044.66
AK		LONE ROCK DAYBEACON NO 4	00	57-27.90	134-33.40	14710.56	28012.83
AK		ROSE ISLAND ROCK LIGHT NO 19	00	57-27.30	135-32.30	14610.63	28250.07
AK		McCLELLAN ROCK LIGHT	00	57-27.20	135-01.50	14662.12	28120.80
AK		WEST FRANCIS ROCK BUOY NO 6	00	57-24.30	135-38.30	14586.11	28247.55
AK		BRAD ROCK BUOY NO 3	00	57-22.40	135-41.30	14571.92	28242.81
AK		HIGHWATER ISLAND SHOAL NO 23	00	57-16.90	135-36.00	14555.70	28170.02
AK		WYVILLE REEF BUOY NO 22	00	57-16.30	135-35.40	14553.99	28162.00
AK		ROUND ROCK LIGHT	00	57-15.60	133-56.10	14714.40	27742.24
AK		NEVA POINT REEF LIGHT NO 12	00	57-14.10	135-33.00	14548.11	28131.75
AK		BIRD ROCK LIGHT NO 2	00	57-12.50	133-35.30	14732.65	27629.74
AK		OLD SITKA ROCKS LIGHT NO 2	00	57-06.90	135-24.60	14530.23	28030.53
AK		EAST PINTA ROCKS NO 1	00	57-05.60	133-58.40	14668.17	27652.79
AK		KASIANA ISLAND SHOAL NO 1	00	57-05.40	135-24.30	14524.01	28015.79
AK		WEST PINTA ROCKS LIGHT	00	57-05.20	134-00.60	14663.02	27657.89
AK		CHANNEL ROCK BUOY NO 7	00	57-03.80	135-21.80	14521.27	27990.59
AK		CHANNEL ROCK LIGHT NO 8	00	57-03.60	135-22.10	14519.84	27990.12
AK		USHER ROCK SHOAL NO 5	00	57-03.10	135-23.70	14514.76	27992.65
AK		MAKHNATI ROCK WHISTLE NO 2	00	57-02.20	135-23.70	14510.73	27984.65
AK		ROCKWELL LIGHT	00	57-02.20	135-19.90	14517.49	27968.03
AK		ROCKY PATCH BUOY RP	00	57-01.70	135-18.30	14518.10	27956.57
AK		TSARITSA ROCK BUOY NO 7	00	57-01.30	135-19.40	14514.37	27957.83
AK		SIMPSON ROCK BUOY NO 5	00	57-01.20	135-20.60	14511.79	27962.20

FISH'N

STATE/COUNTRY	COUNTY/PROV	NAME	DEPTH	LAT	LON	TD#1	TD#2
AK		KULICHKOF ROCK BUOY NO 2	00	56-60.00	135-26.90	14495.17	27979.24
AK		YASHA ISLAND SHOAL NO 2	00	56-58.90	134-34.50	14581.17	27740.77
AK		AKHOIK REEF BUOY NO 1	00	56-54.80	154-07.70	11040.93	31231.60
AK		ELOVOI ROCK DAYBEACON NO 1	00	56-49.30	135-22.60	14455.73	27867.19
AK		MIDWAY ROCK LIGHT MR	00	56-31.80	132-57.80	14625.12	27073.18
AK		FOREMOST ROCK DAYBEACON	00	56-30.10	133-00.30	14614.71	27066.80
AK		POINT HIGHFIELD REEF	00	56-28.90	132-23.60	14665.33	26910.20
AK		VICHNEFSKI ROCK LIGHT	00	56-26.30	133-00.80	14599.30	27032.01
AK		McARTHUR REEF BUOY	00	56-23.70	133-10.60	14573.99	27049.44
AK		HELM ROCK BUOY NO 8	00	56-22.20	133-38.40	14523.49	27160.01
AK		FIVE FATHOM SHOAL BUOY	00	56-21.70	133-13.90	14561.07	27045.36
AK		WEST ROCK LIGHT	00	56-21.20	133-38.10	14520.08	27149.83
AK		CALDER ROCKS WHISTLE NO 6	00	56-15.50	133-43.30	14489.32	27124.67
AK		NESBITT REEF LIGHT	00	56-13.20	132-51.70	14563.77	26868.54
AK		VILLAGE ISLANDS ROCK NO 15	00	56-13.20	132-18.90	14613.95	26730.47
AK		VILLAGE ROCK DAYBEACON NO 12	00	56-12.90	132-17.50	14614.94	26721.90
AK		MIDCHANNEL ROCK DAYBEACON	00	56-12.20	132-16.20	14614.33	26709.68
AK		BUTTON ISLAND SHOAL NO 5	00	56-12.10	132-14.80	14616.05	26703.18
AK		TRAP ROCK BUOY NO 3	00	56-11.30	132-13.30	14615.37	26689.16
AK		FOUND ISLAND ROCK NO 2	00	56-11.10	132-12.70	14615.54	26684.78
AK		AMELIUS ISLAND SHOAL A	00	56-10.20	133-49.60	14458.27	27110.44
AK		KEY REEF LIGHT	00	56-09.60	132-49.80	14553.30	26826.84
AK		FOUND ISLAND ROCK DAYBEACON	00	56-06.80	132-04.30	14612.46	26608.22
AK		LEMON POINT ROCK LIGHT	00	56-04.40	134-06.60	14406.75	27146.47
AK		LINCOLN ROCK WEST LIGHT	00	56-03.40	132-41.80	14542.93	26734.34
AK		EDNA BAY SHOAL BUOYS	00	55-57.80	133-37.30	14431.90	26953.26
AK		HUB ROCK DAYBEACON NO 3	00	55-56.50	133-17.70	14459.80	26847.19
AK		BROWNSON ISLAND ROCKS BI	00	55-56.00	132-06.70	14570.23	26509.62
AK		SALMON RIVER SHOAL NO 3	00	55-54.50	130-00.20	14742.86	26315.88
AK		AIKENS ROCK DAYBEACON NO 3	00	55-54.10	133-15.60	14454.41	26818.30
AK		VILLAGE ROCK DAYBEACON VR	00	55-53.50	133-15.30	14452.69	26812.23
AK		PEEP ROCK LIGHT	00	55-49.20	133-19.80	14429.44	26802.58
AK		POINT SWIFT SHOAL NO 2	00	55-46.30	133-18.80	14420.53	26776.81
AK		DESCONOCIDA REEF BUOY NO 10	00	55-41.30	133-31.40	14381.04	26806.54
AK		CURACAO REEF BUOY NO 8	00	55-39.30	133-28.20	14379.25	26777.29
AK		LARZATITA ISLAND REEF LIGHT	00	55-35.10	133-19.60	14378.79	26706.93
AK		HERMANOS ISLANDS REEF NO 8	00	55-33.80	133-17.70	14377.38	26689.26
AK		PIEDRAS ISLAND REEF NO 9	00	55-33.70	133-17.80	14376.85	26689.17
AK		HIGHWATER ROCK DAYBEACON NO 1	00	55-33.60	133-06.20	14396.02	26628.85
AK		KLAWOCK LEDGE DAYBEACON NO 3	00	55-33.40	133-06.10	14395.48	26627.11
AK		KLAWOCK INLET SHOAL NO 8	00	55-32.60	133-07.00	14391.14	26626.95
AK		KLAWOCK REEF BUOY NO 1	00	55-30.60	133-11.10	14377.19	26636.35
AK		KLAWOCK REEF BUOY NO 3	00	55-30.50	133-10.40	14378.02	26632.17
AK		KLAWOCK REEF BUOY NO 2	00	55-30.40	133-11.10	14376.48	26635.20

FISH'N

STATE/COUNTRY	COUNTY/PROV	NAME	DEPTH	LAT	LON	TD#1	TD#2
AK		PARIDA ISLAND SOUTH REEF NO 5	00	55-30.10	133-13.30	14371.71	26644.82
AK		CRAIG SHOAL NO 7	00	55-29.20	133-08.70	14376.30	26615.96
AK		FERN REEF BUOY NO 3A	00	55-29.10	133-15.80	14363.94	26652.03
AK		SALTERY POINT SHOAL NO 6	00	55-28.90	133-08.70	14375.25	26614.26
AK		BALANDRA SHOAL NO 3	00	55-28.60	133-13.70	14365.74	26638.40
AK		FISH EGG REEF BUOY NO 3	00	55-28.50	133-09.50	14372.49	26616.15
AK		BALLENA ISLAND SHOAL NO 2	00	55-28.30	133-13.10	14365.70	26633.62
AK		POND REEF NO 16	00	55-26.30	131-48.80	14494.94	26180.83
AK		ST IGNACE ROCK LIGHT	00	55-25.70	133-23.60	14338.63	26673.49
AK		SOLA ROCK DAYBEACON SR	00	55-25.60	133-28.80	14329.30	26699.63
AK		ROSA REEF NO 15	00	55-24.80	131-48.10	14490.99	26169.56
AK		OHIO ROCK BUOY	00	55-23.80	131-46.20	14490.56	26154.89
AK		PENINSULA POINT REEF NO 2	00	55-23.10	131-44.30	14491.15	26141.89
AK		LEWIS REEF LIGHT NO 11	00	55-22.50	131-44.20	14489.30	26138.97
AK		IDAHO ROCK BUOY NO 4	00	55-20.90	131-41.00	14488.89	26116.78
AK		WRECK BUOY WR6 (Barge)	00	55-20.70	131-40.30	14489.30	26112.59
AK		PENNOCK ISLAND REEF PR	00	55-20.30	131-40.00	14488.44	26109.90
AK		CALIFORNIA ROCK BUOY NO 3	00	55-18.90	131-36.10	14489.78	26087.27
AK		POTTER ROCK BUOY	00	55-18.10	131-34.50	14489.59	26078.31
AK		CUTTER ROCKS DAYBEACON CR	00	55-17.40	131-31.40	14492.01	26063.50
AK		WALDEN ROCK LIGHT WR	00	55-16.30	131-36.60	14480.45	26085.27
AK		SPIRE ISLAND REEF LIGHT SI	00	55-16.10	131-29.90	14490.03	26056.28
AK		MASTIC ROCK DAYBEACON	00	55-15.50	131-23.90	14497.18	26034.17
AK		BAILEY ROCK DAYBEACON BR	00	55-15.40	131-35.90	14478.56	26081.06
AK		HOG ROCKS LIGHT	00	55-10.70	131-16.90	14492.19	26019.31
AK		KELP ROCKS NO 1	00	55-09.50	131-37.80	14456.36	26084.77
AK		LIVELY ROCK BUOY NO 9	00	55-09.50	131-35.10	14460.53	26074.38
AK		MOIRA ROCK LIGHT	00	55-05.00	131-59.80	14407.13	26173.77
AK		REEF ISLAND LIGHT	00	55-04.80	130-12.10	14568.26	26030.01
AK		HID REEF WHISTLE NO 2	00	55-04.20	131-40.40	14435.12	26093.24
AK		INDIAN ROCK NO 6	00	55-01.80	131-20.70	14457.86	26035.01
AK		MELLEN ROCK LIGHT	00	55-01.60	132-39.90	14330.49	26354.26
AK		BLACK ROCK LIGHT	00	55-01.40	131-03.50	14482.67	26008.44
AK		AJAX REEF LIGHT NO 3	00	55-00.10	131-27.60	14441.83	26053.38
AK		SHOE ISLAND SHOAL BUOY NO 2	00	54-57.40	132-45.40	14307.39	26369.99
AK		WALLACE ROCK BUOY NO 2	00	54-51.10	132-26.90	14317.84	26273.68
AK		GUIDE ROCKS DAYBEACON NO 4	00	54-49.60	132-21.40	14322.13	26248.20
AK		CENTER ISLAND REEF NO 3	00	54-48.20	132-22.90	14315.15	26252.96
AK		TONGASS REEF DAYBEACON	00	54-47.20	130-44.60	14466.80	26004.10
AK		BOAT ROCK LIGHT	00	54-46.80	130-47.90	14460.63	26005.76
AK		LORD ROCK LIGHT	00	54-43.60	130-49.10	14449.04	26008.01
AK	ALEUTIANS	CROW REEF BUOY NO CR	00	55-45.60	160-43.40	18586.94	46385.59
AK	ALEUTIANS	BLUFF POINT SHOAL NO 1	00	55-11.50	161-52.30	18490.30	46838.40
AK	ALEUTIANS	ROCKY POINT SHOAL RP	00	53-53.50	166-31.20	17942.40	48388.85

F I S H ' N

STATE/COUNTRY	COUNTY/PROV	NAME	DEPTH	LAT	LON	TD#1	TD#2
AK	ALEUTIANS	ILIULIUK HARB S CHAN NO 11	00	53-52.60	166-32.70	17935.33	48394.46
AK	ALEUTIANS	ILIULIUK HARB S CHAN NO 10	00	53-52.60	166-32.70	17935.33	48394.46
AK	ALEUTIANS	BAILEY LEDGE DAYBEACON	00	53-51.60	166-33.40	17929.15	48395.79
AK	ALEUTIANS	KULUK SHOAL BUOY NO 2	00	51-52.10	176-36.40	14829.05	49774.35
AK	ALEUTIANS	GANNET ROCKS LIGHT NO 4	00	51-52.10	176-36.40	14829.05	49774.35
AK	ALEUTIANS	GANNET ROCKS BUOY 4A	00	51-51.90	176-36.50	14827.70	49774.07
AK	ALEUTIANS	SWEEPER COVE JETTY NO 6	00	51-51.70	176-37.60	14820.57	49775.01
AK	ALEUTIANS	FINGER SHOAL BUOY NO 3	00	51-51.50	176-33.90	14841.20	49770.08
AK	BERING SEA	NOME HARBOR E JETTY LIGHT	00	64-29.90	165-24.70	17950.97	47238.10
AK	BERING SEA	UNALAKLEET RIVER S SPIT LIGHT	00	63-52.10	160-47.00	18297.55	46392.55
AK	BERING SEA	YUKON RIVER S ENTRANCE LIGHT	00	62-35.40	164-59.50	18238.26	47366.42
CA	DEL NORTE	ST GEORGE REEF BUOY SG (LNB)	00	41-50.20	124-23.80	14311.69	43868.41
CA	HUMBOLDT	READING ROCKS LIGHT	00	41-20.50	124-10.60	14573.06	43840.29
CA	HUMBOLDT	TURTLE ROCKS BUOY NO 28	00	41-08.20	124-11.80	14664.71	43822.08
CA	HUMBOLDT	PILOT ROCK BUOY NO 2	00	41-02.60	124-09.20	14712.86	43814.98
CA	HUMBOLDT	BLUNTS REEF BUOY B (ELB)	00	40-26.40	124-30.20	14915.38	43735.50
CA	LOS ANGELES	VESSEL STAR OF SCOTLAND	42	33-59.80	118-31.20	28169.45	41145.71
CA	LOS ANGELES	STA BARBARA BANK	300	33-59.70	118-44.10	28136.11	41207.86
CA	LOS ANGELES	ST DUME FISHING	600	33-59.50	118-55.90	28105.01	41262.95
CA	LOS ANGELES	TWIN TOWERS FISHING	30	33-59.50	118-29.20	28174.25	41134.82
CA	LOS ANGELES	OCEAN PARK REEF	60	33-59.20	118-30.20	28171.42	41138.65
CA	LOS ANGELES	VENICE PIER REEF	20	33-59.10	118-28.60	28175.39	41130.43
CA	LOS ANGELES	VENICE ART REEF	60	33-58.70	118-29.60	28172.46	41133.91
CA	LOS ANGELES	VENICE FISHING PIER	00	33-58.60	118-28.20	28175.91	41126.68
CA	LOS ANGELES	SANTA CRUZ FISHING	47	33-57.80	119-29.30	28014.33	41407.00
CA	LOS ANGELES	FORTY SEVEN FATHOM SPOT	280	33-57.80	119-29.30	28014.33	41407.00
CA	LOS ANGELES	MARINA DEL RAY ART REEF	60	33-57.50	118-29.05	28172.68	41126.95
CA	LOS ANGELES	EL SEGUNDO FISHING	24	33-56.00	118-26.50	28177.65	41109.19
CA	LOS ANGELES	FORTY EIGHT SPOT	48	33-55.85	119-50.85	27954.71	41490.43
CA	LOS ANGELES	SANTA MONICA CANYON	00	33-55.80	118-33.80	28159.00	41144.08
CA	LOS ANGELES	DOUBLE BUBBLE FISHING	15	33-55.22	118-26.66	28176.49	41107.28
CA	LOS ANGELES	EL SEGUNDO FISHING BANKS	100	33-55.20	118-33.80	28158.44	41141.96
CA	LOS ANGELES	MALIBU SPOT	672	33-54.60	118-36.80	28150.26	41154.31
CA	LOS ANGELES	SOUTH FISHING BANKS	50	33-53.40	118-37.00	28148.66	41151.04
CA	LOS ANGELES	MANHATTAN BEACH PIER REEF	20	33-53.00	118-24.80	28178.98	41090.59
CA	LOS ANGELES	HERMOSA BEACH ART REEF	20	33-51.70	118-24.30	28178.96	41083.77
CA	LOS ANGELES	HERMOSA BEACH ART REEF	20	33-51.18	118-24.36	28178.31	41082.33
CA	LOS ANGELES	KINGS HARBOR ART REEF	80	33-50.30	118-24.60	28176.87	41080.57
CA	LOS ANGELES	REDONDO BEACH ART REEF	110	33-50.20	118-24.35	28177.39	41079.03
CA	LOS ANGELES	REDONDO CANYON	250	33-49.20	118-27.20	28169.37	41089.53
CA	LOS ANGELES	TORRANCE BCH ART REEF	60	33-48.80	118-24.30	28176.17	41074.18
CA	LOS ANGELES	VOLCANIC REEF	300	33-47.60	118-29.80	28161.43	41096.75
CA	LOS ANGELES	BELMONT PIER ART REEF	15	33-45.30	118-08.80	28210.39	40987.49
CA	LOS ANGELES	AVALON BAY, CATALINA IS	00	33-20.83	118-19.42	28162.59	40969.15

F I S H ' N

STATE/COUNTRY	COUNTY/PROV	NAME	DEPTH	LAT	LON	TD#1	TD#2
CA	MARIN	NAPA RIVER WRECK NO 4WR	00	38-09.40	122-17.60	16043.01	43304.81
CA	MARIN	MIDDLE GROUND OBSTRUCTION B	00	38-03.70	121-58.60	16123.30	43268.10
CA	MARIN	MIDDLE GROUND OBSTRUCTION A	00	38-03.60	121-58.30	16124.57	43267.43
CA	MARIN	CASTRO ROCKS NO 2CR	00	37-55.90	122-25.20	16058.42	43234.72
CA	MARIN	SOUTHAMPTON SHOAL NO 5	00	37-55.30	122-25.60	16058.85	43231.66
CA	MARIN	SOUTHAMPTON SHOAL NO 4	00	37-55.00	122-25.30	16060.67	43229.93
CA	MARIN	SOUTHAMPTON SHOAL NO 1	00	37-54.00	122-25.30	16063.50	43224.54
CA	MARIN	SOUTHAMPTON SHOAL NO 2	00	37-54.00	122-25.10	16064.15	43224.46
CA	MARIN	SOUTHAMPTON SHOAL LIGHT	00	37-52.90	122-24.00	16070.75	43218.04
CA	MARIN	CONE ROCK LIGHT	00	37-51.80	122-28.10	16060.73	43213.90
CA	MARIN	DUXBURY REEF WHISTLE 1DR	00	37-51.60	122-41.70	16018.04	43218.51
CA	MARIN	HARDING ROCK HR	00	37-50.30	122-26.70	16069.35	43205.20
CA	MARIN	YELLOW BLUFF LIGHT	00	37-50.20	122-28.30	16064.55	43205.40
CA	MARIN	BLOSSOM ROCK BELL BR	00	37-49.10	122-24.20	16080.55	43197.49
CA	MARIN	BART OBSTRUCTION LIGHTS	00	37-48.70	122-20.20	16094.28	43193.28
CA	MARIN	ANITA ROCK LIGHT	00	37-48.50	122-27.20	16072.69	43195.71
CA	MENDOCINO	SAUNDERS REEF BUOY NO 16	00	38-50.80	123-40.00	15605.87	43483.25
CA	ORANGE	SEVENTEEN FATHOM SPOT	102	33-43.73	119-02.51	28075.68	41235.71
CA	ORANGE	SEVENTEEN FATHOM REEF	102	33-43.60	119-09.70	28057.12	41267.41
CA	ORANGE	FISH HARBOR CHANNEL NO 2	00	33-43.50	118-15.60	28192.28	41015.21
CA	ORANGE	ESTHER PLATFORM	30	33-43.11	118-06.80	28212.94	40971.17
CA	ORANGE	CABRILLO PIER ART REEF	20	33-42.70	118-16.80	28188.61	41018.58
CA	ORANGE	W HUNTINGTON FLATS	85	33-40.80	118-08.50	28206.59	40972.71
CA	ORANGE	HORSESHOE KELP BEDS	75	33-40.00	118-13.50	28193.92	40994.56
CA	ORANGE	HUNTINGTON BCH REEF A	50	33-40.00	118-03.00	28218.75	40943.65
CA	ORANGE	EMMY PLATFORM	42	33-39.72	118-02.61	28219.38	40940.96
CA	ORANGE	EVA PLATFORM	60	33-39.69	118-03.66	28216.89	40945.99
CA	ORANGE	BOLSA CHICA 4 ART REEF	85	33-39.32	118-06.40	28210.08	40958.26
CA	ORANGE	BOLSA CHICA 6 ART REEF	83	33-39.28	118-06.09	28210.77	40956.64
CA	ORANGE	POTTERS BANK FISHING	180	33-38.80	118-16.30	28186.09	41004.48
CA	ORANGE	SOUTHWEST FISHING BANKS	180	33-38.70	118-16.40	28185.75	41004.66
CA	ORANGE	HUNTINGTON BCH FISHING	97	33-38.60	118-10.60	28199.46	40976.50
CA	ORANGE	HUNTINGTON FLATS	60	33-38.50	118-03.30	28216.54	40940.90
CA	ORANGE	BULL KELP FISHING	151	33-38.10	118-14.05	28190.79	40991.64
CA	ORANGE	HUNTINGTON BCH PIPELINE	48	33-38.10	118-00.30	28223.13	40925.21
CA	ORANGE	HUNTINGTON BCH REEF B	66	33-37.27	117-59.48	28224.19	40918.97
CA	ORANGE	HUNTINGTON BCH REEF D	45	33-37.00	117-58.50	28226.19	40913.48
CA	ORANGE	RUEBEN E LEE OBSTRUCTION	00	33-36.90	117-54.20	28235.99	40892.29
CA	ORANGE	NEWPORT BEACH ART REEF	120	33-36.07	117-57.54	28227.46	40906.33
CA	ORANGE	SOUTHEAST FISHING BANKS	300	33-35.80	118-06.80	28205.67	40950.30
CA	ORANGE	EDITH PLATFORM	150	33-35.75	118-08.44	28201.78	40958.04
CA	ORANGE	NEWPORT BCH BIO-STRUCTURE D	00	33-35.60	117-53.50	28236.25	40885.48
CA	ORANGE	NEWPORT BCH BIO-STRUCTURE C	00	33-35.60	117-53.30	28236.71	40884.51
CA	ORANGE	NEWPORT BCH BIO-STRUCTURE A	00	33-35.50	117-53.50	28236.15	40885.23

F I S H ' N

ATE/COUNTRY	COUNTY/PROV	NAME	DEPTH	LAT	LON	TD#1	TD#2
CA	ORANGE	NEWPORT BCH BIO-STRUCTURE B	00	33-35.50	117-53.40	28236.38	40884.74
CA	ORANGE	ELLY ELLEN PLATFORM	150	33-34.98	118-07.69	28202.79	40952.31
CA	ORANGE	KIDNEY BANKS	750	33-34.50	119-01.00	28073.00	41197.62
CA	ORANGE	NEWPORT KELP BEDS	900	33-34.12	118-09.23	28198.36	40957.29
CA	ORANGE	EUREKA PLATFORM	60	33-33.82	118-07.00	28203.28	40945.82
CA	ORANGE	NEWPORT SPOT	702	33-32.70	119-12.40	28043.21	41241.75
CA	ORANGE	LAGUNA KELP BEDS	1500	33-30.50	117-51.00	28236.71	40860.57
CA	ORANGE	SANTA ROSA FLATS FISHING	00	33-29.50	119-60.00	27920.84	41427.93
CA	ORANGE	HIDDEN SEVEN FATHOM REEF	45	33-29.50	119-04.40	28061.16	41196.35
CA	ORANGE	SEVEN & HALF FATHOM SPOT	45	33-29.50	119-04.40	29134.49	41773.63
CA	ORANGE	SHIP ROCK LIGHT	00	33-27.80	118-29.40	28145.04	41033.95
CA	ORANGE	HUNTINGTON BCH REEF C	66	33-27.12	117-59.18	28214.81	40891.17
CA	ORANGE	HARBOR REEF E BUOY	00	33-26.90	118-29.40	28144.29	41031.38
CA	ORANGE	HARBOR REEF S BUOY	00	33-26.80	118-29.30	28144.45	41030.64
CA	ORANGE	MARLIN 228 AREA	00	33-24.50	118-13.42	28180.11	40949.85
CA	ORANGE	LASVEN MARLIN AREA	342	33-23.33	117-57.83	28209.42	40888.09
CA	ORANGE	BEGG ROCK WHISTLE NO 4	00	33-22.00	119-41.80	27964.01	41329.42
CA	ORANGE	BEGG ROCKS	00	33-21.76	119-41.60	27964.41	41327.81
CA	ORANGE	OSBORN FISHING BANK	00	33-21.55	119-02.52	28060.65	41163.26
CA	ORANGE	FARNSWORTH BANK	54	33-21.00	118-31.50	28134.53	41024.43
CA	S LUIS OBISPO	MOUSE ROCK NO 3MR	00	35-26.30	120-54.40	27777.85	42175.92
CA	S LUIS OBISPO	CONSTANTINE ROCK NO 1CR	00	35-26.20	120-56.60	27769.98	42182.40
CA	S LUIS OBISPO	MORRO CREEK OUTFALL "B"	00	35-23.20	120-52.40	27785.07	42151.82
CA	S LUIS OBISPO	CHURCH ROCKS @ MORRO BAY	00	35-20.50	120-59.90	27758.80	42160.86
CA	S LUIS OBISPO	DIABLO CANYON FISHING	00	35-12.60	120-51.60	27787.94	42090.13
CA	S LUIS OBISPO	PECHO ROCKS	90	35-10.70	120-48.90	27797.14	42070.67
CA	S LUIS OBISPO	LANSING ROCK BUOY	00	35-09.70	120-44.80	27811.06	42051.22
CA	S LUIS OBISPO	WESTDAHL ROCK NO 1	00	35-08.80	120-47.00	27803.53	42053.87
CA	S LUIS OBISPO	SOUZA ROCK GONG	00	35-07.70	120-44.30	27812.60	42038.61
CA	SAN DIEGO	C PENDELTON ART REEF	40	33-19.30	117-31.42	28268.24	40743.32
CA	SAN DIEGO	THE CATHEDRALS FISHING	1200	33-19.02	118-31.76	28132.35	41020.20
CA	SAN DIEGO	HIPOINT FISHING	2340	33-19.00	118-31.82	28132.20	41020.41
CA	SAN DIEGO	PENDLETON ART REEF	40	33-18.92	117-33.20	28264.03	40750.88
CA	SAN DIEGO	THREE MILE REEF	66	33-18.60	119-27.60	27997.63	41260.23
CA	SAN DIEGO	BARN KELP FISHING	24	33-18.60	117-29.10	28272.47	40731.18
CA	SAN DIEGO	SILVER CANYON FISHING	00	33-18.20	118-23.40	28151.17	40980.36
CA	SAN DIEGO	CHURCH ROCKS, CATALINA IS	00	33-17.80	118-19.60	28159.61	40962.13
CA	SAN DIEGO	BOILER REEF	18	33-16.50	119-36.40	27975.05	41289.60
CA	SAN DIEGO	SEVEN FATHOM REEF	42	33-15.80	119-37.80	27971.32	41293.04
CA	SAN DIEGO	OCEANSIDE'S CLAM BEDS	50	33-14.30	117-17.30	28292.72	40669.24
CA	SAN DIEGO	BUTTERFLY BANK FISHING	267	33-14.00	118-51.50	28082.15	41093.38
CA	SAN DIEGO	OCEANSIDE ART REEF	60	33-11.00	117-24.00	28275.36	40694.25
CA	SAN DIEGO	OCEANSIDE SPOT	672	33-02.80	117-21.50	28272.24	40670.04
CA	SAN DIEGO	NINE FATHOM REEF	54	33-02.60	118-37.50	28106.86	41002.82

FISH'N

STATE/COUNTRY	COUNTY/PROV	NAME	DEPTH	LAT	LON	TD#1	TD#2
CA	SAN DIEGO	MACKERAL FISHING BANK	2052	33-02.40	118-23.50	28138.40	40941.88
CA	SAN DIEGO	POWERHOUSE FISHING	60	33-02.20	117-18.40	28277.97	40655.55
CA	SAN DIEGO	ELEVEN FATHOM SPOT	66	33-00.50	118-37.60	28105.17	40998.07
CA	SAN DIEGO	TORREY PINES REEF NO 2	60	32-53.35	117-15.35	28275.36	40630.27
CA	SAN DIEGO	TORREY PINES REEF NO 1	55	32-53.12	117-15.50	28274.84	40630.60
CA	SAN DIEGO	LA JOLLA KELP BEDS	40	32-50.00	117-17.50	28267.82	40635.01
CA	SAN DIEGO	PT LOMA BIRD ROCKS	15	32-48.90	117-16.57	28268.62	40629.72
CA	SAN DIEGO	POINT LOMA SPOT	342	32-47.90	118-31.50	28110.14	40943.23
CA	SAN DIEGO	THIRTY MILE FISHING BANK	00	32-47.50	117-46.60	28206.14	40753.84
CA	SAN DIEGO	FORTY MILE BANK	245	32-44.50	118-10.00	28154.34	40846.67
CA	SAN DIEGO	POINT LOMA SPOT	750	32-44.50	117-47.80	28201.10	40753.96
CA	SAN DIEGO	NORTH FISHING SPOT	33	32-44.00	117-35.30	28226.38	40701.10
CA	SAN DIEGO	POINT LOMA SPOT	516	32-43.60	118-27.50	28115.96	40917.50
CA	SAN DIEGO	POINT LOMA SPOT	486	32-43.10	118-24.30	28122.56	40903.26
CA	SAN DIEGO	PT LOMA KELP BEDS	50	32-42.50	118-16.30	28139.37	40868.99
CA	SAN DIEGO	TANNER FISHING BANKS	165	32-42.00	119-08.00	28025.50	41078.19
CA	SAN DIEGO	FORTY THREE FATHOM SPOT	258	32-39.30	117-58.30	28175.03	40788.87
CA	SAN DIEGO	TWENTY FOUR FATHOM SPOT	144	32-39.00	119-34.10	27965.55	41172.53
CA	SAN DIEGO	NINE MILE FISHING BANK	00	32-37.10	117-24.70	28241.58	40648.39
CA	SAN DIEGO	POINT LOMA SPOT	654	32-33.50	119-29.70	27973.34	41141.80
CA	SAN DIEGO	FLATS AREA	81	32-28.00	117-11.00	28260.18	40584.28
CA	SAN DIEGO	CORTEZ BANK FISHING	00	32-26.50	119-07.50	28019.13	41040.25
CA	SAN DIEGO	ROCKPILE FISHING	60	32-25.60	117-08.00	28263.76	40570.52
CA	SAN DIEGO	BOOMERANG FISHING	940	32-22.50	118-27.60	28101.97	40877.09
CA	SAN DIEGO	BOX CANYON FISHING	36	32-20.00	117-32.10	28212.53	40657.12
CA	SAN DIEGO	SOUTH FISHING SPOT	43	32-10.50	117-51.90	28166.43	40720.96
CA	SAN DIEGO	POINT LOMA SPOT	360	32-03.67	118-13.14	28119.72	40791.33
CA	SAN DIEGO	FORTY FATHOM SPOT	240	32-02.40	119-36.00	27949.27	41093.54
CA	SAN DIEGO	POINT LOMA SPOT	306	31-37.00	116-48.40	28258.45	40471.73
CA	SAN MATEO	NOONDAY ROCK WHISTLE NR	00	37-47.70	123-10.70	27091.38	43210.13
CA	SAN MATEO	MILE ROCKS LIGHT	00	37-47.60	122-30.60	27210.18	43192.53
CA	SAN MATEO	MILE ROCKS LIGHT	00	37-47.60	122-30.60	16064.42	43192.53
CA	SAN MATEO	MISSION ROCK NE LIGHT	00	37-46.50	122-22.80	16091.92	43182.55
CA	SAN MATEO	MISSION ROCK SE LIGHT	00	37-46.30	122-22.80	16092.44	43181.45
CA	SAN MATEO	SAN BRUNO SHOAL NO 1	00	37-41.70	122-20.30	16112.08	43154.56
CA	SAN MATEO	SOUTHEAST REEF NO 1S	00	37-27.90	122-28.10	27272.27	43083.59
CA	STA BARBARA	KIDNEY BANKS	378	34-33.50	119-01.00	28121.27	41431.85
CA	STA BARBARA	KINNETIC LABS BUOY	00	34-30.20	120-42.80	27814.78	41842.98
CA	STA BARBARA	PLATFORM HARVEST MOORING	00	34-28.30	120-40.50	27821.52	41825.72
CA	STA BARBARA	NAPLES REEF	48	34-25.00	119-57.80	27947.96	41645.18
CA	STA BARBARA	THREE FATHOM SPOT	18	34-24.58	119-34.60	28016.11	41544.71
CA	STA BARBARA	MOHAWK REEF	45	34-24.20	119-45.30	27984.48	41589.18
CA	STA BARBARA	ARROYO BURRO BEACH REEF	60	34-23.80	119-44.90	27985.43	41585.63
CA	STA BARBARA	HONDO PLATFORM	00	34-23.42	120-07.19	27919.48	41675.96

FISH'N

STATE/COUNTRY	COUNTY/PROV	NAME	DEPTH	LAT	LON	TD#1	TD#2
CA	STA BARBARA	STA BARBARA CAMBY'S REEF	120	34-22.60	119-42.20	27992.65	41568.59
CA	STA BARBARA	RINCOR ISLAND ART REEF	45	34-20.50	119-26.41	28037.09	41489.97
CA	STA BARBARA	SANTA BARBARA ARCH REEF	18	33-28.90	119-03.50	28063.00	41190.48
CA	VENTURA	HILLHOUSE PLATFORM	00	34-19.88	119-36.20	28008.45	41530.35
CA	VENTURA	RINCOR REEF	100	34-19.40	119-27.00	28034.62	41487.70
CA	VENTURA	PITAS PT ART REEF	24	34-18.08	119-22.06	28047.79	41459.72
CA	VENTURA	VENTURA ART REEF	55	34-14.30	119-19.19	28053.14	41430.32
CA	VENTURA	FOOTPRINT REEF	525	34-14.00	119-42.00	27988.33	41529.31
CA	VENTURA	TWELVE MILE REEF	525	34-14.00	119-42.00	27988.33	41529.31
CA	VENTURA	VENTURA FISHING REEF	60	34-14.00	119-19.00	28053.46	41428.17
CA	VENTURA	VENTURA FISHING	90	34-11.20	119-21.60	28044.18	41427.94
CA	VENTURA	GILDA PLATFORM	00	34-10.93	119-25.11	28034.18	41442.47
CA	VENTURA	GRACE PLATFORM	00	34-10.78	119-28.08	28025.77	41454.98
CA	VENTURA	CHANNEL IS ART REEF	36	34-09.00	119-16.12	28057.82	41394.01
CA	VENTURA	HOLLYWOOD BEACH ART REEF	60	34-09.00	119-16.10	28057.87	41393.91
CA	VENTURA	GINA PLATFORM	00	34-07.02	119-16.57	28055.14	41387.86
CA	VENTURA	BASS ROCK	78	34-06.40	119-11.60	28068.30	41362.75
CA	VENTURA	FINGERS AREA	600	34-03.60	119-10.50	28069.19	41346.42
CA	VENTURA	SEAMOUNT FISHING	356	34-02.60	121-03.80	27755.77	41793.23
CA	VENTURA	HARRISON'S REEF	60	34-02.60	118-58.00	28102.00	41284.73
CA	VENTURA	BEL AIR REEF	26	34-02.22	118-33.00	28167.19	41163.39
CA	VENTURA	TOPANGA CREEK FISHING	24	34-02.20	118-34.95	28162.15	41172.87
CA	VENTURA	BURNT HOUSE REEF	40	34-02.00	118-36.00	28159.24	41177.26
CA	VENTURA	CARBON BCH ART REEF	30	34-01.90	118-39.20	28150.86	41192.46
CA	VENTURA	TEMESCAL FISHING REEF	22	34-01.90	118-31.75	28170.09	41156.07
CA	VENTURA	BIG KELP REEF	120	34-01.80	118-45.30	28134.86	41221.49
CA	VENTURA	LAS FLORES ROCKS	33	34-01.80	118-37.80	28154.39	41185.29
CA	VENTURA	CORRAL BEACH REEF	25	34-01.70	118-44.55	28136.73	41217.52
CA	VENTURA	COLONY KELP BEDS	36	34-01.60	118-42.30	28142.52	41206.32
CA	VENTURA	MALIBU REEFS	36	34-01.54	118-39.72	28149.17	41193.63
CA	VENTURA	PT LOMA DEEP HOLE FISHING	180	34-01.50	118-57.50	28102.42	41278.11
CA	VENTURA	MALIBU ROCKPILE FISHING	60	34-01.50	118-39.70	28149.19	41193.38
CA	VENTURA	SCATTERED ROCKS	50	34-01.50	118-34.22	28163.36	41166.71
CA	VENTURA	OBSTRUCTION REEF	50	34-01.50	118-33.40	28165.46	41162.70
CA	VENTURA	SUNSET BEACH REEF	39	34-01.50	118-33.30	28165.72	41162.20
CA	VENTURA	MARINA DEL REY E CABLE AREA	00	34-01.40	118-32.20	28168.45	41156.45
CA	VENTURA	DECKER CANYON FISHING	92	34-01.20	118-54.20	28110.92	41261.48
CA	VENTURA	HUNTINGTON BEACH REEFS	54	34-01.00	119-21.50	28037.51	41385.50
CA	VENTURA	ESCONDIDO BEACH ART REEF	60	34-01.00	118-46.00	28132.31	41221.82
CA	VENTURA	STA MONICA FISH HAVEN	00	34-00.60	118-31.70	28168.95	41151.07
CA	VENTURA	YELLOW BANKS FISHING	00	34-00.50	119-29.30	28015.95	41417.79
CA	VENTURA	PT DUME FISHING	82	34-00.50	118-49.50	28122.70	41236.60
CA	VENTURA	SANTA MONICA ART REEF	48	34-00.36	118-31.80	28168.46	41150.68
CANADA	B COLUMBIA	SLIPPERY ROCK LIGHT	00	54-24.00	130-29.70	11738.32	30614.15

FISH'N

STATE/COUNTRY	COUNTY/PROV	NAME	DEPTH	LAT	LON	TD#1	TD#2
CANADA	B COLUMBIA	RYAN POINT REEF LIGHT	00	54-21.60	130-29.90	11756.95	30609.75
CANADA	B COLUMBIA	WESTERLY JETTY LIGHT	00	49-15.50	123-16.70	15236.95	29096.21
CANADA	B COLUMBIA	THRASHER ROCK LIGHT	00	49-09.00	123-38.40	15160.54	29078.87
CANADA	B COLUMBIA	GABRIOLA REEFS BUOY UM	00	49-07.70	123-39.30	15156.50	29068.22
CANADA	B COLUMBIA	ROBERTS BANK LIGHT	00	49-05.20	123-18.60	15220.90	28996.98
CANADA	B COLUMBIA	ROBERTS BANK BUOY TA	00	49-04.40	123-22.80	15207.04	28998.91
CANADA	B COLUMBIA	DANGER REEF LIGHT	00	49-03.30	123-42.80	15141.41	29033.64
CANADA	B COLUMBIA	GRAPPLER ROCK LIGHT	00	48-56.40	123-36.10	15157.89	28952.70
CANADA	B COLUMBIA	VICTORIA SHOAL BUOY U43	00	48-55.20	123-30.90	15173.43	28928.83
CANADA	B COLUMBIA	GOVERNOR ROCK U45	00	48-54.80	123-29.80	15176.55	28922.33
CANADA	B COLUMBIA	BEN MOHR ROCK BUOY UK	00	48-51.60	123-23.40	15193.56	28875.76
CANADA	B COLUMBIA	CONCONI REEF LIGHT	00	48-49.40	123-17.40	15209.65	28839.15
CANADA	B COLUMBIA	SEABIRD ROCKS LIGHT	00	48-45.00	125-09.20	14825.19	29049.66
HAWAII	HONOLULU	KEEHI LAGOON PIPELING B	00	21-19.80	157-54.10	12366.08	37182.89
HAWAII	HONOLULU	KEEHI LAGOON PIPELINE A	00	21-19.70	157-53.90	12363.92	37183.33
HAWAII	HONOLULU	DIAMOND HEAD REEF NO 2	00	21-15.00	157-49.10	12309.73	37204.73
HAWAII	MAUI	KAMALO BAY REEF BUOY NO 2	00	21-02.10	156-52.70	11711.36	37250.67
HAWAII	MAUI	WAIHEE REEF BUOY NO 2	00	20-55.90	156-28.70	11464.54	37271.04
MARIANAS	GUAM ISLAND	APRA HARBOR W SHOAL WS	00	13-26.90N	144-39.10E	Suggest	GPS
MARIANAS	SAIPAN	OKINO REEF BUOY NO 1	00	15-12.60N	145-41.60E	Suggest	GPS
MARSHALL ISLANDS	KWAJALEIN ATOLL	KWAJALEIN EBEYE REEF ER2	00	08-45.50N	167-43.90E	Suggest	GPS
OR	COOS	JARVIS DIKE 6.8 LIGHT 19	00	43-25.00	124-16.50	13510.40	27797.38
OR	COOS	COOS BAY FISH PEN LIGHT A	00	43-23.90	124-17.00	13519.88	27794.33
OR	COOS	COOS BAY FISH PEN LIGHT D	00	43-23.90	124-17.00	13519.88	27794.33
OR	COOS	COOS BAY FISH PEN LIGHT B	00	43-23.80	124-17.10	13520.72	27793.94
OR	COOS	COOS BAY FISH PEN LIGHT C	00	43-23.80	124-16.90	13520.82	27794.36
OR	COOS	COOS BAY DREDGE BUOY F	00	43-22.50	124-21.60	13529.83	27782.29
OR	COOS	BALTIMORE ROCK NO 2BR	00	43-21.30	124-22.90	13539.65	27777.40
OR	DOUGLAS	UMPQUA RIVER NO 23	00	43-44.90	124-07.80	13335.96	27849.66
OR	LANE	SIUSLAW RIVER DIKE NO 16	00	43-58.90	124-07.50	13210.34	27872.36
OR	LANE	SIUSLAW RIVER DIKE NO 18A	00	43-58.80	124-07.50	13211.24	27872.20
OR	LANE	SIUSLAW RIVER DIKE NO 20	00	43-58.70	124-07.60	13212.13	27871.85
OR	LANE	SIUSLAW RIVER DIKE NO 22	00	43-58.40	124-07.40	13214.82	27871.79
OR	LINCOLN	CLEFT OF THE ROCK LIGHT	00	44-17.50	124-06.50	13044.04	27901.49
PHILIPPINES	LUZON ISLAND	CUBI SHOAL LIGHT NO 8	00	14-48.60N	120-15.50E	Suggest	GPS
PHILIPPINES	LUZON ISLAND	SIXTEEN FOOT SHOAL NO 6	16	14-47.90N	120-14.50E	Suggest	GPS
PHILIPPINES	LUZON ISLAND	GRAND ISLAND SHOAL NO 4	00	14-46.70N	120-13.10E	Suggest	GPS
PHILIPPINES	LUZON ISLAND	TWENTY-FOUR FOOT SHOAL NO 2	24	14-45.20N	120-13.40E	Suggest	GPS
WA	CLALLAM	DUNTZE ROCK WHISTLE 2D	00	48-24.90	124-44.90	11500.53	28071.28
WA	CLALLAM	DUNTZE ROCK WHISTLE 2D	00	48-24.90	124-44.90	11500.53	28071.28
WA	CLALLAM	SCROGGS ROCKS LIGHT	00	48-24.40	123-26.30	11341.84	28166.19
Canada	B Columbia	RACE ROCKS LIGHT	00	48-17.90	123-31.80	11373.29	28156.39
WA	CLALLAM	CLALLAM REEF NO 1	00	48-16.10	124-15.40	11471.33	28101.46
Canada	B Columbia	RACE ROCKS E BUOY VG	00	48-16.10	123-27.70	11370.10	28160.72

F I S H ' N

STATE/COUNTRY	COUNTY/PROV	NAME	DEPTH	LAT	LON	TD#1	TD#2
WA	CLALLAM	UMATILLA REEF WHISTLE 2UR	00	48-11.20	124-49.20	11557.25	28057.52
Canada	B Columbia	ROSENFELD ROCK NO U59	00	48-48.20	123-01.60	11232.47	28205.73
WA	GEORGIA STRAIT	BOUNDARY PASS SHOAL B	00	48-45.90	123-00.80	11235.83	28205.88
WA	GEORGIA STRAIT	CLEMENTS REEF BUOY	00	48-45.80	122-52.00	11219.24	28216.46
WA	GEORGIA STRAIT	EWING ISLAND REEF DAYBEACON	00	48-45.70	122-52.50	11220.40	28215.82
WA	GEORGIA STRAIT	POINT FRANCIS SHOAL NO 4	00	48-41.70	122-38.20	11201.19	28231.91
WA	GEORGIA STRAIT	ARACHNE REEF LIGHT	00	48-41.10	123-17.60	11279.50	28183.84
WA	GEORGIA STRAIT	INATI BAY REEF BUOY	00	48-40.50	122-37.10	11201.47	28232.90
WA	GEORGIA STRAIT	ROCKS JUNCTION BUOY	00	48-40.50	122-35.40	11198.20	28234.98
WA	GEORGIA STRAIT	LUMMI ROCKS NO 16A	00	48-40.20	122-40.10	11207.89	28229.13
WA	GEORGIA STRAIT	VITI ROCKS LIGHT	00	48-38.00	122-37.30	11206.97	28231.89
WA	GEORGIA STRAIT	HARBOR ROCK DAYBEACON	00	48-37.80	122-58.60	11249.59	28205.68
WA	GEORGIA STRAIT	VITI ROCKS NO 9	00	48-37.80	122-37.10	11207.00	28232.08
WA	GEORGIA STRAIT	JONES ISLAND ROCKS	00	48-37.20	123-02.50	11258.80	28200.69
WA	GEORGIA STRAIT	CYPRESS REEF DAYBEACON C	00	48-36.80	122-43.30	11221.36	28224.13
WA	GEORGIA STRAIT	BIRD ROCKS LIGHT	00	48-35.90	123-00.80	11258.47	28202.30
WA	GEORGIA STRAIT	LYDIA SHOAL NO 13	00	48-35.90	122-46.70	11230.13	28219.64
WA	GEORGIA STRAIT	SHIRT TAIL REEF NO 1	00	48-35.30	123-01.20	11260.72	28201.59
WA	GEORGIA STRAIT	BLIND BAY ROCK DAYBEACON	00	48-35.00	122-55.90	11250.71	28208.00
WA	GEORGIA STRAIT	BLAKELY ISLAND SHOAL BS	00	48-34.20	122-50.70	11242.06	28214.13
WA	GEORGIA STRAIT	SHOAL BAY AQUACULTURE LIGHT	00	48-33.40	122-52.40	11247.38	28211.76
WA	GEORGIA STRAIT	KELP REEFS LIGHT	00	48-32.90	123-14.10	11292.99	28184.83
WA	GEORGIA STRAIT	REID ROCK BUOY	00	48-32.90	122-59.30	11262.67	28203.05
WA	GEORGIA STRAIT	BLACK ROCK LIGHT NO 9	00	48-32.80	122-45.90	11235.55	28219.61
WA	GEORGIA STRAIT	TURN ROCK LIGHT NO 3	00	48-32.00	122-57.80	11261.80	28204.58
WA	GEORGIA STRAIT	LITTLE ZERO ROCK NO V30	00	48-31.90	123-19.70	11307.12	28177.54
WA	GEORGIA STRAIT	LAWSON ROCK JUNCTION	00	48-31.90	122-47.20	11240.30	28217.69
WA	GEORGIA STRAIT	YELLOW BLUFF REEF NO 2	00	48-31.90	122-39.50	11224.58	28227.27
WA	GEORGIA STRAIT	REEF POINT JUNCTION	00	48-31.70	122-43.50	11233.20	28222.23
WA	GEORGIA STRAIT	FISHERMAN BAY SECTOR LIGHT	00	48-31.50	122-55.10	11257.47	28207.75
Canada	B Columbia	ZERO ROCK LIGHT	00	48-31.40	123-17.40	11303.71	28180.16
WA	GEORGIA STRAIT	UNDERTAKERS REEF NO 8	00	48-31.40	122-49.70	11246.61	28214.41
WA	GEORGIA STRAIT	FIDALGO BAY SHOAL NO 2	00	48-30.60	122-35.00	11218.32	28232.48
WA	GEORGIA STRAIT	CENTER ISLAND REEF DAYBEACON	00	48-29.10	122-50.10	11253.00	28213.13
WA	GEORGIA STRAIT	RAM ISLAND ROCKS NO 4	00	48-28.40	122-50.20	11254.94	28212.76
WA	GEORGIA STRAIT	DENNIS SHOAL NO 6	00	48-27.50	122-42.80	11241.67	28221.72
WA	GEORGIA STRAIT	WILLIAMSON ROCKS NO 4	00	48-26.90	122-42.30	11242.08	28222.15
WA	GEORGIA STRAIT	TWIN ROCKS DAYBEACON	00	48-26.80	122-54.60	11268.20	28206.69
WA	GEORGIA STRAIT	AMERICAN AQUA FISH PEN LIGHTS	00	48-24.50	122-33.60	11229.53	28232.36
WA	GEORGIA STRAIT	LAWSON REEF JUNCTION BELL	00	48-24.10	122-42.90	11250.26	28220.46
WA	GEORGIA STRAIT	SEAL ROCKS LIGHT NO 12	00	48-22.40	122-33.70	11234.84	28231.58
WA	GRAYS HARBOR	CHARLEY CREEK DIKE NO 2	00	46-57.40	123-50.60	11776.76	28085.74
WA	PUGET SOUND	ONAMAC POINT REEF A	00	48-11.30	122-32.40	11261.07	28229.73
WA	PUGET SOUND	ONAMAC POINT REEF B	00	48-11.10	122-32.40	11261.63	28229.66

FISH'N

STATE/COUNTRY	COUNTY/PROV	NAME	DEPTH	LAT	LON	TD#1	TD#2
WA	PUGET SOUND	CAMANO HEAD ROCKS NO 1	00	48-03.00	122-21.20	11258.90	28241.87
WA	PUGET SOUND	GEDNEY ISLAND FISHING REEF B	00	47-59.90	122-18.40	11261.50	28244.67
WA	PUGET SOUND	GEDNEY ISLAND FISHING REEF A	00	47-59.80	122-18.60	11262.28	28244.38
WA	PUGET SOUND	CLINTON SHOAL BUOY	00	47-58.60	122-20.90	11271.57	28240.94
WA	PUGET SOUND	KLAS ROCKS NO 2	00	47-57.70	122-40.20	11321.33	28214.82
WA	PUGET SOUND	COLVOS ROCKS LIGHT	00	47-57.10	122-40.10	11323.12	28214.74
WA	PUGET SOUND	POSSESSION POINT REEF A	00	47-53.80	122-23.60	11293.77	28235.81
WA	PUGET SOUND	POSSESSION POINT REEF B	00	47-53.80	122-23.20	11292.78	28236.35
WA	PUGET SOUND	CASE SHOAL DAYBEACON	00	47-51.50	122-40.40	11343.52	28212.29
WA	PUGET SOUND	SISTERS ROCK NO 4	00	47-51.50	122-38.40	11338.57	28215.00
WA	PUGET SOUND	CASE SHOAL NO 6	00	47-50.70	122-40.10	11345.69	28212.41
WA	PUGET SOUND	CASE SHOAL NO 5	00	47-49.50	122-38.80	11346.86	28213.73
WA	PUGET SOUND	CASE SHOAL NO 8	00	47-48.80	122-42.80	11359.45	28208.03
WA	PUGET SOUND	EDMONDS FISHING REEF	00	47-48.70	122-23.30	11310.70	28234.58
WA	PUGET SOUND	QUILCENE BAY FISH PEN B	00	47-47.30	122-51.00	11385.58	28196.30
WA	PUGET SOUND	BOEING CREEK REEF A	00	47-45.10	122-23.10	11323.36	28233.69
WA	PUGET SOUND	BOEING CREEK REEF B	00	47-44.90	122-23.10	11324.11	28233.63
WA	PUGET SOUND	SEAL ROCK DAYBEACON	00	47-42.90	122-52.90	11407.81	28191.91
WA	PUGET SOUND	TREASURE ISLAND SHOAL NO 2	00	47-41.90	122-32.10	11358.93	28220.17
WA	PUGET SOUND	POINT BOLIN REEF NO 6	00	47-41.80	122-34.50	11365.52	28216.81
WA	PUGET SOUND	JUANITA BAY SHOAL DAYBEACON	00	47-41.80	122-13.00	11309.42	28246.64
WA	PUGET SOUND	MISERY POINT REEF BUOY A	00	47-39.60	122-49.60	11413.14	28195.08
WA	PUGET SOUND	MISERY POINT REEF BUOY B	00	47-39.40	122-49.90	11414.74	28194.58
WA	PUGET SOUND	LAKE UNION SHOAL NO 2	00	47-37.80	122-20.20	11344.21	28235.33
WA	PUGET SOUND	ELLIOTT BAY FISH HAVEN A	00	47-37.50	122-22.40	11351.28	28232.15
WA	PUGET SOUND	ELLIOTT BAY FISH HAVEN B	00	47-37.50	122-22.30	11351.01	28232.29
WA	PUGET SOUND	WING POINT REEF NO 2	00	47-36.80	122-29.10	11371.89	28222.53
WA	PUGET SOUND	TYEE SHOAL LIGHT	00	47-36.60	122-29.20	11372.99	28222.31
WA	PUGET SOUND	BLAKELY ROCK LIGHT	00	47-35.70	122-28.80	11375.72	28222.55
WA	PUGET SOUND	DECATUR REEF LIGHT NO 2	00	47-34.90	122-28.50	11378.33	28222.69
WA	PUGET SOUND	ORCHARD ROCKS FISH PEN	00	47-34.60	122-31.70	11388.08	28218.08
WA	PUGET SOUND	BAINBRIDGE REEF BUOY NO 4	00	47-34.20	122-31.10	11388.22	28218.78
WA	PUGET SOUND	WEST SEATTLE REEF BUOY	00	47-33.40	122-24.40	11373.85	28227.95
WA	PUGET SOUND	BLAKE ISLAND REEF BUOY A	00	47-31.80	122-29.40	11394.21	28220.31
WA	PUGET SOUND	BLAKE ISLAND REEF BUOY B	00	47-31.70	122-29.40	11394.65	28220.27
WA	PUGET SOUND	POINT HEYER REEF BUOY B	00	47-25.20	122-25.50	11413.94	28223.49
WA	PUGET SOUND	POINT HEYER REEF BUOY A	00	47-25.10	122-25.60	11414.69	28223.31
WA	PUGET SOUND	QUARTERMASTER HARB SHOAL NO 2	00	47-21.00	122-28.60	11442.78	28217.47
WA	PUGET SOUND	FOX ISLAND ROCK NO 1	00	47-16.50	122-38.70	11493.00	28201.00
WA	PUGET SOUND	COMMENCEMENT BAY SHOAL A	00	47-16.30	122-25.90	11459.34	28219.64
WA	PUGET SOUND	STATE FISHERIES SALMON PENS	00	47-16.10	122-38.70	11495.09	28200.83
WA	PUGET SOUND	WYCKOFF SHOAL NO 1	00	47-14.50	122-42.80	11514.47	28194.17
WA	PUGET SOUND	PITT PASSAGE N SHOAL	00	47-13.60	122-42.70	11519.02	28193.92
WA	PUGET SOUND	TOLIVA SHOAL	00	47-12.20	122-36.40	11509.75	28202.59

F I S H ' N

STATE/COUNTRY	COUNTY/PROV	NAME	DEPTH	LAT	LON	TD#1	TD#2
WA	PUGET SOUND	SQUAXIN ISLAND FISH PEN B	00	47-12.10	122-54.20	11557.26	28176.41
WA	PUGET SOUND	PEALE PASSAGE FISH PEN A	00	47-11.70	122-54.20	11559.44	28176.22
WA	PUGET SOUND	EAGLE ISLAND REEF NO 9	00	47-11.40	122-41.90	11528.82	28194.14
WA	PUGET SOUND	ITSAMI LEDGE REEF BUOY A	00	47-10.50	122-50.50	11556.41	28181.09
WA	PUGET SOUND	WEST OLYMPIA SHOAL NO 1	00	47-05.50	122-55.40	11597.22	28171.48
WA	PUGET SOUND	OLYMPIA SHOAL LIGHT	00	47-05.50	122-55.10	11596.45	28171.92

CHAPTER 14

SEA BOUNTY

This chapter is very near and dear to my heart. I would rather eat seafood that Susie cooks than some of the things that great chefs have built their reputations on. Susie always complains about my weight, yet at dinner time she'll make a meal fit for six King Henry the Eighths. She is inventive and willing to try just about anything (on me).

One nice thing about planning a cruise or a camping trip is that we are home when we're thinking about menus and how to prepare the meals. Heat and humidity are the major drawbacks to cooking inside the boat in Florida between April and December.

We have two solutions. During the summer months, we barbecue most of the foods on board. We purchased one of those neat stainless steel things that mounts of the stern of the boat and hangs over the side. We like using the easy-starting kind of charcoal the best, rather than starter fluids, because they are so highly flammable and hazardous.

Lighting the charcoal in a breeze can be a real challenge, however. A friend of ours showed us the following method of firing up the barbecue with no fuss or mess. We call this the Joe Potts Barbecue Chimney Method. We are sure that Joe didn't invent the method, but we can't prove he didn't and he ain't talkin', so we are going to be safe and name it after him.

First, always have a large can of V-8 juice on the boat for breakfast (any can about the same size will do). We pour the juice into a plastic container and keep it on ice for frequent sipping. Next, take a can opener and remove the top and bottom of the can, then take a beer can opener (of the church key variety) and make several triangular openings around the perimeter of one end. A small hole at the top will serve as a pick-up point or a wire can be hooked through the hole for the purpose of picking up the chimney when it is hot. What you end up with is a fine little chimney to stack self-starting charcoal in.

The size of the can is just about the right measure for the charcoal to fill the bottom of the grill. When the chimney is placed into the barbecue grill, the triangular openings must be on the bottom. It is through these holes that we light the briquettes, but more important, they are the air draft holes that fire the charcoal briquettes into rosy red cinders packed with pure cooking power in short order.

Once all the briquettes are aglow and a perky red, lift the chimney with a fork or knife, and, being careful not to touch it to any plastic parts of the boat, lower it into water. After a loud hiss and a couple of seconds, it is ready to be stowed away.

We space the hot briquettes evenly about the bottom of the barbecue grill and add only enough more regular briquettes on top of the hot ones to cook our dinner. Usually, in 10 to 20 minutes we can start our steaks, fish, or whatever else is in need of barbecuing.

HELPFUL HINT

We have learned that we can increase our visibility range while underway in the fog by having the First Mate or Captain stand on the bow. A rain coat, a life jacket, and a thermos full of hot coffee are also very helpful.

We almost always barbecue the first night out. This way we can cook several things in a row. We have learned that cooked food lasts longer in the cooler than raw food, especially meats of any kind. Once the food is cooked, we divert our talents to the generator and the microwave.

The combination of a generator and a microwave on a boat is hard to beat. Our baked potatoes, fresh veggies, baked apples for dessert — to say nothing about freshly caught poached fish — make Susie the envy of the fleet. We installed a regular icemaking unit under the seat, and while making ice, we can also keep food frozen. The ice maker becomes a freezer.

The second method of solving the cooking problem, of course, is to precook all of the food in the comfort of your air-conditioned home. As mentioned before, the additional benefit of using this method is that food lasts a lot longer once cooked and on ice than raw foods do.

Now, for the things you catch, find, spear, or grab while on a cruise: Preserving seafood for any length of time is at least complicated and at best uncertain. So we have become what our friends term "opportunity eaters."

Creatures like lobster, crabs, and clams are very hearty animals and survive well for a day or so in the livewell, where they get a constant supply of fresh salt water. Crabs are very fond of the heads of freshly caught fish (leftovers from the filleting operation) and will survive for some time. The only problem with crabs, unless they're King crab, is that you have to have lots of them to make a meal.

Clams, scallops, and oysters don't last long, as they are either eaten right away or put in the perpetual chowder pot. We have never been able to put too many of any of these into our pot, and the chowder makes for a terrific snack source during the day.

Scallops should never be eaten raw, because if you start eating the little fellers right away, there will never be any left over for the stew pot. Scallops, freshly caught, freshly cleaned, and eaten immediately are our favorite morsels from the sea. We also like to include them in our salads, soups, egg dishes, and chowders, or to cook them by themselves in garlic and drawn butter with just a touch of rice wine vinegar added for dash.

When we catch a fish that is to be our dinner, we immediately fillet it and put the meat on ice within a plastic zipper-type bag. We catch only what we can eat that day and release everything else.

The following recipes are some that Susie prepares exceptionally well. She has become deservedly famous for them among our boating friends, and once you try them, you'll become the envy of your friends, too. Though Susie developed these recipes using South Florida fish and shellfish, they will work as well with local substitutions. Experiment — take a chance — and even odds, you will love the results.

WIT & WISDOM

He who trusts his fuel gauge must also be a good swimmer.

RECIPES

POTATO-OYSTER STEW

This dish is our perpetual chowder. As the days go on, you can add more potatoes, onions, clams, crab meat, and leftover fish to the pot and in no time have a splendid dish. Do not salt the chowder each time you add ingredients, however, or it will soon begin to taste like the Gulf of Mexico! Serves four.

INGREDIENTS:

- 1 large handful of shucked raw oysters
- 3 cups of water
- 1 teaspoon of salt
- 1 large onion, diced
- 1 stalk of celery
- 1 bay leaf
- 2 dried tarragon leaves
- 2 potatoes, peeled and diced
- 2 cups of milk (or cream)
- 1 cup of whole small mushrooms

PREPARATION:

Place the potatoes, onion, water, and salt in a pot and simmer for 20 minutes or until the potatoes are tender. Stirring constantly, add everything else to the pot and simmer for three to five minutes, being careful not to burn the milk. Cover and turn the fire off. Let stand for 20 to 30 minutes. Heat again to bring stew to serving temperature, stirring constantly. Add pepper as needed.

When "perpetuating the pot," remember that any kind of fish that has been previously prepared in any way may be dumped into this pot, even if it has been breaded. Never add salt to the pot. As the various veggies are consumed, just add more with milk or cream, but don't burn the milk. The milk or cream will tone down the flavor of the chowder's previous incarnation and allow the new mess to develop its own character. If you like the dish thicker, add more cream, and don't be afraid to experiment with spices. There will come a time (at about the fourth generation) when you will want to start over!

CLAMS A LA SUSIE

The preparation of this dish is as simple as throwing everything into a pot! This soup is very rich and is great served with French garlic bread. We especially enjoy it during the winter months when the evenings are a bit cool and on winter days while fishing — this and hot coffee. Mmmmmmmm. This soup is best made ahead of time at home and carried to the boat. Serves four.

INGREDIENTS:

- 2 large handfuls of fresh clams
- 2 quarts of water
- 1 teaspoon of salt
- 1 medium onion, diced
- 2 stalks of celery
- 1 bay leaf
- 4-6 whole peppercorns
- 2 tablespoons of minced parsley
- 4 tablespoons of butter or margarine
- 4 tablespoons of all-purpose flour
- 2-3 tablespoons of lemon juice
- 1 10-ounce package of frozen carrots
- 1 10-ounce package of frozen peas
- 2 potatoes, peeled and diced
- 1 half quart of milk
- 1/4 cup of whipping cream

PREPARATION:

Place the clams in the bathtub (or in a large sink or bowl) and cover with fresh water for two to three hours. It helps to stir them a couple of times. This encourages the clams to spit out sand instead of saving it for the soup.

Put two quarts of water in the bottom of a double-boiler pot and bring to a boil (don't use the water the clams have been sitting in). Place all of the fresh clams, still in their shells, in the top of the double-boiler and steam the clams until they open.

Remove the meat, being careful to save the juices. Put all of the meat and juices into the boiling water in the bottom of the double-boiler. (You may have to add water to bring the level back to two quarts.) Add all the raw veggies and spices and return to a rolling boil.

After five minutes, reduce the heat to a slow simmer and cover the pot. Simmer for one to one and half hours, then add the butter to the pot. Add the flour to one cup of cold water and blend completely. Slowly add the flour-water mixture to the pot, stirring constantly. Cook, two or three minutes. Add lemon juice and the frozen carrots. Cover and simmer for about five to seven minutes.

Add the peas and simmer two to three minutes. Stir in the cream and then add the milk. Add salt and pepper to taste. Refrigerate the whole mess and take to the boat. Keep the soup on ice, then heat it up and serve it.

CORNY FISH CHOWDER

This dish is a neat way to serve fish to those who are not real fish-eating aficionados, and also makes use of fish fillets that got too small during the cleaning operation. Serve with hot buttered French bread and a glass of chilled light white wine of your choice. This is a dinner that can be enjoyed on the bridge while slowly putt-putting back to home port. Serves four.

INGREDIENTS:

- 1 pound of fresh fish fillets, cut into "fingers"
- 1 medium onion, diced
- 1/2 cup finely diced celery
- 2 tablespoons butter or margarine
- 1 tablespoon of all-purpose flour
- 2 chicken bouillon cubes
- 2 cups of water
- 1 bay leaf
- 2 dried tarragon leaves
- 2 cups of potatoes, peeled and diced
- 1 13-ounce can of evaporated milk
- 1 8.5-ounce can of cream-style corn
- 1 teaspoon dill weed
- 1/2 cup of chopped parsley

PREPARATION:

Saute dill weed, onion, and celery in butter until the onion is clear and tender. Stir in flour and add bouillon cubes, water, and potatoes. Bring to a boil. Cover and simmer for 15 to 20 minutes until potatoes are tender.

Add fish and corn, and stir in milk and the rest of the ingredients. Add salt and pepper to taste. Cover and simmer until the fish is tender, but not overcooked. Turn the fire off and let stand for 10 to 15 minutes before serving.

Just before serving, heat to serving temperature. When serving, be very careful not to get in the way of the mad rush to the table!

BAKED FISH WITH DILLY CHEESE SAUCE

Many varieties of fish are especially suitable for this dish. Try snapper, grouper, shark, halibut, cod, sea bass, barracuda, flounder, or just about anything that has gills and swims. We fold small fillets when we don't have fillets that are three quarters of an inch thick, as called for. If you are going to fold fillets, try stuffing them with a bit of pimento and anchovies. Another variation is to spread the inside of the fillet with a bit of Miracle Whip. Experimenting with this dish is fun. Serves four.

INGREDIENTS:

1.5	pounds of fish fillets (three quarters of an inch thick)
3	tablespoons of butter or margarine
3	tablespoons of all-purpose flour
1	tablespoon of salt
1/2	teaspoon of dry mustard
1/4	teaspoon of dried dill weed
1	dash of cayenne
1.5	cups half and half cream
1.5	cups shredded cheddar cheese
1	four-ounce can of mussels, drained
1	four-ounce can of diced clams, drained
1/4	pound of small shrimp, cooked and peeled

PREPARATION:

Preheat oven to 400 degrees. Cut fish fillets into serving pieces and place them into a greased two-quart baking dish. In a two-quart sauce pan, melt the butter. Stir in the flour and cook until it bubbles. Add salt, dry mustard, dill, and cayenne. Remove from heat and gradually stir in half and half cream.

Return sauce to heat and cook, stirring constantly until thickened. Mix in one cup of cheese, stirring until melted. Mix in the mussels, small shrimp, and clams. Pour cheese sauce evenly over the fish. Sprinkle with the remaining cheese.

Bake at 400 degrees for about 20 minutes or until top browns and fish flakes evenly when tested with a fork in the thickest part. This dish is best served with white wine or ice cold beer, green beans, and a baked potato.

SUSIE'S POTATO-FISH PIE

The fish that are especially suitable for this dish are snapper, grouper, shark, halibut, cod, sea bass, barracuda, flounder, and spotted sea trout. The leftovers are great when reheated in the oven or microwave and served with ice cold milk. Serves four.

INGREDIENTS:

1/2	pound of fish fillets
4	cups of potatoes, peeled and thinly sliced
3/4	teaspoon of salt
2	tablespoons of minced parsley
1	small onion, minced
1/8	teaspoon of black pepper
2	tablespoons of butter or margarine
1/2	teaspoon of dried dill weed
1/2	cup of whipping cream
1/2	cup fresh parsley for garnish
1	anchovy
1	pie crust

TO MAKE PIE CRUST:

Mix two cups of all-purpose flour and three quarters of a teaspoon of salt. Cut in half a cup of softened butter or margarine and a third of a cup of lard (shortening) until small particles are formed. Mix well with a fork while adding a couple of tablespoon of cold water a few drops at a time, stirring until particles hold together. Form this mess into a ball and divide into two equal parts. Roll half of the dough until it is an eighth of an inch thick and will fit over a nine-inch pie plate. Trim edges evenly around the plate. (The second half will cover the pie once the other ingredients have been added.)

PREPARATION:

Preheat oven to 375 degrees. Prepare a nine-inch pie shell as above. Toss together the potatoes, salt, parsley, onion, and black pepper, and spread half around the bottom of the pie crust. Place the fish fillets over the potato mess and sprinkle the dill weed over the fillets. Add remaining potatoes and dot with butter. Roll out remaining crust and cover the pie filling. Cut slits to allow the steam to escape. Trim the edges and crimp the crusts together with a fork.

Bake at 375 degrees for about one hour. Remove from the oven and carefully cut out a round hole in the middle of the pie and save. Then, *very* gradually pour the cream into the pie through the hole just cut, allowing the cream to settle before continuing. Replace the pastry cut-out and place the one anchovy over the plug. Return the pie to the oven and bake for 10 more minutes. Cut into wedges and serve warm. Garnish with the fresh parsley.

FISHY HOME FRIED POTATOES

This dish is great in the morning when there are leftover fried or oven-baked fish. Try this dish along with eggs or your favorite breakfast dish. It can be prepared in minutes and is very tasty. We guarantee the crew will love it. This is an outstanding recipe for shark, dolphin, large grouper, yellowfin tuna, king mackerel, and large jacks (all de-boned). Serves four.

INGREDIENTS:

1	pound fresh fish fillets, cut into "fingers"
3	cups of potatoes, peeled and diced
3	tablespoons of butter or margarine
2-4	green onions, chopped
1	cup sliced mushrooms, if available
1/2	teaspoon of salt
1	teaspoon of dill weed
1	dash of black pepper
1	dash of cayenne

PREPARATION:

Remove all skin and bones from the fish after baking for 20 minutes and then break fish meat into small pieces. Set aside. In a large frying pan, saute the potatoes in two tablespoons of the butter or margarine for about 15 minutes or until lightly browned and tender. Remove potatoes and keep warm.

In the same pan, melt the remaining butter or margarine and add the onions. Saute for 10 minutes or until the onions are just clear, then stir in black pepper, salt, dill, and cayenne. Roll in the potatoes and the fish without stirring too much. Heat through on very low flame or in the microwave. Transfer to the serving dish, and sprinkle with the fresh parsley.

For variety, try placing a couple of butter-basted eggs on the plate, lightly sprinkled with paprika, salt, and pepper.

SUSIE'S KOREAN SHARK STEAKS

We are very fond of shark and look for every opportunity to put small ones (less than four feet long) on our table. Once we have caught one, we clean our catch as soon as possible (immediately is best). We tie the shark's tail to a line attached to the aft cleat, then we clean the feller and let him "bleed" for a bit while he's in the water before we start carving out thick fillets. We remove the blood line from the fillets, and keep a supply of freezer-type plastic bags on board to store them (our ice maker doubles as a small freezer). This recipe serves four.

INGREDIENTS:

1.5	pounds of fresh shark steaks (one-inch thick)
2	tablespoons of soy sauce
2	tablespoons of rice wine vinegar
2	tablespoons of lemon juice
2	tablespoons of vegetable oil
1/2	tablespoon of chopped parsley
1	clove garlic, minced or pressed
1/2	teaspoon of freshly ground pepper
1/2	teaspoon of minced green onion

PREPARATION:

Place the steaks in a bowl. Combine the soy sauce, vinegar, lemon juice, oil, parsley, garlic, and black pepper to create a marinade. Pour the marinade over the steaks and allow them to soak for about 30 minutes. Turn often to expose all surfaces of the steaks to the marinade.

Remove the steaks from the marinade and barbecue them on the boat's grill (over charcoal). Cover the barbecue and grill for about four to five minutes per side. Brush on a little marinade after turning.

When the steaks are done, serve them on a dish and sprinkle the steaks lightly with the minced green onions and parsley. We like to serve them with baked sweet potatoes, garlic bread, and a large salad. Top the meal off with your favorite red or white wine (full bodied port is our favorite), chilled to a pucker.

For variety, Susie likes to ladle nacho-type melted cheese over the fish, topped with sliced jalapenos. When Susie does this we play Mexican music and dance a lot. It seems the more jalapenos we eat, the better we dance.

SUSIE'S HOT-DAMN SHRIMP CASSEROLE

This dish is for the romantics who have a flair for the unusual and for those who like the wonderful combination of spices from the Orient coupled with a dash of Americana. This dish teems with flavor, and it will drive you to say, "Hot damn, got any more?" If you are not too fond of spices, you may exclaim, "Hot damn pass the ice cream!"

This is one of Susie's best creations, and it's made from the fresh bait shrimp that are still alive and left over after fishing. Fresh scallops can be used instead of the shrimp, or you can try a fifty-fifty combination. Serves four.

INGREDIENTS:

2	cups (one and a quarter pounds) fresh peeled shrimp
3	tablespoons of butter or margarine
3/4	cup of chopped celery
1/2	cup coarsely chopped green peppers
4	onions, chopped
1/2	cup diced mushrooms
3	tablespoons of all-purpose flour
1	tablespoon of salt
1/4	teaspoon of curry powder
1/4	teaspoon of red pepper
2	teaspoons of Worcestershire sauce
1	tablespoon of soy sauce
1	13-ounce can of evaporated milk, warmed
1/4	cup of grated Parmesan cheese
1/4	teaspoon of paprika
4	Prayers

PREPARATION:

Preheat oven to 425 degrees. In a large skillet, melt the butter or margarine over medium heat. Add celery, green pepper, mushrooms, and onions. Saute for about 10 minutes or until the onions are clear, stirring constantly (stirring here is essential). Add flour, salt, all of the spices, Worcestershire and soy sauces, stirring until well blended. Saute for about three minutes or until everything is well cooked and heated.

Stir in the warmed condensed milk. Cook, stirring continuously, until sauce is smooth and thickened. Add shrimp and cook for three to six minutes. Taste and correct seasoning to suit. Pour this mess into a buttered six-inch by 10-inch casserole dish. Sprinkle top with Parmesan cheese and paprika and cover. Bake at 425 degrees for 20 minutes and serve hot.

Use the prayers freely to keep everyone's fingers out of the mess before baking in the casserole. For dessert, try French vanilla ice cream! Talk about good!

KOREAN CIOPPINO

Cioppino is a combination of various fish and shellfish, and here is Susie's variation on this classic dish. We often make this when we have been fishing and have caught a mixture of all kinds of fish. Obviously, we use up the bait shrimp that are still alive, fresh scallops from our freezer, clams (diced or minced, canned or fresh), and any available crab meat. All are chucked into the stew with no holds barred. Just about anything goes, because this dish is so forgiving. Garfeldasteinski (the Damned Cat) could make it. Serves four.

INGREDIENTS:

1-1/2	pounds fresh fish fillets, cut into "fingers"
1/2	pound of scallops
1	pound fresh shelled shrimp
2	tablespoons of vegetable oil
2	tablespoons of butter or margarine
1-1/2	cups sliced onions
2	cloves of garlic, pressed
1	can (one pound, 12 ounces) Italian plum tomatoes
1	can (10-3/4 ounces) chicken broth
1	cup dry white drinking wine
1	cup of water
2	tablespoons of chopped parsley
1-1/2	teaspoons dried basil leaves
1-1/2	teaspoons of salt
1/2	teaspoon of dried oregano leaves
1	eight-ounce can minced or diced clams; not drained
5 to 6	cups cooked white, brown, or wild rice
1-1/2	cups sliced mushrooms
2	large chicken breasts (boned and cooked)

PREPARATION:

Cut fish fillets into one-inch chunks and set aside. Heat oil, butter or margarine, onions, and garlic in a heavy skillet. Saute about two minutes or until onions are soft. Add tomatoes, wine, water, parsley, basil, salt, and oregano. Cover and simmer for about 20 minutes.

Add fish and chicken and simmer for about 10 minutes. Add the rest of the seafood (shrimp, clams, etc.) and simmer for about five minutes. Avoid stirring the stew at all after adding the fish. Using a large wooden spoon, "roll" the seafood into the sauce. (Overcooking and stirring will make the stew mushy.)

To serve, spoon hot rice into large, shallow soup dishes. Ladle the stew over the top of the rice and cap with a pat of butter. Place a sprig of parsley into the stew and call it a tree. Serve this dish with a light, dry white wine, tossed salad, French garlic bread, and a mound of your favorite veggies. A hug from the captain and crew is guaranteed.

CHAPTER 15

DAFFYNITIONS

The following "daffynitions" are being provided to clarify recreational boating terminology, not to confuse our dear readers. The Captains of small vessels use certain words for deep-seated psychological reasons, while other words just need defining. In all our wisdom (guessing), we will attempt to clear the air and to put doubt to rest forever.

ANCHOR: A heavy device usually found at the bow of the boat. Its intended use is to hold the boat firmly when you want to go home and to slip its grip at night when you're laying to.

BOAT: (1) Anything that floats, carries people, passengers, guests, animals, food, drinks, and costs lots of money. (2) Also, a vessel that consumes excess cash proportionately to the availability of same. (3) An object of senseless love. (4) A personal yacht.

BOW: Pointed end of the vessel or the end of the vessel that usually parts the water and leaves the port first, i.e., the front of the boat.

BUMPERS: Improper boating form of the word "fender."

CABIN: The area on the boat where cooking and all sorts of fun games take place.

CAPTAIN: Lord and Master.

CAPTAIN'S CHAIR: A place to park the Captain so that work can get done.

CAPTAIN'S PRIVILEGE: Those things the Captain's wife or First Mate says that the Captain can or cannot do.

CHART: A sailor's map.

COCKPIT: (1) A place that is usually surrounded by a gunnel. (2) A weather deck usually found near or at the stern of the boat. (3) A convenient place to observe sunsets and feed the First Mate a line.

COVE: (1) A quiet indentation within the landmass where sailors and powerboat drivers attempt to anchor their boats for the night so that they can use the phrase "trust me." (2) A place where boats gather to tell lies about their adventures. (3) A haven. (4) A wonderful place to camp on the boat while playing soft music, cooking dinner, relaxing, and making plans for the next day's journey while your neighbor shows off his bigger boat.

DECK: Floor.

DECK, WEATHER: A floor that gets rained on.

DEPTH INDICATOR: (1) Indicates depth and quits working in shallow water. (2) A "passifier."

DINGHY: (1) Very small boat, see TENDER, BOAT. (2) What the Captain usually is.

DOCK: (1) A place where one might want to put his boat. (2) To some, home base.

FENDER: (1) Inflated rubber "things" that hang over the side of the boat to protect it from rubbing and bumping. (2) Bumper.

FISH: Those things that become scarcer proportionate to the amount of money spent to catch them.

FISHFINDER: (1) A device that is believed to be able to alert fishermen regarding where to catch a fish. (2) Fancy name for a depth indicator. (3) A device that helps the Captain frustrate fishermen who can't catch fish.

FISHING: The art of attempting to catch fish while presenting live, frozen, dead, cut, wood, or plastic baits with sharp hooks so designed to catch grass, rocks, and coral while at the same time providing frustration and lessons in patience.

FLASHLIGHT: Sometimes called a search light, it always works during the day, it works only intermittently at night, and it never works in tight channels.

GALLEY: Kitchen.

HALYARD: (1) A line used to raise or lower a sail or flag. (2) Line. (3) Rope.

HEAD: (1) A place where a cap or hat is placed. (2) Toilet. (3) A place that is too small for the Captain and just right for people who don't know how to operate the equipment.

HELM: Driving or steering station.

HELMSMAN: The driver of the boat.

LINE: (1) "Thing" used to tie the boat to the dock, pier, or other boat with. (2) Proper boating term for the words rope, string, or cord. (3) The one "thing" that always has knots in it. (4) The "thing" the Captain tries to feed to the First Mate while apologizing for yelling, hoping for forgiveness and secretly anticipating good things to come.

NAVIGATION: (1) The art of knowing where one is going. (2) The ability to figure out where one is.

NAVIGATOR: A person able to find shore; which usually excludes the Captain, who can find the shore only when he's not trying to.

PFD: Personal Flotation Device, or life jacket.

PORT: (1) Opposite of starboard; the left side of the vessel when one is looking at the bow. (2) Place where all good Captains hope to get to often. (3) A spot where services such as repairs, food, marinas, restaurants, and supplies abound and where they always cost more.

RADAR: An electronic device that works all of the time when the sun is shining, seldom at night, and almost never in the fog.

ROPE: Line.

SEARCH LIGHT: See FLASHLIGHT.

STARBOARD: The right side of the vessel when one is looking at the bow.

STATEROOM: The place where the beds are kept.

STERN: The blunt end of the vessel or the end of the vessel that leaves port last.

SUNSETS: An invention designed to impress the First Mate into a sense of nostalgia and lesser resistance; filled with a special something that is never present during sunrises.

TENDER, BOAT: A very small boat that is always in the way.

THING: The word "thing" is used as a substitute word for any other word the Captain of the vessel cannot remember, or never knew.

"Get me that thing. Tie the boat to that thing. That thing over there. Bring me the thing to fix this thing." REAL MEANING: I don't know what I'm talking about, but I sure hope you do.

TOILET: See HEAD.

TROLLING: The act of washing artificial lures while pretending to fish.

WAKE: Waves left behind the boat that will most certainly cause someone to express profanities on the nicest days.

WAVES: (1) A natural saltwater phenomenon which, when encountered, causes violent motion; waves are guaranteed to be present when pouring hot drinks. (2) "Things" that Captains make to irritate the First Mate, as in "Don't make waves, honey!" (3) Female sailors.

WHITE LINE RECORDER: (1) Makes mysterious writings on small paper to tease the operator into believing that fish are waiting to pounce on anything presented in the form of bait. (2) Draws profiles of the sea bottom in sufficient detail to identify ledges, rocks, and other shapes, such as wrecks and reefs. (3) Substitute for an inoperative depth indicator.

WINDLASS: An electrical and/or mechanical device designed to haul in line, such as the anchor windlass, halyard windlass.

YACHT: A boat owned by a proud person.

CHAPTER 16

WAYPOINT LOG

Most all modern loran machines have some kind of waypoint memory for storing your waypoints. The following log will allow you to list your waypoints right in this book for easy reference. We suggest leaving the first 10 waypoints in your memory open for special entries.

We have entered the coordinates we use all of the time at the very end of our log. This way, we can flip directly to our pass coordinates without having to look them up.

This is your very own log book; please enjoy it.

MEMORY	DESTINATION	TD #1	TD #2
WPT 01	_____	_____	_____
WPT 02	_____	_____	_____
WPT 03	_____	_____	_____
WPT 04	_____	_____	_____
WPT 05	_____	_____	_____
WPT 06	_____	_____	_____
WPT 07	_____	_____	_____
WPT 08	_____	_____	_____
WPT 09	_____	_____	_____
WPT 10	_____	_____	_____
WPT 11	_____	_____	_____
WPT 12	_____	_____	_____
WPT 13	_____	_____	_____
WPT 14	_____	_____	_____

MEMORY	DESTINATION	TD #1	TD #2
WPT 15			
WPT 16			
WPT 17			
WPT 18			
WPT 19			
WPT 20			
WPT 21			
WPT 22			
WPT 23			
WPT 24			
WPT 25			
WPT 26			
WPT 27			
WPT 28			
WPT 29			
WPT 30			
WPT 31			
WPT 32			
WPT 33			
WPT 34			
WPT 35			
WPT 36			

MEMORY	DESTINATION	TD #1	TD #2
WPT 37			
WPT 38			
WPT 39			
WPT 40			
WPT 41			
WPT 42			
WPT 43			
WPT 44			
WPT 45			
WPT 46			
WPT 47			
WPT 48			
WPT 49			
WPT 50			
WPT 51			
WPT 52			
WPT 53			
WPT 54			
WPT 55			
WPT 56			
WPT 57			
WPT 58			

MEMORY	DESTINATION	TD #1	TD #2
WPT 59			
WPT 60			
WPT 61			
WPT 62			
WPT 63			
WPT 64			
WPT 65			
WPT 66			
WPT 67			
WPT 68			
WPT 69			
WPT 70			
WPT 71			
WPT 72			
WPT 73			
WPT 74			
WPT 75			
WPT 76			
WPT 77			
WPT 78			
WPT 79			
WPT 80			

MEMORY	DESTINATION	TD #1	TD #2
WPT 81			
WPT 82			
WPT 83			
WPT 84			
WPT 85			
WPT 86			
WPT 87			
WPT 88			
WPT 89			
WPT 90			
WPT 91			
WPT 92			
WPT 93			
WPT 94			
WPT 95			
WPT 96			
WPT 97			
WPT 98			
WPT 99			
WPT 100			
WPT 101			
WPT 102